Learn to *Lattice Smock*

Learn to Lattice Smock

Landauer Publishing, www.landauerpub.com, is an imprint of Fox Chapel Publishing Company, Inc.

Nuno de Tsukuru Rittai Moyo Lattice Smocking
© 2025 Miyuki Uemura
© 2025 Graphic-sha Publishing Co., Ltd.
This book was first designed and published in Japan in 2025 by Graphic-sha Publishing Co., Ltd.
This English edition was published in 2026 by FOX CHAPEL PUBLISHING
English translation rights arranged with GRAPHIC-SHA PUBLISHING CO., LTD. through Japan UNI Agency, Inc., Tokyo

Original Edition Creative Staff:
Book design: Motoko Kitsukawa
Photos: Kimiko Kaburagi
Pattern: Miyuki Oshima
Editing: Ayako Enaka (Graphic-sha Publishing Co., Ltd.)

Material offered by
ARTEMONDO CO., LTD.
KIJINOMORI CO., LTD.
KIYOHARA & CO., LTD.
COSCLOTH
YOKOTA CO., LTD
la droguerie
nunocoto fabric
SUNWELL.CO., LTD.
MARCHENART
the linen bird.

Translator for the English Edition: Nick Bennett
Indexer for English Edition: Jay Kreider

ISBN 978-1-63981-173-1

Library of Congress Control Number: 2026937853

To learn more about the other great books from Fox Chapel Publishing, or to find a retailer near you, call toll-free at 800-457-9112 or visit us at www.FoxChapelPublishing.com.
We are always looking for talented authors.
To submit an idea, please send a brief inquiry to acquisitions@foxchapelpublishing.com.
Or write to:
Fox Chapel Publishing
903 Square Street
Mount Joy, PA 17552

Printed in China
First printing

MIX
Paper | Supporting responsible forestry
FSC® C147414
FSC www.fsc.org

Learn to Lattice Smock

Creating Three-Dimensional Patterns with Fabric

MIYUKI UEMURA

CONTENTS

Introduction 6
About this Book 8
Lattice Smocking Basics 9
Tools 40
Materials 41
About Fabric 42
Customizing Patterns 44

13

14

16

17

20

21

23

25

26

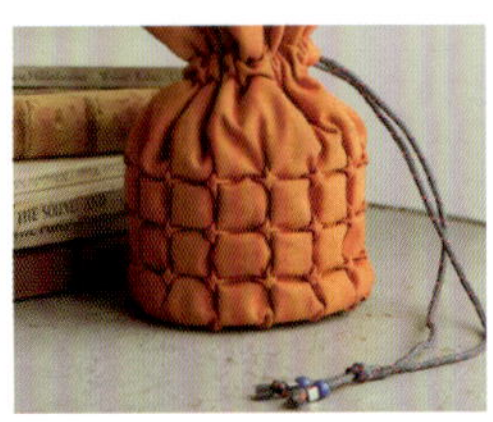
29

31

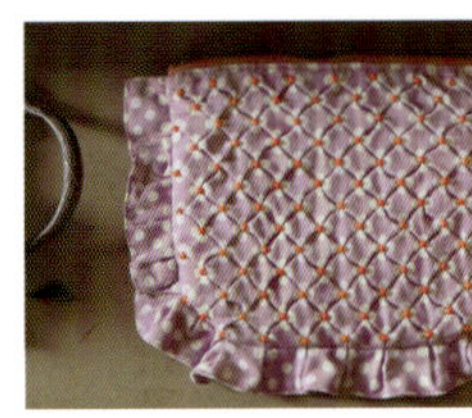
32

34

35

36

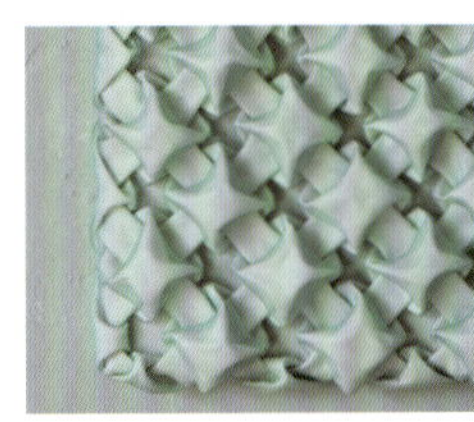
39

Straight and Diagonal Lines

LATTICE 46

BRAID 52

SHELL 54

LEAF 56

BONE 58

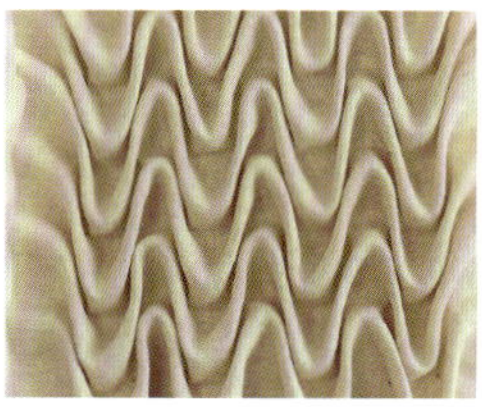
WAVE 60

CRISSCROSS BONE 62

ARROW 64

BRICK 66

BUBBLE 72

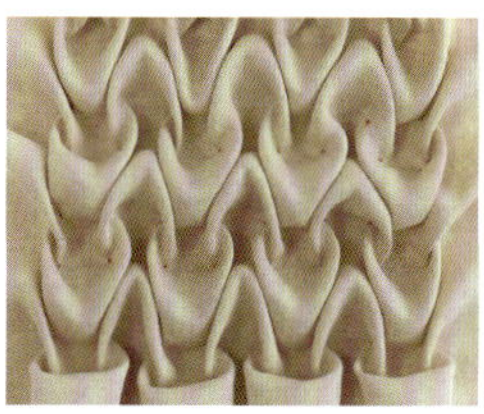
HEART 74

LOZENGE 76

DOUBLE LATTICE 78

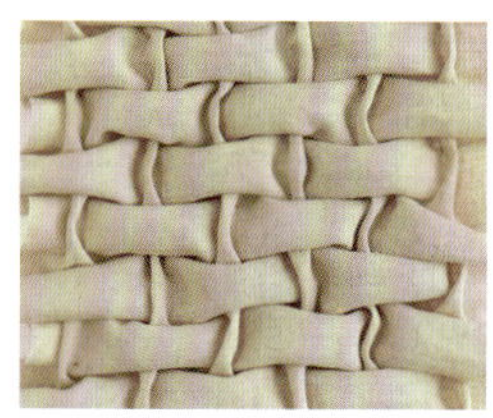
RATTAN 80

DRAGON SCALE 84

PUZZLE 88

Four Corners

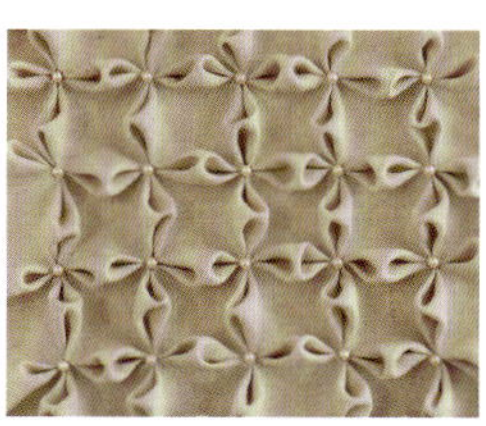
FLOWER 94

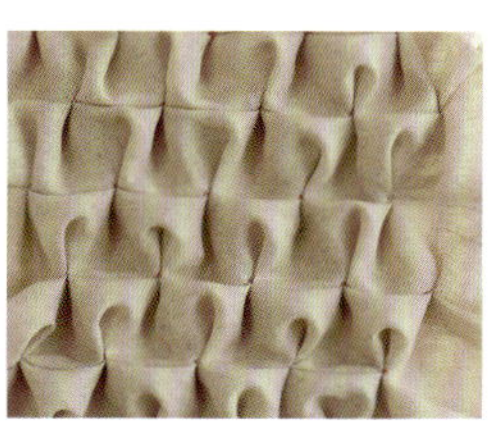
HOURGLASS 98

DIAMOND 100

BOX 102

Lattice Stitching 48
Brick Stitching 68
Rattan Stitching 82
Dragon Scale Stitching 86
Puzzle Stitching 90
Flower Stitching 96
Making a Shoulder Bag 104
How to Make the Projects 109
Index 150
About the Author 152

INTRODUCTION

Lattice smocking is a technique in which fabric is gathered and stitched in a grid pattern on the reverse side (wrong side) to create a design on the front (right side). It is an example of Canadian smocking, also called North American smocking. The earliest known examples of lattice smocking appear on dresses made in the 1780s, and it is believed that its use as decoration on pillows and cushions in the 1970s led to its wider popularity.

Applying lattice smocking to a single piece of fabric produces an almost sculptural three-dimensionality. Endless variations can be created by combining different grid sizes, fabric types and patterns.

When I first encountered this technique, I completely immersed myself in it, captivated by the interesting forms it produces and the rhythmic pleasure of moving my hands. In this book, I introduce the patterns that particularly fascinate me in a way that makes them easy to adapt for any project. The thickness created by the three-dimensionality functions as built-in padding or support, making it suitable for bags and pouches, while the naturally formed ruffles and drapes will surely offer new ideas for garment decoration.

I encourage you to try working on a small swatch first; a needle, thread, and fabric are all you need. Once started, you'll find it difficult to stop creating the 3D patterns that emerge from your stitching. I hope this book helps you discover an absorbing hobby that opens the door to fun and enjoyment.

Miyuki Uemura

ABOUT THIS BOOK

This book contains two technique chapters, showing you how to stitch smocking patterns using different stitching methods. The first technique involves joining fabric by picking up both ends of diagonal or straight grid lines, while the second technique involves scooping up fabric by picking up all four corners of the squares in a grid. Every chapter begins with simpler patterns and ones that use similar stitching techniques.

The examples shown on the pattern pages are made using linen (Artemondo's Number 5 Collection® J Linen). Each example is approximately 20 × 20cm. Because the stretch level varies depending on the pattern, there may be slight differences in the finished sizes.

Leaf (diagonal)

Lozenge (horizontal)

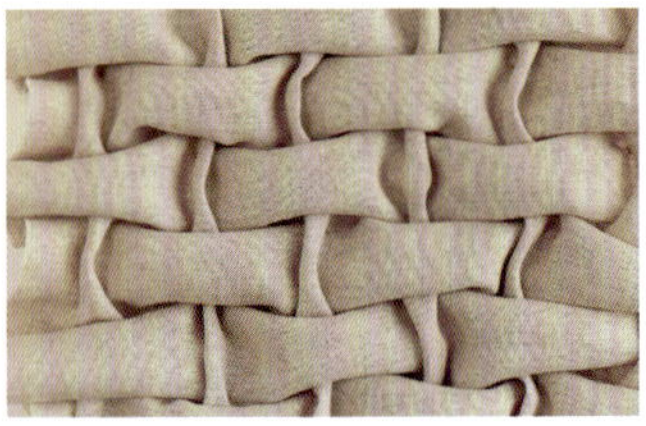

Rattan (vertical)

Flower (four corners)

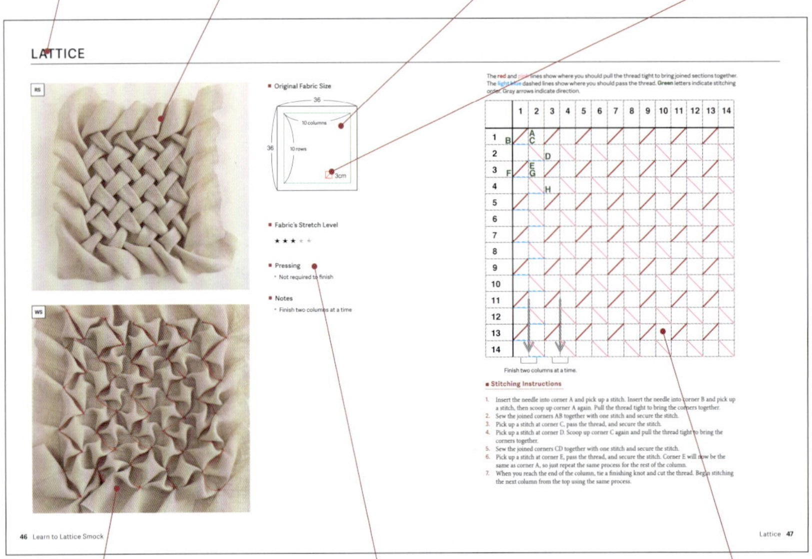

Each lattice smocking pattern is explained across a two-page spread. On the left page, you will find photographs of the pattern from both the RS and WS, the fabric size required to make an approximately 20 × 20cm swatch, the fabric's stretch level, whether pressing is required, and notes. On the right page, you will find the stitching diagram and step-by-step stitching instructions. The thread paths, the sections where the corners are lifted to align the fabric, and the sections where the thread is passed through are color-coded. For basic patterns and key techniques, the stitching method is also explained with photographs.

LATTICE SMOCKING BASICS

In lattice smocking, you draw a grid on the fabric, then either scoop up the corners to bring pieces of fabric together or pull the fabric taut to create three-dimensional shapes.

The finished shape varies depending on which corners are brought together and how the thread is carried.

Because the stitching method is a repetition of the same steps, once you learn the sequence, you can stitch smoothly and easily.

About the Stitching Diagrams

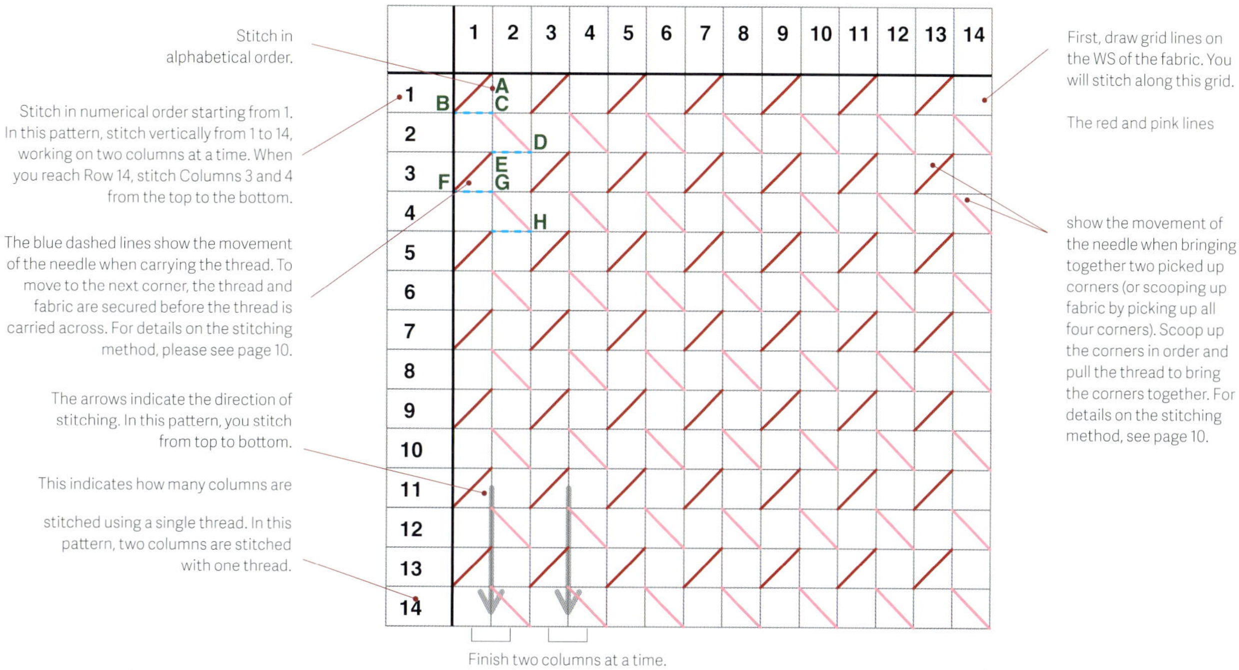

About Markings

Before stitching, draw both the base grid and the stitching lines all the way to the edges of the fabric. In the photo, the lines are drawn so that the Brick pattern (page 66) is worked vertically. Only the lines for bringing the fabric together are drawn; the lines for carrying the thread are not marked.

The grid does not need to be aligned with the warp and weft of the fabric, as long as the grid itself is accurate. Markings should be drawn so they do not show on the RS of the fabric. Pencils or pens that do not bleed into the fabric and can be erased later are recommended. Pens that air-erase may fade while you are still stitching, so take care when using them. Also, when drawing many grid lines, an ink pen may be used up quickly. Learn more on page 40.

About Thread

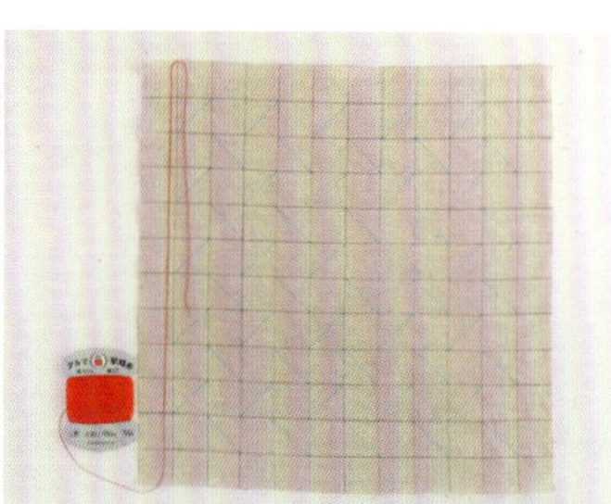

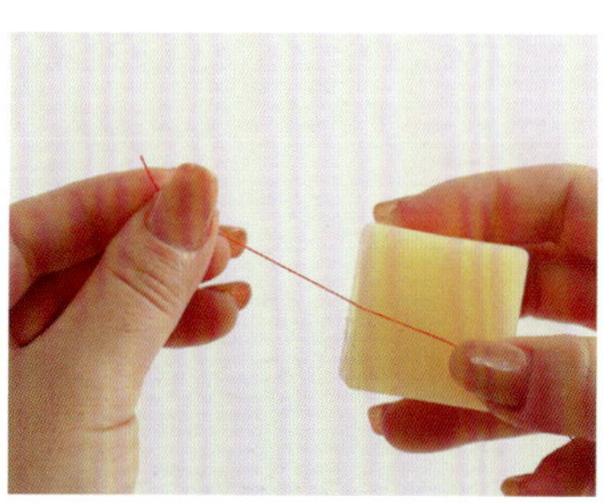

Use hand-sewing thread, from fine to thick, depending on the fabric. As shown in the left photo, prepare a length of thread about 1.5 to 2 times the length of the fabric you plan to stitch. Applying thread wax beforehand helps prevent fraying and makes stitching easier. Learn more on pages 40–41.

Stitching Diagram Lines

Red and Pink Lines

Bring picked-up corners together. See more in Lattice Stitching (page 48).

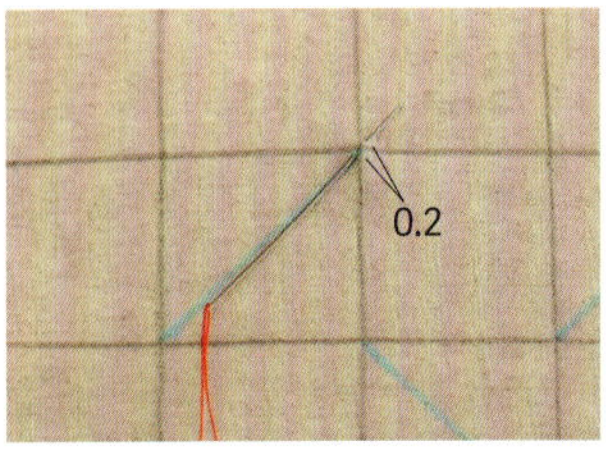

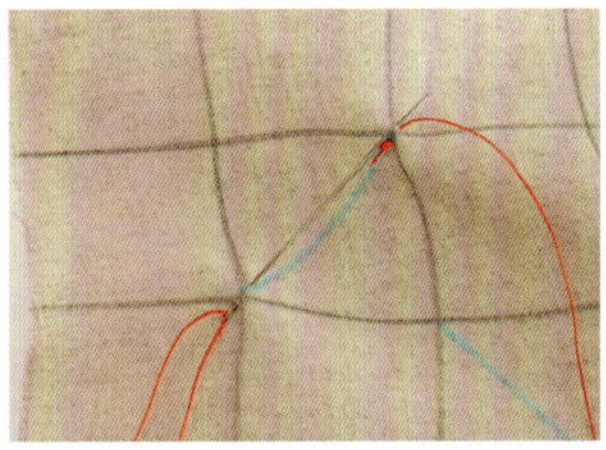

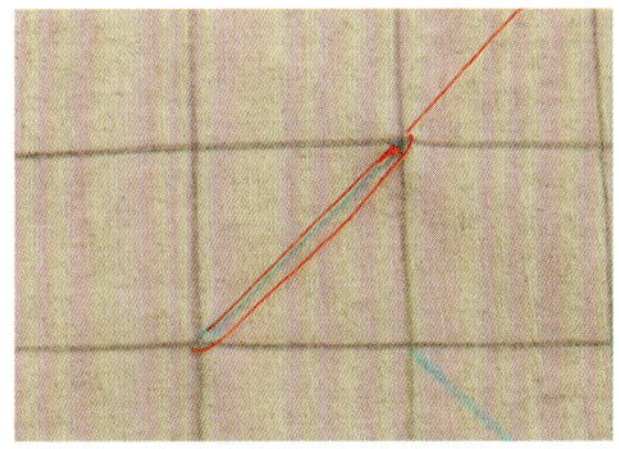

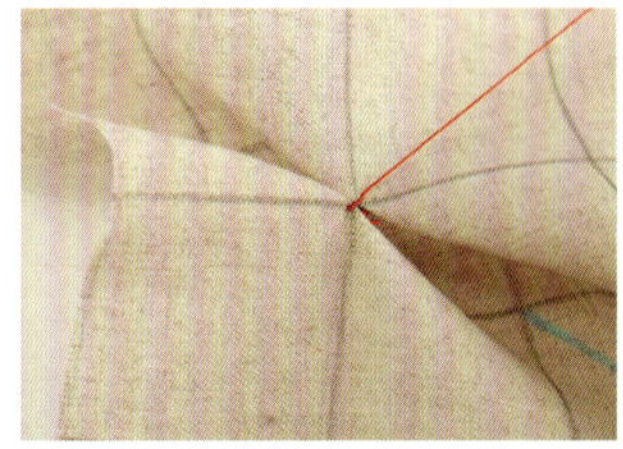

01 Draw a grid on the WS (shown here in light blue), then draw following the red lines on the stitching diagram. Thread the needle and tie a finishing knot with a single strand of thread. Pick up a stitch from inside out at the top-right corner of the square. Each stitch should be about 0.2cm long.

02 Pick up a stitch from outside in at the bottom-left corner, then scoop up the top-right corner from **Step 01** in the same way.

03 Pull the thread. You will see two strands of threads running diagonally.

04 Pull the thread tight to bring the top-right and bottom-left corners together.

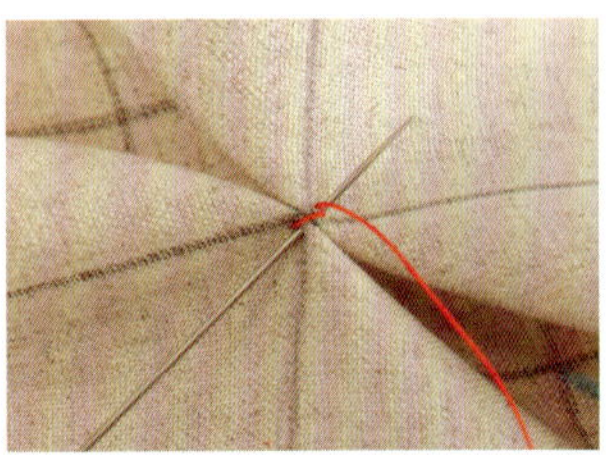

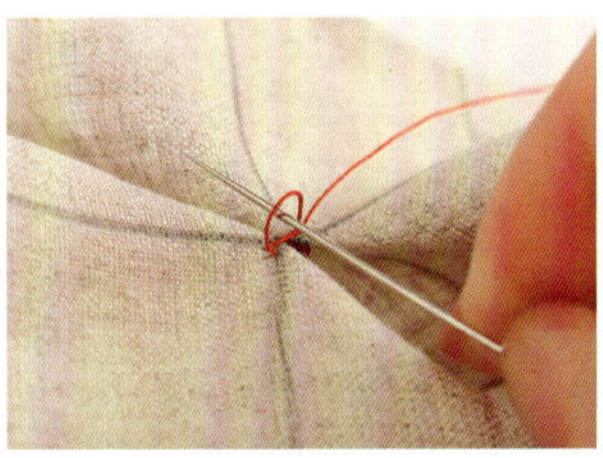

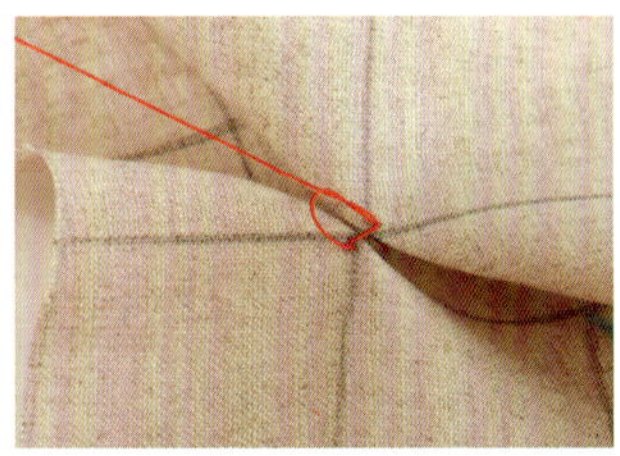

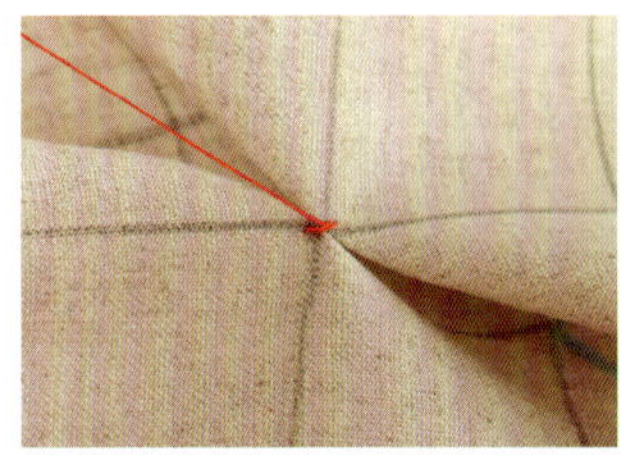

05 Sew the two joined corners together with one stitch.

06 Pull the thread, creating a small loop just before pulling it tight. Pass the needle through the loop from bottom to top.

07 Pass the needle through the loop and pull the thread tight to lock the stitch and secure the fabric. This sequence of scooping corners that have been bought together and securing the stitch comprises the whole process.

Blue Dashed Lines

Pass the thread.

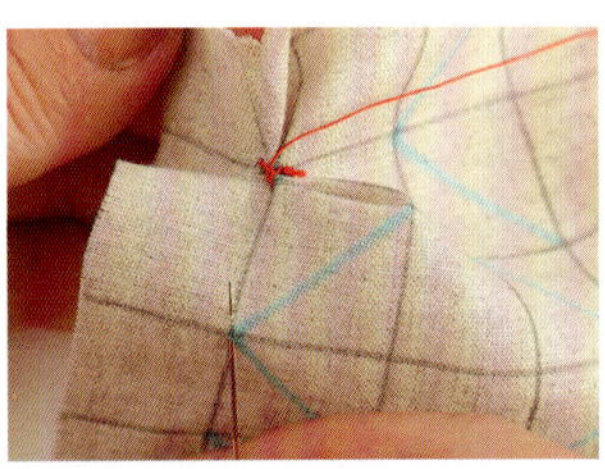

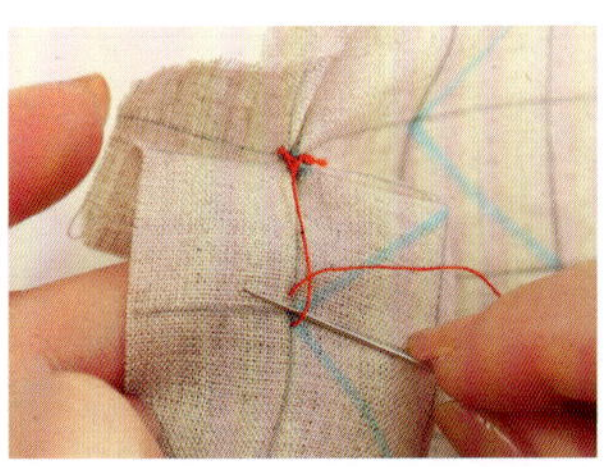

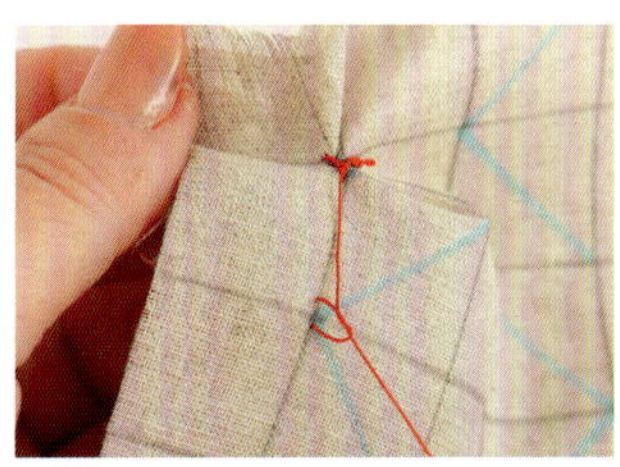

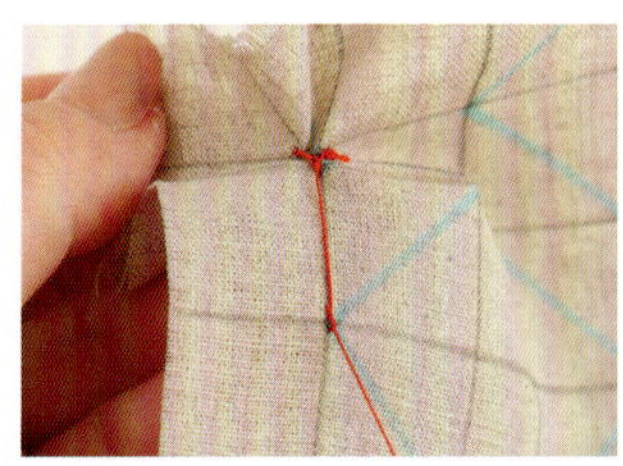

01 Pick up a stitch at the lower corner. Pass the thread from top to bottom along the grid. Only red lines are drawn on the wrong side of the fabric, but no blue dashed lines are. It's okay to draw dashed lines until you get used to it. Pick up a stitch at the bottom corner.

02 Pull the thread along the grid without tightening it. Pass the thread over the thread you just pulled to make a loop, then pass the needle under the thread you just pulled.

03 Pull the thread and secure the stitch. The thread runs along the gridline, and the knot at the corner holds the fabric in place.

How to Pass the Thread

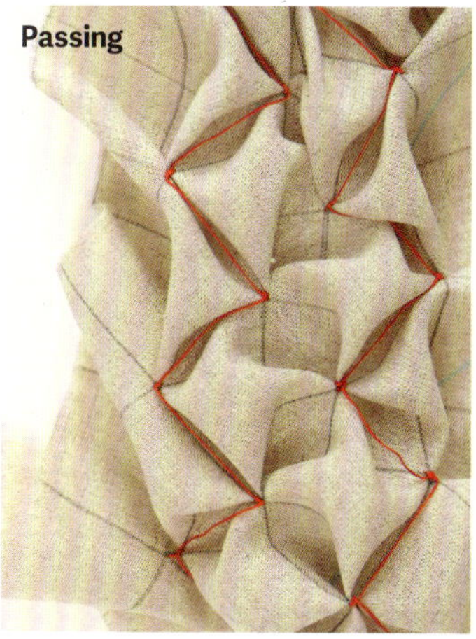

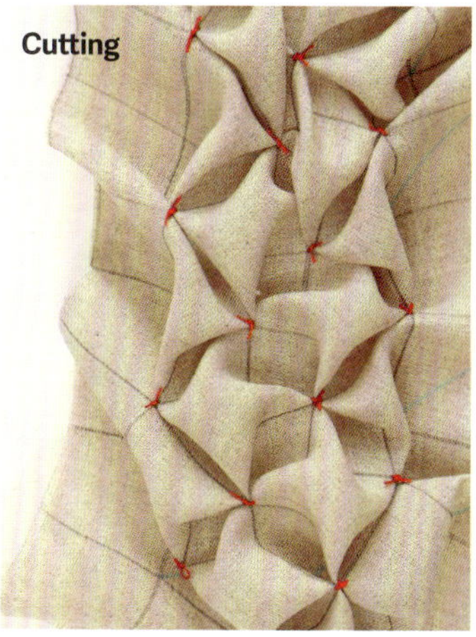

The blue dashed lines in the stitching diagrams indicate where to carry the thread. There are two ways to carry the thread: 1) move to the next grid square without cutting the thread, 2) fasten off and cut the thread each time the corners are brought together and secured. The example on the left shows carrying the thread, while the example on the right shows cutting the thread instead of carrying it. When working many stitches, it is more convenient to carry the thread without cutting it, but if you want to preserve elasticity, cutting the thread is more suitable. In this book, the thread is cut when skipping two or more grid squares. Since cutting the thread instead of carrying it can sometimes make the process easier to understand, feel free to choose the method you prefer.

How to Press the Fabric

Once the shape is set, it will not return to its original state, so apply steam gradually when pressing. Do not press down; hold the iron slightly above the fabric and apply the steam gently. For some fabrics, use a pressing cloth when ironing.

About Seam Allowances

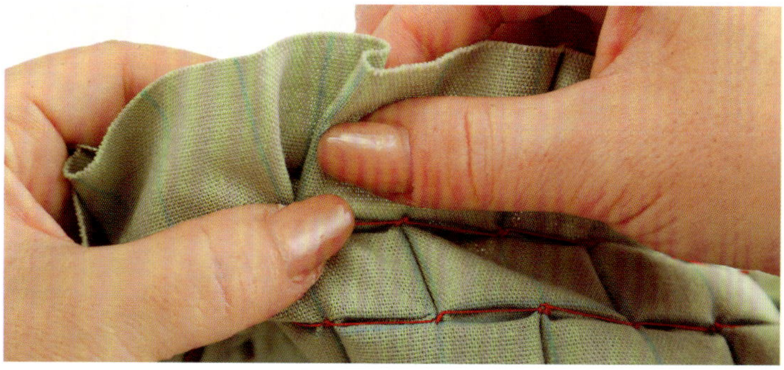

Once all the stitching is complete, the fabric will be gathered, and the seam allowances around the edges will appear wavy. Since this makes construction difficult, fold the seam allowances along the stitch lines in advance. Marking all the way to the edge of the fabric makes it easier to shape the seam allowances neatly.

In the Brick pattern shown in the photo above, match the markings and fold small pleats like box pleats. If you press them firmly to set the shape, construction will be easier later. If pressing alone does not set the folds well, basting the folds in place first will help.

About Washing

Hand washing is the best way to clean smocked fabric. Wash gently to avoid crushing the three-dimensional shape. If the threads on the back are visible, be careful not to snag or cut them.

Bone One-Handle Bag

This bag is made using bias-cut fabric and finished with a softly rounded shape. A vertical smocking pattern was chosen to suit the one-handle style. The opening is wide and the inside is easy to see, so this is a project where you'll want to pay attention to the lining as well.

Bone Pattern: page 58
How to Make: page 110

Wave Pocket Tote

Smocking is incorporated into the external pocket of this simple, vertically elongated bag. The body of the bag is made from sturdy canvas while the pocket is made from lightweight ramie fabric for a softer feel. The Wave pattern stands out beautifully against the combination of two different textures in white-on-white.

Wave Pattern: page 60
How to Make: page 113

Crisscross Bone Ruffle Handle Bag

I added stitching to the zipper opening and handles, which added texture to match the smocking, before finishing the bag stylishly with faux leather. These created a well-balanced, eye-catching design.

Crisscross Bone Pattern: page 62
How to Make: page 116

Arrow Triangle Bag

I added smocking at the opening and then gathered it to create a permanent triangular shape. The soft, relaxed texture of the linen also helps show off the gathers beautifully.

Arrow Pattern: page 64
How to Make: page 119

Brick and Bow Clutch

Pinch the center of the Brick pattern to form a bow shape. I used beads in a similar color to the main fabric to create a subtle look with just a hint of sparkle. Try different combinations of fabric and bead colors to match your style.

Brick Pattern: page 66
How to Make: page 122

Brick Shoulder Bag

I used the smocking pattern vertically and kept the design clean with elongated lines that follow the shape of the bag. Although the stitching is less visible in black, it still has a strong presence, making it easy to use in a subtle way.

Brick Pattern: page 66
How to Make: page 104

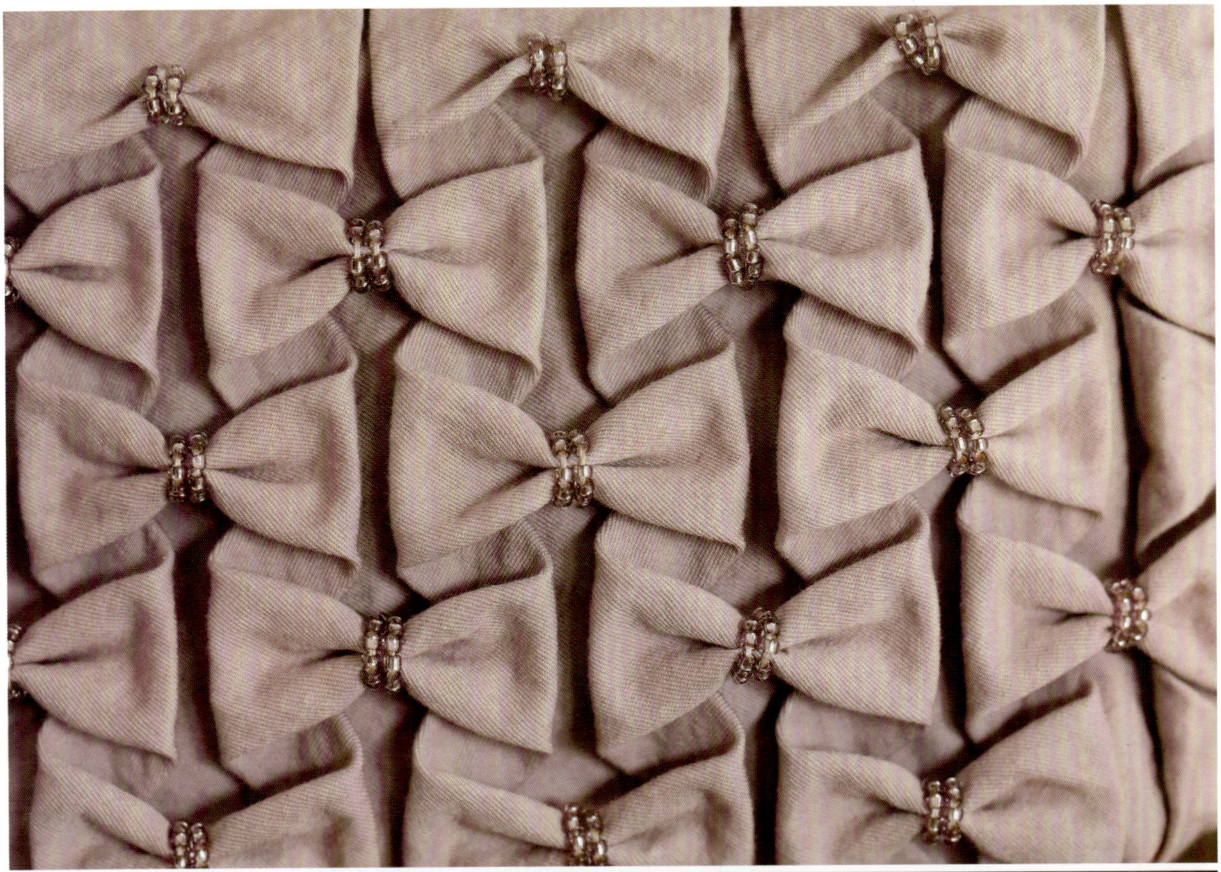

Lozenge Cushion

The Lozenge shape resembles an elongated version of the Brick pattern, but it has both the beauty and impact of a geometric design. As an interior piece, you'll never get bored of its modern simplicity. The fabric texture with *tsumugi*-style slubs also suits the pattern perfectly.

Lozenge Pattern: page 76
How to Make: page 124

Shell Circle Cushion

This is a striking round cushion. I used soft crepe fabric to enhance the beauty of the circular shape and the curved pleats and Shell smocking. It's also important that the pleats lie neatly in one direction.

Shell Pattern: page 54
How to Make: page 126

Flower Drawstring Bag

I added smocking at the base of this bag to create a rounded shape. By matching the colors of the beads and the cord, the design feels cohesive and stylish without looking busy. Satin has both softness and body, which helps show lattice smocking at its best.

Flower Pattern: page 94
How to Make: page 128

Box Drawstring Pouch

I used slightly heavier Oxford cotton fabric to enhance the lattice smocking and stop the stitching from dominating the pouch. This is a good example of how even small smocking can stand out.

Box Pattern: page 102
How to Make: page 134

Heart Chain Clutch

Although it's handbag-sized, I gave this clutch a sturdy gusset so it's practical and reliable. Remove the chain and it can also be used as a pouch. While it looks like leather, I chose a leather-like satin for ease of sewing.

Heart Pattern: page 74
How to Make: page 131

Diamond Ruffle Pouch

I used check and polka-dot fabrics to smock while threading on beads. Using print fabric adds an interesting effect, as new patterns emerge in the gathered areas created by the stitching.

Diamond Pattern: page 100
How to Make: page 136

Hourglass Crescent Bag

I use the spacing of the print to guide the smocking. The stripes within the stitched areas form an Hourglass pattern. Although the finished bag has a half-moon shape, the original fabric is cut slightly wider than a square. This is a handbag that lets you enjoy the visual interest of its shape.

Hourglass Pattern: page 98
How to Make: page 139

Rattan Bamboo-Handle Bag

True to the word "rattan" (meaning woven cane), I added smocking at the bottom of the bag to create a basket-like feel. Thanks to the stitching, the body of the bag also takes on a softly rounded shape, which is another charming feature.

Rattan Pattern: page 80
How to Make: page 142

Dragon Scale Drawstring Bag

This drawstring bag features bold smocking on diagonally striped fabric. Even after smocking, the stripes connect cleanly and remain visually continuous. By changing the fabric color, this scale pattern could also resemble pinecones or even a Christmas tree.

Dragon Scale Pattern: page 84
How to Make: page 145

Puzzle Wall Art

I turned lattice-smocked fabric into a simple decorative piece by layering organza over Oxford fabric and stitching them together. The transparency and the layered three-dimensional effect give it a beautiful, ethereal appearance.

Puzzle Pattern: page 88
How to Make: page 148

TOOLS

This section introduces the tools needed for lattice smocking. These are the same basic tools used for sewing. Please use your preferred tools.

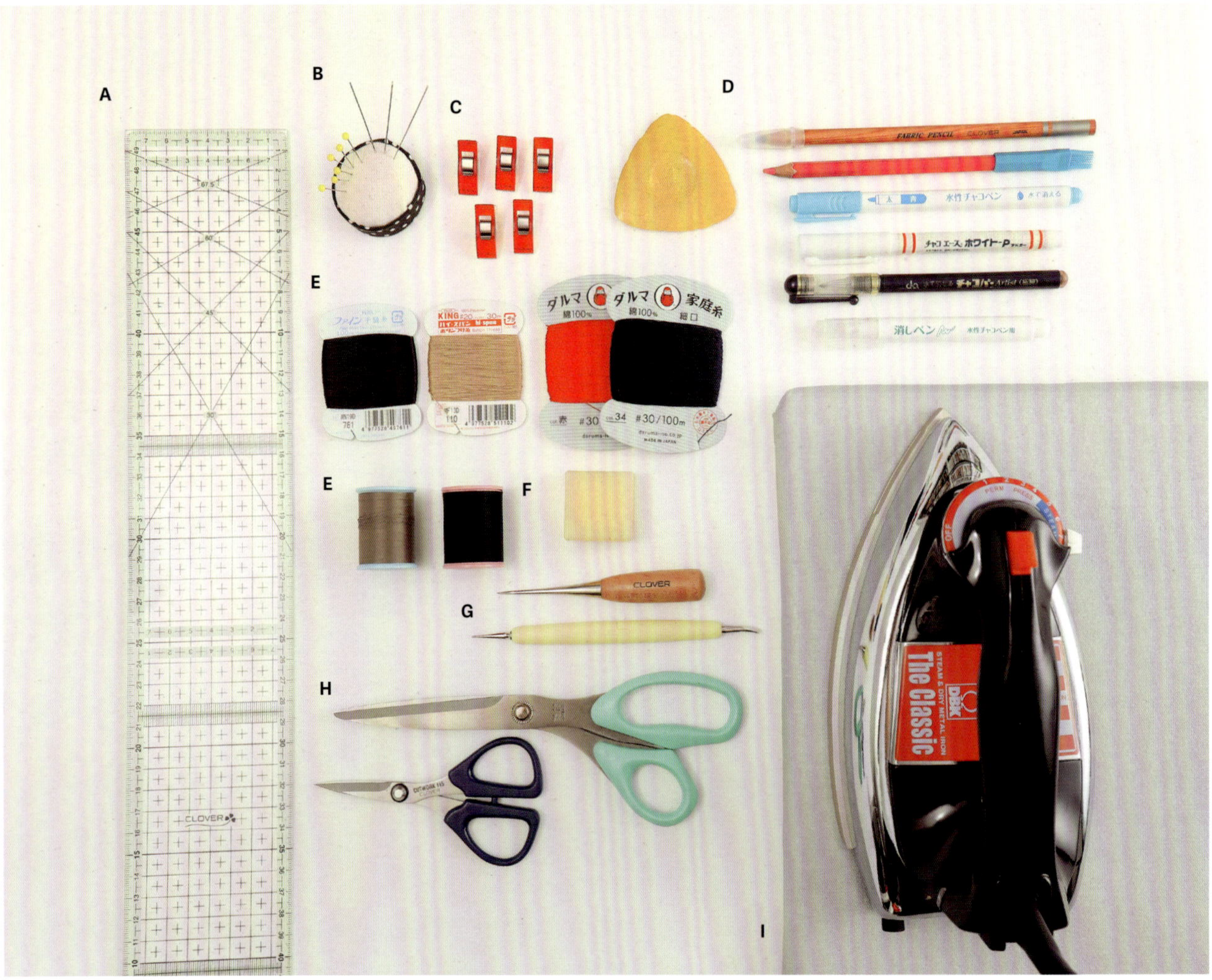

A. Ruler
Even more useful if it has a grid consisting of vertical and horizontal lines.

B. Sewing Needles, Pins, and Pincushion
Longer needles make it easier to pick up stitches over longer distances, but any needle you find comfortable to use is fine.

C. Sewing Clips
Used during construction. You can choose to use either clips or pins for basting.

D. Marking Tools
You can use any marking tool you prefer, as long as it does not affect the right side of the fabric. Pencils or pens that don't dye the fabric and that can be erased later are recommended.

E. Thread
Use hand-sewing thread such as fine household thread or embroidery thread. A sewing machine is convenient for the construction stage.

F. Thread Wax
Apply this to the thread to make it stronger. It is not essential to use, so feel free to use it according to your preference.

G. Awl, Tracing Wheel, and Hera Marker
These are used to shape and adjust the lattice smocking. Since they are often used on areas of the fabric that remain visible, an awl may damage the fabric or leave holes. If that is a concern, use a tracing wheel or hera marker instead.

H. Scissors
Use fabric shears for cutting fabric, and thread snips for cutting thread while stitching.

I. Iron and Ironing Board
Use an iron with a steam function.

MATERIALS

Fabric is very important for lattice smocking. It can change the appearance of a piece, so please try out various fabrics while referring to page 42. Prepare materials according to the project you wish to make.

A. Fabric for Lattice Smocking
Solid fabrics are recommended; if using a print, checks, polka dots, or stripes work best. With checks, dots, or stripes, aligning the print with the grid size when stitching can create interesting designs. Be careful with floral or large-scale prints, as the overall motif may become unclear. Depending on the print, however, some fabrics may produce unexpectedly interesting results.

B. Fabric for the Lining
Any fabric is fine as long as it does not show through to the right side. Choose a fabric that works well with the outer fabric.

C. Fusible Interfacing
If you want to maintain a softly padded shape for items like bags, apply knit interfacing or lightweight, nonwoven interfacing to the wrong side.

D. Handles
These are used when finishing bags. Choose handles according to the project. For drawstring items, thread a cord of your choice.

E. Magnetic Snaps and D-Rings
Use these to close flaps or attach straps, as appropriate for the project.

F. Beads
These can be stitched in together with the smocking or added as a final decorative detail. Choose the bead size to suit the size of the stitching.

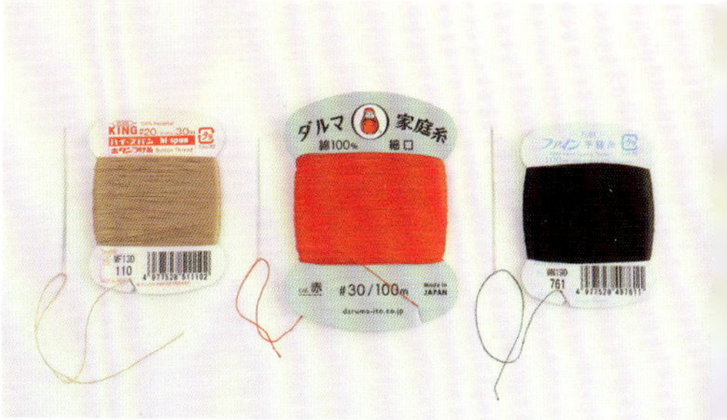

These are examples of needle length and thread thickness. Choose the thread thickness to suit the fabric. Very short needles are not suitable, so use a needle length that is easy to work with.

ABOUT FABRIC

You can use any type of fabric for lattice smocking. However, some are more suitable than others depending on what you're trying to achieve. If you're going to make the effort to make a piece, you might as well learn about their compatibility before you choose your fabric and pattern.

Stretch Level

For some smocking patterns, the fabric stretch will affect the beauty of the finished piece. Diagonal patterns require soft and stretchy fabric, while horizontal and vertical patterns can be made with stiffer fabric. Use the chart below as a reference when choosing fabric.

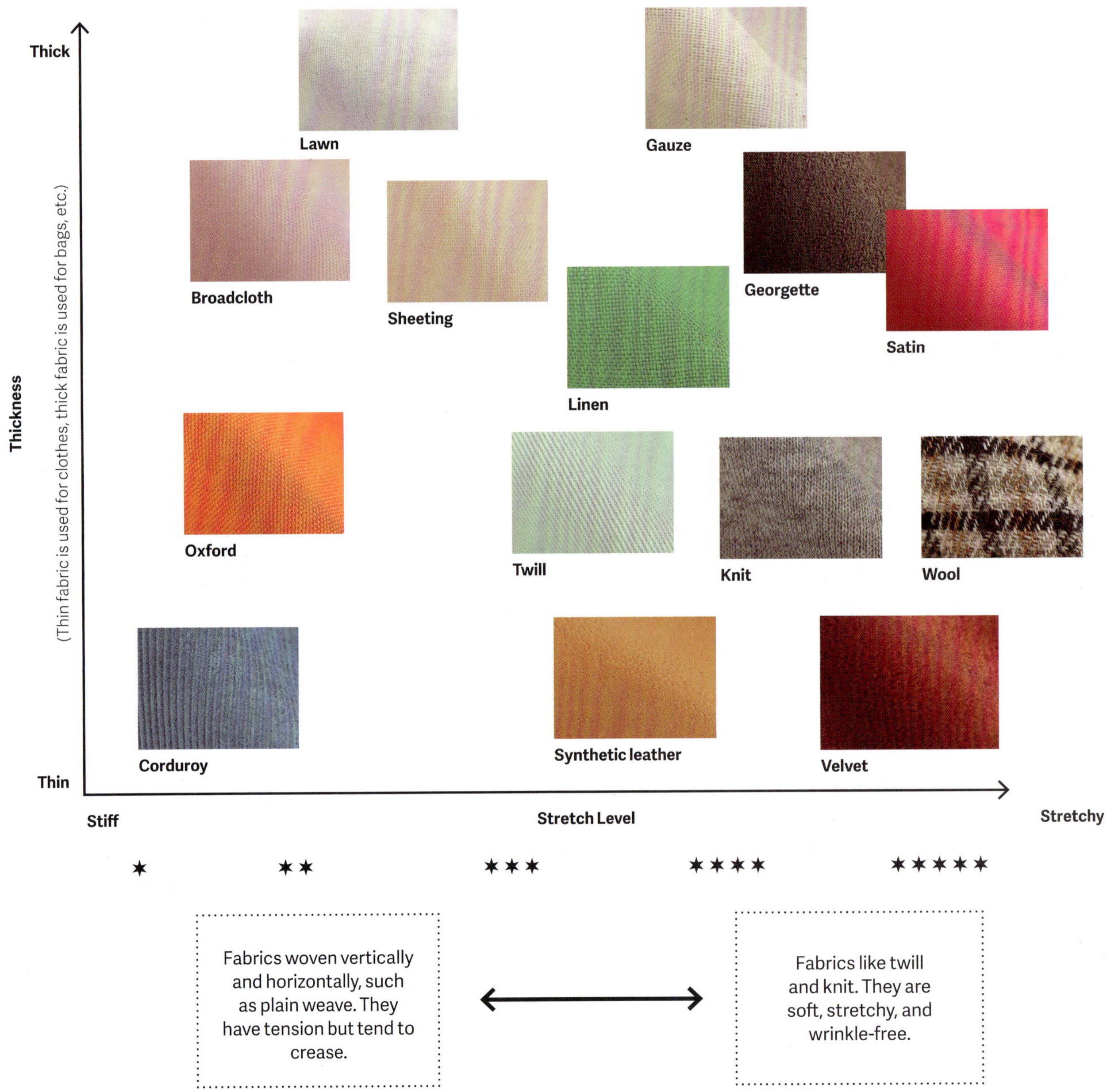

About Washing

If you use water to erase marks or other lines after stitching, the fabric may shrink if it is very wet. If the fabric can be prewashed, be sure to wash it before smocking to shrink the fabric so that it does not change shape later.

Finishing with Different Fabrics

Even with the same pattern, the finished piece will differ depending on the fabric used. Let's take a look at the differences between three types of fabric using the Lattice pattern (page 46).

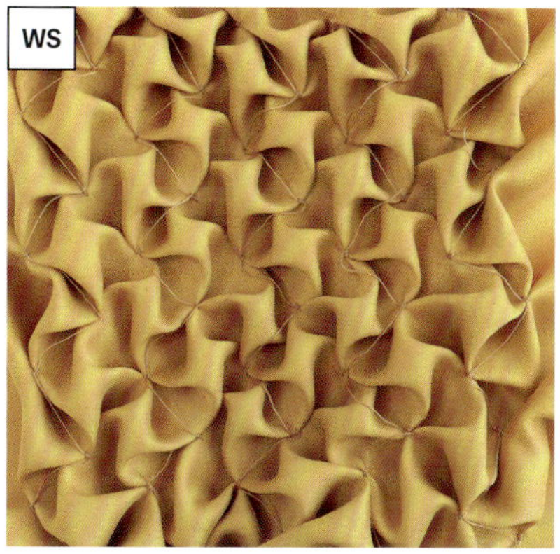

1. Satin

The stretchy and taut nature of satin allows for beautifully defined patterns. Its sheen creates an elegant impression. While it may or may not suit your project or personal taste, it definitely provides a plump, well-defined shape for a beautiful finish.

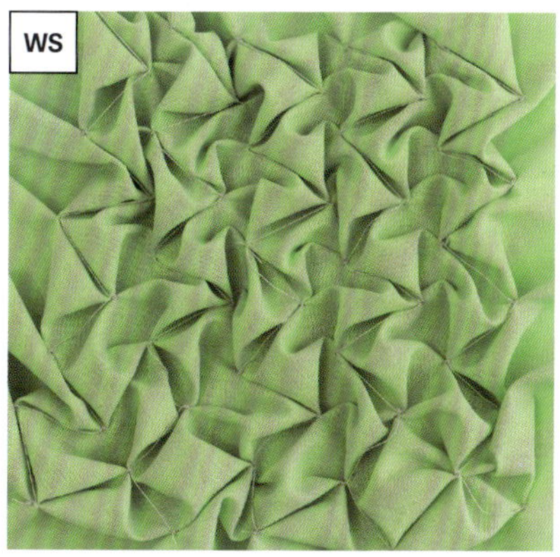

2. Sheeting

Sheeting has a coarser weave than lawn or broadcloth and is thinner than Oxford. It's inexpensive and available in a wide variety of colors and patterns, making it a popular fabric. While not as stretchy as corduroy, it does have some wrinkles and can lose its shape.

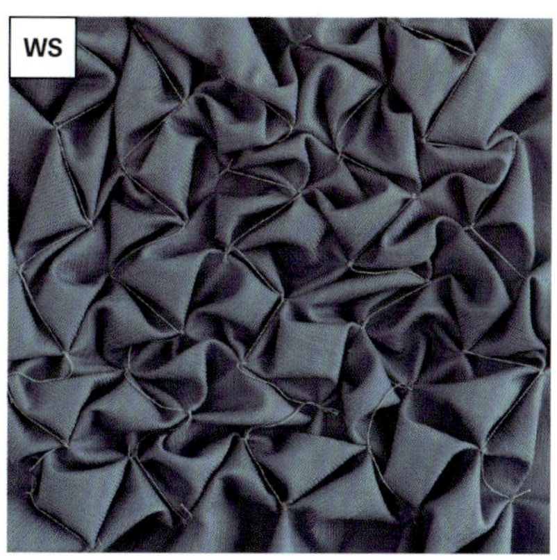

3. Corduroy

Corduroy, with its vertical ribbing, is a somewhat challenging material. Its strengths, such as its thickness and texture, can also create problems when it comes to shaping. Some areas of the pattern wrinkle easily, resulting in a poorly shaped garment

As you can see, even with the same smocking pattern, the finished product will vary depending on the fabric. Consider your fabric selection based on how well the pattern and fabric work together, how you want to use it, and the effect you want to achieve. Also, remember that the piece will shrink to about half its size when stitched. If you're using a heavy material, you'll need roughly twice the amount of fabric as the finished product, so consider the weight of the piece when choosing your design and materials.

CUSTOMIZING PATTERNS

In the next two sections, I will explain how to stitch 20 different smocking patterns. Here, I will also explain three ways to further customize these stitches for creative projects. I will use the Flower, Wave, and Leaf patterns, but the same techniques can also be applied to other patterns.

■ Reverse

Reversing the thread feed direction will flip the WS to the front.

Picking Up Both Ends

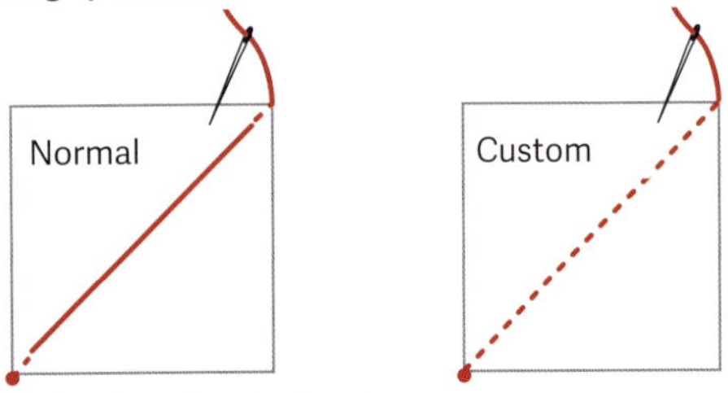

Pass the thread to the front.

When picking up all four corners

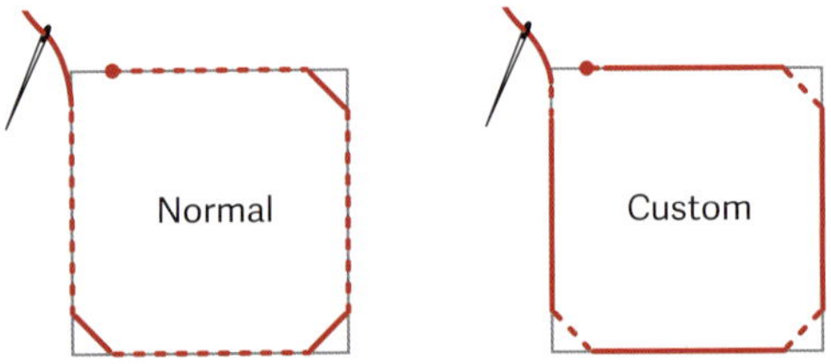

Pick up a stitch near the starting point, then follow the thread along the back to pick up the four corners.

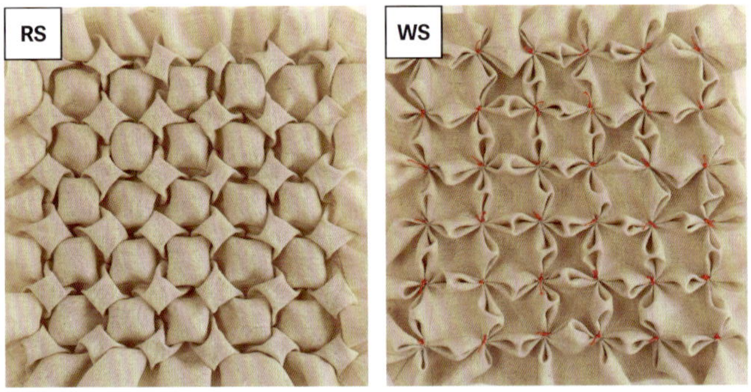

The WS features a Flower pattern, while the RS displays a Box pattern with smaller square sections.

In both cases, don't run the thread to the next square; instead, tie a finishing knot and cut the thread each time.

■ Number of Empty Squares

Changing the number of the empty squares where no thread is passed will alter the shape of the pattern.
Wave (page 60)
Example: Change the interval between stitches to two squares.

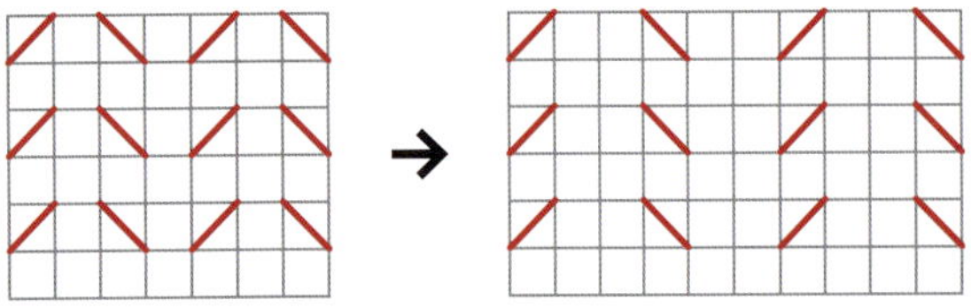

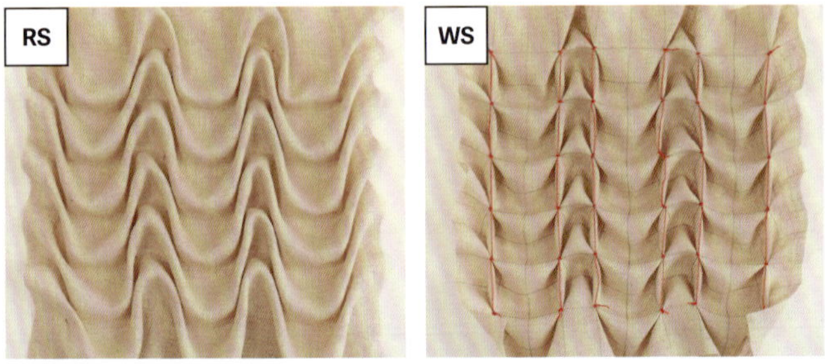

This creates a Wave pattern with large curves.

■ Stitch on the Bias

If you draw the grid diagonally, the pattern will be diagonal (with a bias).
Leaf (page 56)
Example: Draw the lattice diagonally.

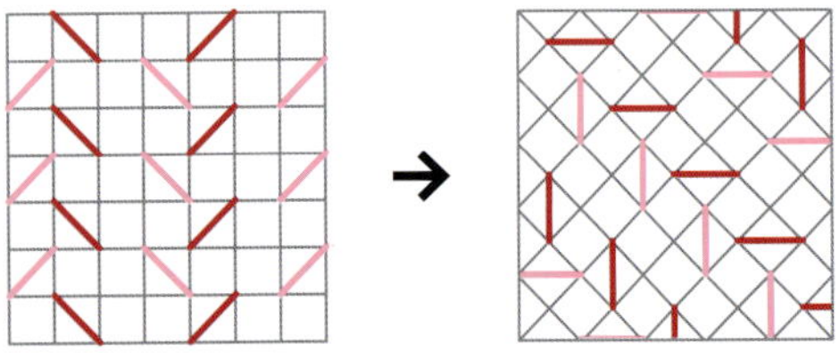

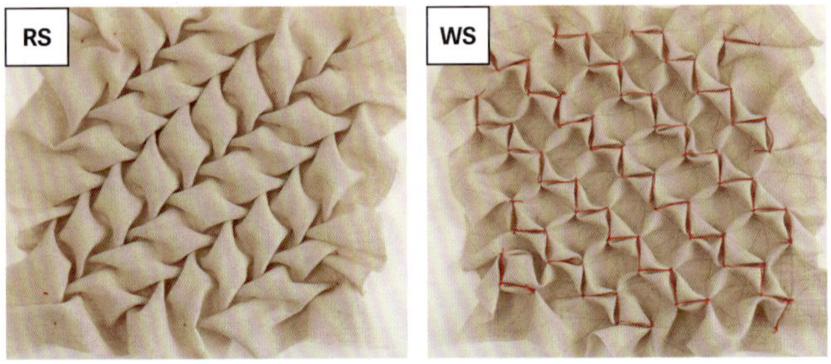

The Leaf pattern is applied diagonally. It stretches diagonally but resists stretching or shrinking lengthwise and widthwise, resulting in a slightly stiffer finish than usual.

Straight and Diagonal Lines

These smocking patterns join fabric by picking up both ends of the diagonal or straight lines of a grid.

LATTICE

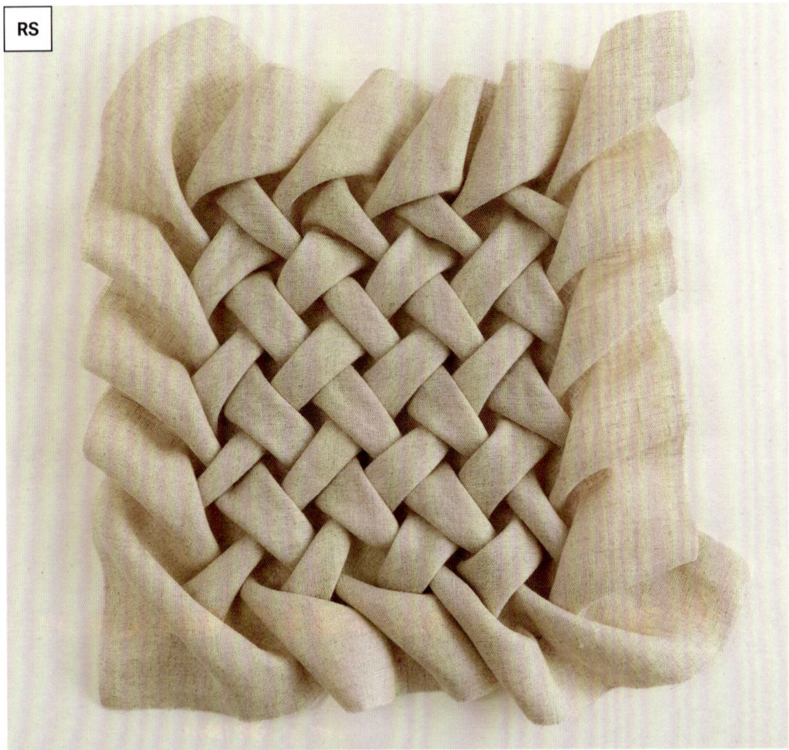

■ **Original Fabric Size**

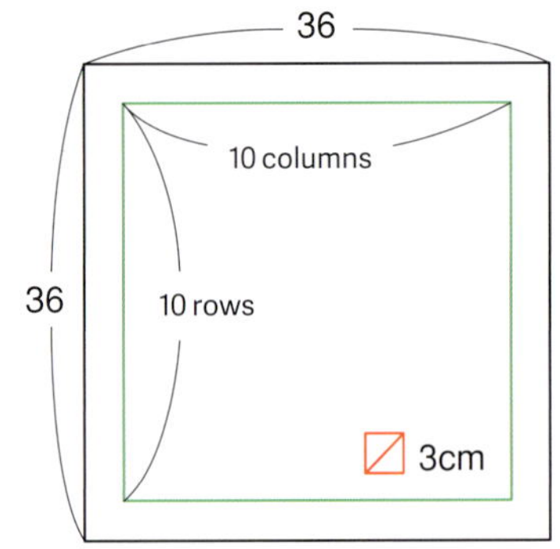

■ **Fabric's Stretch Level**

★ ★ ★ ☆ ☆

■ **Pressing**

- Not required to finish

■ **Notes**

- Finish two columns at a time

The **red** and **pink** lines show where you should pull the thread tight to bring joined sections together. The **light blue** dashed lines show where you should pass the thread. **Green** letters indicate stitching order. **Gray** arrows indicate direction.

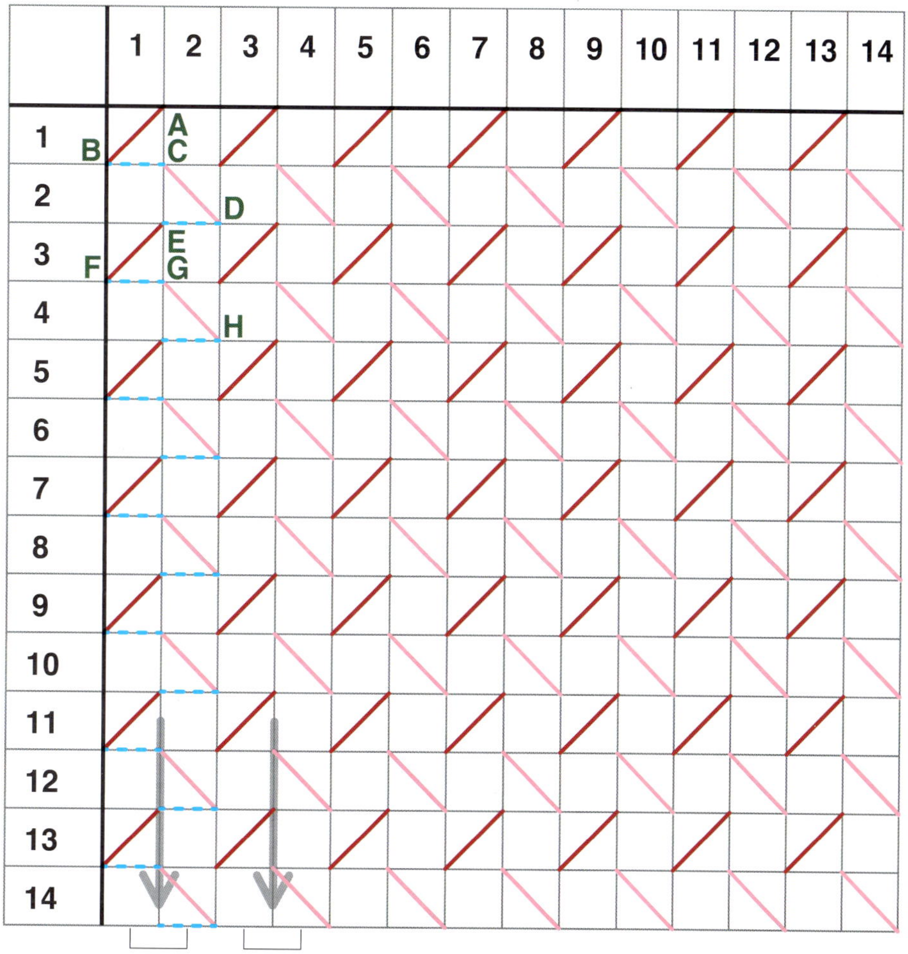

Finish two columns at a time.

■ Stitching Instructions

1. Insert the needle into corner A and pick up a stitch. Insert the needle into corner B and pick up a stitch, then scoop up corner A again. Pull the thread tight to bring the corners together.
2. Sew the joined corners AB together with one stitch and secure the stitch.
3. Pick up a stitch at corner C, pass the thread, and secure the stitch.
4. Pick up a stitch at corner D. Scoop up corner C again and pull the thread tight to bring the corners together.
5. Sew the joined corners CD together with one stitch and secure the stitch.
6. Pick up a stitch at corner E, pass the thread, and secure the stitch. Corner E will now be the same as corner A, so just repeat the same process for the rest of the column.
7. When you reach the end of the column, tie a finishing knot and cut the thread. Begin stitching the next column from the top using the same process.

Bring A and B together.

01 Draw a grid on the wrong side of the fabric and then draw diagonal lines connecting the corners that will be scooped together, as shown on p. 51.

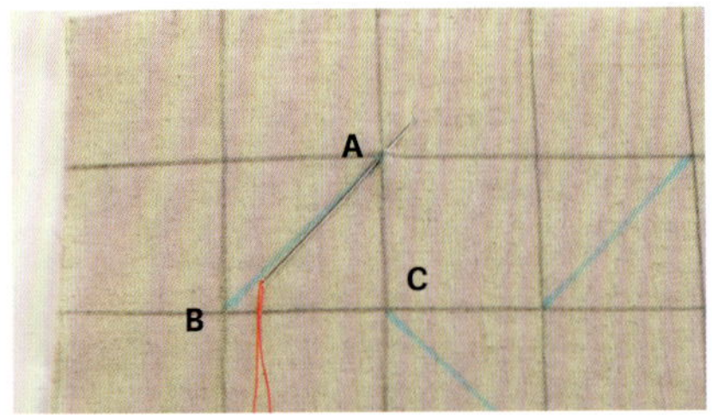

02 Thread the needle and tie a finishing knot with a single strand of thread. Pick up a stitch from inside the square to outside at corner A. Each stitch should be about 0.2cm long.

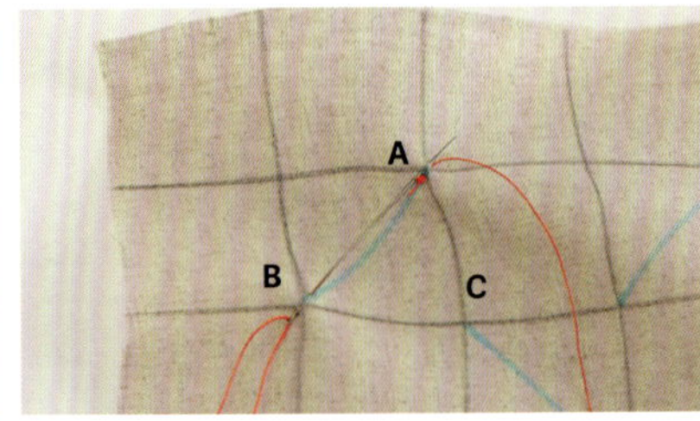

03 Pick up a stitch from outside the square to inside at corner B. Scoop up corner A from **Step 02** in the same way.

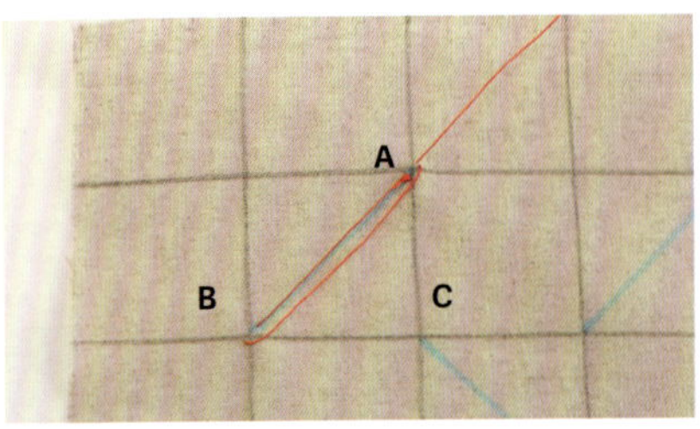

04 Pull the thread. You will see two strands of thread running diagonally.

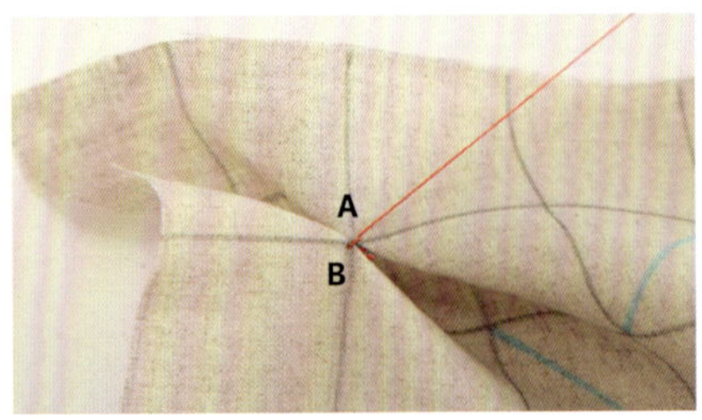

05 Pull the thread tight to .bring corners A and B together.

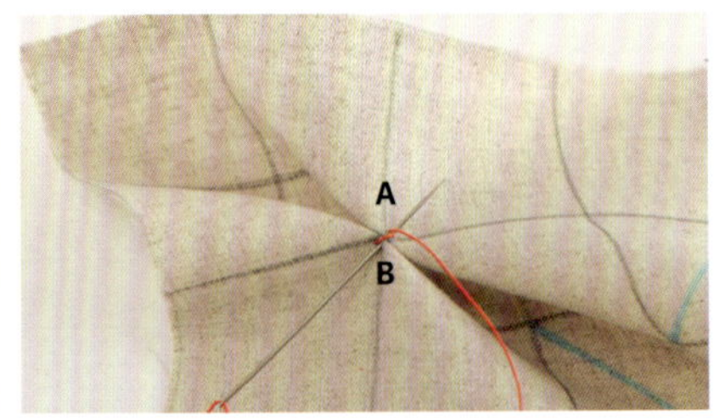

06 Sew the joined corners AB together with one stitch.

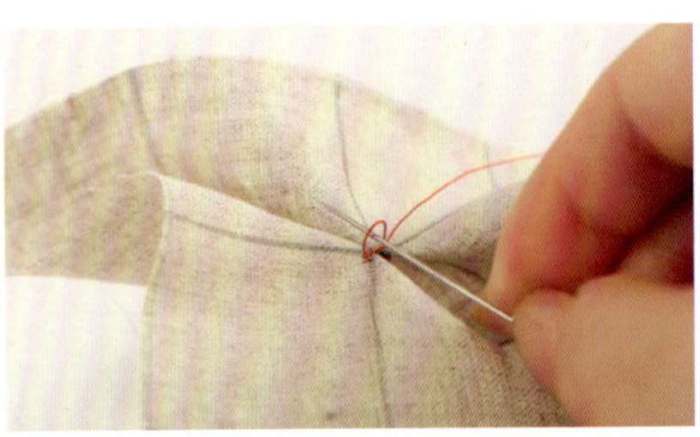

07 Pull the thread, creating a small loop just before pulling it tight. Pass the needle through the loop from bottom to top.

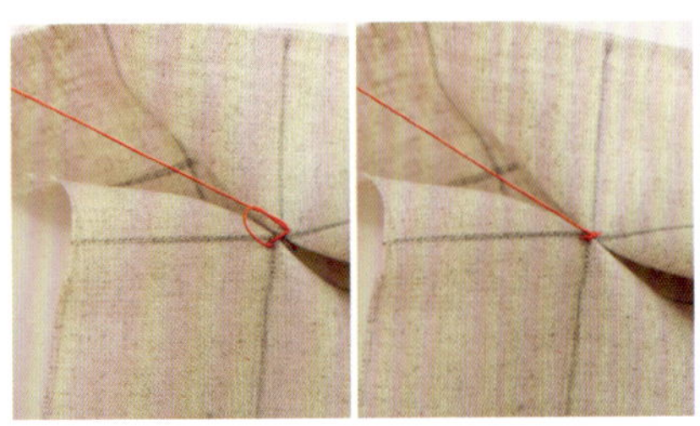

08 Pull the thread tight to lock the stitch and secure the fabric.

Pass the thread from AB to C.

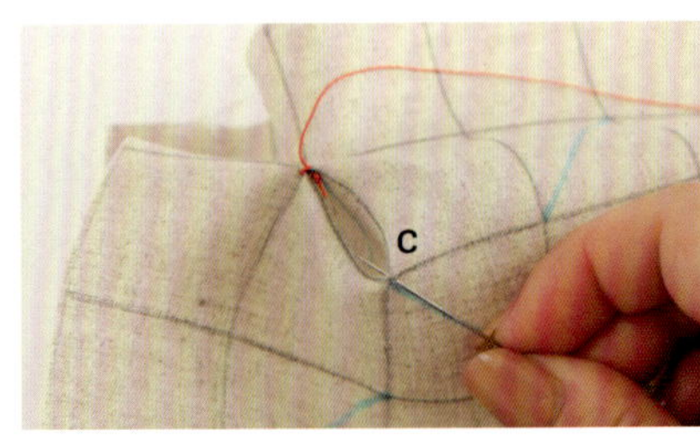

09 Move to the next row and scoop up one stitch at corner C.

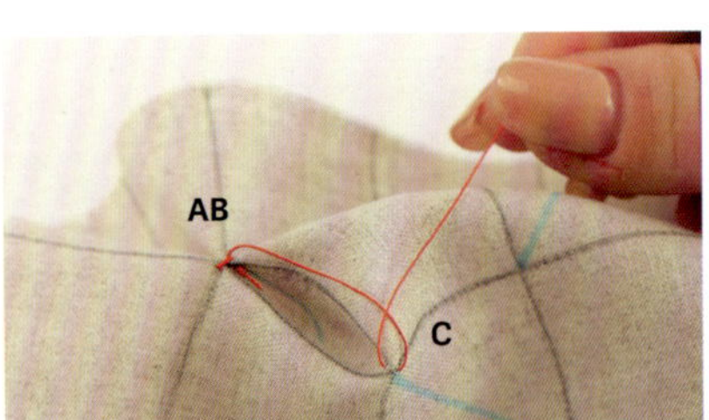

10 Pull the thread along the gridline from AB to C.

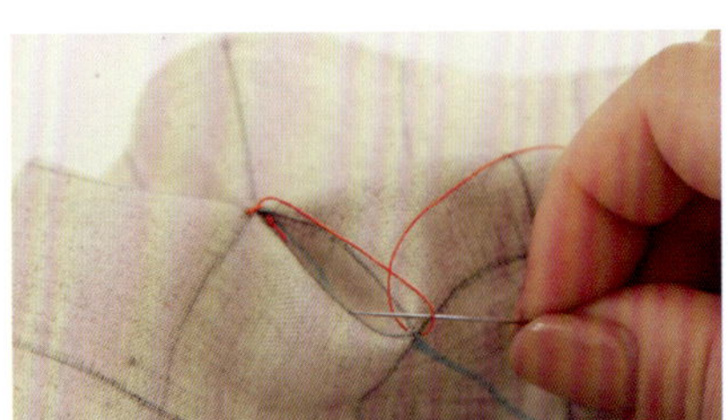

11 Without pulling the thread all the way through, pass it over the thread that you just pulled to create a loop, then bring the needle back under the thread and through the loop.

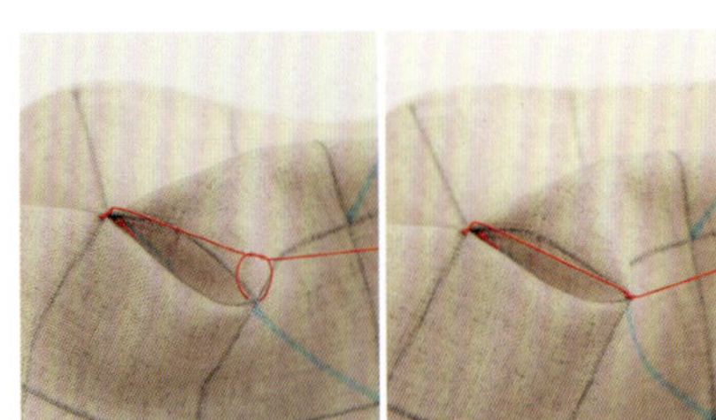

12 Pull the thread to make a knot. This will run the thread along the gridline and create a knot at the corner, securing the fabric in place.

‣ Bring C and D together.

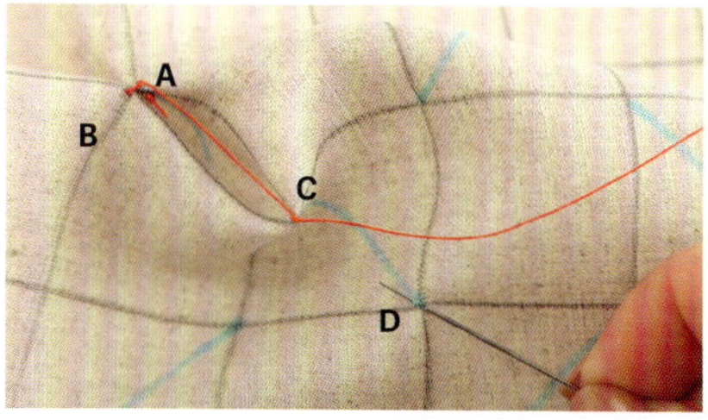

13 Pick up a stitch at the opposite corner to corner C, which is corner D. You'll be bringing the two corners together in the same way that you did in **Steps 02** to **08**.

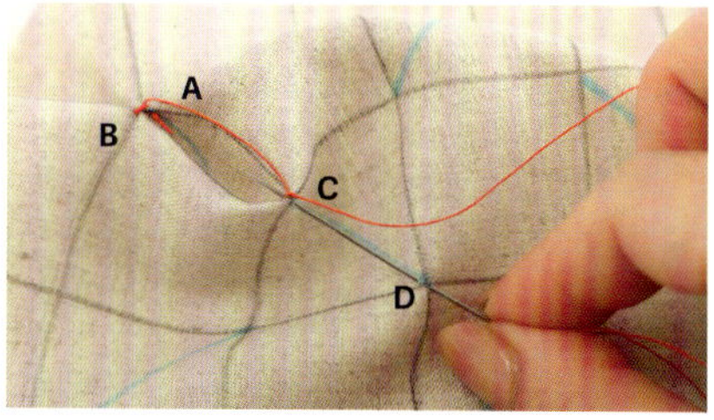

14 Pick up a stitch at corner C again.

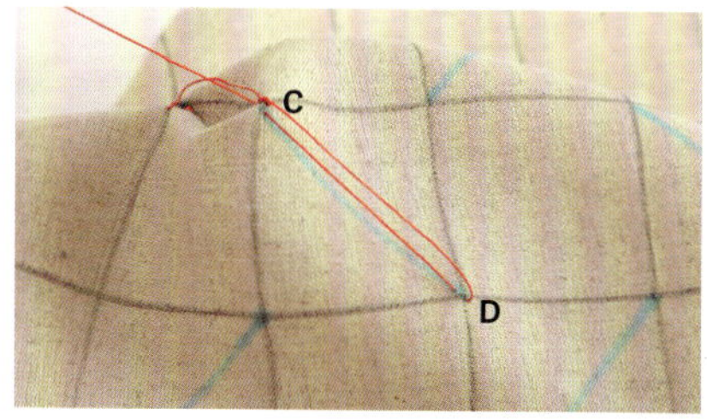

15 Pull the thread. You will see two strands of thread running diagonally.

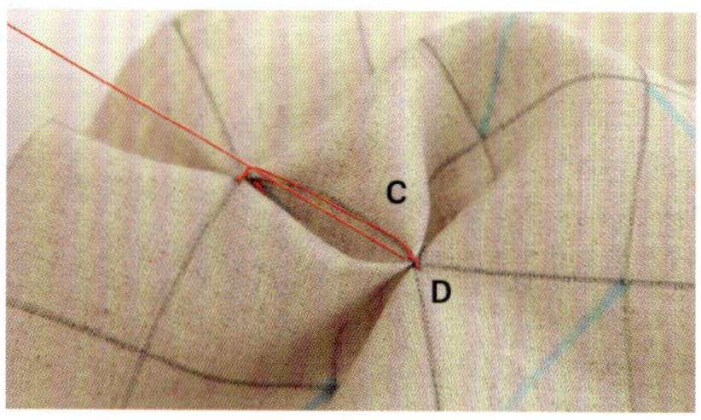

16 Pull the thread tight to bring corners C and D together.

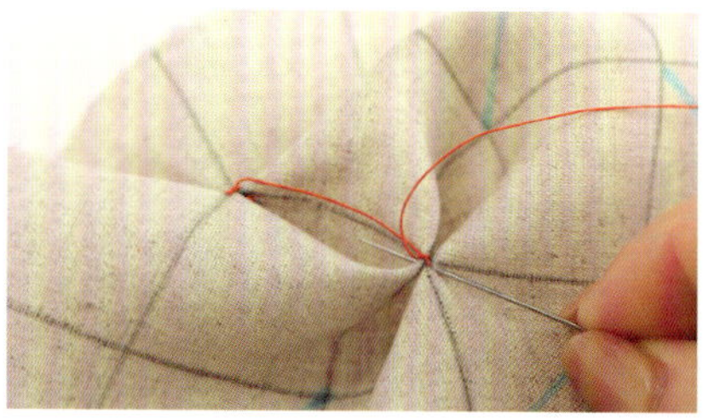

17 Sew the joined corners CD together with one stitch.

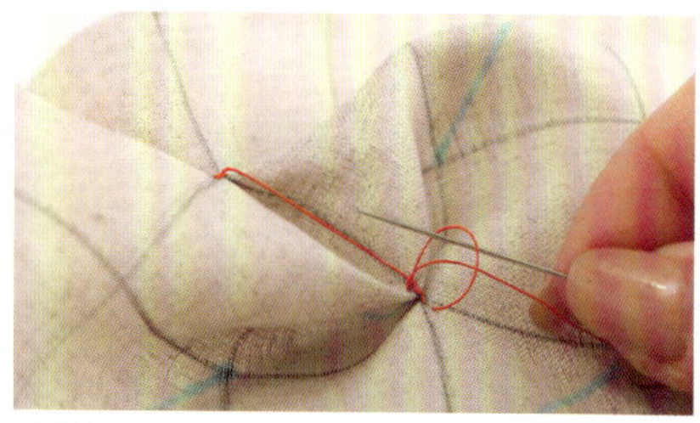

18 Pull the thread, creating a small loop just before pulling it tight. Pass the needle through the loop from bottom to top.

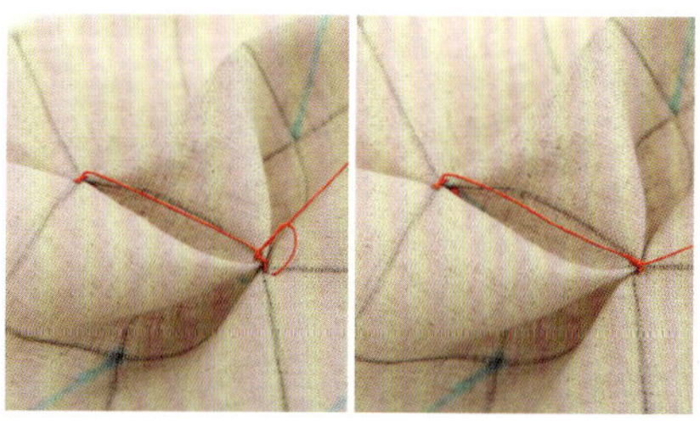

19 Pull the thread tight to lock the stitch and secure the fabric. This creates AB and CD, with the thread running between them.

‣ Pass the thread from CD to E.

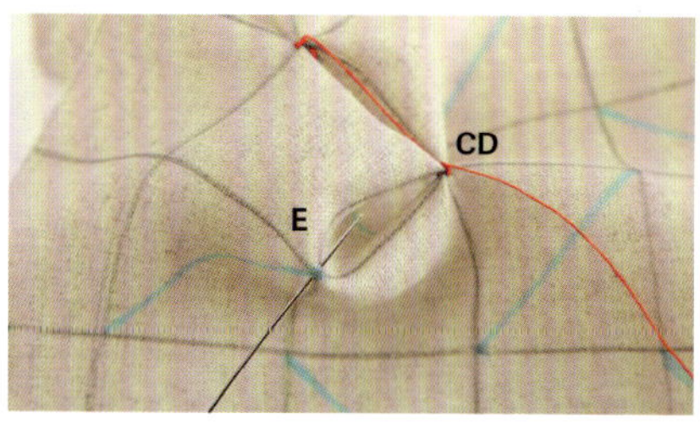

20 Move to the first column and pick up a stitch at corner E. You'll be passing the thread in the same way that you did in **Steps 09** to **12**.

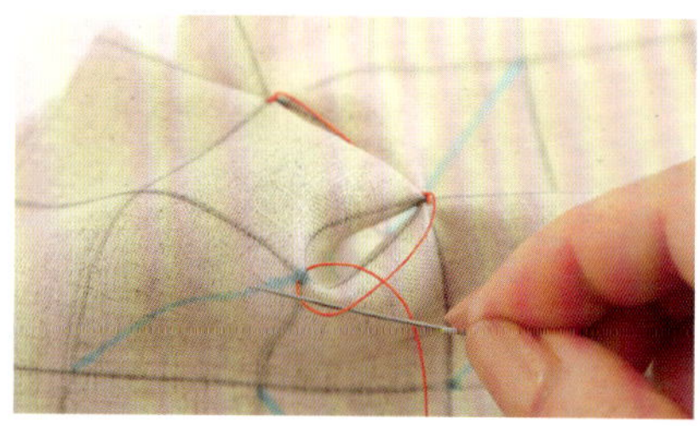

21 Pull the thread along the gridline from CD to E. Without pulling it all the way through, pass it over the thread that you just pulled to create a loop, then bring the needle back under and through the loop.

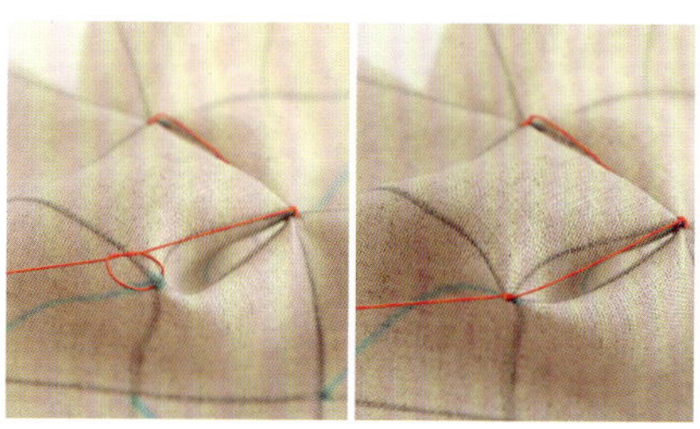

22 Pull the thread and tie a knot at the corner to secure it.

‣ Bring E and F together.

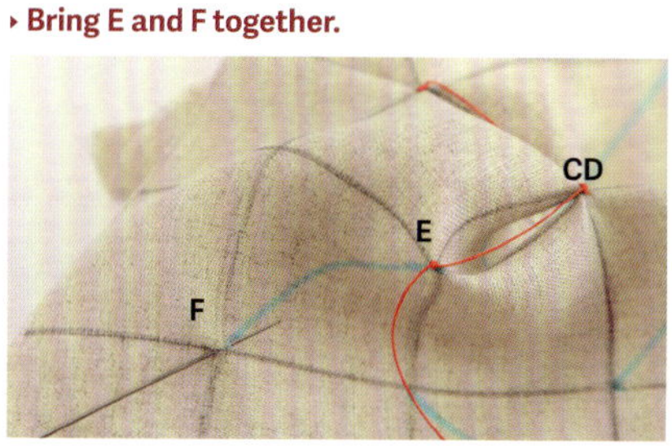

23 Pick up a stitch at the opposite corner to corner E, which is corner F. You'll be bringing the two corners together in the same way that you did in **Steps 02** to **08**.

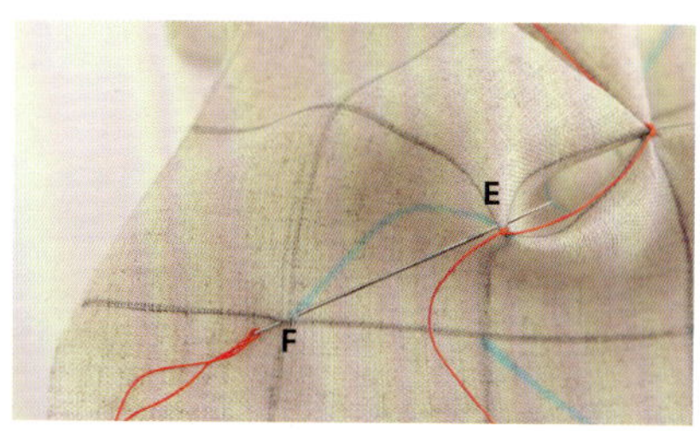

24 Pick up a stitch at corner E again.

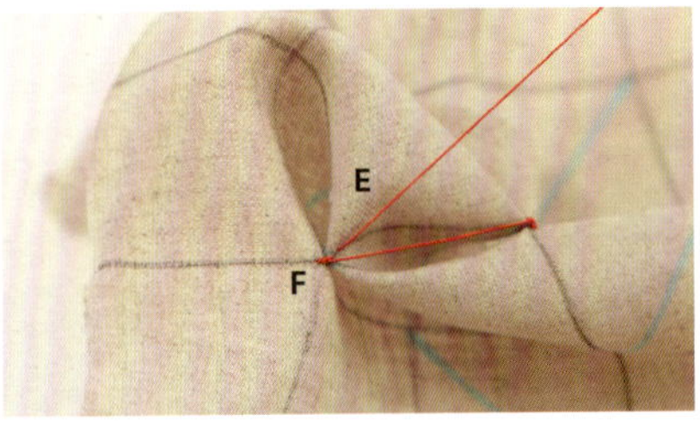

25 Pull the thread tight to bring corners E and F together.

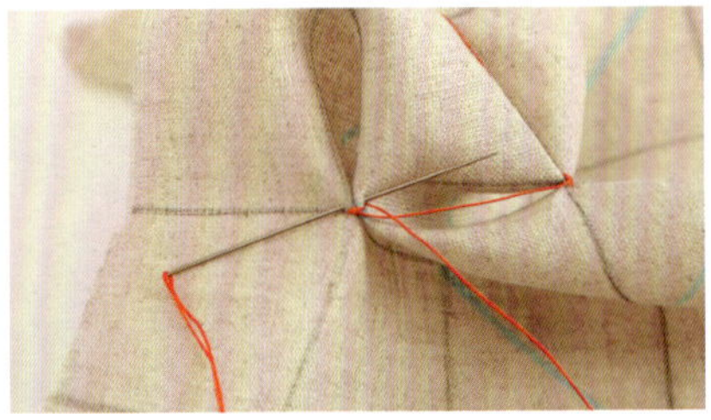

26 Sew the joined corners EF together with one stitch.

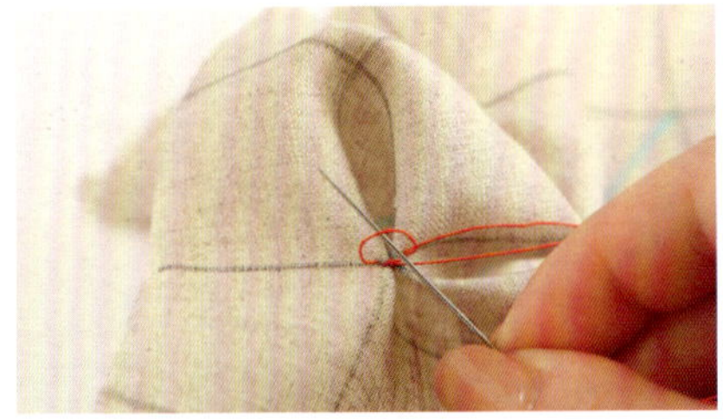

27 Pull the thread, creating a small loop just before pulling it tight. Pass the needle through the loop from bottom to top.

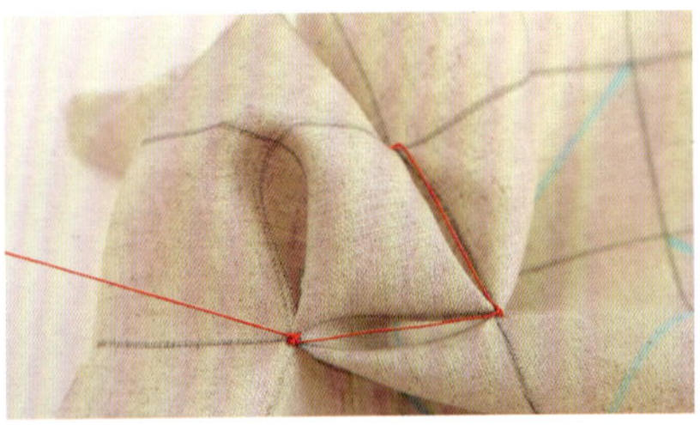

28 Pull the thread tight to lock the stitch and secure the fabric.

▸ Pass the thread from EF to G.

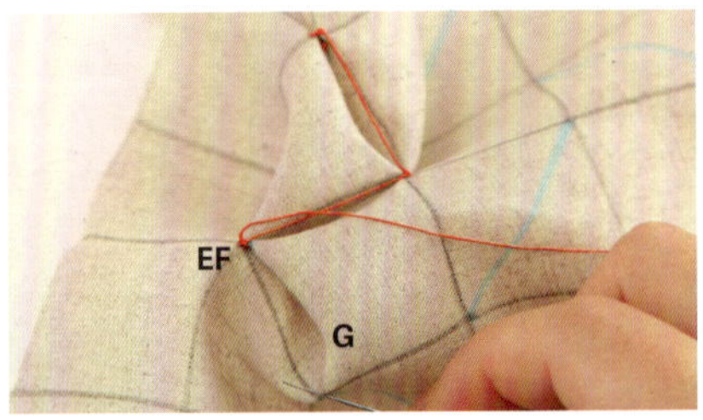

29 Move to the next row and pick up a stitch at corner G. You'll be passing the thread in the same way that you did **Steps 09** to **12**.

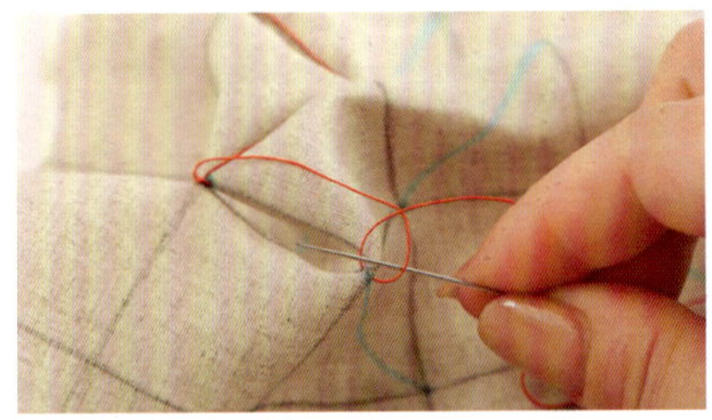

30 Pull the thread along the gridline from EF to G. Pass it over the thread to create a loop, then bring the needle back through the loop. Pull the thread and tie a knot at the corner.

▸ Bring G and H together.

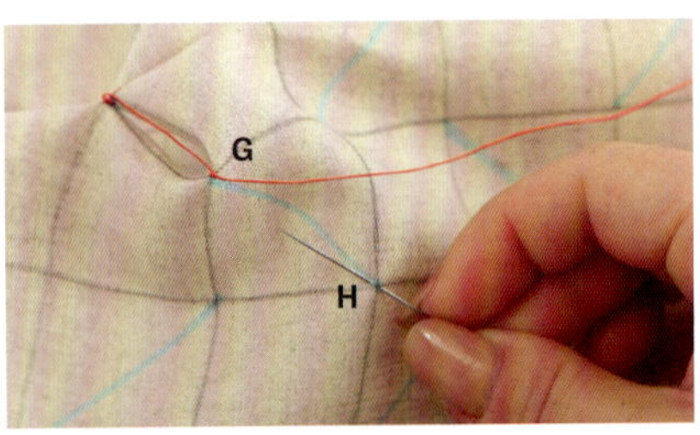

31 Pick up a stitch at the opposite corner to corner G which is corner H. You'll be bringing the two corners together in the same way that you did in **Steps 02** to **08**.

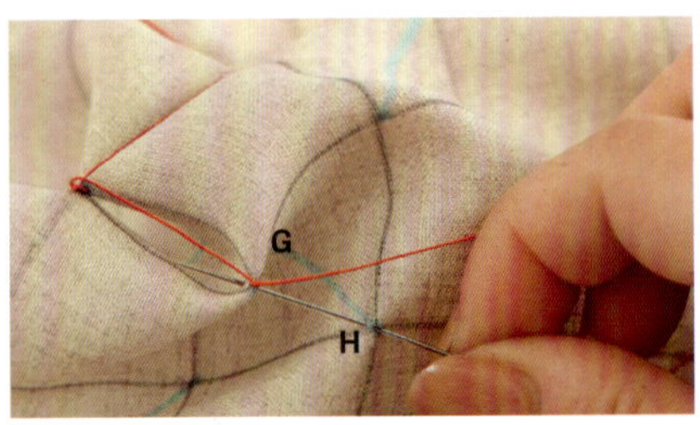

32 Pick up a stitch at corner G again.

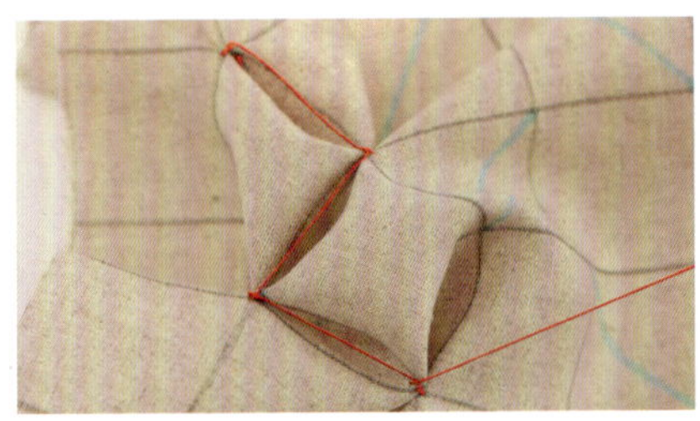

33 Pull the thread tight to bring corners G and H together.

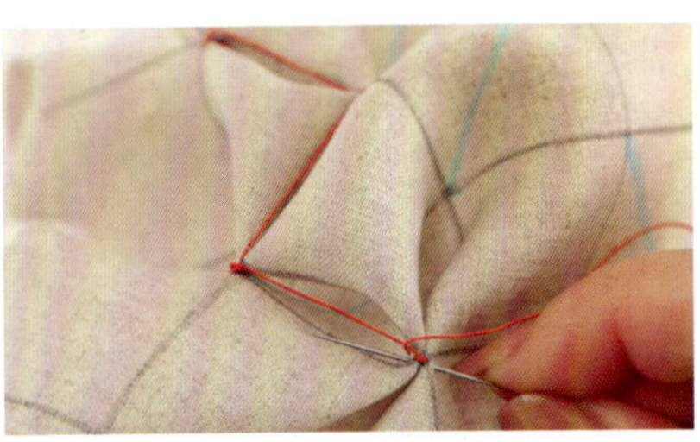

34 Sew the joined corners GH together with one stitch.

35 Pull the thread, creating a small loop just before pulling it tight. Pass the needle through the loop from bottom to top.

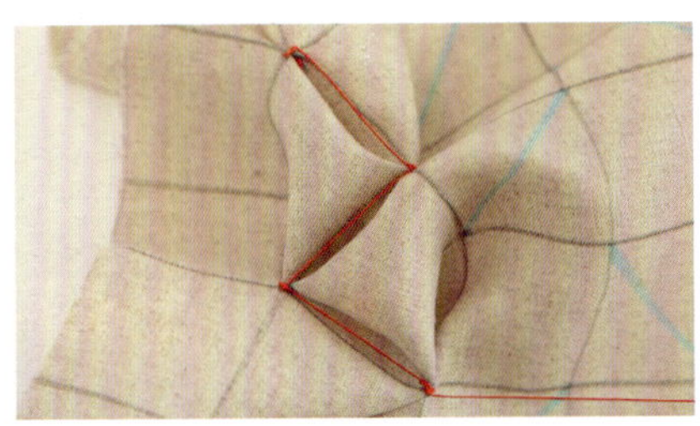

36 Pull the thread tight to lock the stitch and secure the fabric.

▸ **Two columns are complete.**

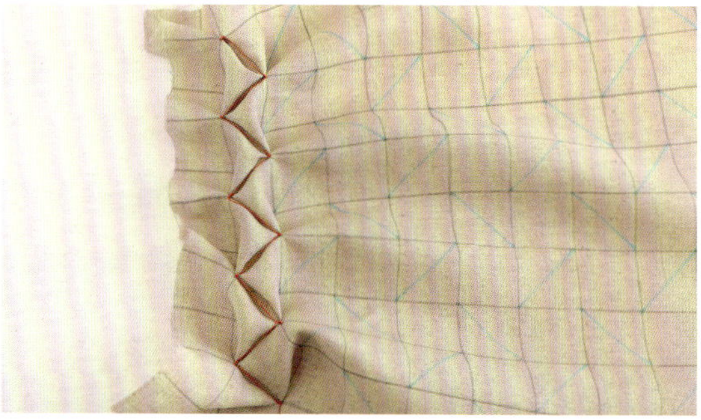

37 Repeat this process to the end of the two-column set. The thread will have zigzagged its way down the columns.

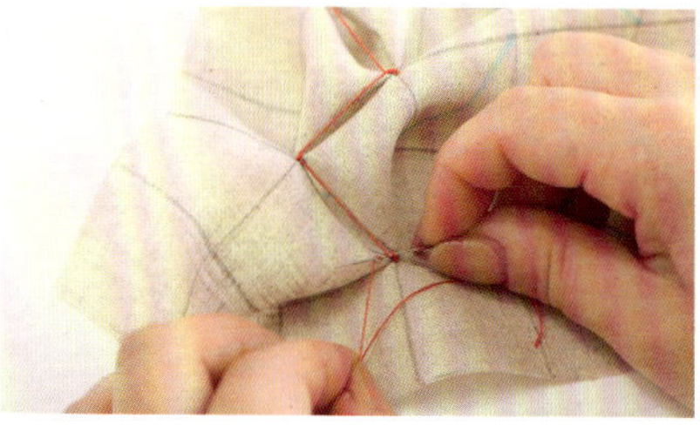

38 At the end, tie a finishing knot and cut the thread.

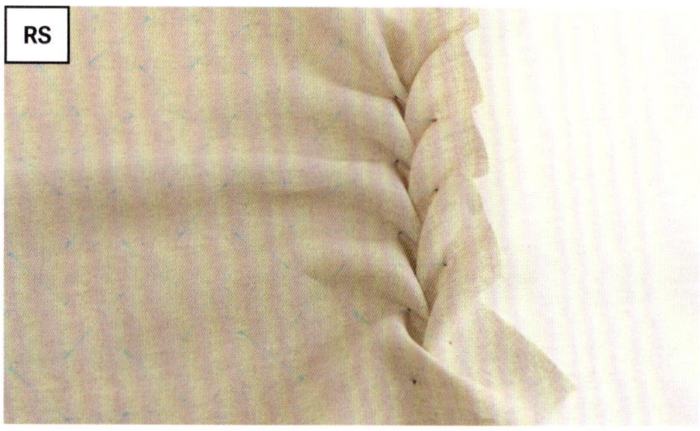

39 Seen from the RS, the fabric will look like this.

▸ **Stitch the next column.**

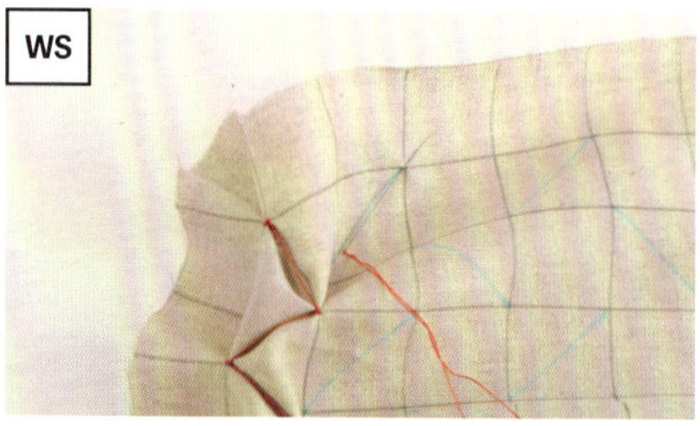

40 Stitch the next two-column set. Pick up a stitch at the top-right corner, which is corner A of the third column, and start stitching.

▸ **Four columns are complete.**

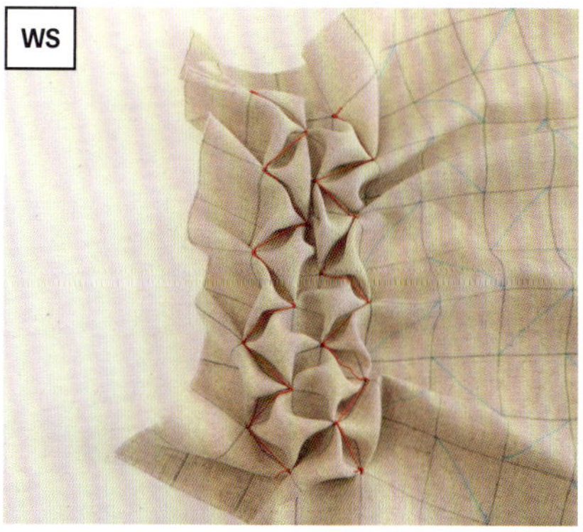

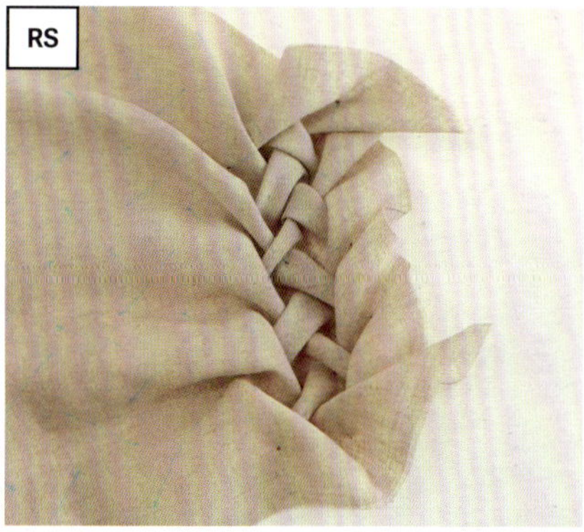

41 Once you have stitched the fourth column, the pattern will become more visible. Repeat this process to finish the entire surface. If the pattern is difficult to see, use an awl or similar tool to pull it out and smooth it out.

BRAID

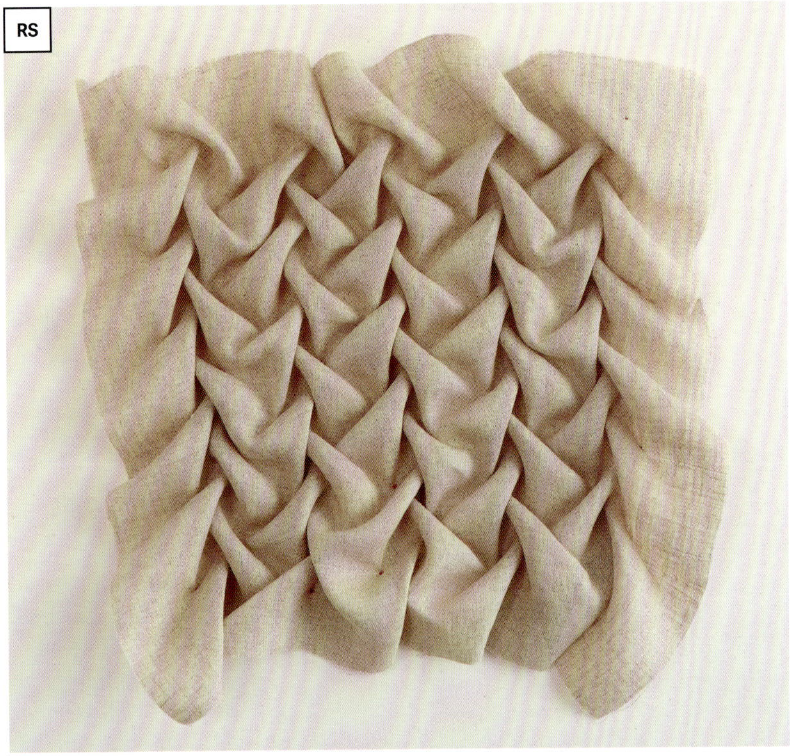

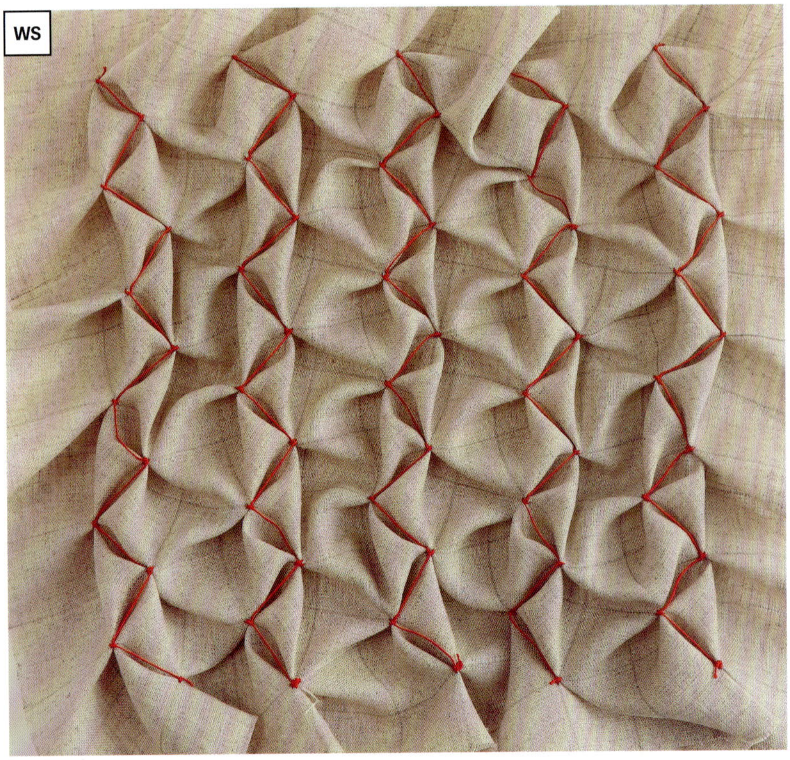

■ **Original Fabric Size**

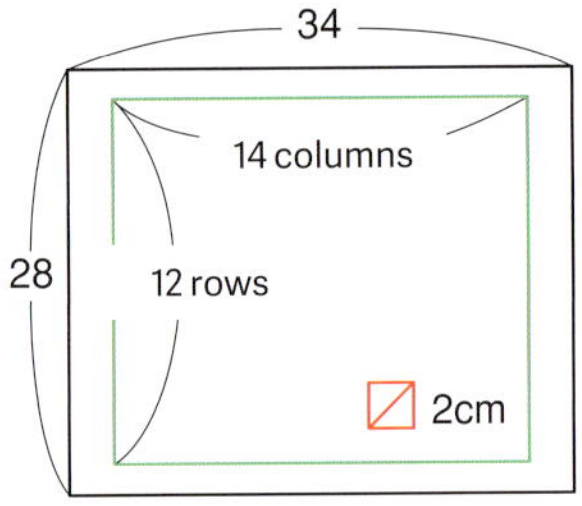

■ **Fabric's Stretch Level**

★ ★ ★ ★ ★

■ **Pressing**

- Not required to finish

■ **Notes**

- Finish two columns at a time

The **red** and pink lines show where you should pull the thread tight to bring joined sections together. The **light blue** dashed lines show where you should pass the thread. **Green** letters indicate stitching order. **Gray** arrows indicate direction.

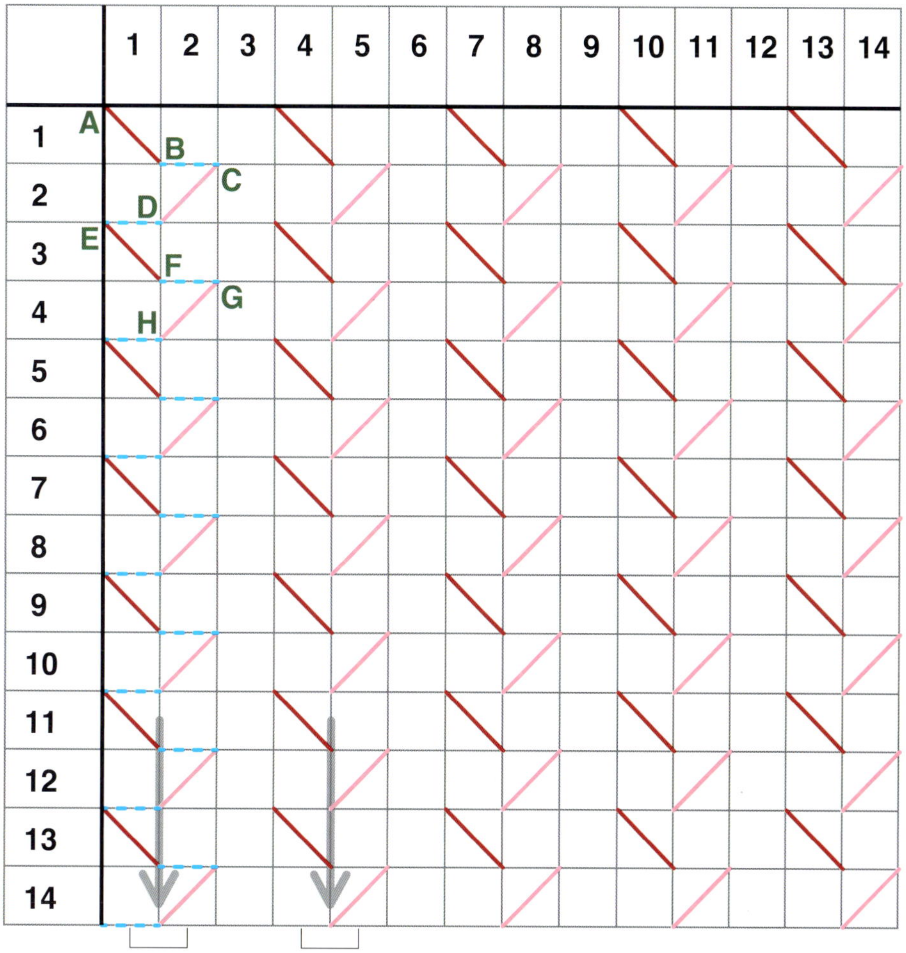

Finish two columns at a time.

■ Stitching Instructions

1. Insert the needle into corner A and pick up a stitch. Insert the needle into corner B and pick up a stitch, then scoop up corner A again. Pull the thread tight to bring the corners together.
2. Sew the joined corners AB together with one stitch and secure the stitch.
3. Pick up a stitch at corner C, pass the thread, and secure the stitch.
4. Pick up a stitch at corner D. Scoop up corner C again and pull the thread tight to bring the corners together.
5. Sew the joined corners CD together with one stitch and secure the stitch.
6. Pick up a stitch at corner E, pass the thread, and secure the stitch. Corner E will now be the same as corner A, so just repeat the same process for the rest of the column.
7. When you reach the end of the column, tie a finishing knot and cut the thread. Skip a column and begin stitching the next column from the top using the same process.

SHELL

RS

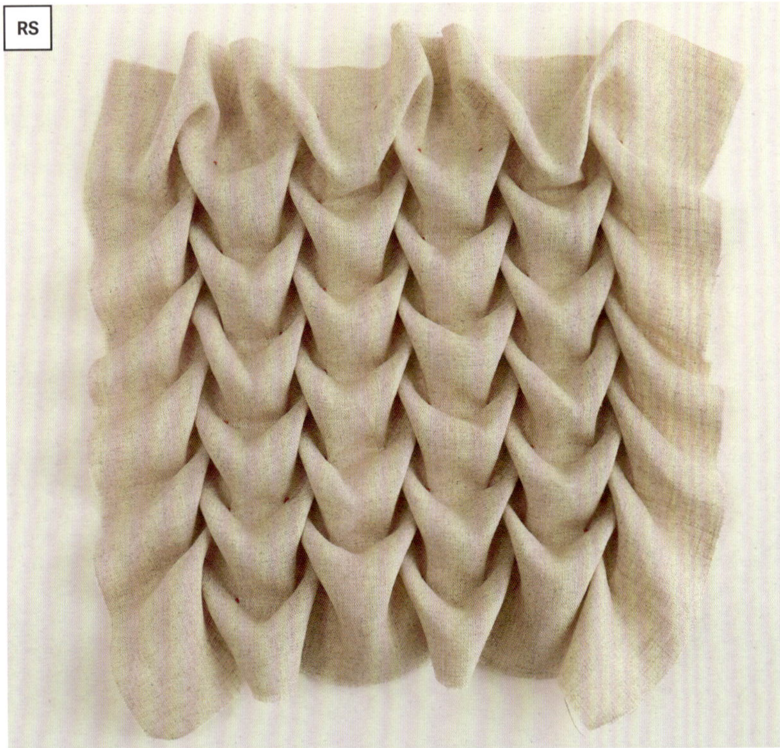

WS

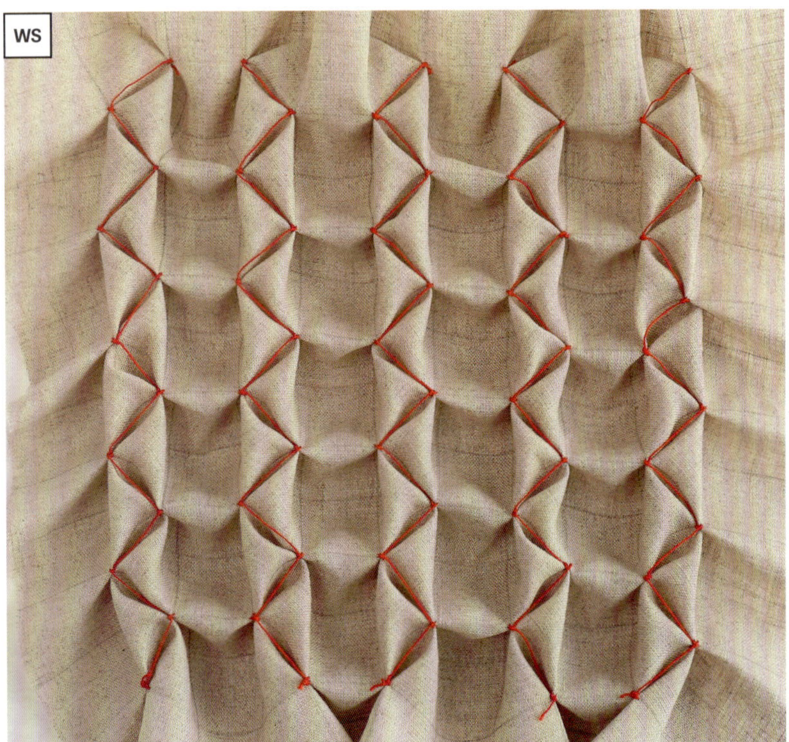

Original Fabric Size

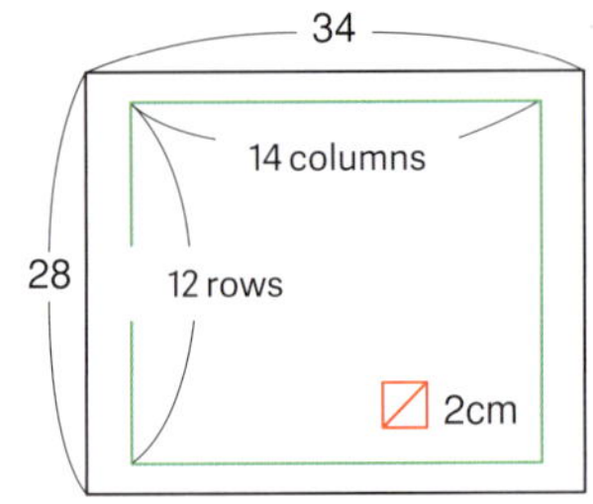

Fabric's Stretch Level

★★★★☆

Pressing

- Not required to finish

Notes

- Finish two columns at a time
- Consists of columns stitched the same way as for Braid (page 52) and columns stitched in reverse

The **red** and **pink** lines show where you should pull the thread tight to bring joined sections together. The **light blue** dashed lines show where you should pass the thread. **Letters** indicate stitching order. **Gray** arrows indicate direction.

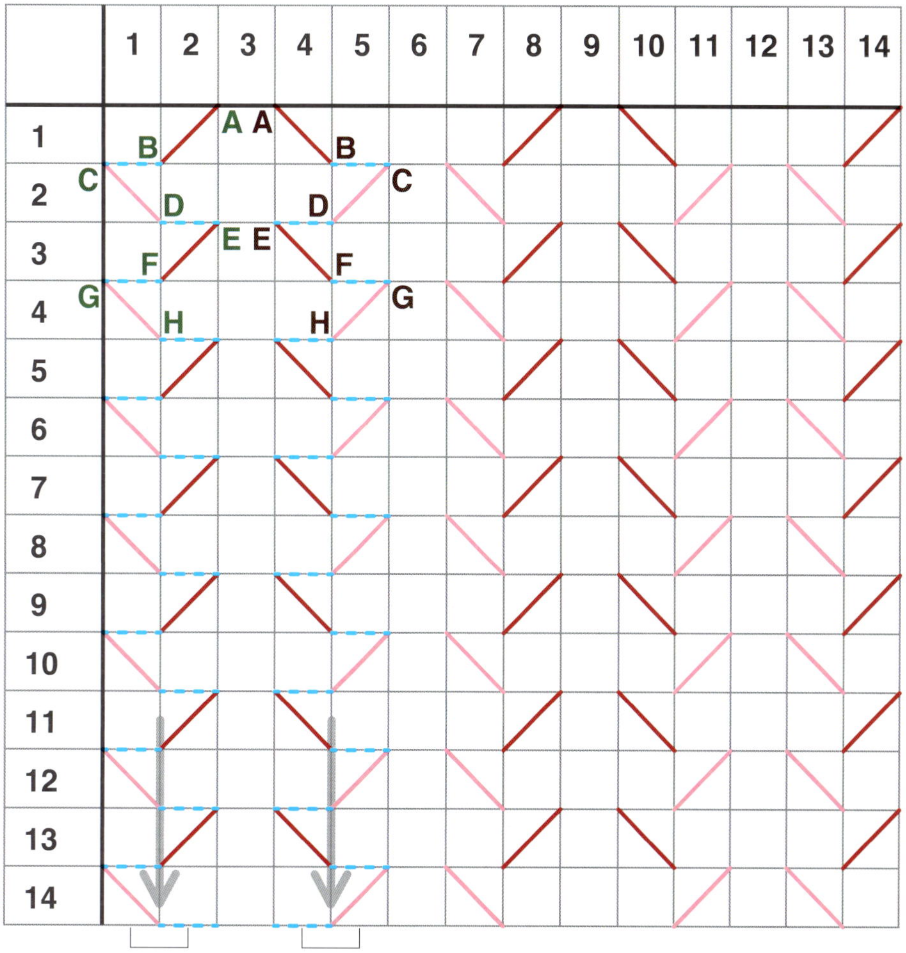

Finish two columns at a time.

■ Stitching Instructions

1. Insert the needle into corner A and pick up a stitch. Insert the needle into corner B and pick up a stitch, then scoop up corner A again. Pull the thread tight to bring the corners together.
2. Sew the joined corners AB together with one stitch and secure the stitch.
3. Pick up a stitch at corner C, pass the thread, and secure the stitch.
4. Pick up a stitch at corner D. Scoop up corner C again and pull the thread tight to bring the corners together.
5. Sew the joined corners CD together with one stitch and secure the stitch.
6. Pick up a stitch at corner E, pass the thread, and secure the stitch. Corner E will now be the same as corner A, so just repeat the same process for the rest of the column.
7. When you reach the end of the column, tie a finishing knot and cut the thread. Skip a column and begin stitching the next column from the top.
8. Stitch the next two-column set in reverse.

LEAF

RS

WS

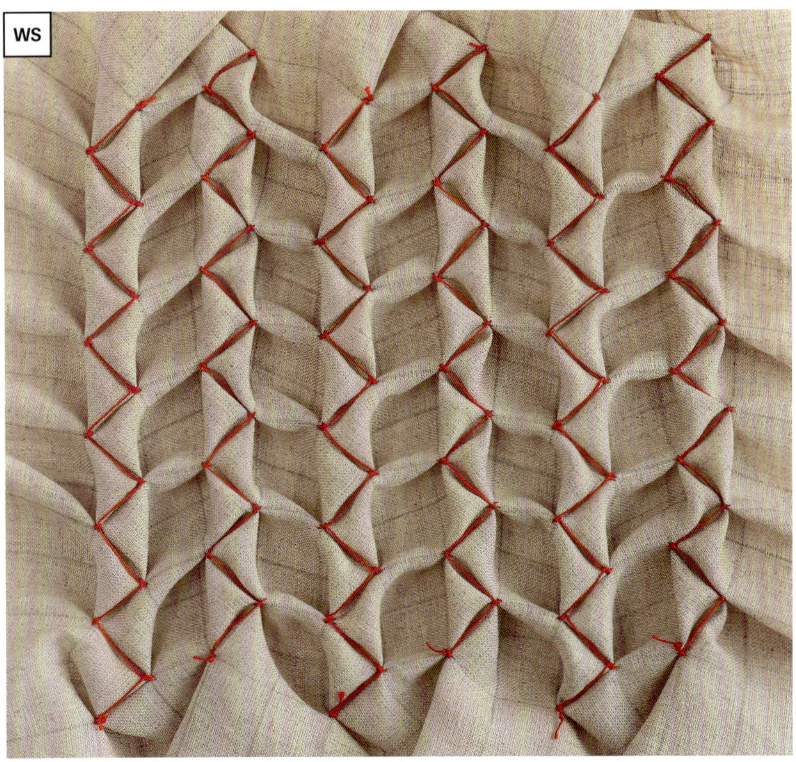

Original Fabric Size

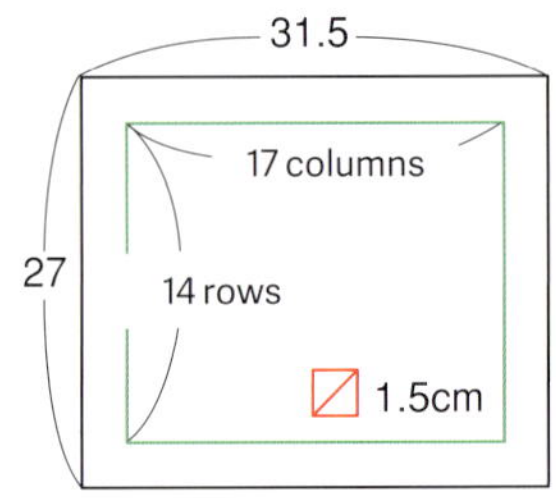

Fabric's Stretch Level

★ ★ ★ ★ ★

Pressing

- Not required to finish

Notes

- Finish two columns at a time

The **red** and **pink** lines show where you should pull the thread tight to bring joined sections together. The **light blue** dashed lines show where you should pass the thread. **Letters** indicate stitching order. **Gray** arrows indicate direction.

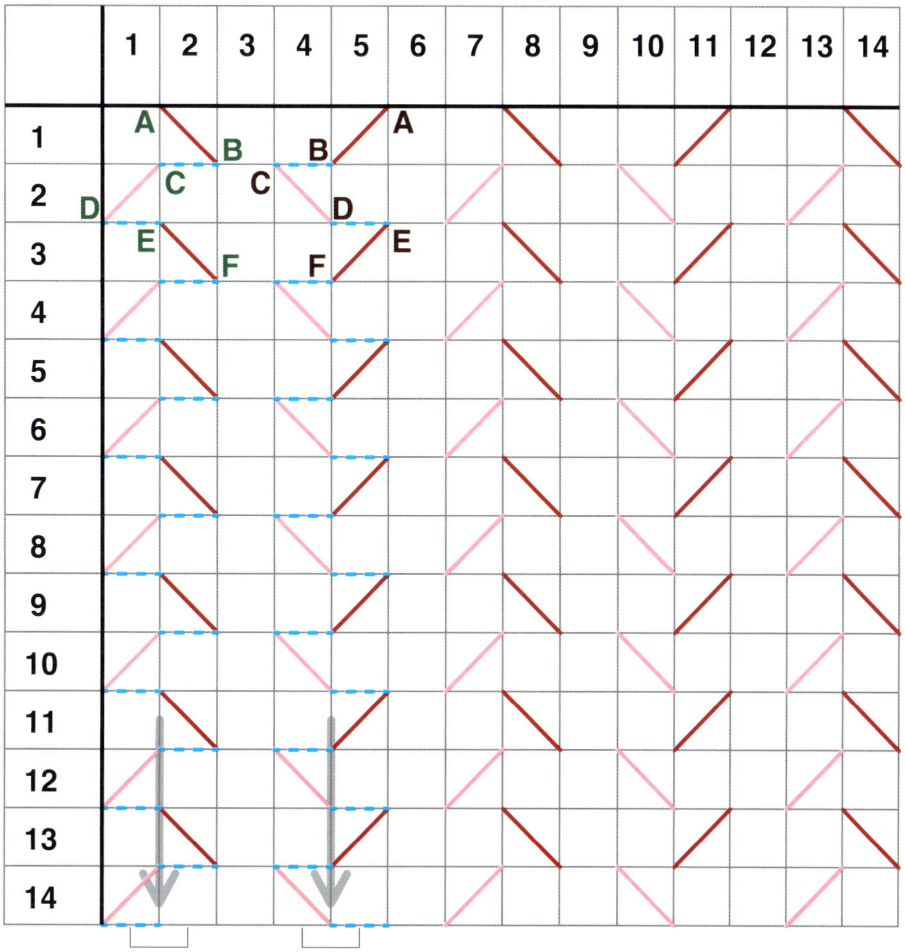

Finish two columns at a time.

■ Stitching Instructions

1. Insert the needle into corner A and pick up a stitch. Insert the needle into corner B and pick up a stitch, then scoop up corner A again. Pull the thread tight to bring the corners together.
2. Sew the joined corners AB together with one stitch and secure the stitch.
3. Pick up a stitch at corner C, pass the thread, and secure the stitch.
4. Pick up a stitch at corner D. Scoop up corner C again and pull the thread tight to bring the corners together.
5. Sew the joined corners CD together with one stitch and secure the stitch.
6. Pick up a stitch at corner E, pass the thread, and secure the stitch. Corner E will now be the same as corner A, so just repeat the same process for the rest of the column.
7. When you reach the end of the column, tie a finishing knot and cut the thread. Skip a column and begin stitching the next column from the top.
8. Stitch the next two-column set in reverse.

BONE

RS

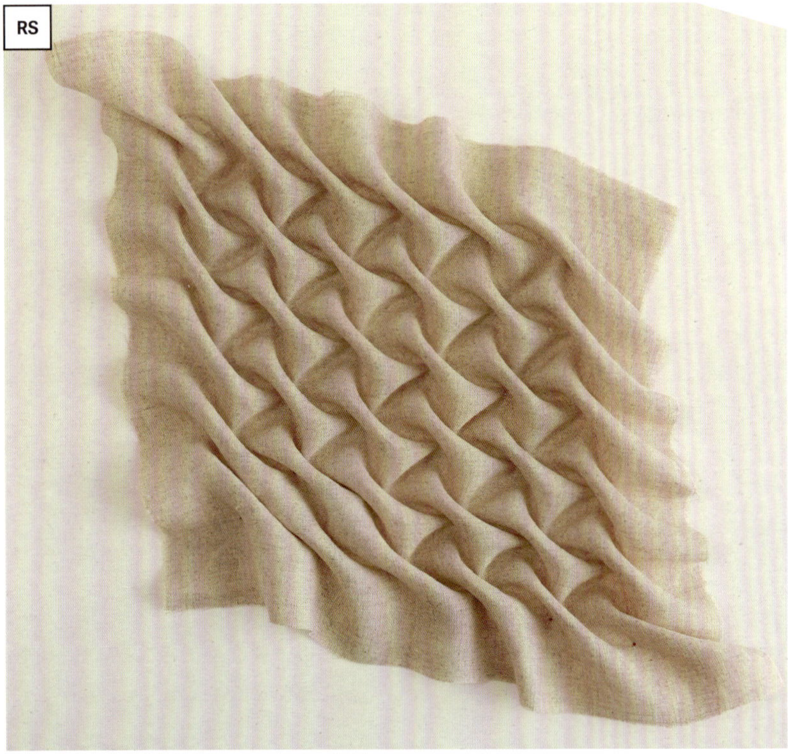

WS

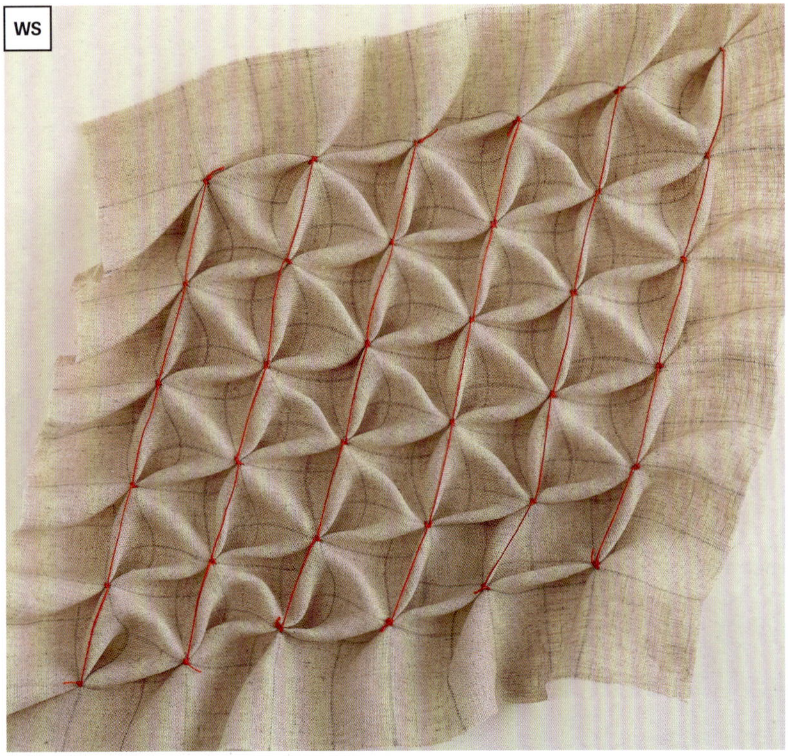

■ **Original Fabric Size**

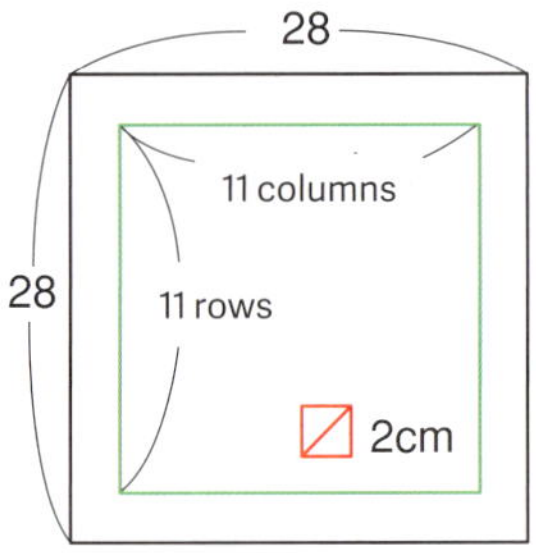

■ **Fabric's Stretch Level**

★★★☆☆

■ **Pressing**

- Not required to finish

■ **Notes**

- Finish one column at a time
- Strong diagonal stretch
- The WS side is also interesting

The **red** lines show where you should pull the thread tight to bring joined sections together. The **light blue** dashed lines show where you should pass the thread. **Green** letters indicate stitching order. **Gray** arrows indicate direction.

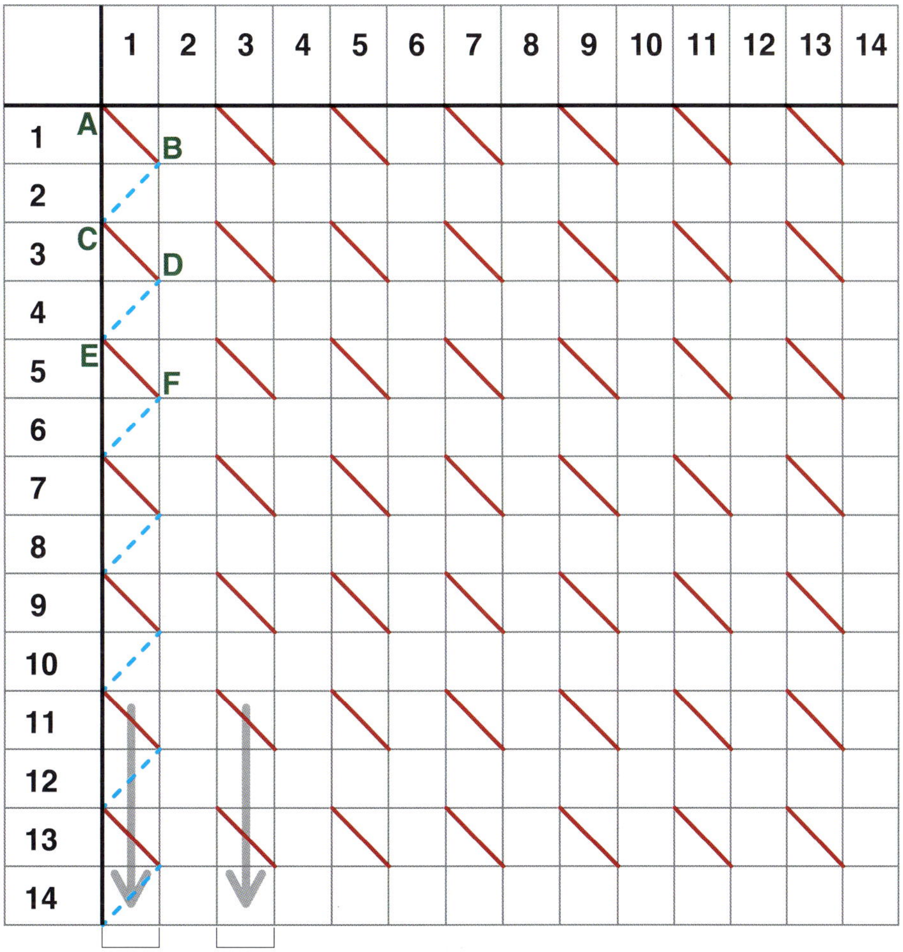

Finish one column at a time.

■ Stitching Instructions

1. Insert the needle into corner A and pick up a stitch. Insert the needle into corner B and pick up a stitch, then scoop up corner A again. Pull the thread tight to bring the corners together.
2. Sew the joined corners AB together with one stitch and secure the stitch.
3. Pick up a stitch at corner C, pass the thread, and secure the stitch. Corner C will now be the same as corner A, so just repeat the same process for the rest of the column.
4. When you reach the end of the column, tie a finishing knot and cut the thread. Skip a column and begin stitching the next column from the top using the same process.

WAVE

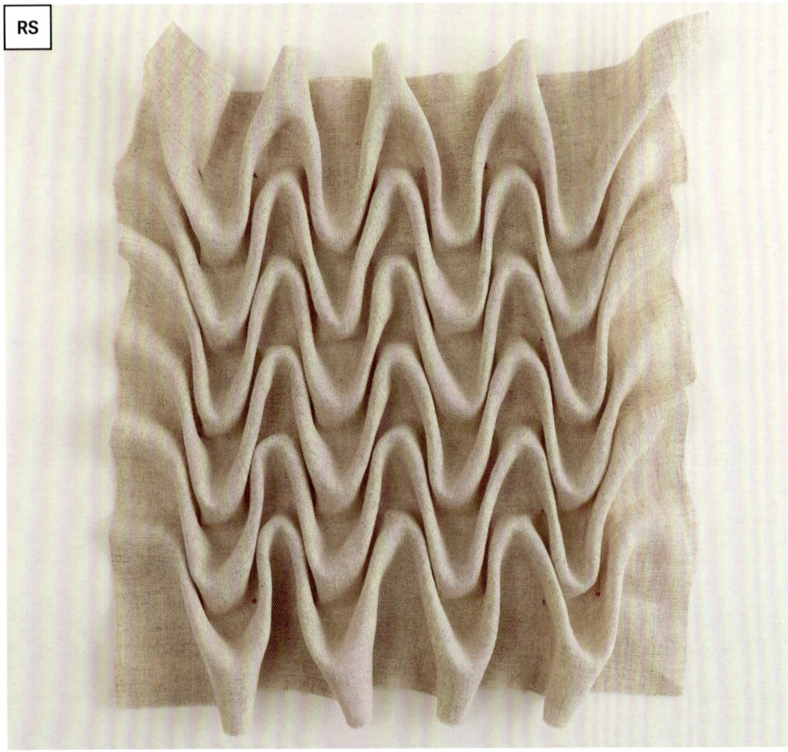

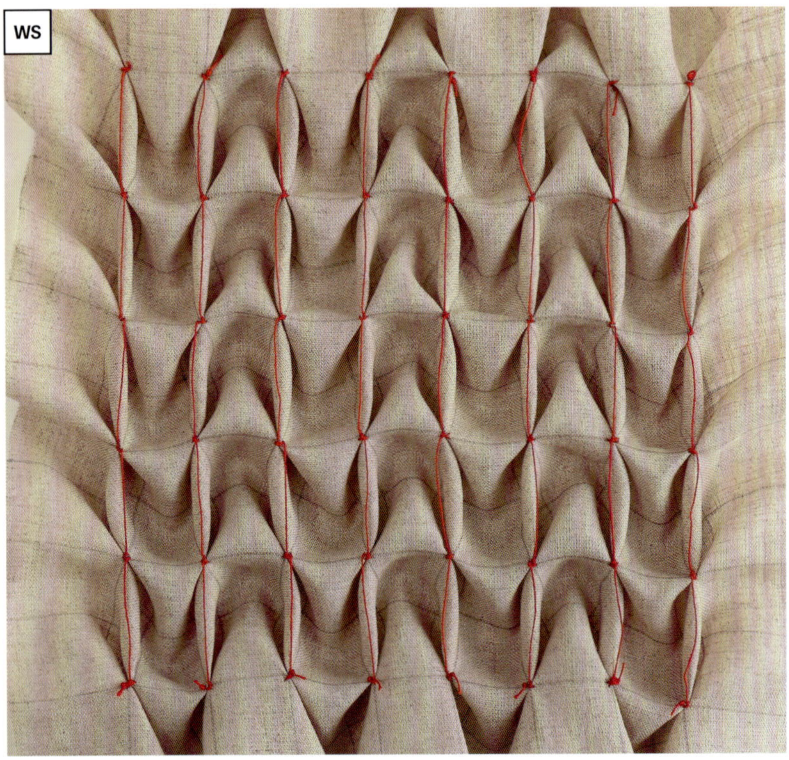

■ Original Fabric Size

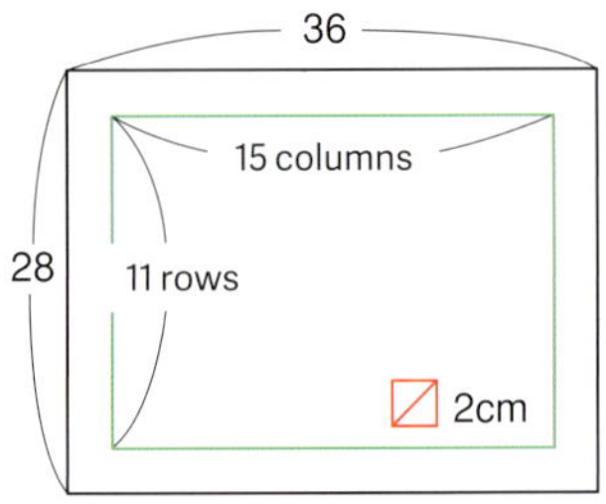

■ Fabric's Stretch Level

★ ★ ★ ★ ★

■ Pressing

- Not required to finish

■ Notes

- Finish one column at a time
- Consists of columns stitched the same way as Bone (page 58) and columns stitched in reverse

The **red** lines show where you should pull the thread tight to bring joined sections together.
The **light blue** dashed lines show where you should pass the thread. **Letters** indicate stitching order.
Gray arrows indicate direction.

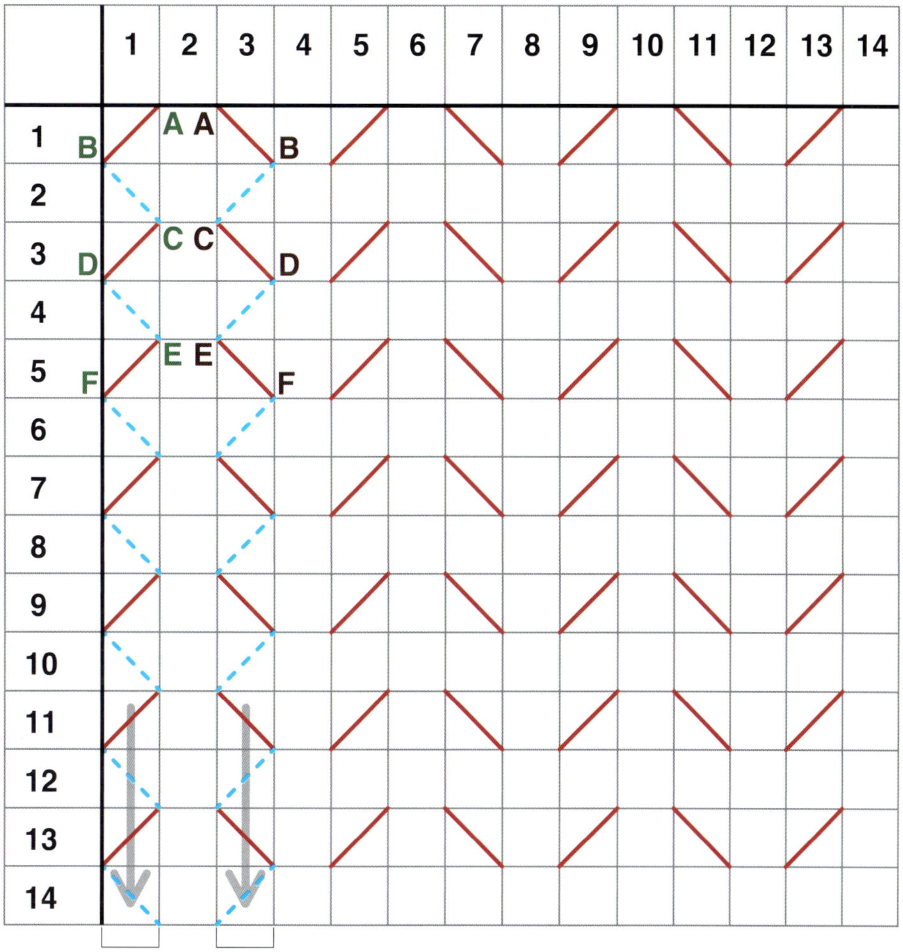

Finish one column at a time.

■ Stitching Instructions

1. Insert the needle into corner A and pick up a stitch. Insert the needle into corner B and pick up a stitch, then scoop up corner A again. Pull the thread tight to bring the corners together.
2. Sew the joined corners AB together with one stitch and secure the stitch.
3. Pick up a stitch at corner C, pass the thread, and secure the stitch. Corner C will now be the same as corner A, so just repeat the same process for the rest of the column.
4. When you reach the end of the column, tie a finishing knot and cut the thread. Skip a column and begin stitching the next column from the top.
5. Stitch the next column in reverse.

CRISSCROSS BONE

RS

WS

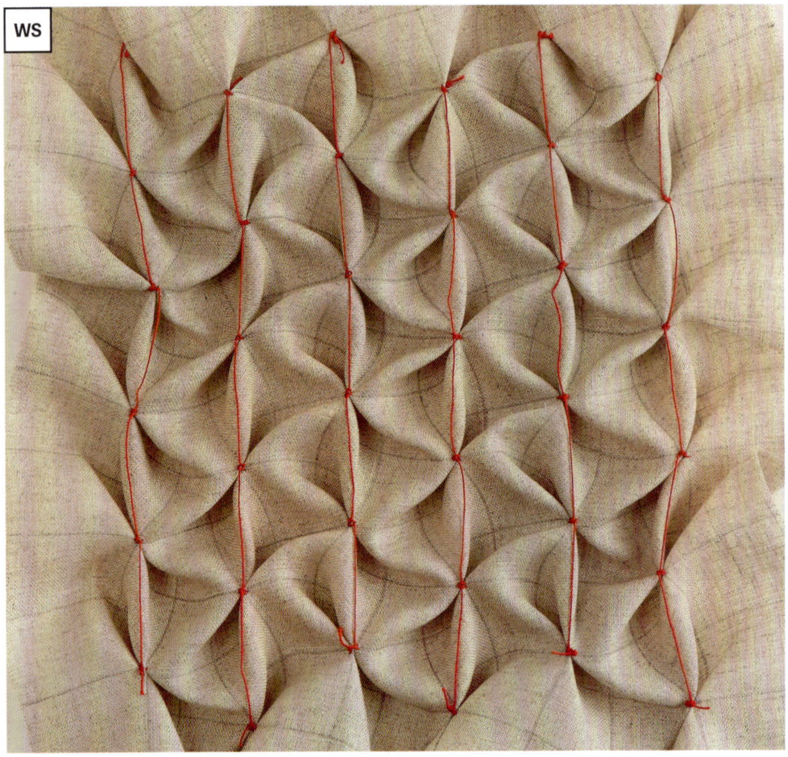

■ **Original Fabric Size**

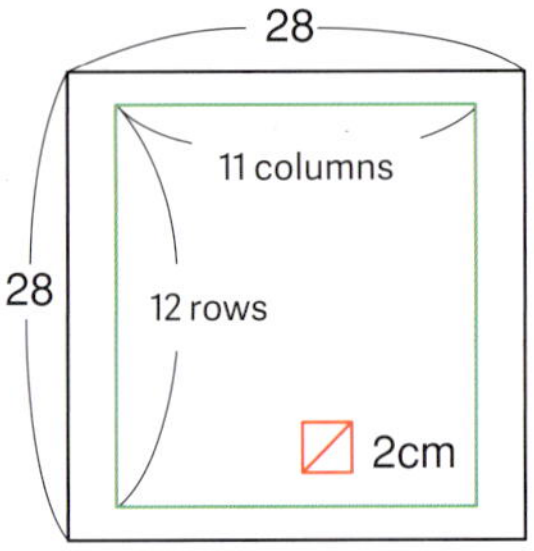

■ **Fabric's Stretch Level**

★★★☆☆

■ **Pressing**

- Not required to finish

■ **Notes**

- Finish one column at a time
- Lowers the third column of Wave (page 60) by one row

The **red** lines show where you should pull the thread tight to bring joined sections together.
The **light blue** dashed lines show where you should pass the thread. **Letters** indicate stitching order.
Gray arrows indicate direction.

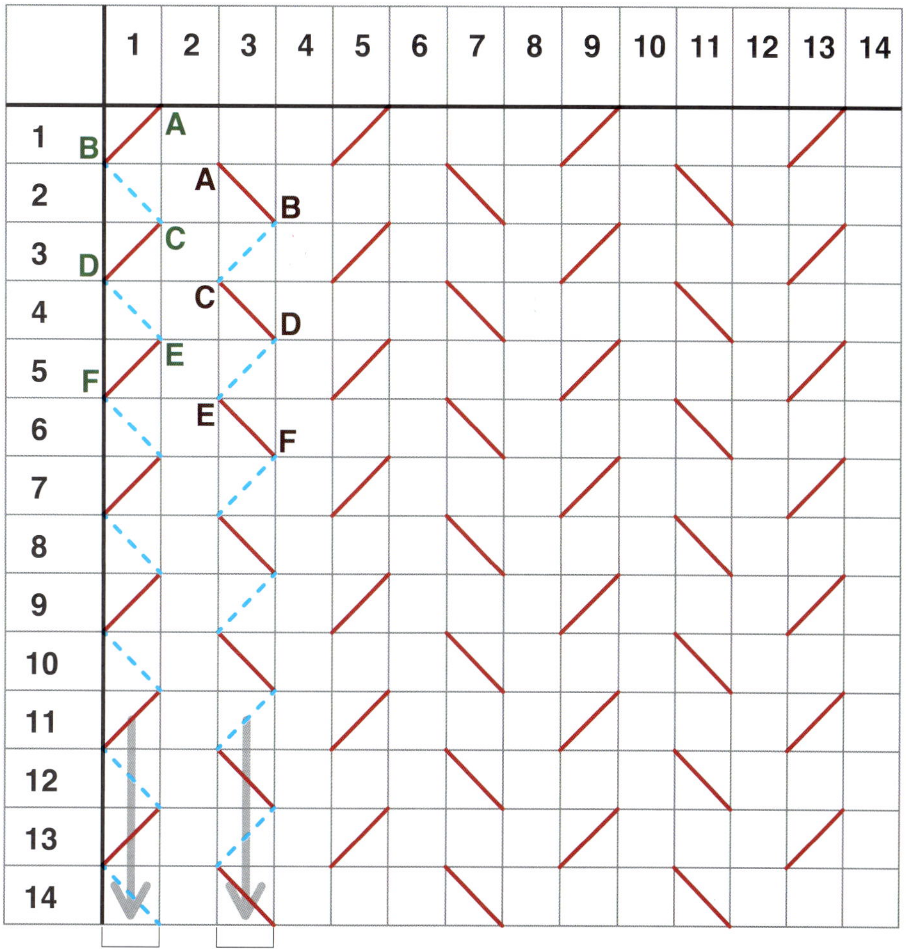

Finish one column at a time.

■ Stitching Instructions

1. Insert the needle into corner A and pick up a stitch. Insert the needle into corner B and pick up a stitch, then scoop up corner A again. Pull the thread tight to bring the corners together.
2. Sew the joined corners AB together with one stitch and secure the stitch.
3. Pick up a stitch at corner C, pass the thread, and secure the stitch. Corner C will now be the same as corner A, so just repeat the same process for the rest of the column.
4. When you reach the end of the column, tie a finishing knot and cut the thread. Skip a column and begin stitching the next column from the top.
5. Stitch the next column in reverse, starting one row lower.

ARROW

RS

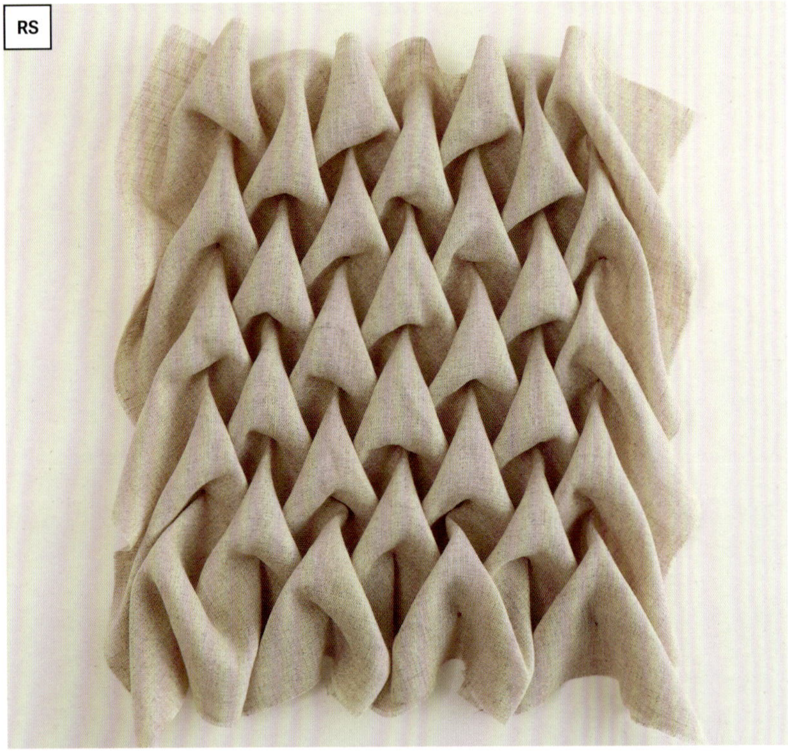

WS

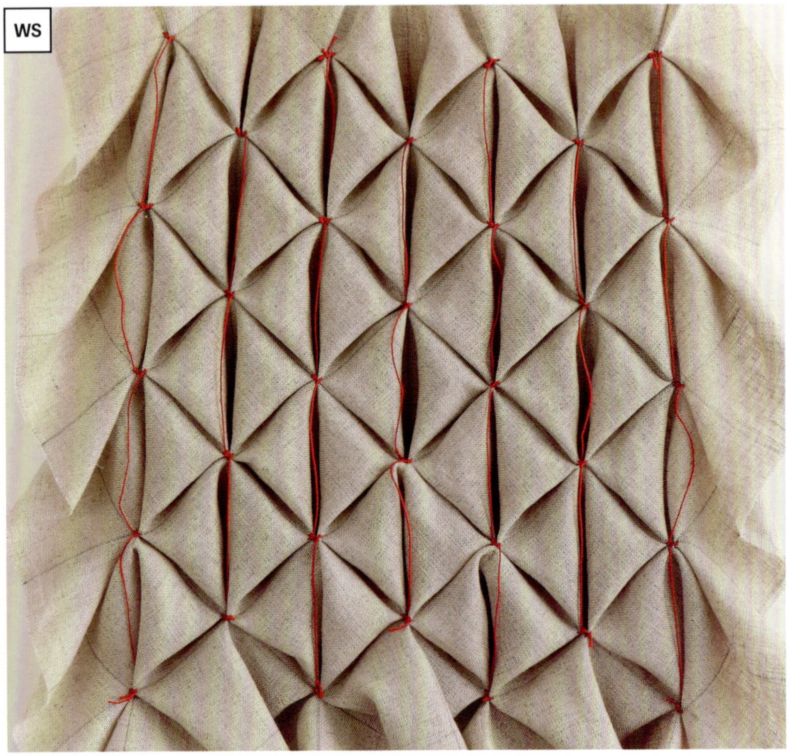

■ Original Fabric Size

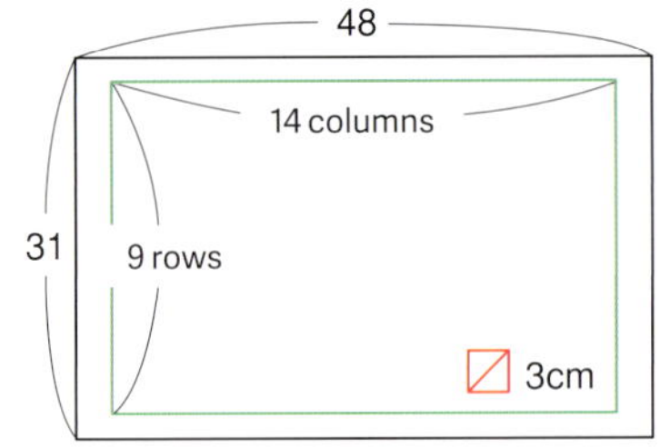

■ Fabric's Stretch Level

★ ★ ★ ☆ ☆

■ Pressing

- Not required to finish

■ Notes

- Finish two columns at a time
- The WS is also interesting

The **red** and **pink** lines show where you should pull the thread tight to bring joined sections together. The **light blue** dashed lines show where you should pass the thread. **Green** letters indicate stitching order. **Gray** arrows indicate direction.

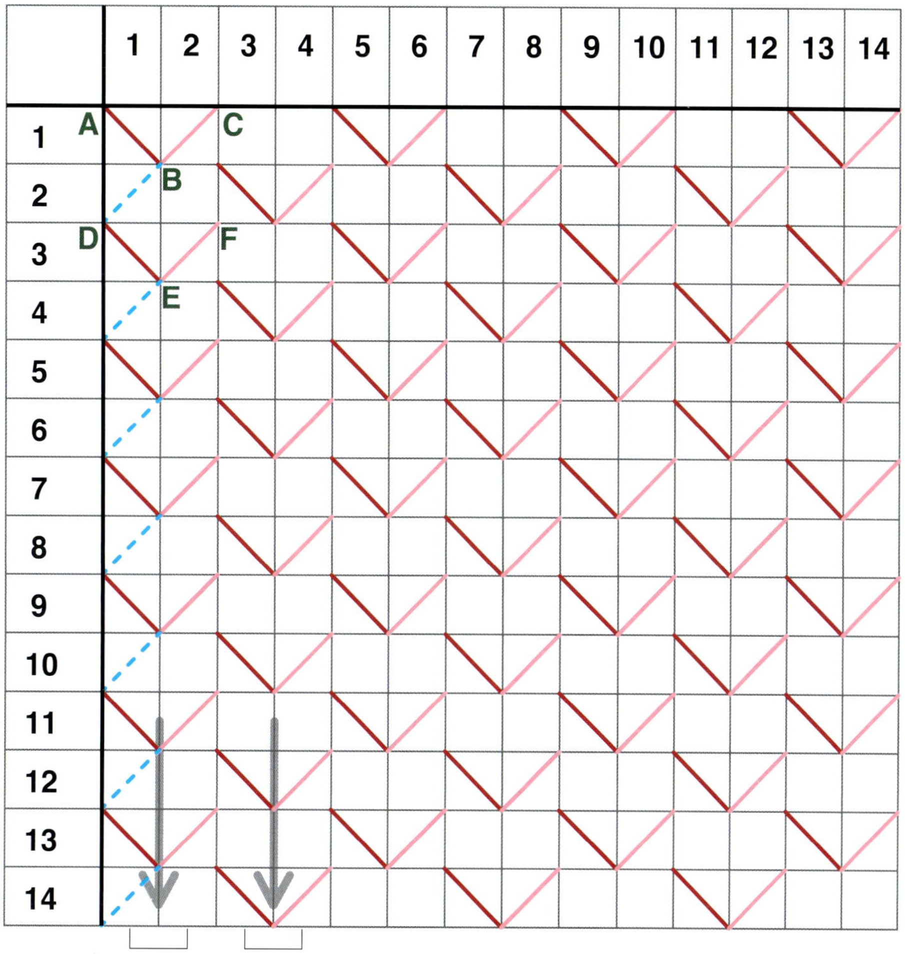

Finish two columns at a time.

■ Stitching Instructions

1. Insert the needle into corner A and pick up a stitch. Insert the needle into corner B and pick up a stitch, then scoop up corner A again. Pull the thread tight to bring the corners together.
2. Sew the joined corners AB together with one stitch and secure the stitch.
3. Insert the needle into corner C, pick up a stitch, then scoop up corner AB again. Pull the thread tight to bring the corners together.
4. Sew the joined corners ABC together with one stitch and secure the stitch.
5. Pick up a stitch at corner D, pass the thread, and secure the stitch. Corner D will now be the same as corner A, so just repeat the same process for the rest of the column.
6. When you reach the end of the column, tie a finishing knot and cut the thread. Begin stitching the next column using the same process, starting one row lower.

BRICK

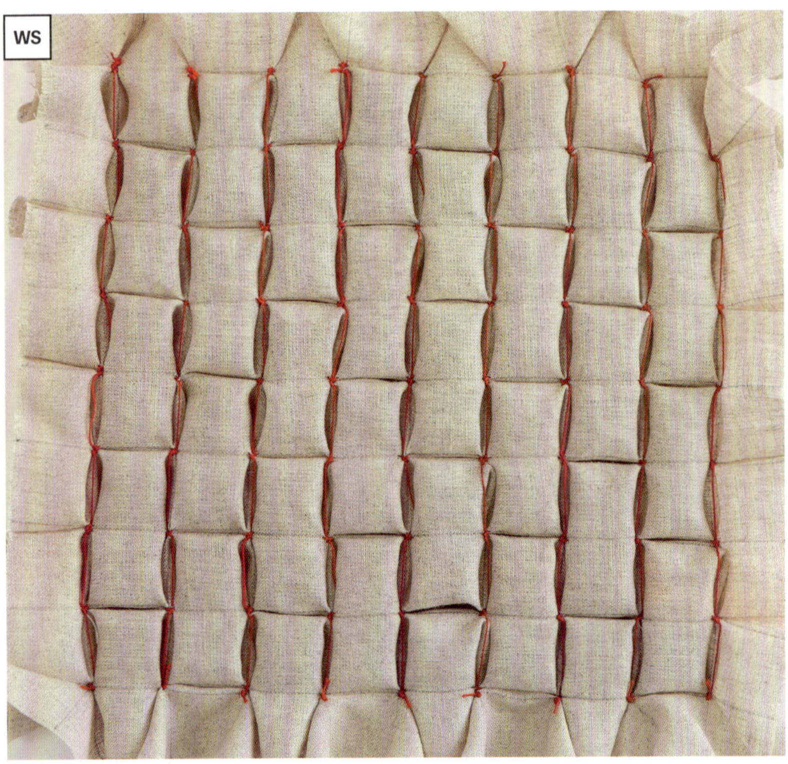

■ Pressed Finish

■ Original Fabric Size

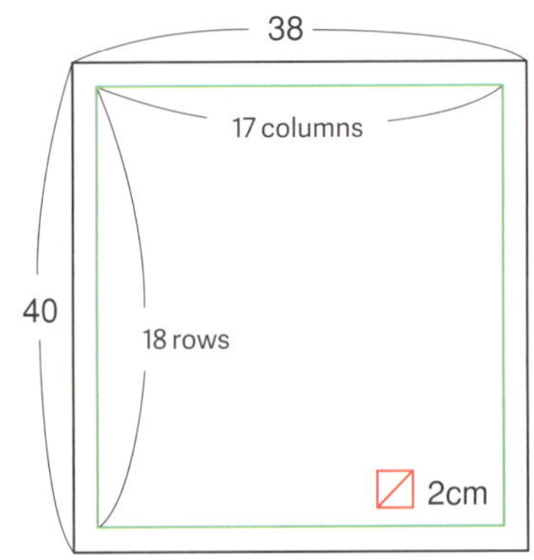

■ Fabric's Stretch Level

★☆☆☆☆

(Depends on the finish)

■ Pressing

- Could be pressed depending on the desired finish

■ Notes

- Finish one column at a time
- Pressing brings out the Brick pattern more
- Sew and pinch the center of the raised pattern to turn the Bricks into Bows

The **red** and **pink** lines show where you should pull the thread tight to bring joined sections together. The **light blue** dashed lines show where you should pass the thread. **Green** letters indicate stitching order. **Gray** arrows indicate direction.

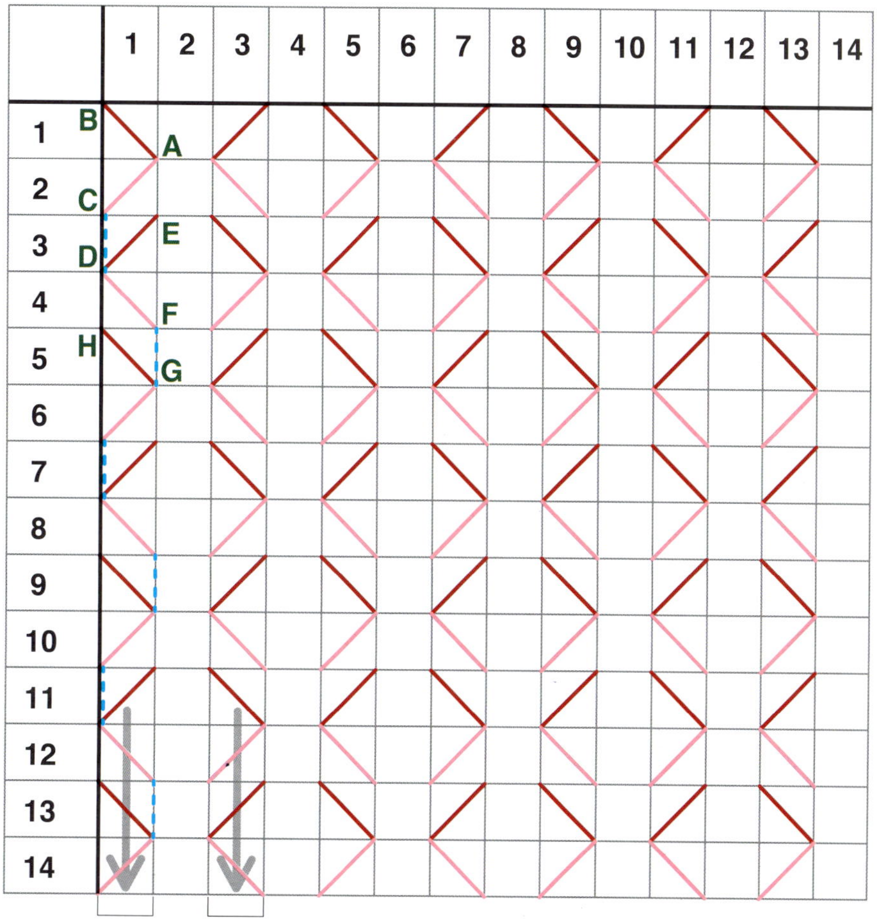

Finish one column at a time.

■ Stitching Instructions

1. Insert the needle into corner A and pick up a stitch. Insert the needle into corner B, pick up a stitch, then scoop up corner A again. Pull the thread tight to bring the corners together.
2. Sew the joined corners AB together with one stitch and secure the stitch.
3. Insert the needle into corner C and pick up a stitch. Insert the needle into corner AB, pick up a stitch, then scoop up corner AB again. Pull the thread tight to bring the corners together.
4. Sew the joined corners ABC together with one stitch and secure the stitch.
5. Pick up a stitch at corner D, pass the thread, and secure the stitch.
6. Pick up a stitch at corner E. Scoop up corner D again and pull the thread tight to bring the corners together.
7. Sew the joined corners DE together with one stitch and secure the stitch.
8. Insert the needle into corner F and pick up a stitch. Insert the needle into corner DE, pick up a stitch, then scoop up corner DE again. Pull the thread tight to bring the corners together.
9. Sew the joined corners DEF together with one stitch and secure the stitch.
10. Pick up a stitch at corner G, pass the thread and secure the stitch. Corner G will now be the same as corner A, so just repeat the same process for the rest of the column.
11. When you reach the end of the column, tie a finishing knot and cut the thread. Skip a column and begin stitching the next column from the top.
12. Stitch the next column in reverse.

BRICK STITCHING

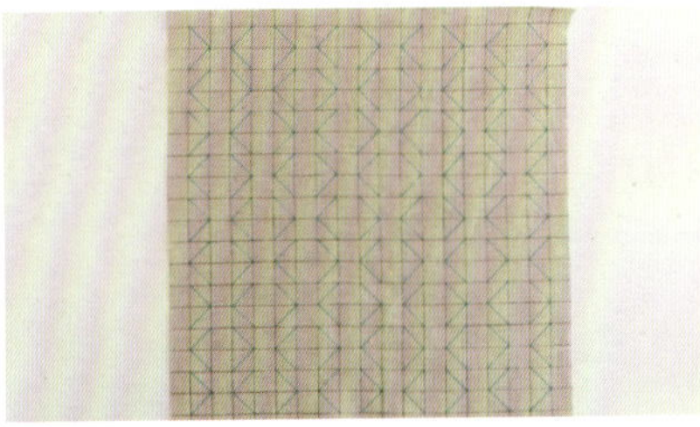

01 Draw a grid on the WS of the fabric. Draw diagonal lines connecting the corners that will be scooped together, as shown on page 67.

Bring A and B together.

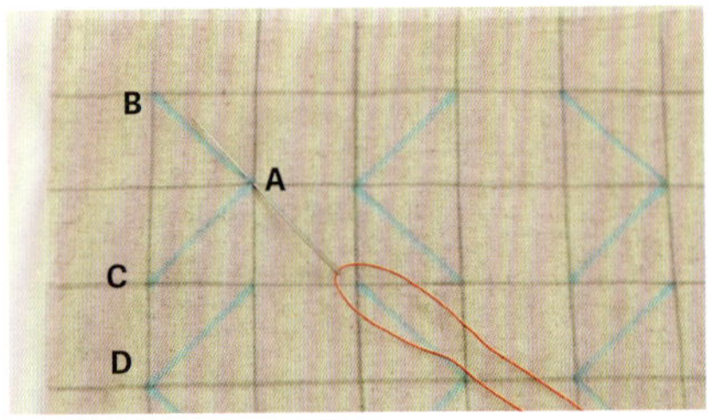

02 Thread the needle and tie a finishing knot with a single strand of thread. Pick up a stitch from inside the square to outside at corner A. Each stitch should be about 0.2cm long.

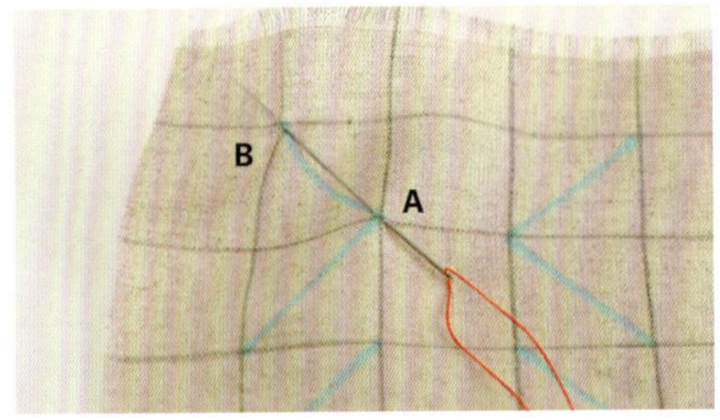

03 Pick up a stitch from outside the square to inside at corner B.

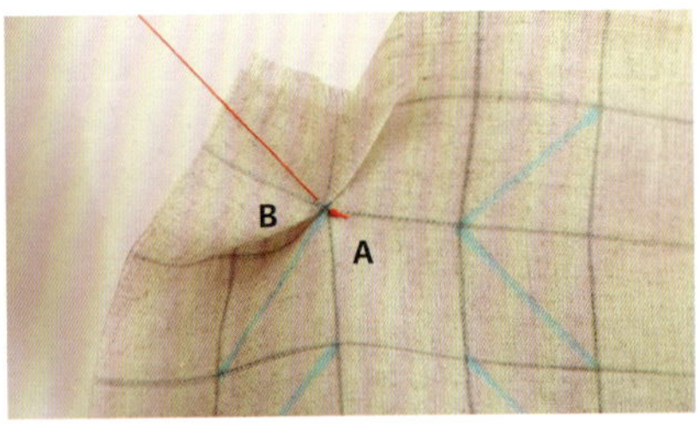

04 Pull the thread tight to bring corners A and B together.

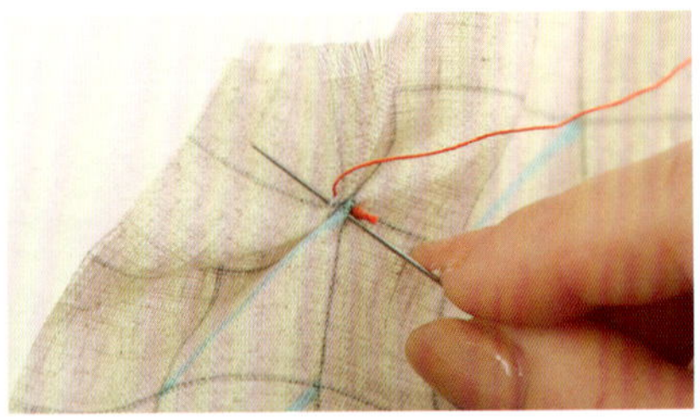

05 Sew the joined corners AB together with one stitch.

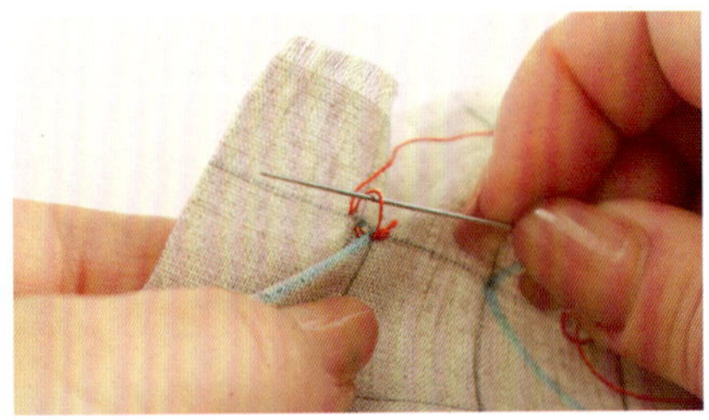

06 Pull the thread, creating a small loop just before pulling it tight. Pass the needle through the loop from bottom to top.

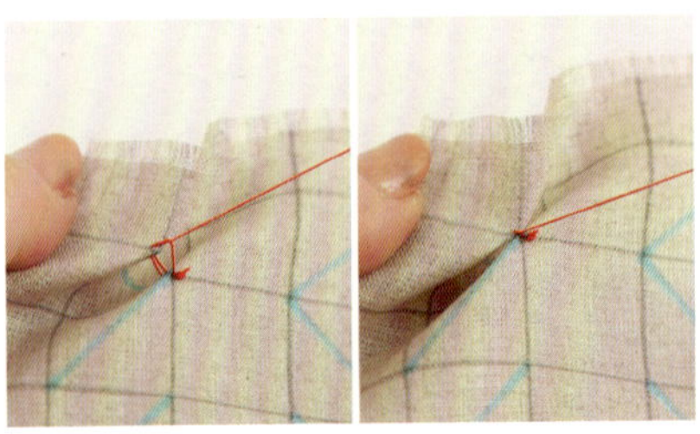

07 Pull the thread tight to lock the stitch and secure the fabric.

Bring AB and C together.

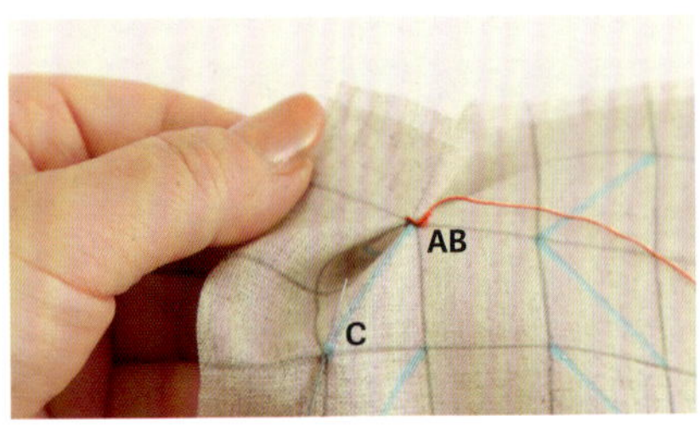

08 Pick up a stitch from outside the square to inside at corner C.

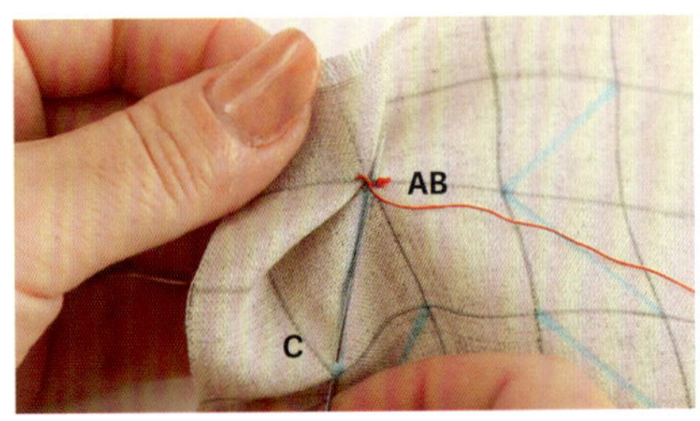

09 Scoop up corners AB with one stitch.

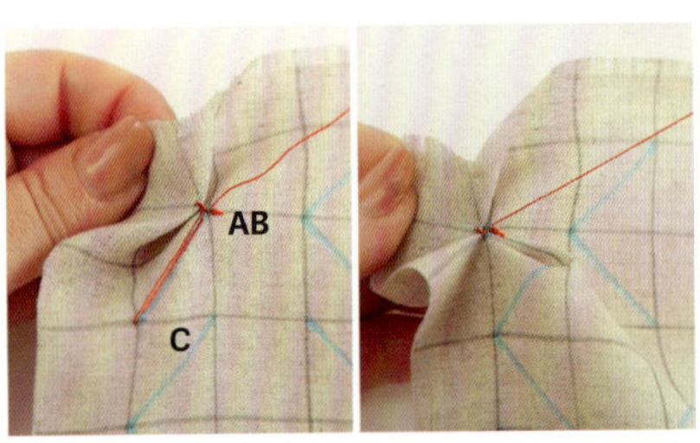

10 Pull the thread. You will see two strands of thread running diagonally. Pull the thread tight to bring corners AB and C together.

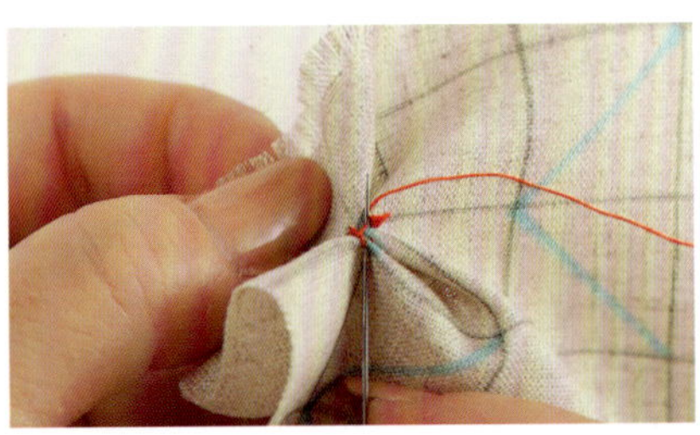

11 Sew the joined corners ABC together with one stitch.

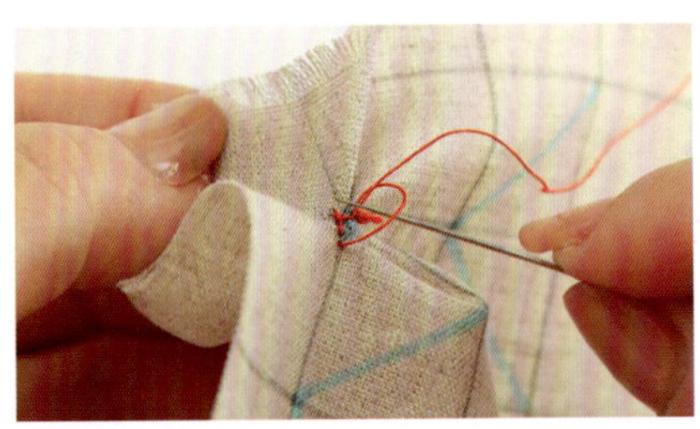

12 Pull the thread, creating a small loop just before pulling it tight. Pass the needle through the loop from bottom to top.

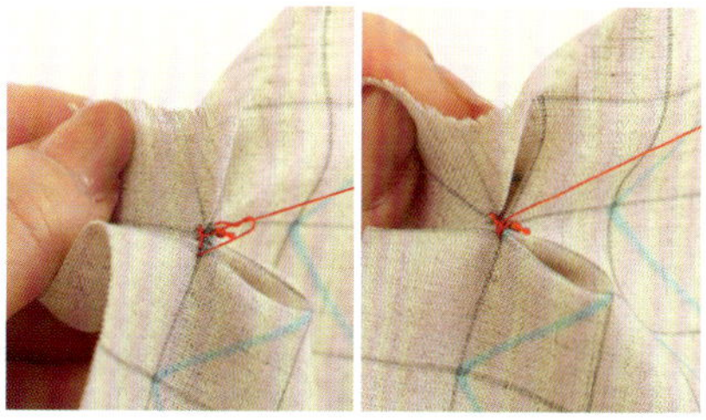

13 Pull the thread tight to lock the stitch and secure the fabric.

‣ Pass the thread from ABC to D.

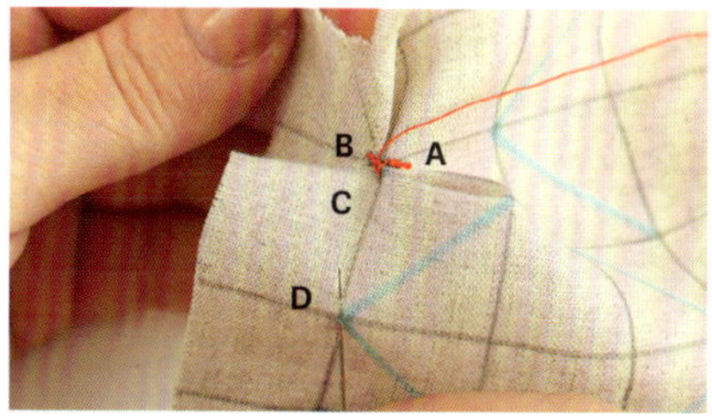

14 Move to the next row and pick up a stitch at corner D.

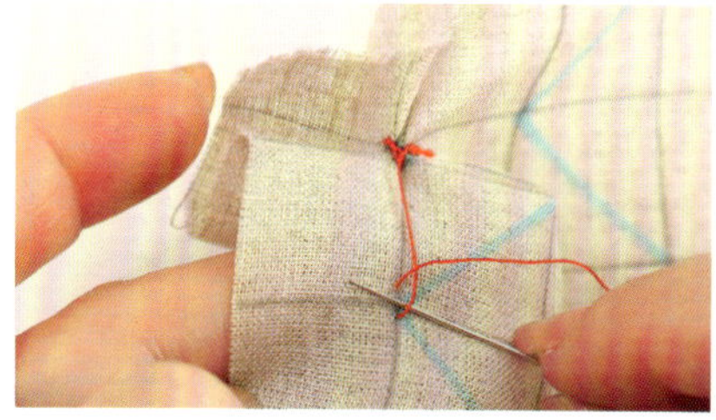

15 Pull the thread along the gridline from ABC to D. Without pulling it all the way through, pass it over the thread that you just pulled to create a loop, then bring the needle back under the thread and through the loop.

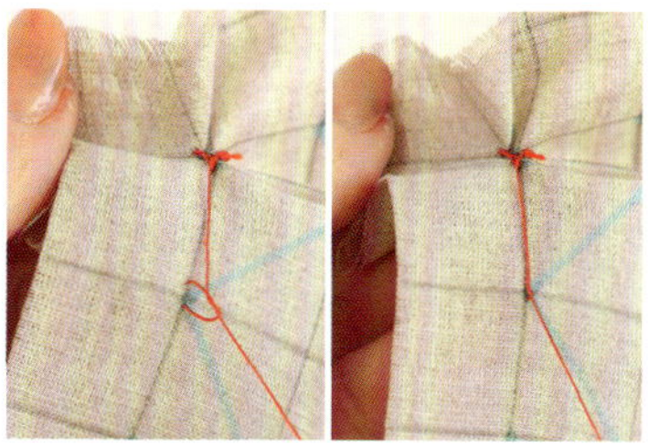

16 Pull the thread to make a knot. This will run the thread along the gridline and create a knot at the corner, securing the fabric in place.

‣ Bring DE and F together.

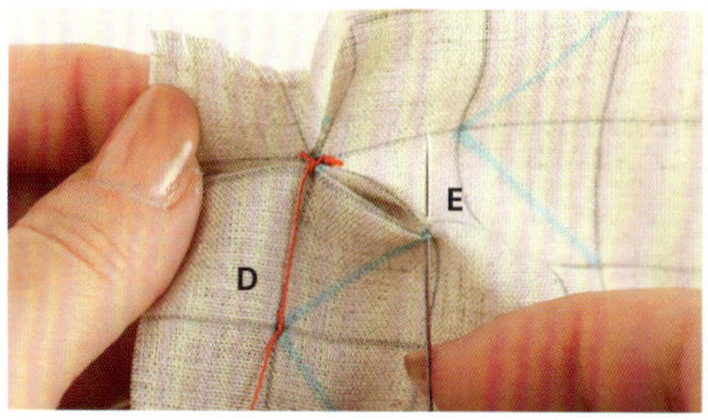

17 Pick up a stitch at the opposite corner to corner D, which is corner E.

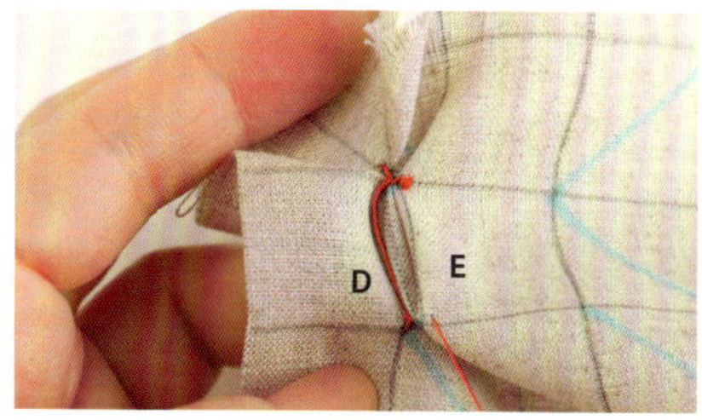

18 Pull the thread tight to bring D and E together.

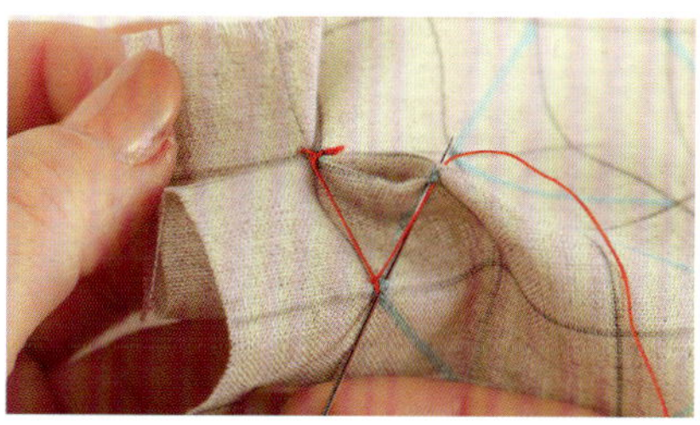

19 Sew the joined corners DE together with one stitch.

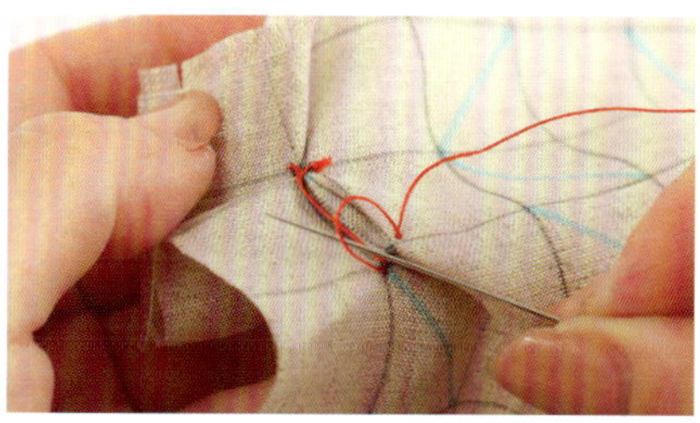

20 Pull the thread, creating a small loop just before pulling it tight. Pass the needle through the loop from bottom to top.

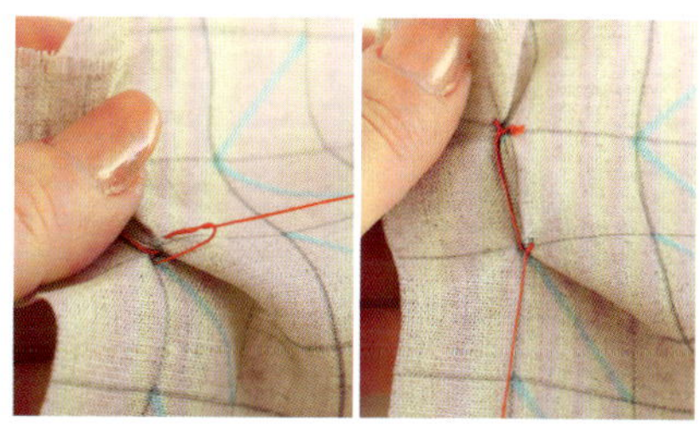

21 Pull the thread tight to lock the stitch and secure the fabric.

‣ Bring DE and F together.

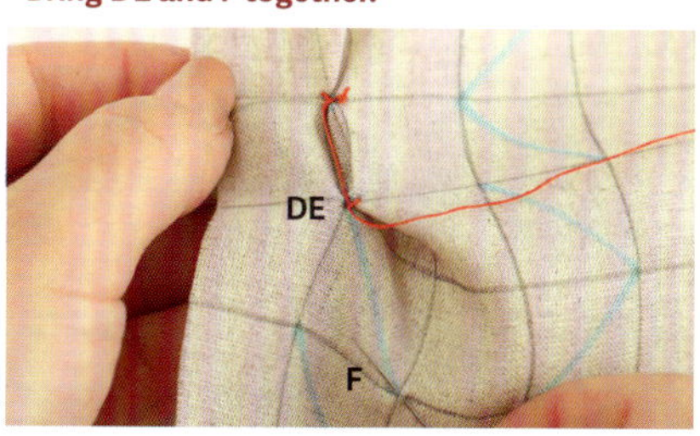

22 Pick up a stitch from outside the square to inside at corner F.

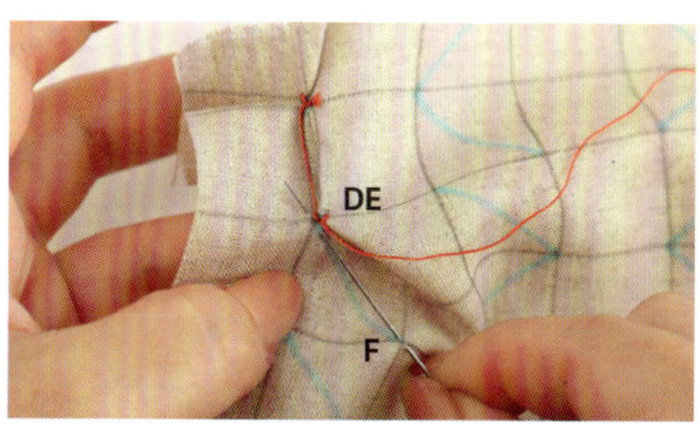

23 Scoop up corners DE with one stitch.

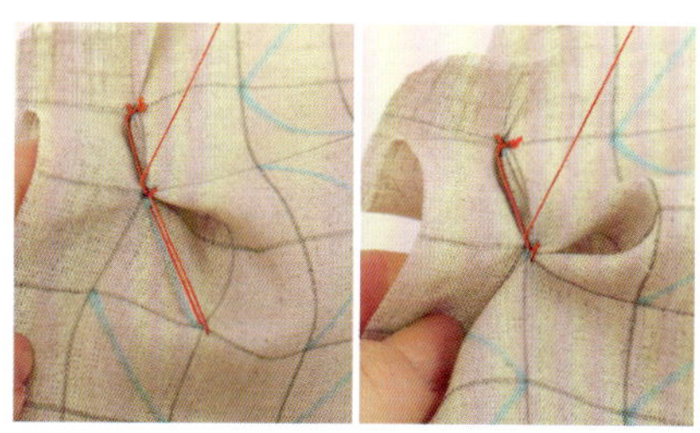

24 Pull the thread tight to bring corners DE and F together.

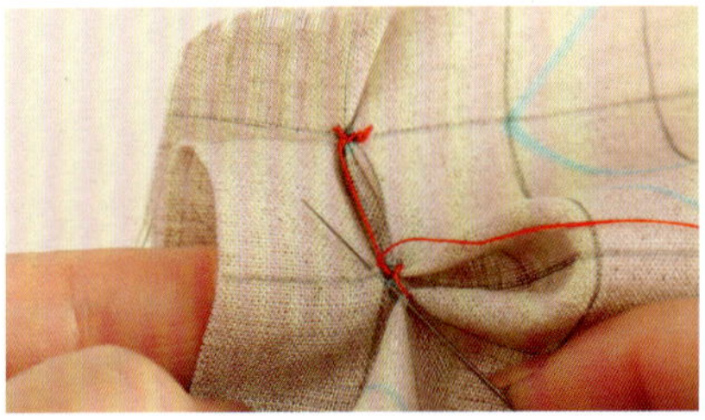

25 Sew the joined corners DEF together with one stitch.

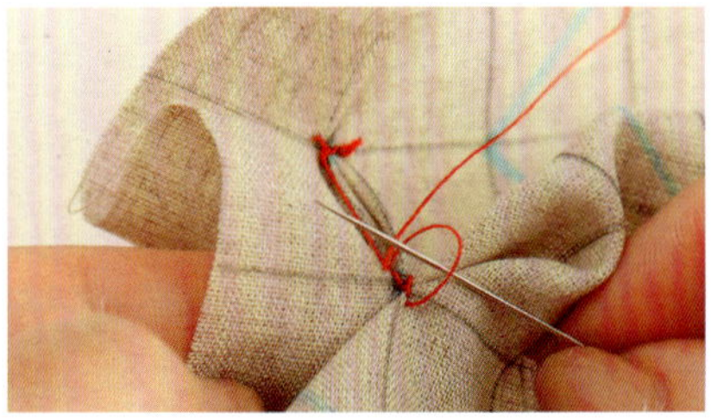

26 Pull the thread, creating a small loop just before pulling it tight. Pass the needle through the loop from bottom to top.

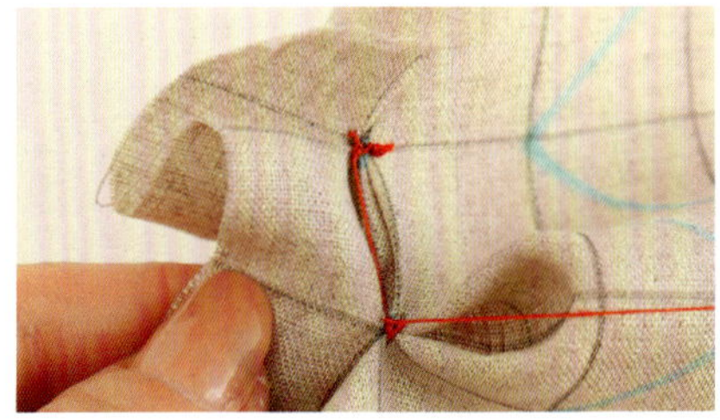

27 Pull the thread tight to lock the stitch and secure the fabric.

▸ Pass the thread from DEF to G.

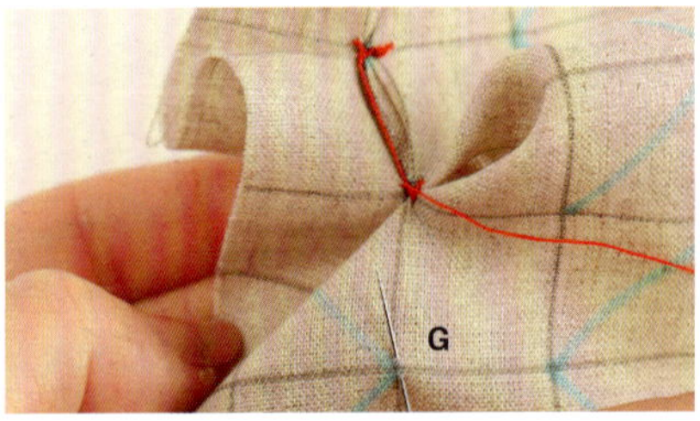

28 Move to the next row and pick up a stitch at corner G.

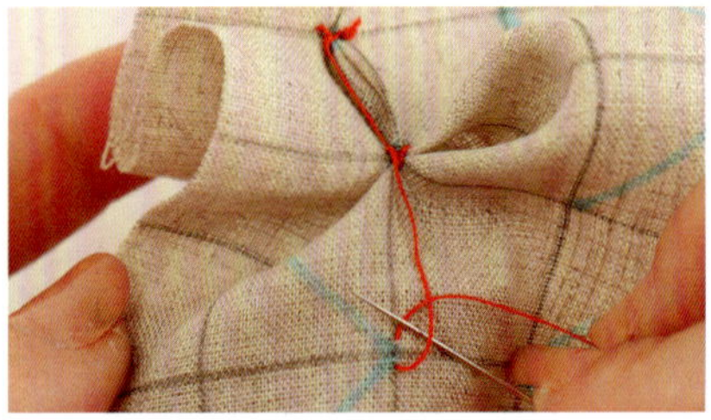

29 Pull the thread along the gridline from DEF to G. Without pulling it all the way through, pass it over the thread that you just pulled to create a loop, then bring the needle back under the thread and through the loop.

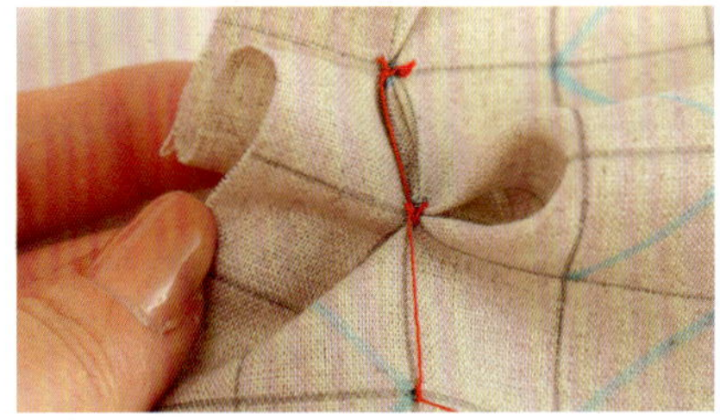

30 Pull the thread tight to lock the stitch and secure the fabric.

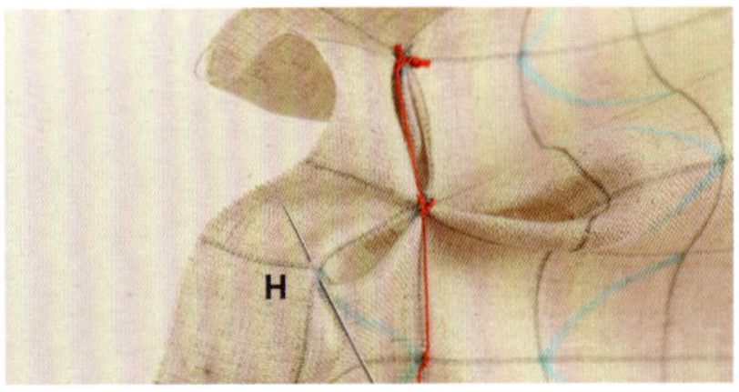

31 Pick up a stitch at corner H. G is now the same as A, so repeat this process to the end of the column.

▸ One column is complete.

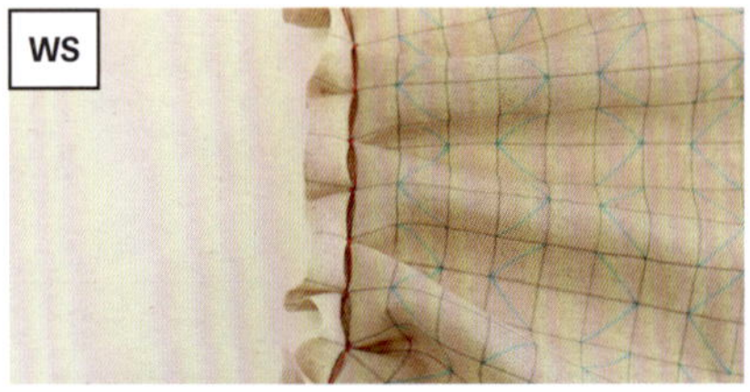

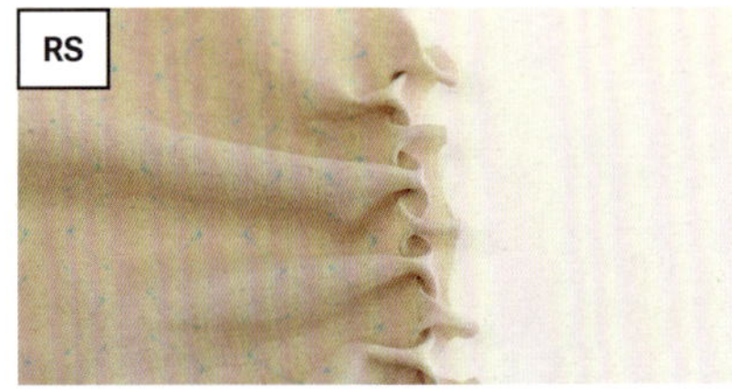

32 At the end, tie a finishing knot and cut the thread. It will look like this.

▸ Two columns are complete.

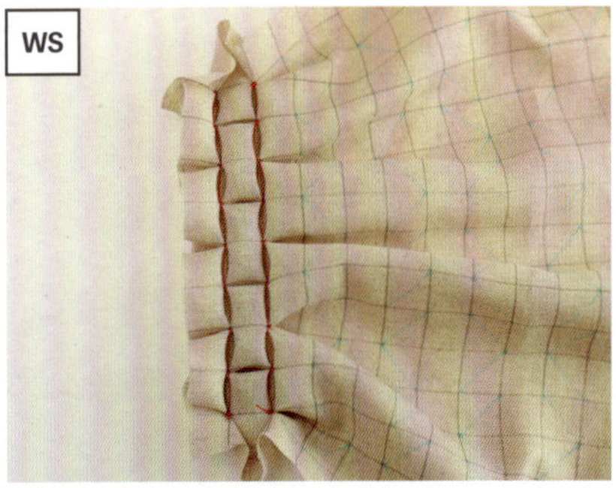

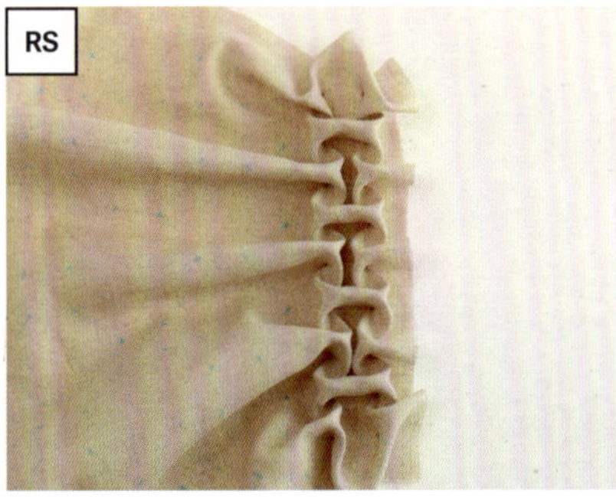

33 In the third column, repeat this process, keeping in mind the pattern is reversed. When you have stitched two columns, the shape becomes more defined. Repeat this process to finish the entire surface.

34 When you have finished smocking, press the fabric to your liking. Gently press down with an iron to flatten the pattern with steam.

You can turn the Bricks into Bows by pinching the middle in the same way that I did with the clutch on page 18.

BUBBLE

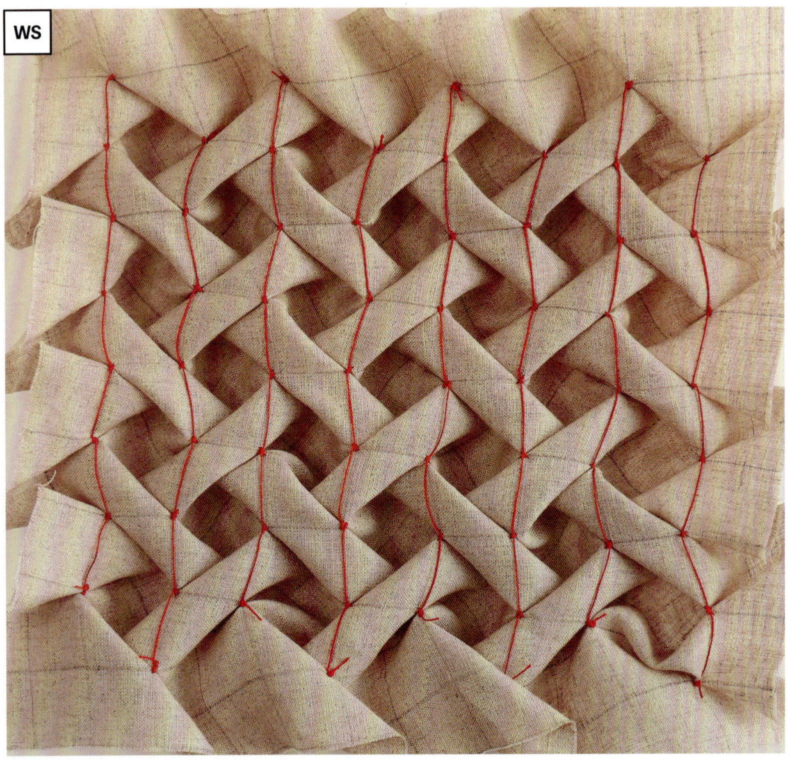

■ **Original Fabric Size**

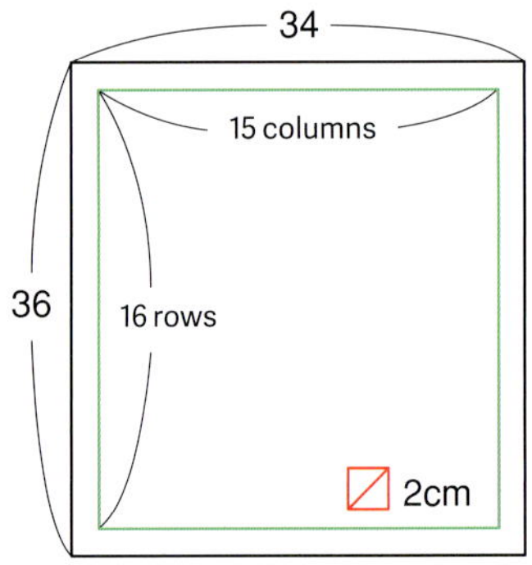

■ **Fabric's Stretch Level**

★★☆☆☆

(Depends on the finish)

■ **Pressing**

- Not required to finish

■ **Notes**

- Finish one column at a time
- The WS is also interesting

The **red** lines show where you should pull the thread tight to bring joined sections together. The **light blue** dashed lines show where you should pass the thread. **Letters** indicate stitching order. **Gray** arrows indicate direction.

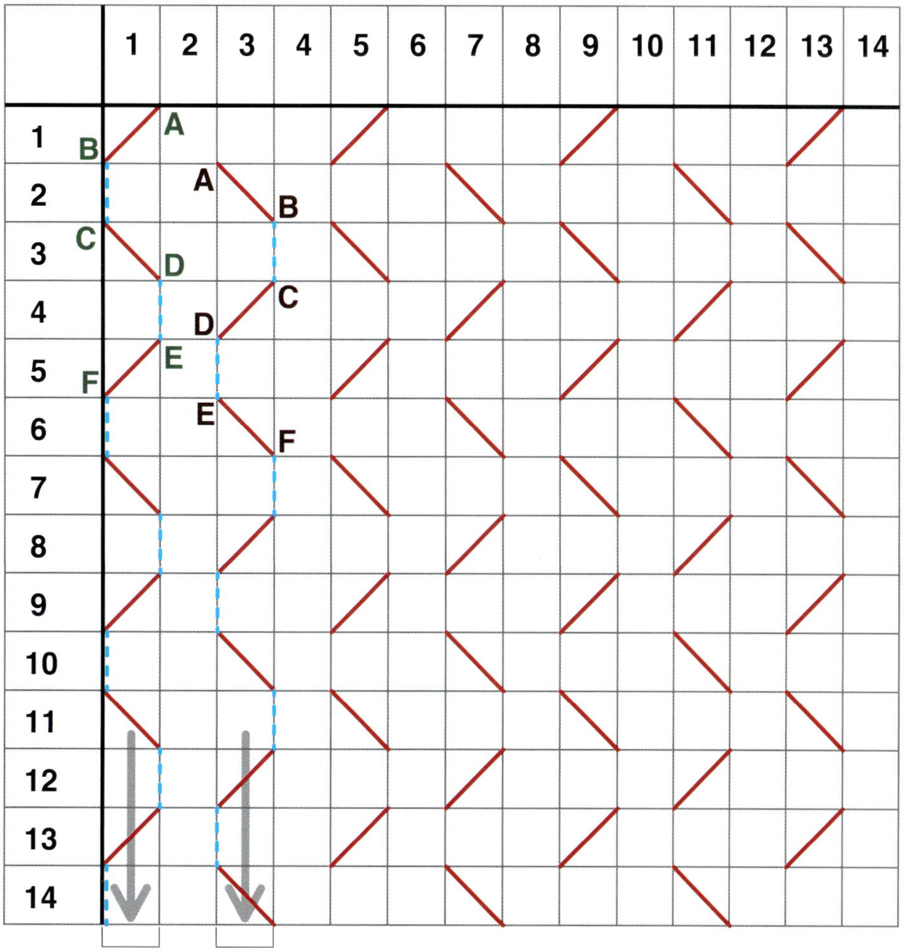

Finish one column at a time.

■ Stitching Instructions

1. Insert the needle into corner A and pick up a stitch. Insert the needle into corner B and pick up a stitch, then scoop up corner A again. Pull the thread tight to bring the corners together.
2. Sew the joined corners AB together with one stitch and secure the stitch.
3. Pick up a stitch at corner C, pass the thread, and secure the stitch.
4. Pick up a stitch at corner D. Scoop up corner C again and pull the thread tight to bring the corners together.
5. Sew the joined corners CD together with one stitch and secure the stitch.
6. Pick up a stitch at corner E, pass the thread, and secure the stitch. Corner E will now be the same as corner A, so just repeat the same process for the rest of the column.
7. When you reach the end of the column, tie a finishing knot and cut the thread. Skip a column and begin stitching the next column.
8. Stitch the next column in reverse starting one row lower.

HEART

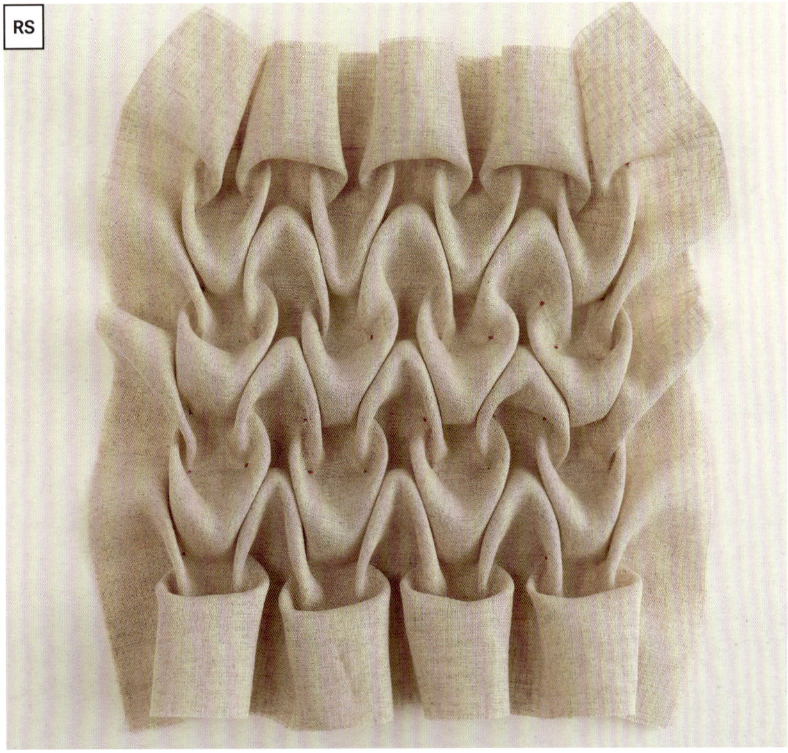

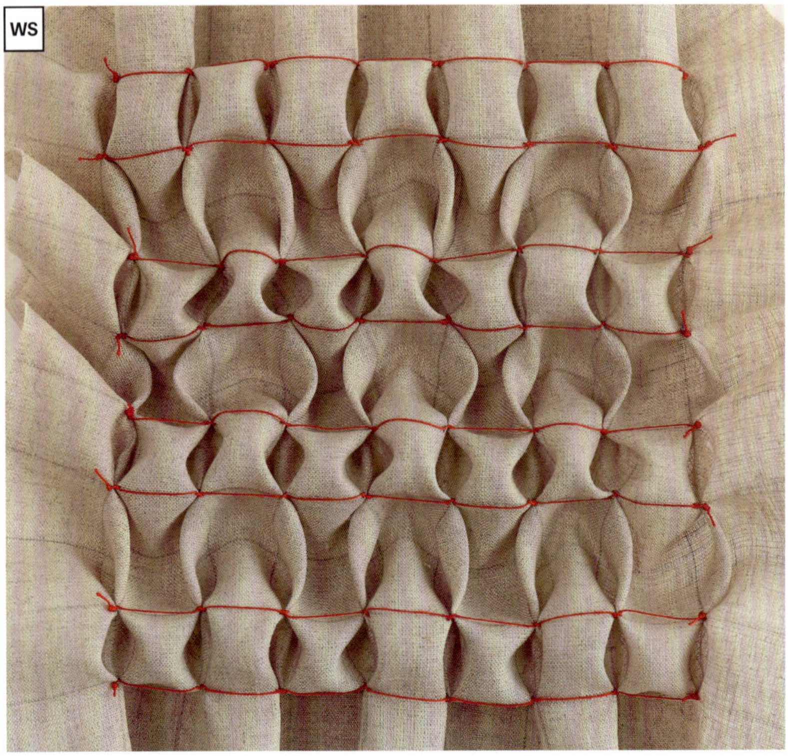

■ **Original Fabric Size**

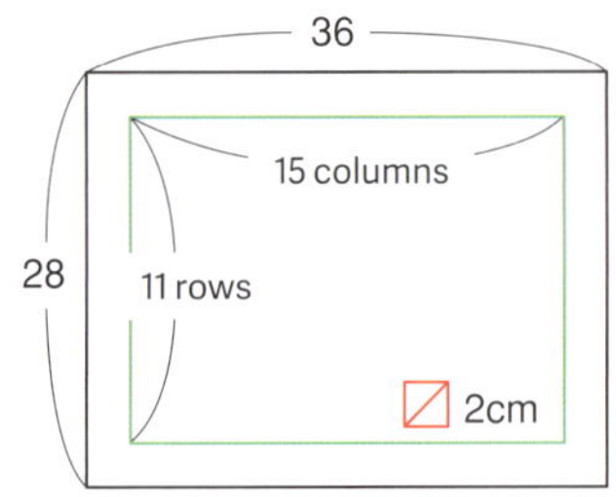

■ **Fabric's Stretch Level**

★★★★☆

■ **Pressing**

- Not required to finish

■ **Notes**

- Proceed horizontally
- Finish one row at a time
- Consists of rows stitched the same way as the first column of Bubble (page 72)

The **red** lines show where you should pull the thread tight to bring joined sections together. The **light blue** dashed lines show where you should pass the thread. **Green** letters indicate stitching order. **Gray** arrows indicate direction.

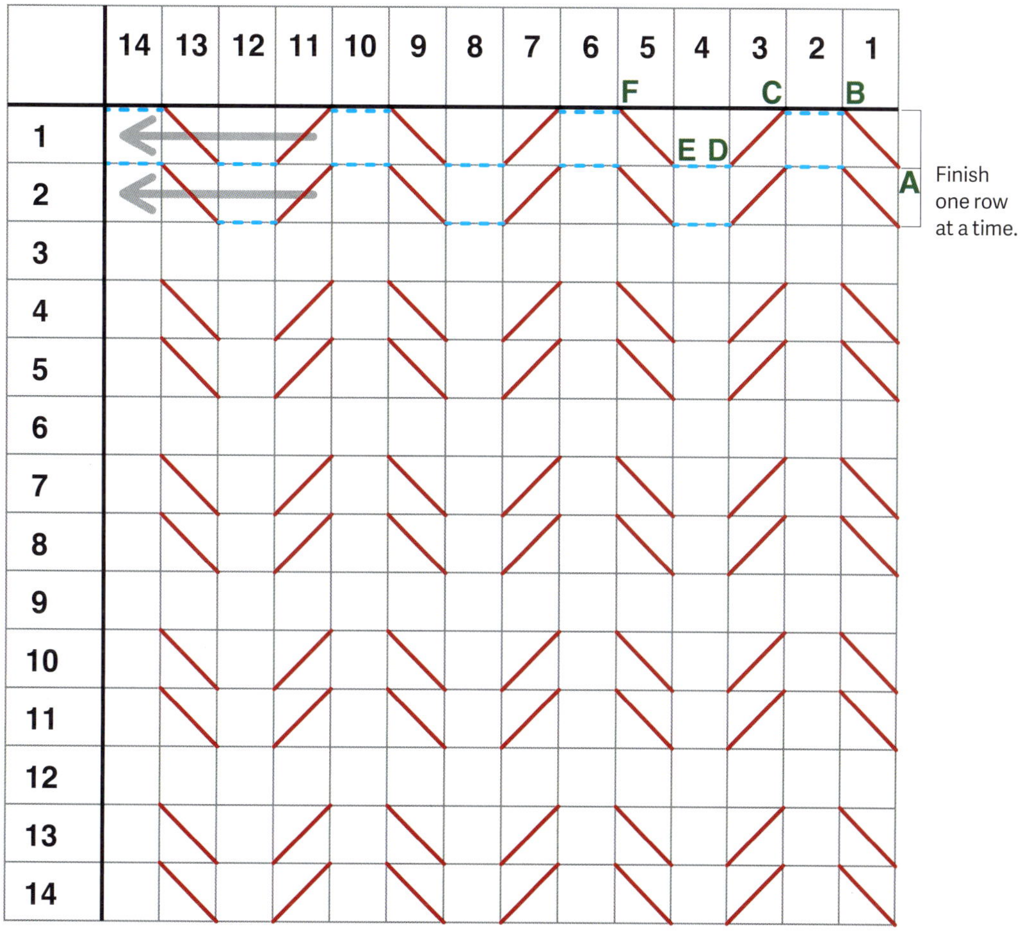

■ Stitching Instructions

1. Insert the needle into corner A and pick up a stitch. Insert the needle into corner B and pick up a stitch, then scoop up corner A again. Pull the thread tight to bring the corners together.
2. Sew the joined corners AB together with one stitch and secure the stitch.
3. Pick up a stitch at corner C, pass the thread, and secure the stitch.
4. Pick up a stitch at corner D. Scoop up corner C again and pull the thread tight to bring the corners together.
5. Sew the joined corners CD together with one stitch and secure the stitch.
6. Pick up a stitch at corner E, pass the thread, and secure the stitch. Corner E will now be the same as corner A, so just repeat the same process for the rest of the row.
7. When you reach the end of the row, tie a finishing knot and cut the thread. Begin stitching the next row from the far right using the same process.
8. When the second row is complete, skip a row and begin stitching the next row from the far right using the same process.

LOZENGE

RS

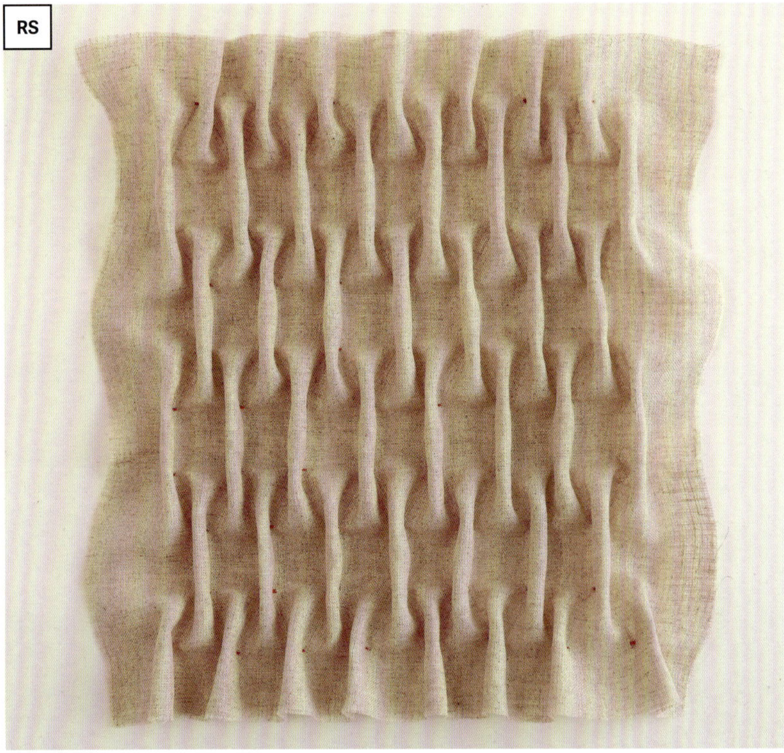

WS

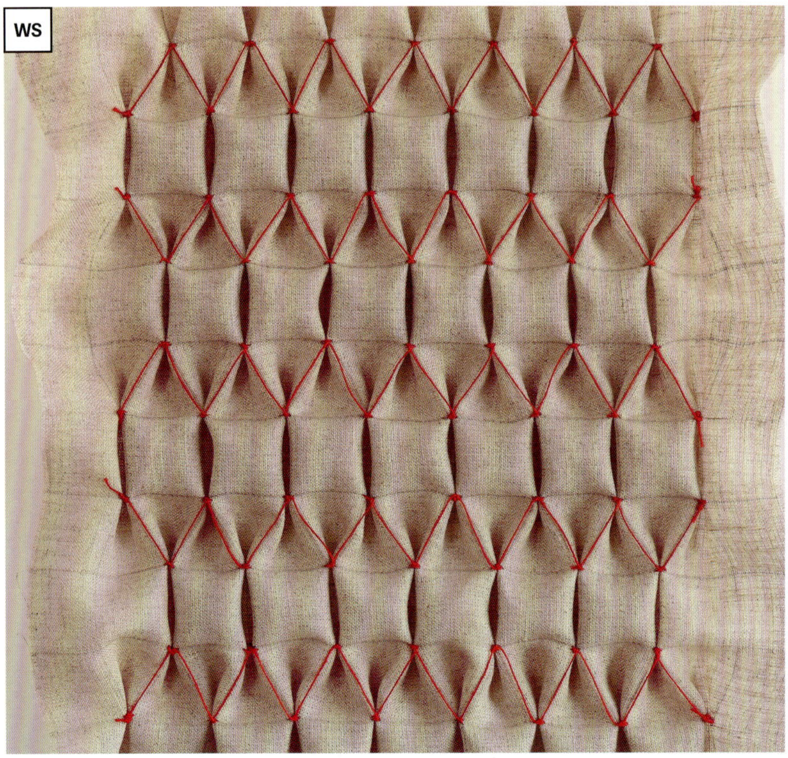

Original Fabric Size

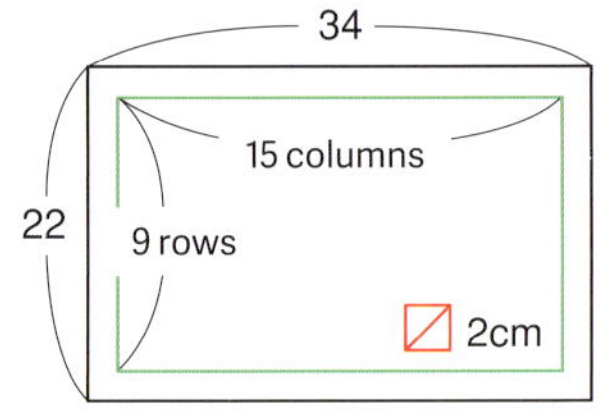

Fabric's Stretch Level

★☆☆☆☆

Pressing

- Could be pressed depending on the desired finish

Notes

- Proceed horizontally
- Finish one row at a time

The **red** lines show where you should pull the thread tight to bring joined sections together. The **light blue** dashed lines show where you should pass the thread. **Green** letters indicate stitching order. **Gray** arrows indicate direction.

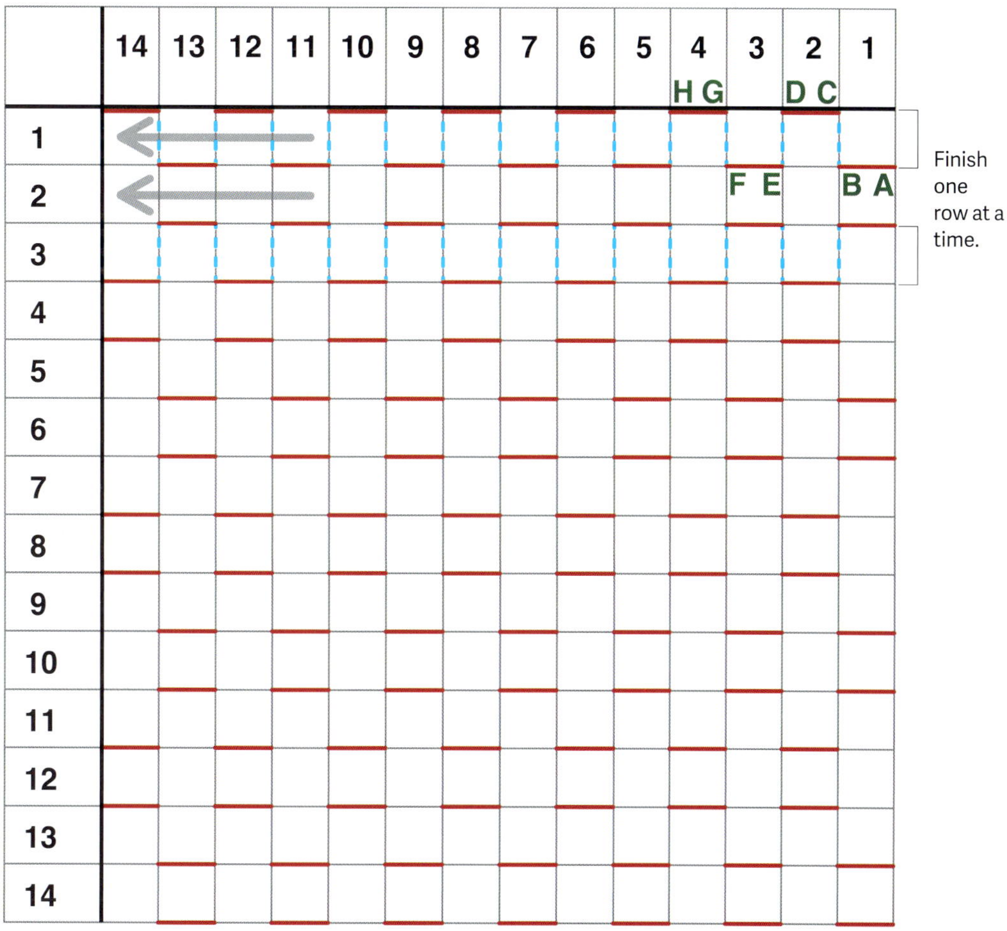

■ Stitching Instructions

1. Insert the needle into corner A and pick up a stitch. Insert the needle into corner B and pick up a stitch, then scoop up corner A again. Pull the thread tight to bring the corners together.
2. Sew the joined corners AB together with one stitch and secure the stitch.
3. Pick up a stitch at corner C, pass the thread, and secure the stitch.
4. Pick up a stitch at corner D. Scoop up corner C again and pull the thread tight to bring the corners together.
5. Sew the joined corners CD together with one stitch and secure the stitch.
6. Pick up a stitch at corner E, pass the thread, and secure the stitch. Corner E will now be the same as corner A, so just repeat the same process for the rest of the row.
7. When you reach the end of the row, tie a finishing knot and cut the thread. Skip a row and begin stitching the next row from the far right.
8. Stitch the next row in reverse.

DOUBLE LATTICE

RS

WS

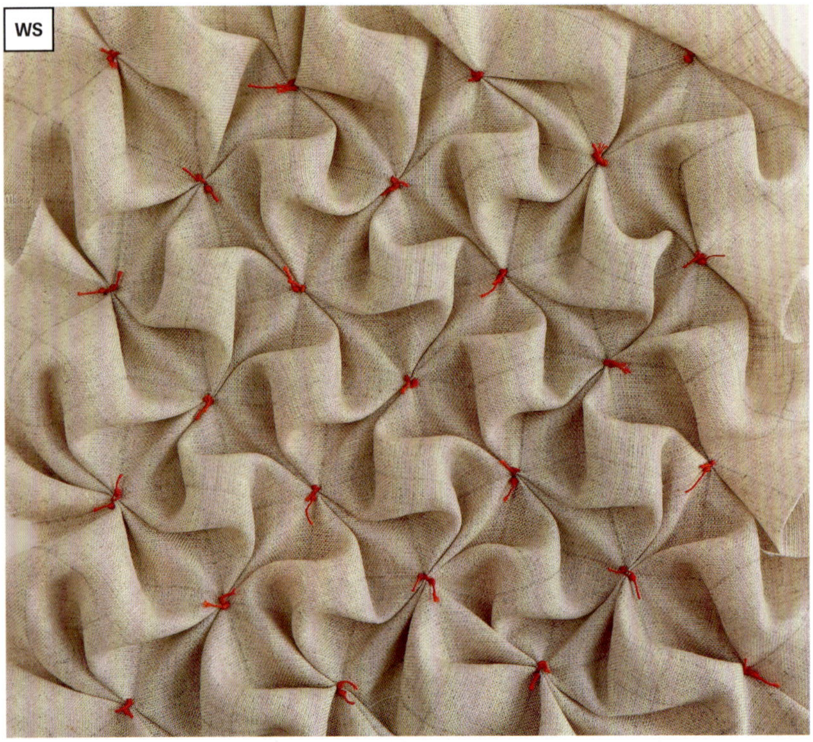

■ Original Fabric Size

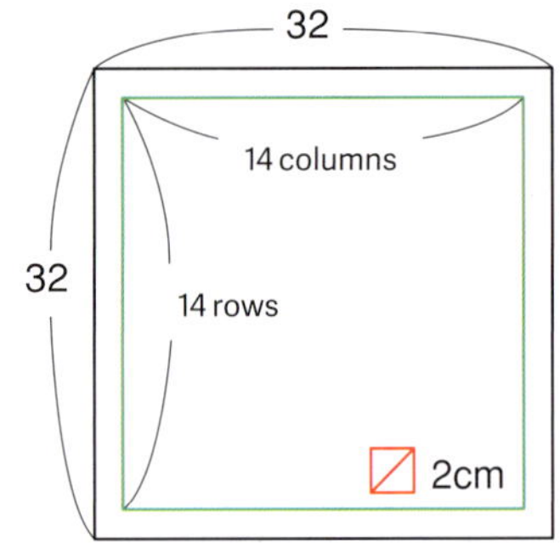

■ Fabric's Stretch Level

★★★★★

■ Pressing

- Not required to finish

■ Notes

- Finish one section at a time
- The WS is also interesting
- Since there will be gaps, instead of continuing to pass the thread, tie a finishing knot each time and cut the thread
- The pattern will be large, so consider making the grid size small

The **red** and **pink** lines show where you should pull the thread tight to bring joined sections together. The **light blue** dashed lines show where you should pass the thread. **Letters** indicate stitching order.

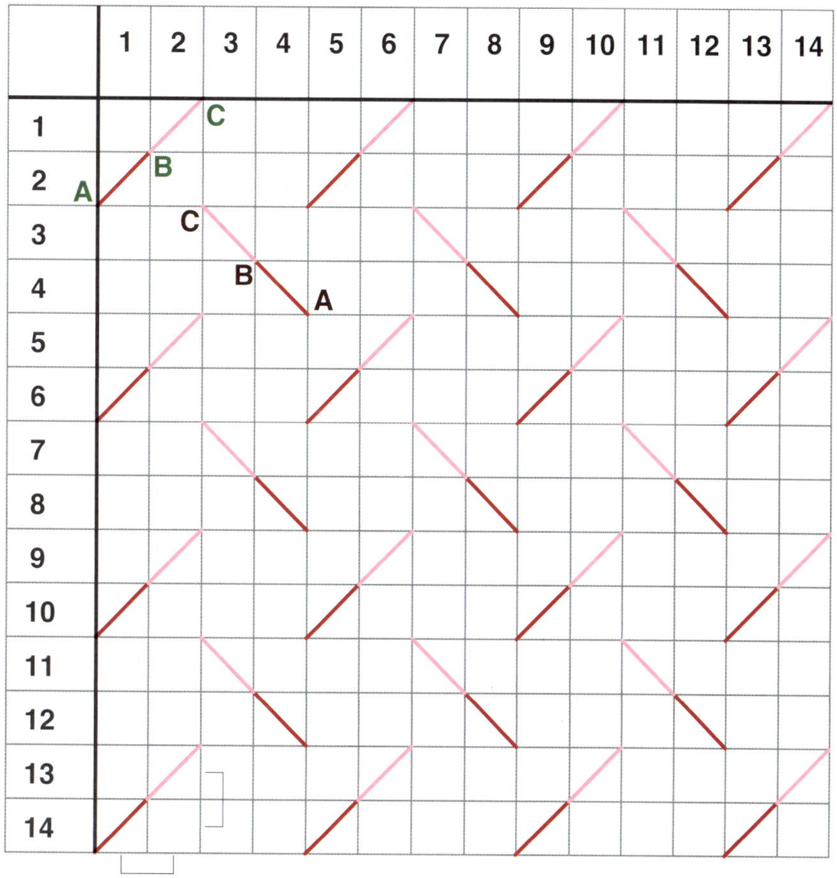

Finish one marked section at a time.

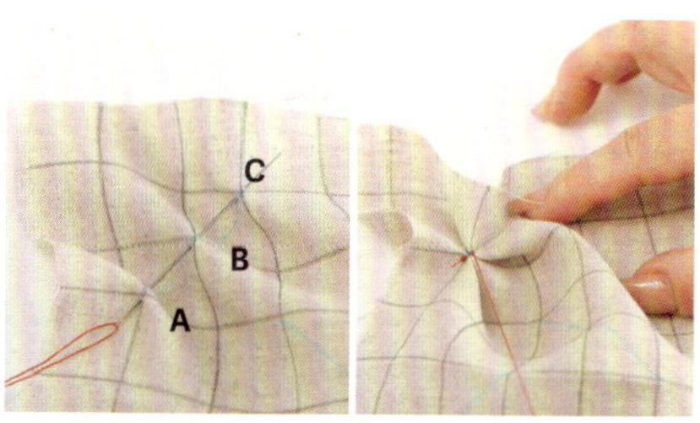

01 Insert the needle into corner A and pick up a stitch. Repeat into corner B and corner C, picking up one stitch each time. Pull the thread tight to bring the corners together.

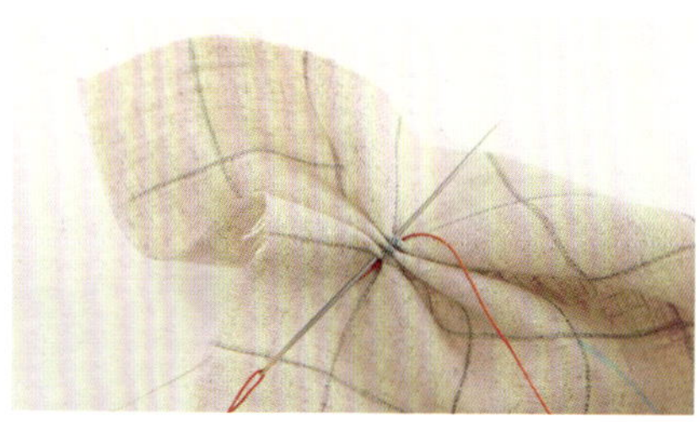

02 Sew the joined corners ABC together with one stitch.

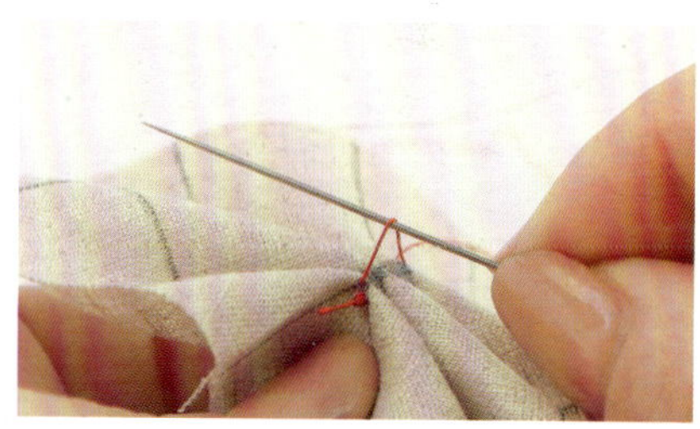

03 Just before you pull the thread through, pass the needle through the loop and secure the stitch.

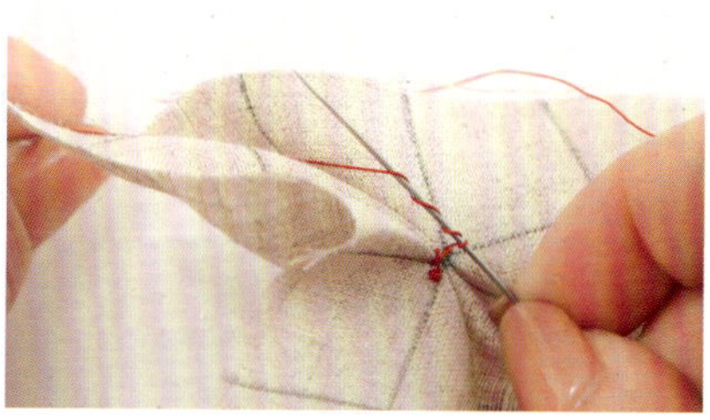

04 Tie a finishing knot and cut the thread.

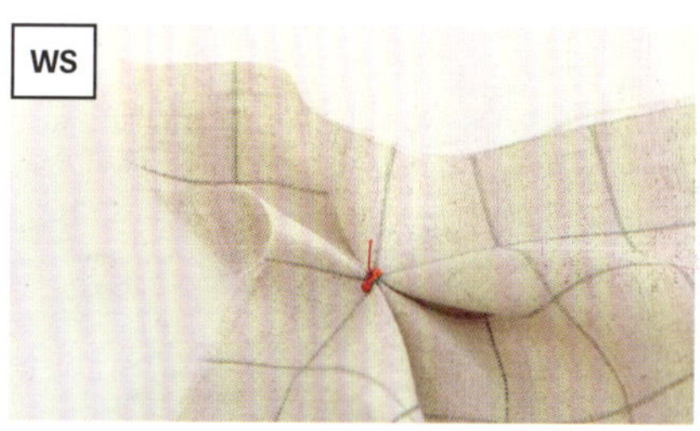

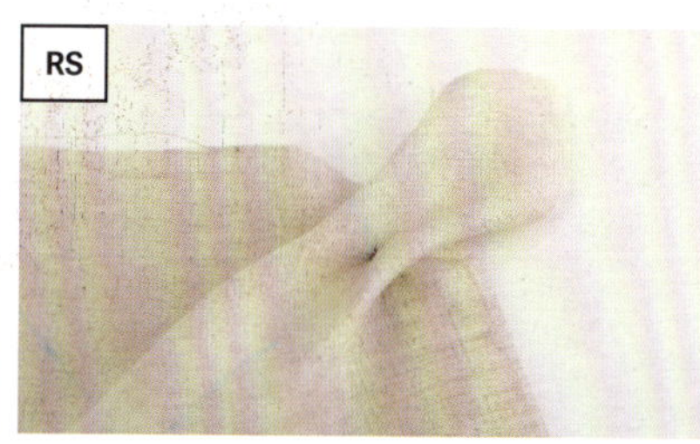

05 This completes one section. Repeat this same process for each section as marked.

RATTAN

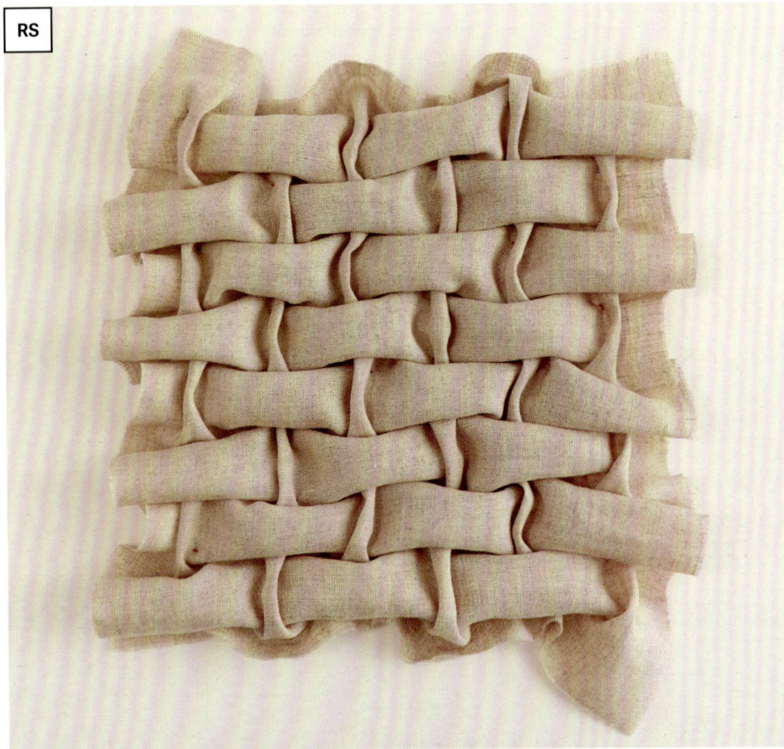

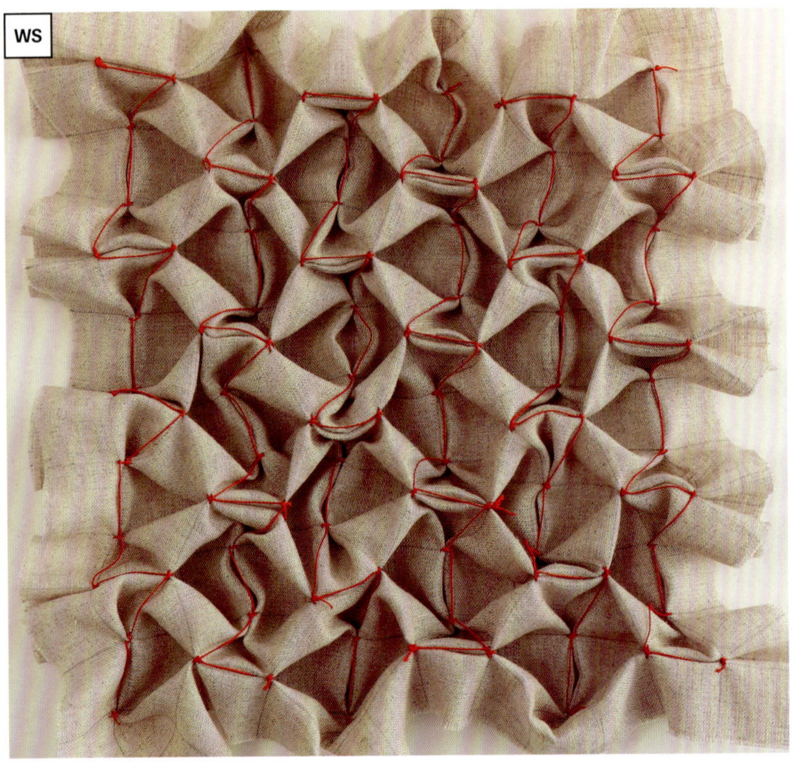

■ **Original Fabric Size**

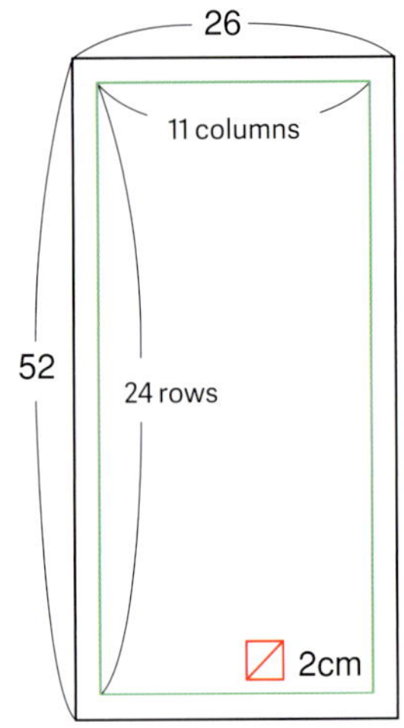

■ **Fabric's Stretch Level**

★★☆☆☆

■ **Pressing**

- Required to finish

■ **Notes**

- Finish one column at a time
- Scoop up three squares at a time

The **red** lines show where you should pull the thread tight to bring joined sections together. The **light blue** dashed lines show where you should pass the thread. **Green** letters indicate stitching order. **Gray** arrows indicate direction.

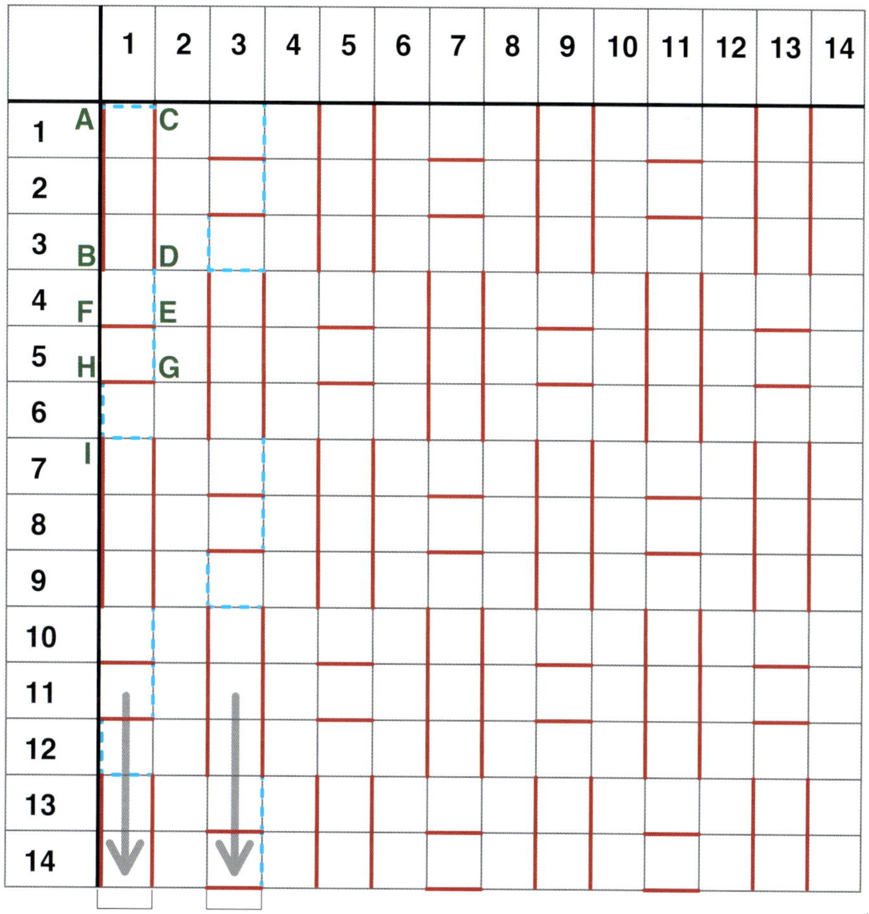

Finish one column at a time.

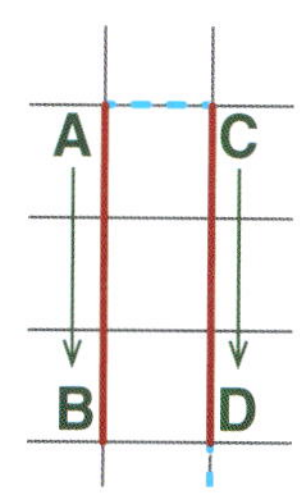

When connecting A to B and C to D, scoop up three squares at a time.

■ Stitching Instructions

1. Insert the needle into corner A and pick up a stitch. Insert the needle into corner B and pick up a stitch, then scoop up corner A again. Pull the thread tight to bring the corners together.
2. Sew the joined corners AB together with one stitch and secure the stitch.
3. Pick up a stitch at corner C, pass the thread, and secure the stitch.
4. Pick up a stitch at corner D. Scoop up corner C again and pull the thread tight to bring the corners together.
5. Sew the joined corners CD together with one stitch and secure the stitch.
6. Pick up a stitch at corner E, pass the thread, and secure the stitch.
7. Pick up a stitch at corner F. Scoop up corner E again and pull the thread tight to bring the corners together.
8. Sew the joined corners E and F together with one stitch and secure the stitch.
9. Pick up a stitch at corner G, pass the thread, and secure the stitch.
10. Pick up a stitch at corner H and pull the thread tight to bring the corners together.
11. Sew the joined corners G and H together with one stitch and secure the stitch.
12. Pick up a stitch at corner I, pass the thread, and secure the stitch. Corner I will now be the same as corner A, so just repeat the same process for the rest of the column.
13. When you reach the end of the column, tie a finishing knot and cut the thread. Skip a column and begin stitching the next column from the top.
14. The pattern of the next column is offset by three squares.

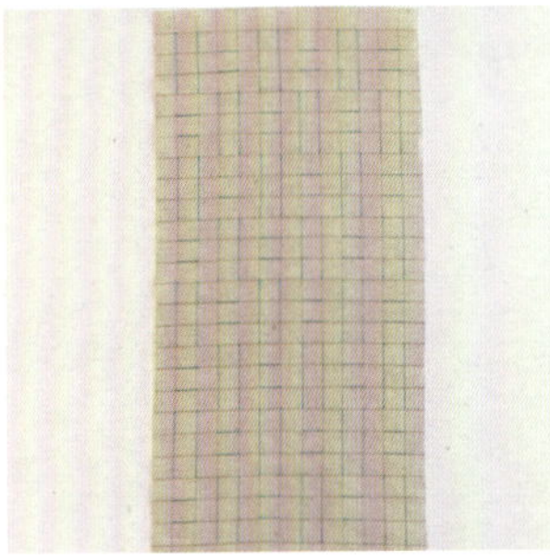

01 Draw a grid on the WS of the fabric. Draw diagonal lines connecting the corners that will be scooped together, as shown on page 81.

▸ Bring A and B together.

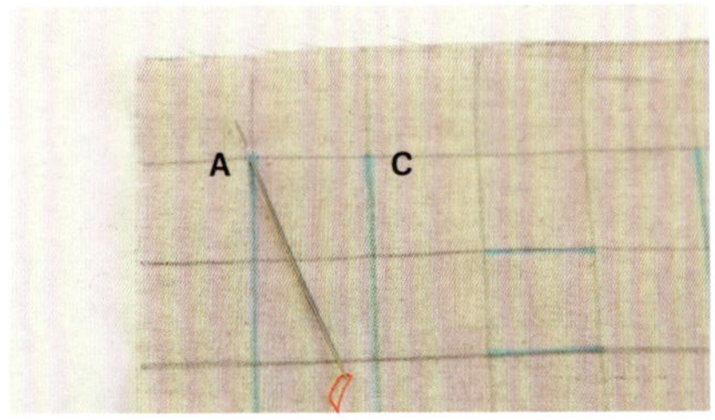

02 Thread the needle and tie a finishing knot with a single strand of thread. Pick up a stitch from inside the square to outside at corner A. Each stitch should be about 0.2cm long.

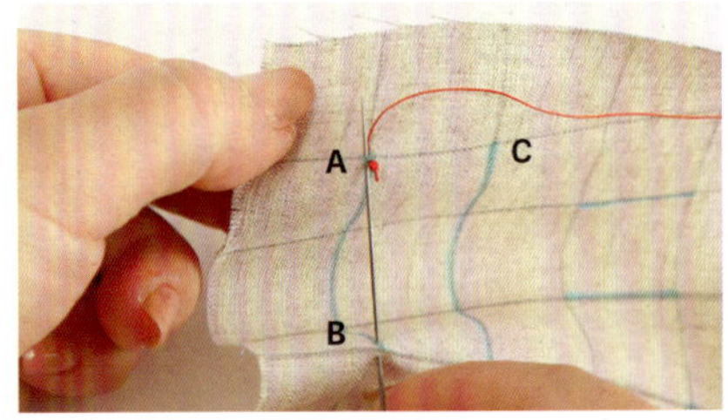

03 Pick on a stitch from outside the square to inside at corner B. Corner B is three squares away from A. Scoop up corner A from **Step 02** in the same way.

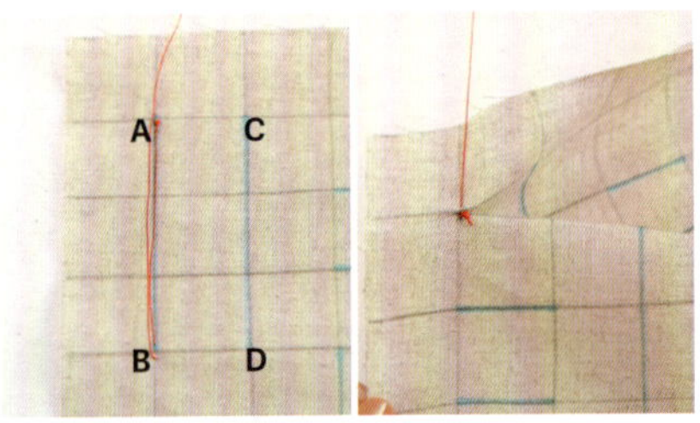

04 Pull the thread tight to bring corners A and B together. You will see two strands of thread running vertically.

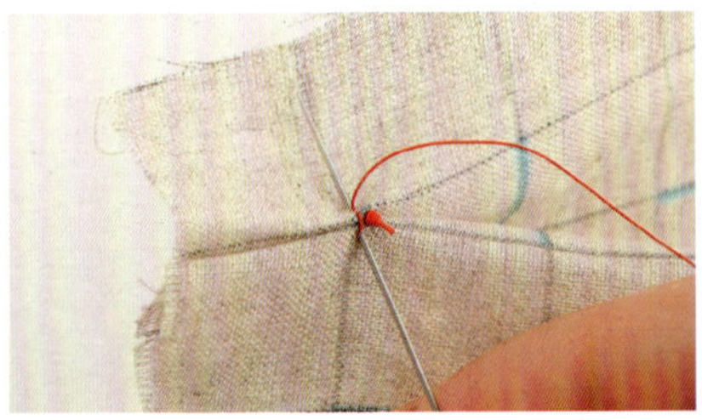

05 Sew the joined corners AB together with one stitch.

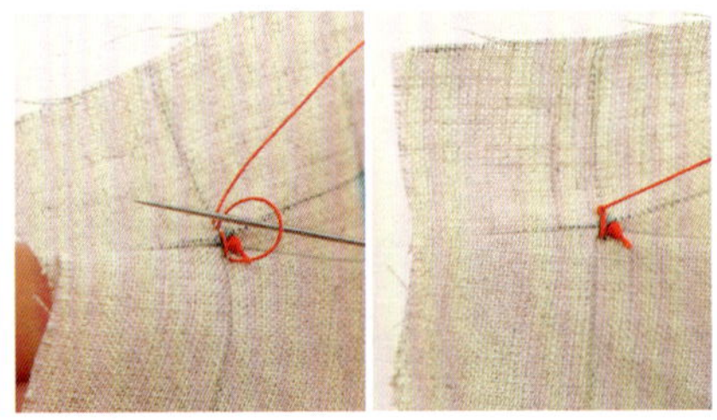

06 Pull the thread, creating a small loop just before pulling it tight. Pass the needle through the loop from bottom to top. Pull the thread tight to lock the stitch and secure the fabric.

▸ Pass the thread from AB to C.

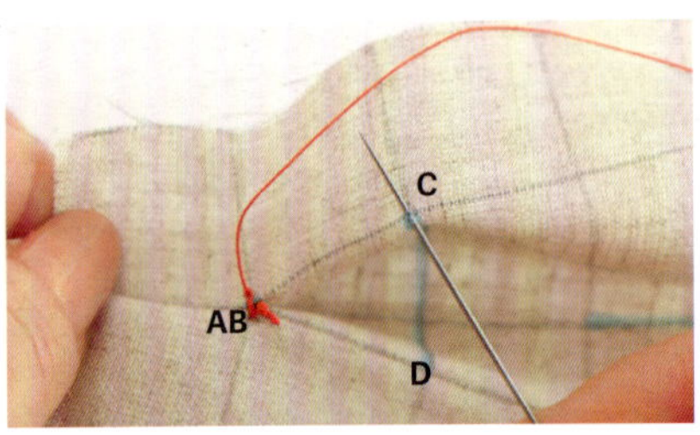

07 Move to the next column and pick up a stitch at corner C. Pull the thread along the gridline from AB to C.

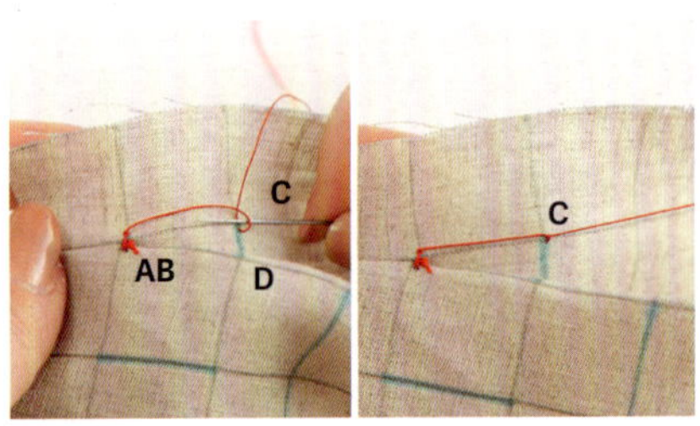

08 Without pulling it all the way through, pass it over the thread that you just pulled to create a loop, then bring the needle back through the loop. Pull the thread and tie a knot.

▸ Bring C and D together.

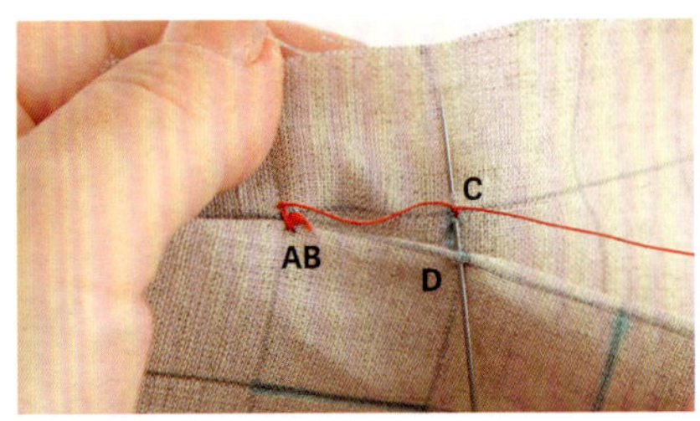

09 Pick up a stitch at corner D, then scoop up corner C again. Pull the thread tight to bring corners C and D together.

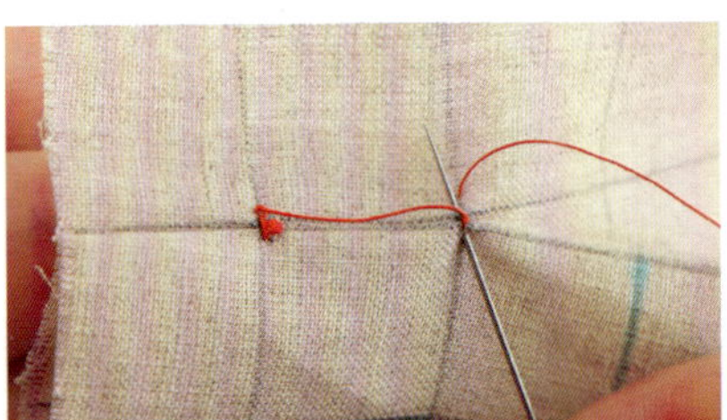

10 Sew the joined corners CD together with one stitch.

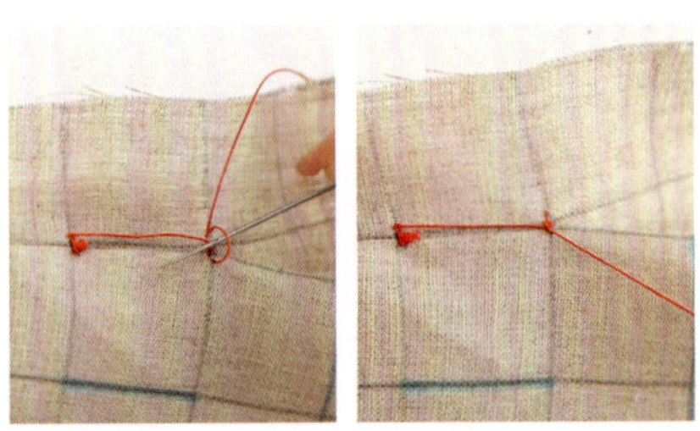

11 Pull the thread, creating a small loop just before pulling it tight. Pass the needle through the loop from bottom to top. Pull the thread tight to secure the stitch.

▸ Pass the thread from CD to E.

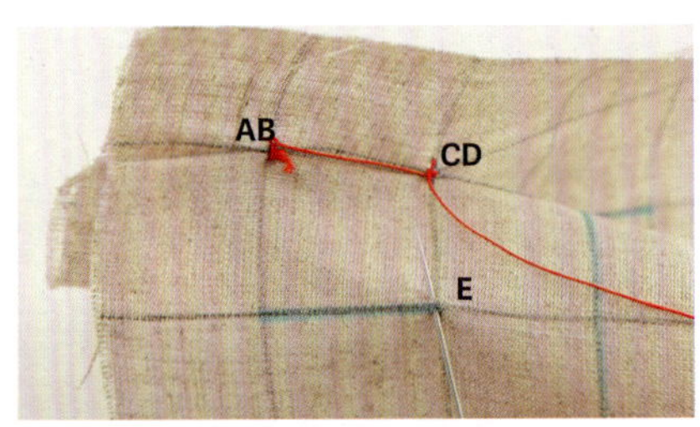

12 Pick up a stitch at corner E. Pull the thread along the gridline from CD to E.

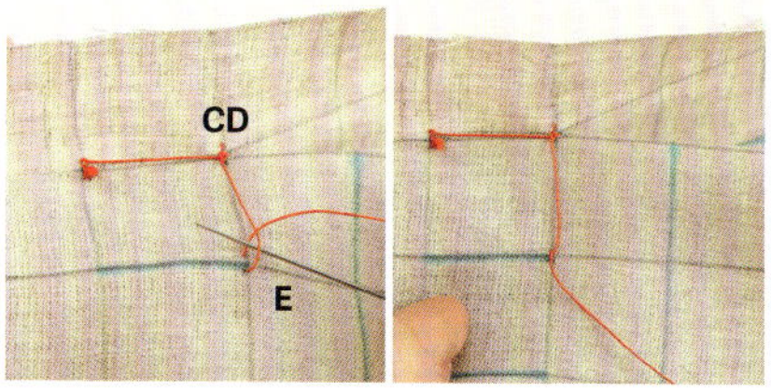

13 Without pulling it all the way through, pass it over the thread that you just pulled to create a loop, then bring the needle back through the loop. Pull the thread and tie a knot.

▸ Bring E and F together.

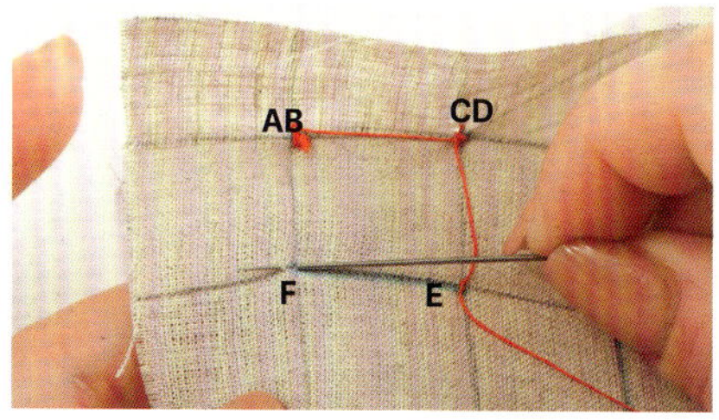

14 Pick up a stitch at corner F, then scoop up corner E again. Pull the thread tight to bring corners E and F together.

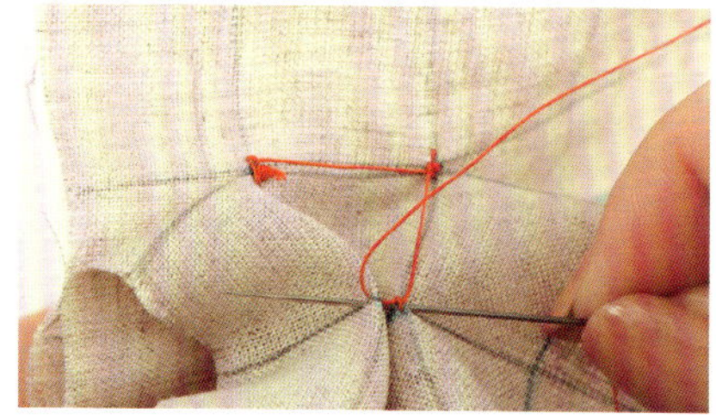

15 Sew the joined corners EF together with one stitch.

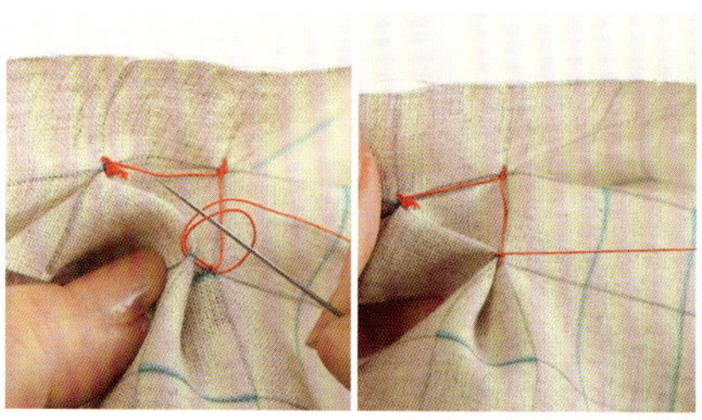

16 Pull the thread, creating a small loop just before pulling it tight. Pass the needle through the loop from bottom to top. Pull the thread tight to secure the stitch.

▸ Pass the thread from EF to G.

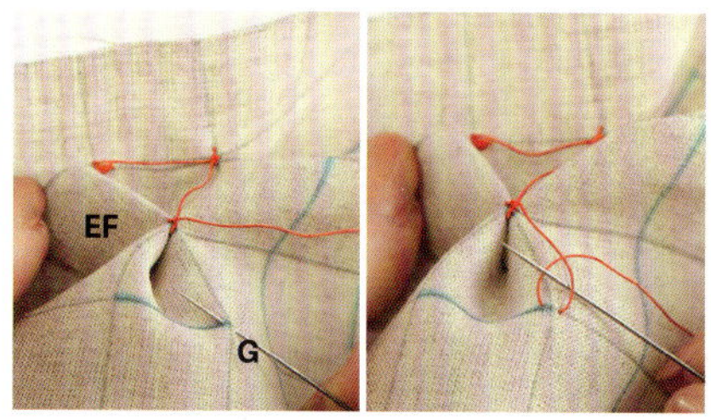

17 Pick up a stitch at corner G and pull the thread along the gridline from EF to G. Without pulling it all the way through, create a loop, pass the needle through it, and secure the stitch.

▸ Bring G and H together.

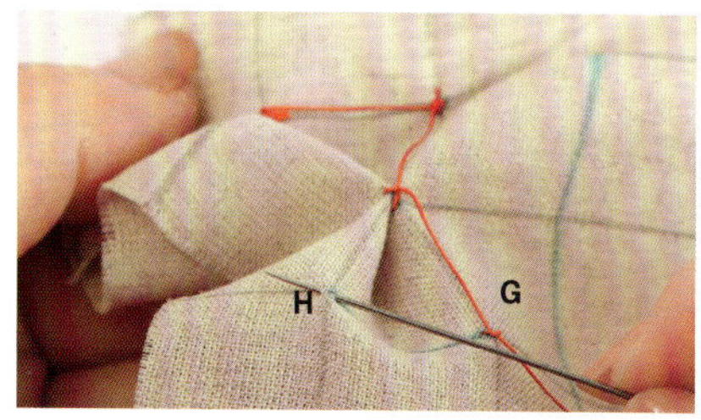

18 Pick up a stitch at corner H, then scoop up corner G again. Pull the thread tight to bring corners G and H together.

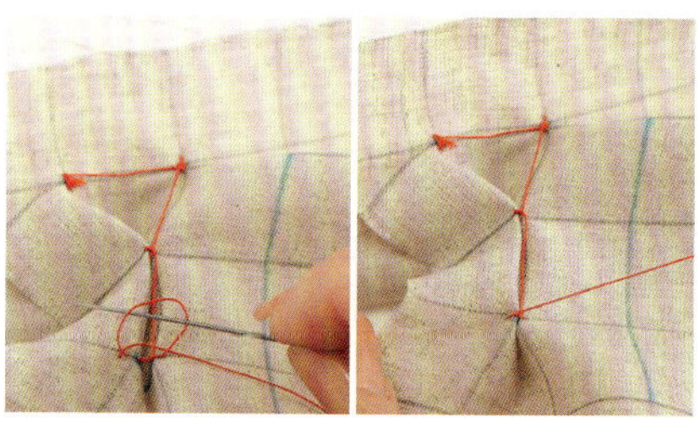

19 Sew the joined corners GH together with one stitch. Create a small loop just before pulling the thread tight. Pass the needle through from bottom to top. Pull the thread tight to secure the stitch.

▸ Pass the thread from GH to I.

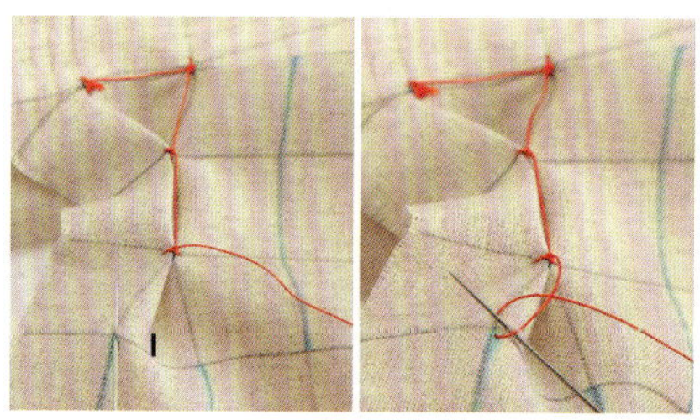

20 Pick up a stitch at corner I and pull the thread along the gridline from GH to I. Without pulling it all the way through, create a loop, pass the needle through it, and secure the stitch.

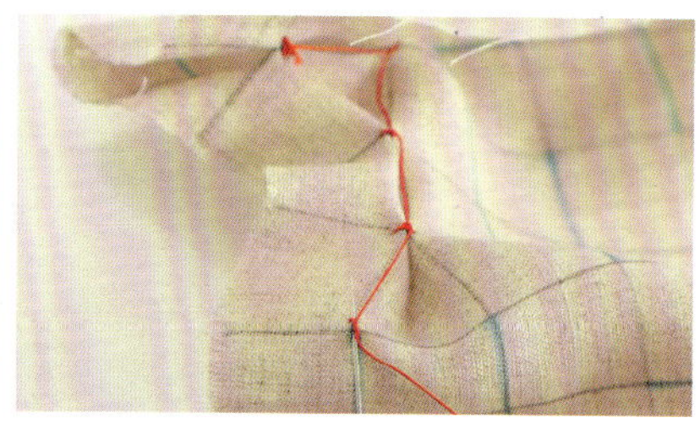

21 I is now the same as A, so repeat this process for the rest of the pattern.

▸ One column is complete.

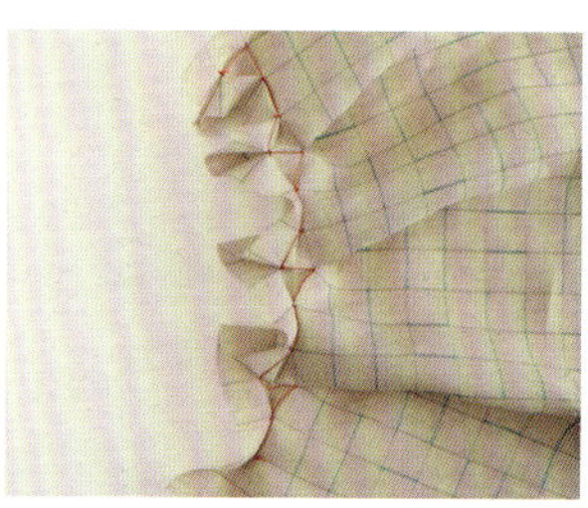

22 After finishing one column, the fabric shrinks considerably. The pattern is not yet clearly visible.

▸ Two columns are complete.

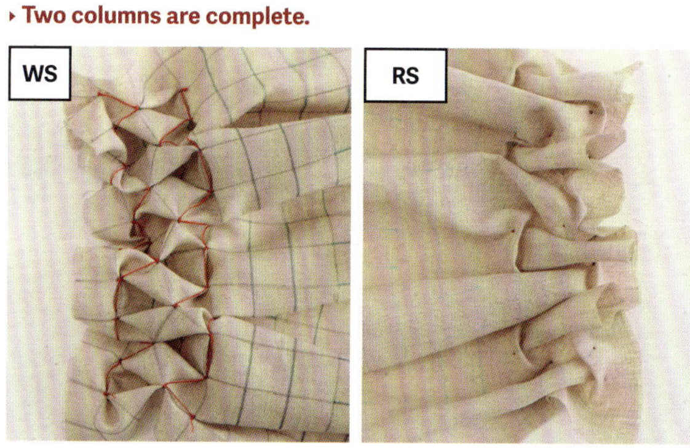

23 After completing two columns, a knit-like pattern begins to emerge. If any areas are not aligned properly, use an awl or similar tool to pull them into shape and adjust. Press lightly to finish.

DRAGON SCALE

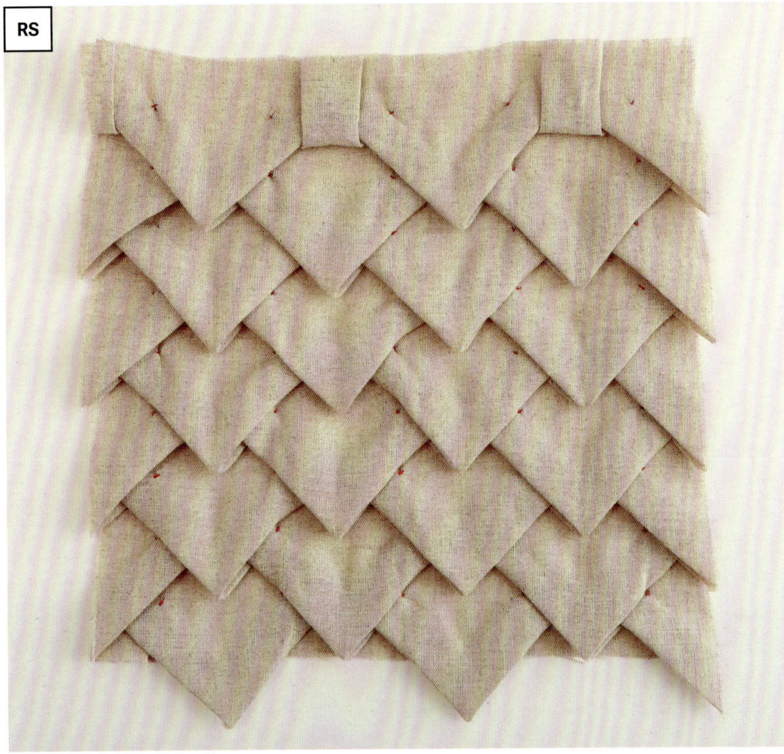

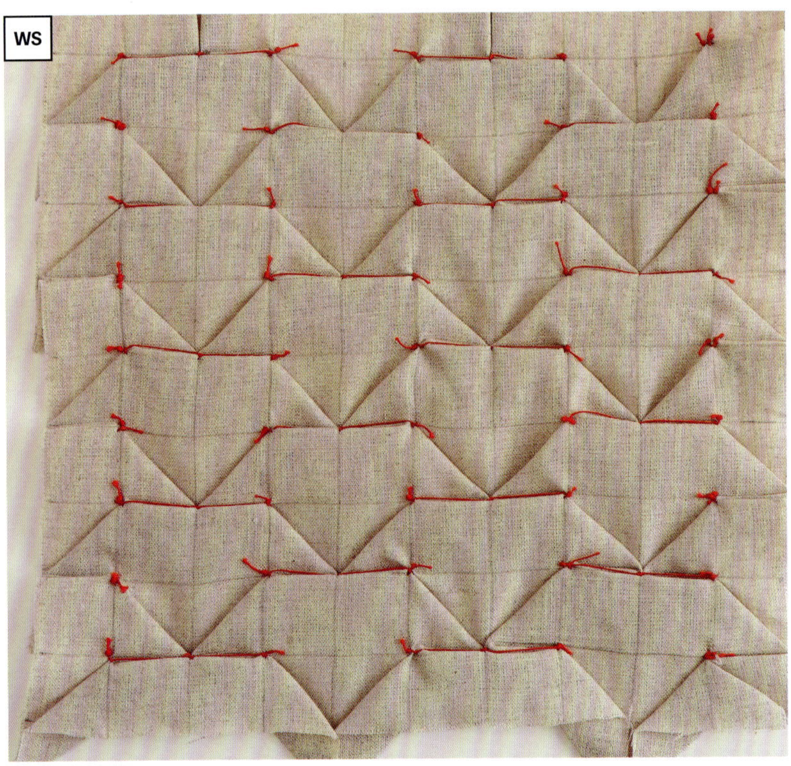

■ **Original Fabric Size**

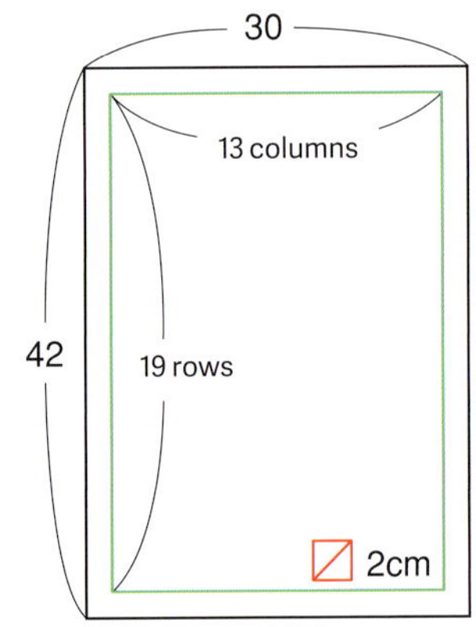

■ **Fabric's Stretch Level**

★☆☆☆☆

■ **Pressing**

- Required to finish

■ **Notes**

- Finish one section at a time
- Since there will be gaps, instead of continuing to pass the thread, tie a finishing knot each time and cut the thread
- Scoop up two squares at a time

The **red** lines show where you should pull the thread tight to bring joined sections together. The **light blue** dashed lines show where you should pass the thread. **Green** letters and arrows indicate stitching order.

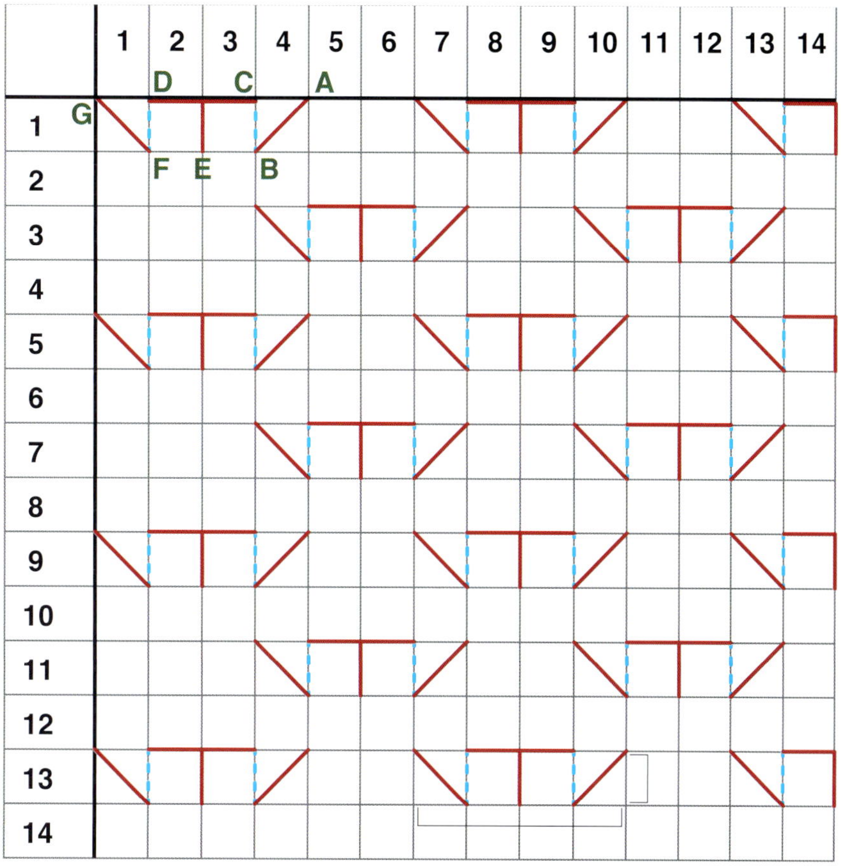

Finish one marked section at a time

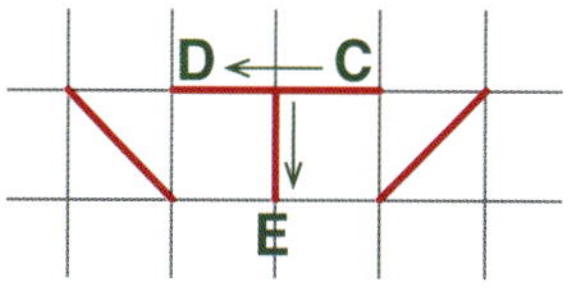

When connecting C to D, scoop up two squares at once then scoop up corner E.

■ Stitching Instructions

1. Insert the needle into corner A and pick up a stitch. Insert the needle into corner B and pick up a stitch, then scoop up corner A again. Pull the thread tight to bring the corners together.
2. Sew the joined corners AB together with one stitch and secure the stitch.
3. Pick up a stitch at corner C, pass the thread and secure the stitch.
4. Pick up a stitch at corner D. Scoop up corner C again and pull the thread tight to bring the corners together.
5. Sew the joined corners CD together with one stitch and secure the stitch.
6. Pick up a stitch at corner E. Scoop up corners CD again and pull the thread tight to bring the corners together.
7. Pick up a stitch at corner F, pass the thread, and secure the stitch.
8. Pick up a stitch at corner G. Scoop up corner C again and pull the thread tight to bring the corners together.
9. Sew the joined corners FG together with one stitch and secure the stitch.
10. Tie a finishing knot, cut the thread, and repeat this same process for each section as marked.

DRAGON SCALE STITCHING

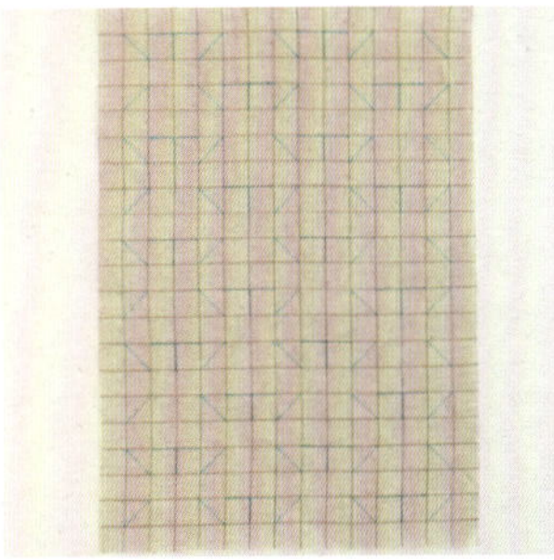

01 Draw a grid on the WS of the fabric. Draw lines connecting the corners that will be scooped together, as shown on page 85.

▸ **Bring A and B together.**

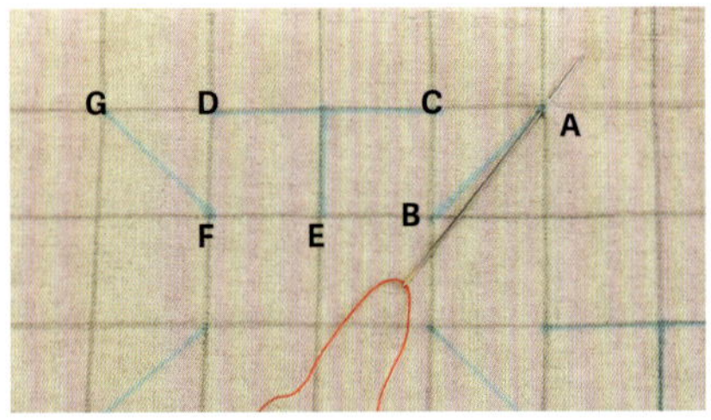

02 Thread the needle and tie a finishing knot with a single strand of thread. Pick up a stitch from inside the square to outside at corner A. Each stitch should be about 0.2cm.

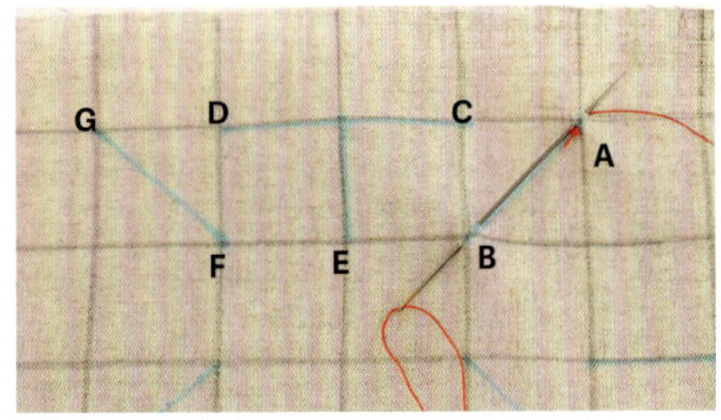

03 Pick up a stitch from outside the square to inside at corner B. Scoop up corner A from **Step 02** in the same way.

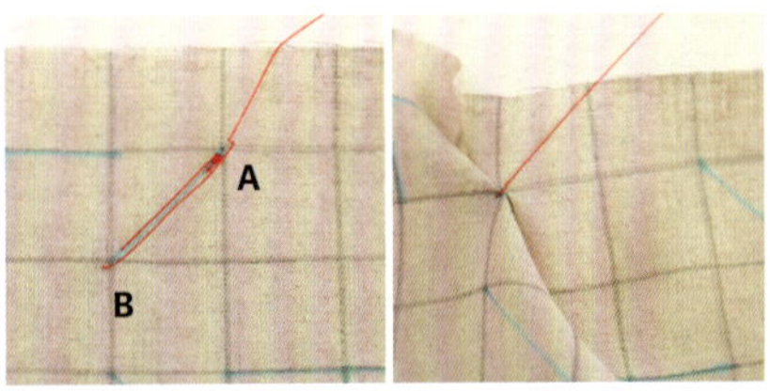

04 Pull the thread. You will see two strands of thread running diagonally.

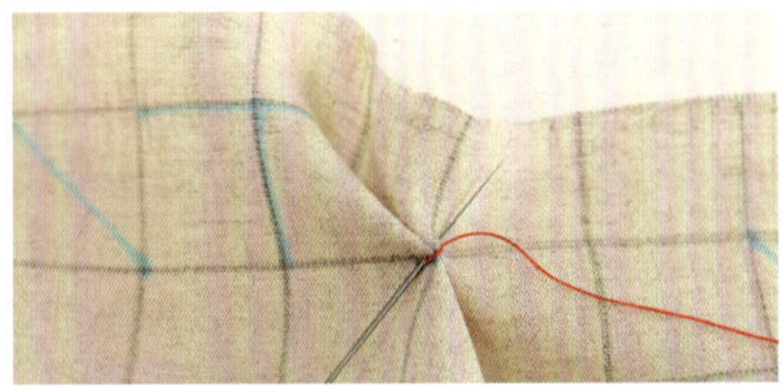

05 Sew the joined corners AB together with one stitch.

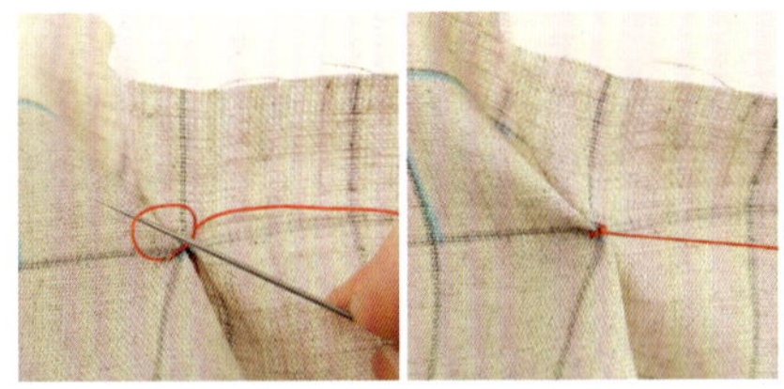

06 Pull the thread, creating a small loop just before pulling it tight. Pass the needle through the loop from bottom to top. Pull the thread tight to secure the fabric.

▸ **Pass the thread from AB to C.**

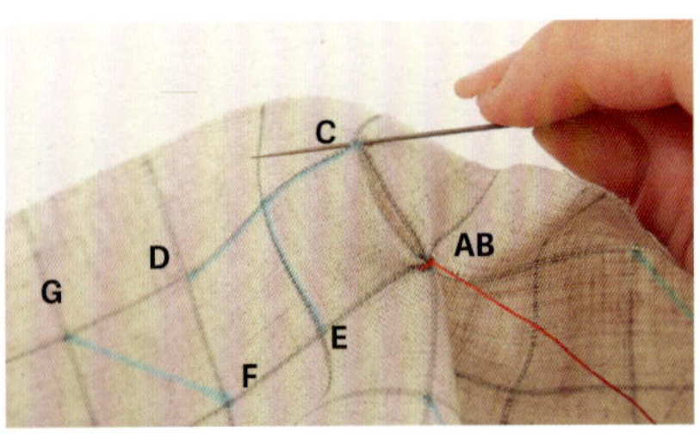

07 Pick up a stitch at corner C. Pull the thread along the gridline from AB to C.

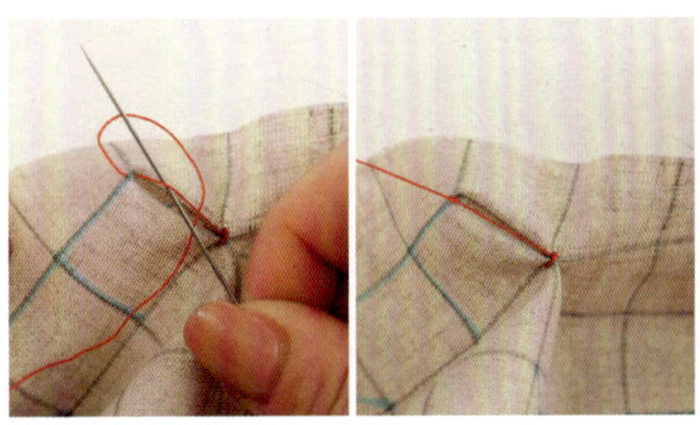

08 Without pulling the thread all the way through, pass it over the thread that you just pulled to create a loop, then bring the needle back under the thread. Pull the thread and tie a knot.

▸ **Bring C, D and E together.**

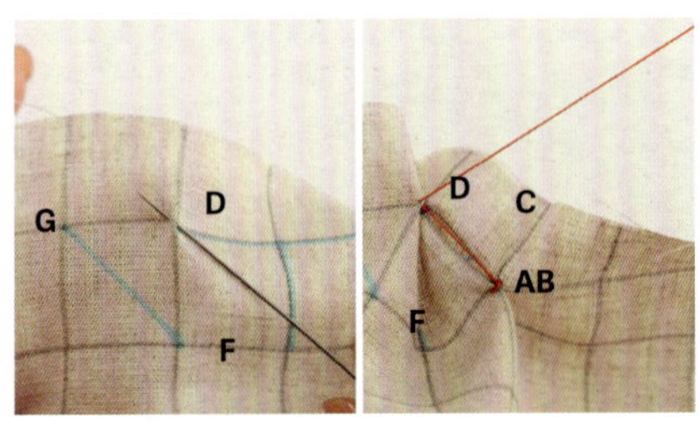

09 Pick up a stitch at corner D. Pull the thread tight to bring corners C and D together.

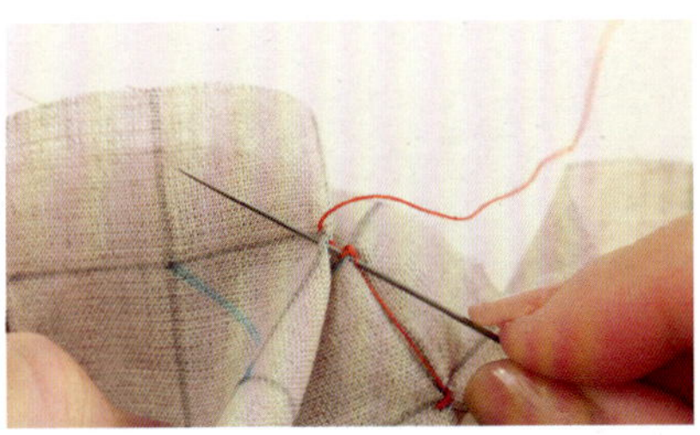

10 Sew the joined corners CD together with one stitch.

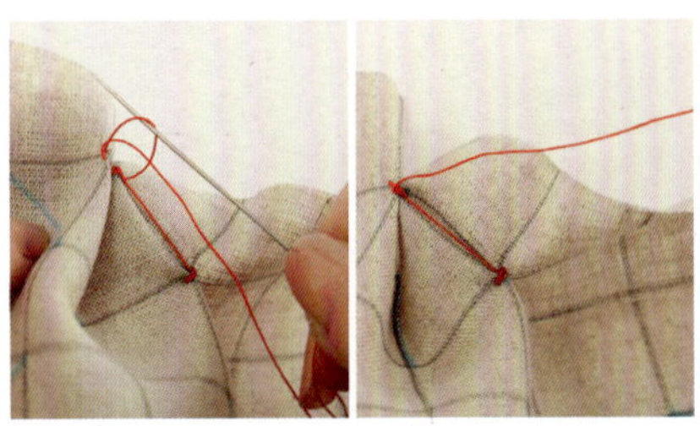

11 Pull the thread, creating a small loop just before pulling it tight. Pass the needle through the loop from bottom to top. Pull the thread tight and secure the stitch.

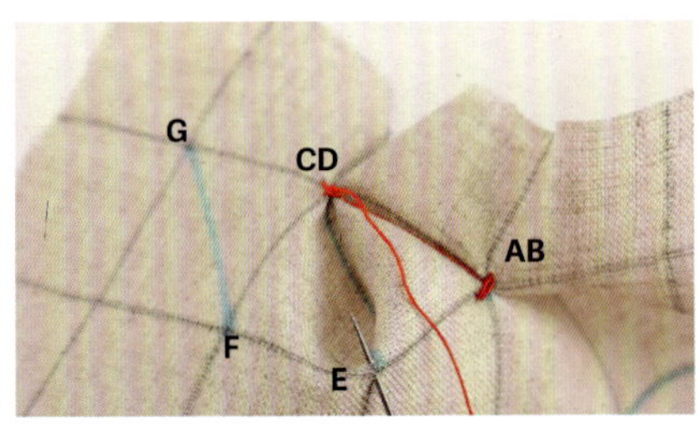

12 Pick up a stitch from outside the square to inside at corner E.

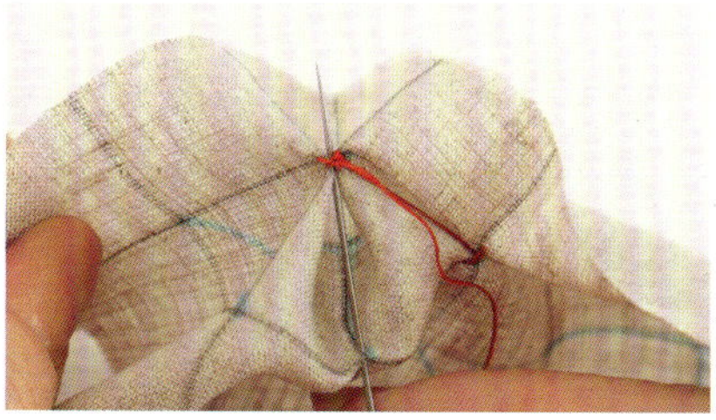

13 Pick up corner CD. Do not pick up the fabric; pick up only the thread.

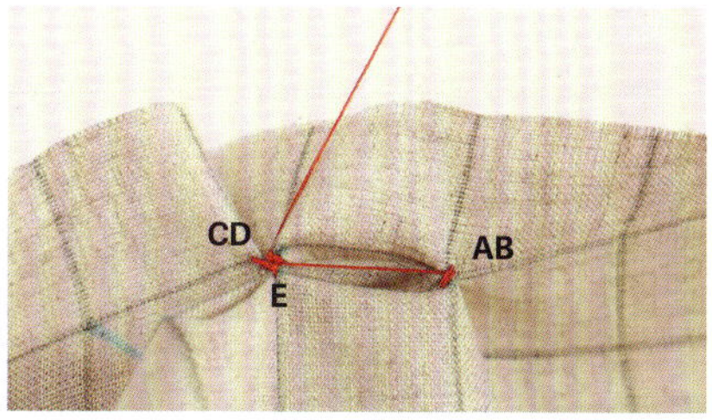

14 Pull the thread tight to bring corners CD and E together. Here as well, do not pick up the fabric at CD; pass the needle under the thread only.

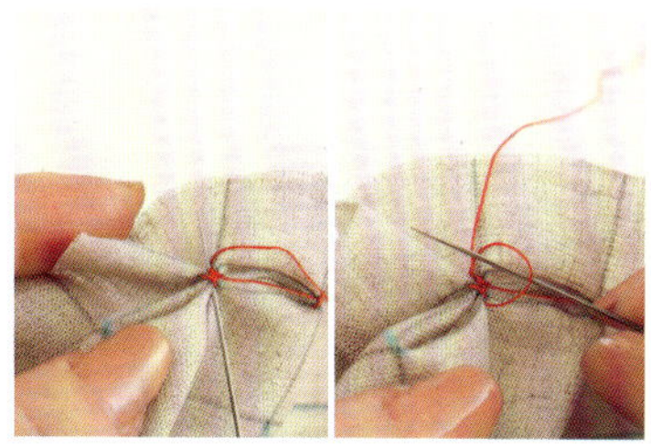

15 Pull the thread, creating a small loop just before pulling it tight. Pass the needle through the loop from bottom to top. Pull the thread tight and secure the stitch.

▸ Pass the thread from CDE to F.

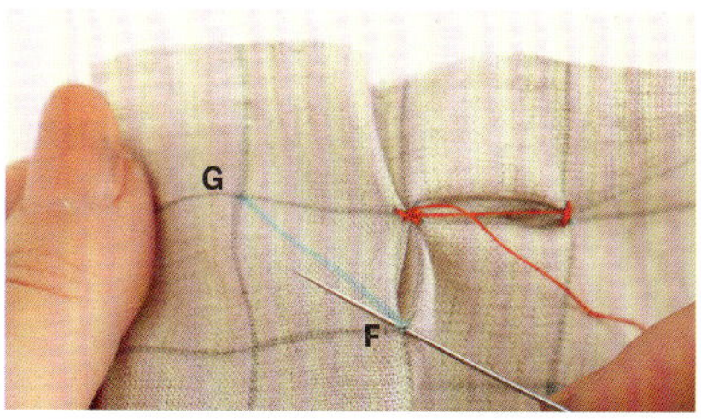

16 Pick up a stitch at corner F.

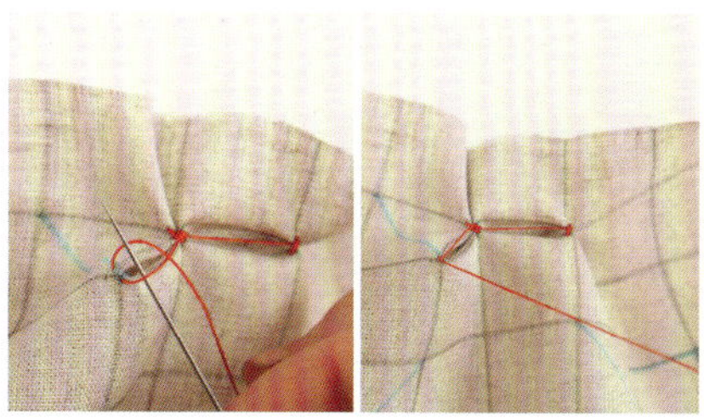

17 Without pulling the thread all the way through, pass it over the thread to create a loop, then bring the needle back under. Pull the thread and secure the stitch.

▸ Bring F and G together.

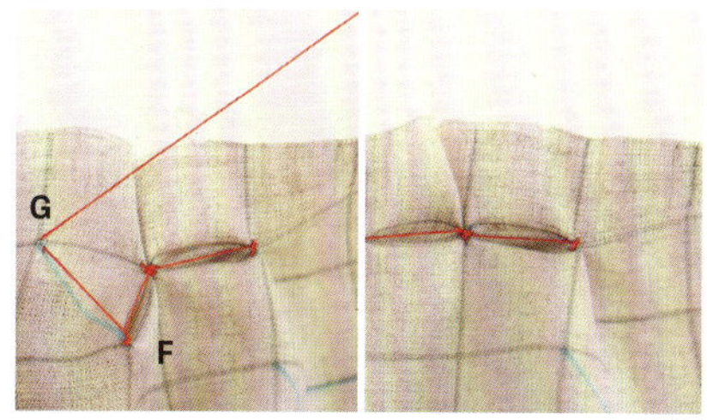

18 Pick up a stitch from inside the square to outside at corner G. Pull the thread tight to bring corners F and G together.

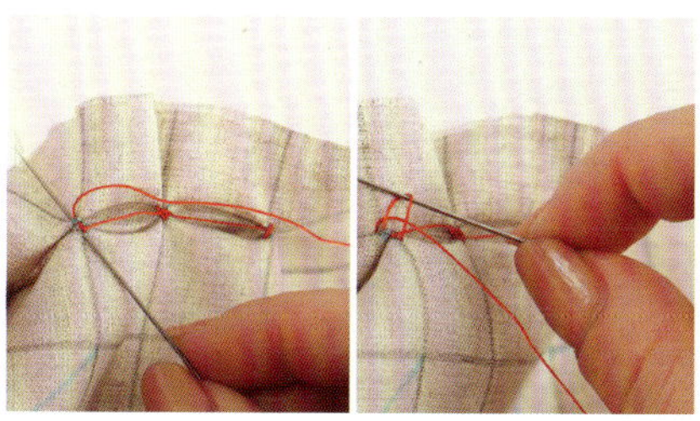

19 Sew the joined corners FG together with one stitch. Form a loop and pass the needle through. Pull the thread tight to lock the stitch and secure the fabric.

▸ One section is complete.

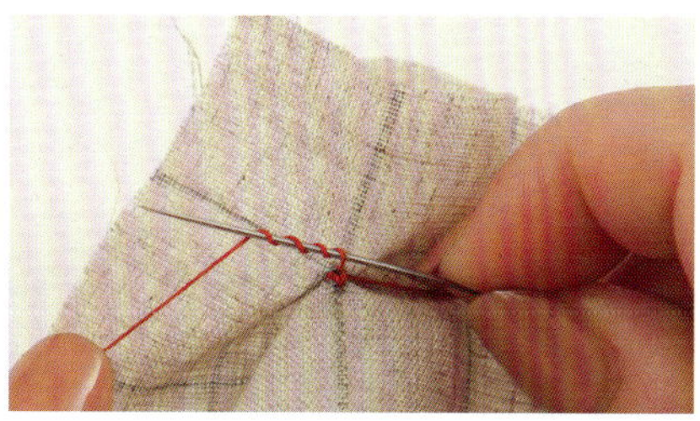

20 Tie a finishing knot and cut the thread.

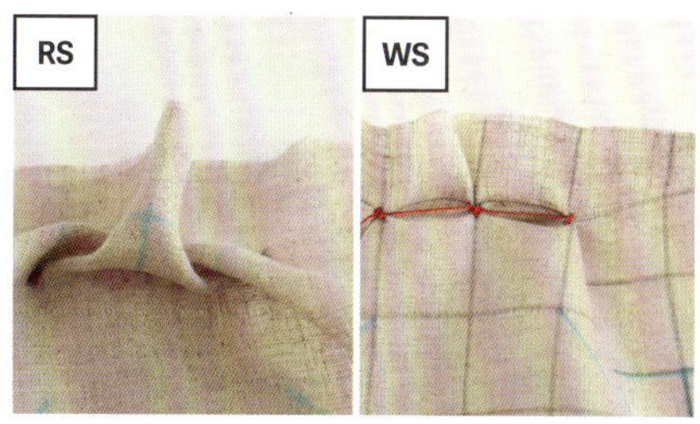

21 You have now created one section.

▸ Seven rows are complete.

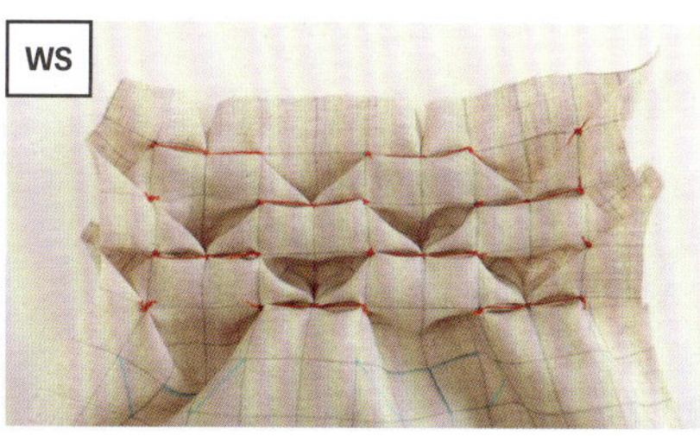

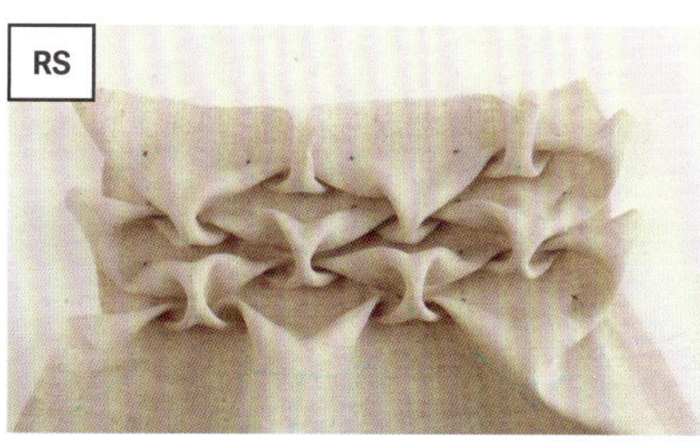

22 This is what it looks like after you have finished stitching seven rows. Stitch one section at a time.

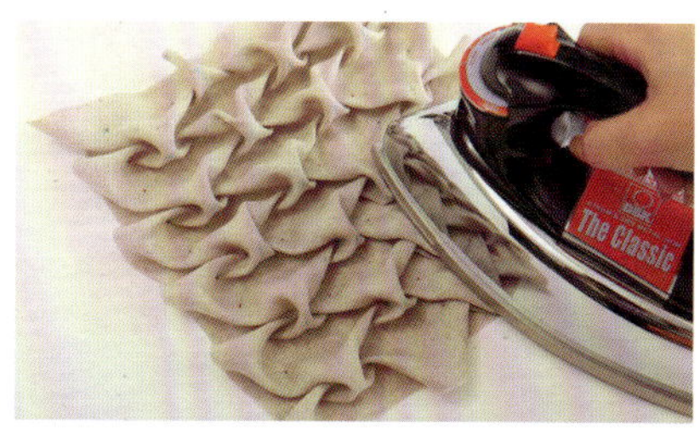

23 Use an awl or similar tool to pull out any uneven parts or straighten the shape. Press with an iron to finish.

PUZZLE

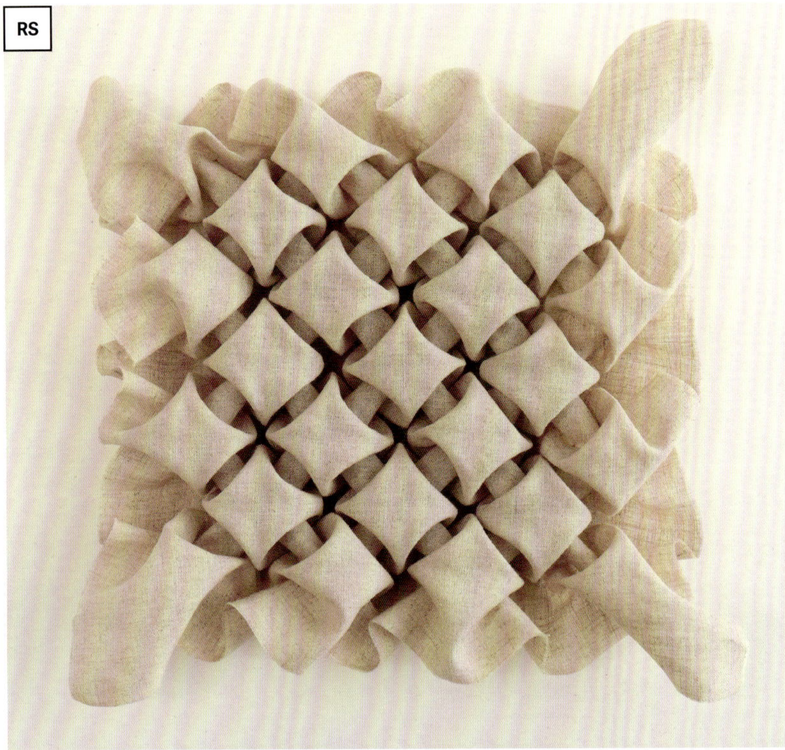

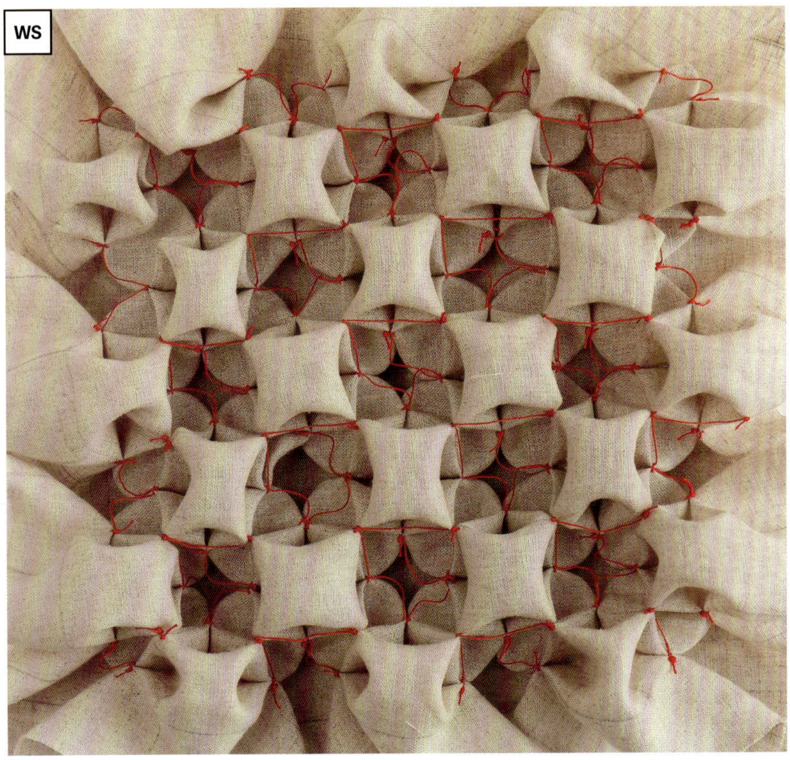

Original Fabric Size

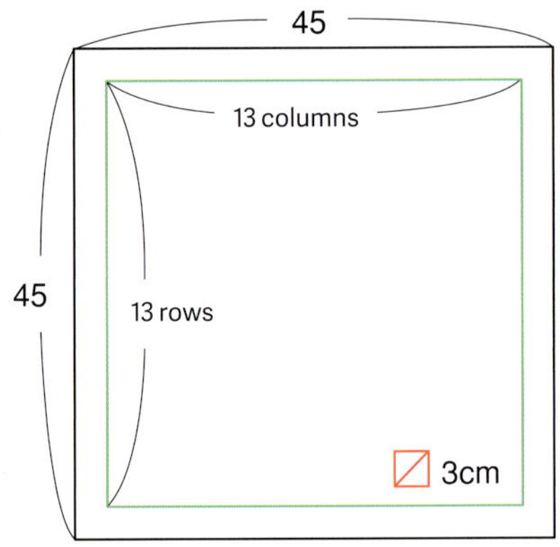

Fabric's Stretch Level

★★☆☆☆

Pressing

- Could be pressed depending on the desired finish

Notes

- Stitch one section at a time
- The WS is also interesting
- This involves scooping up both the corners and the centers of squares in the grid

The **red** and pink lines show where you should pull the thread tight to bring joined sections together. The light blue dashed lines show where you should pass the thread. **Green** letters indicate stitching order.

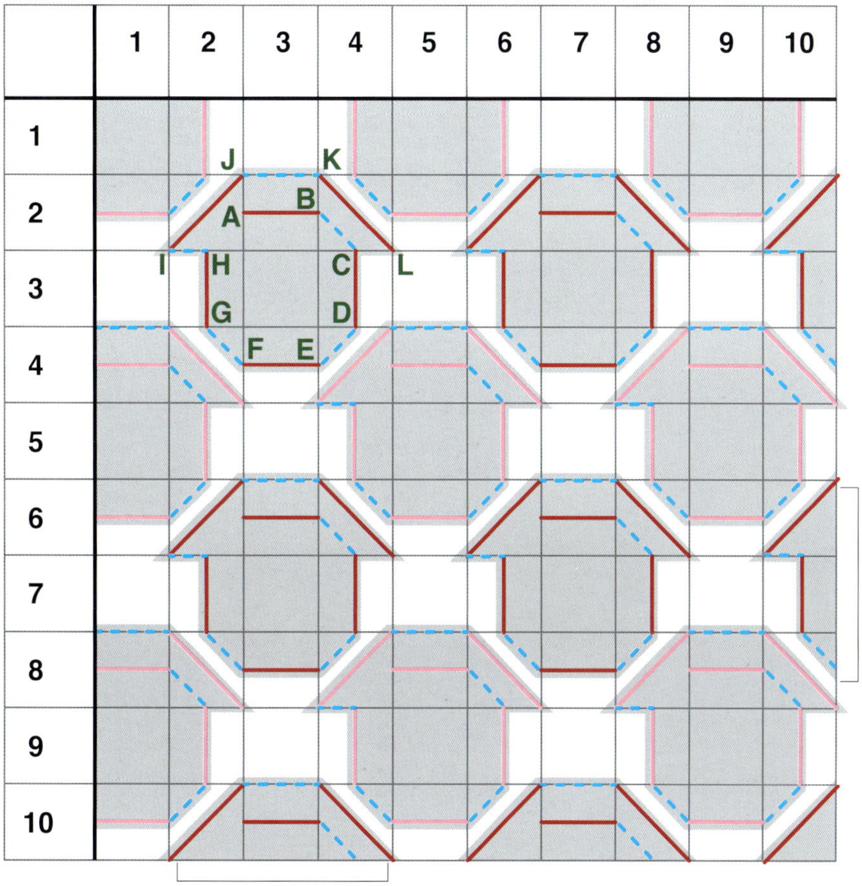

Finish one marked section at a time.

■ Stitching Instructions

1. Insert the needle into A, in the center of the grid, and pick up a stitch. Insert the needle into B and pull the thread tight to bring them together.
2. Sew the joined AB together with one stitch and secure the stitch.
3. Pick up a stitch at C, pass the thread, and secure the stitch.
4. Pick up a stitch at D. Pick up C again and pull the thread tight to bring them together.
5. Sew the joined CD together with one stitch and secure the stitch.
6. Pick up a stitch at E, pass the thread, and secure the stitch.
7. Pick up a stitch at F. Pick up E again and pull the thread tight to bring them together.
8. Sew the joined EF together with one stitch and secure the stitch.
9. Pick up a stitch at G, pass the thread, and secure the stitch.
10. Pick up a stitch at H. Pick up G again and pull the thread tight to bring them together.
11. Sew the joined GH together with one stitch and secure the stitch.
12. Pick up a stitch at corner I, pass the thread, and secure the stitch.
13. Pick up a stitch at corner J. Scoop up corner I again and pull the thread tight to bring the corners together.
14. Sew the joined corners IJ together with one stitch and secure the stitch.
15. Pick up a stitch at corner K, pass the thread, and secure the stitch.
16. Pick up a stitch at corner L. Scoop up corner K again and pull the thread tight to bring the corners together.
17. Sew the joined corners KL together with one stitch and secure the stitch.
18. Tie a finishing knot, cut the thread, and repeat this same process for each section as marked.

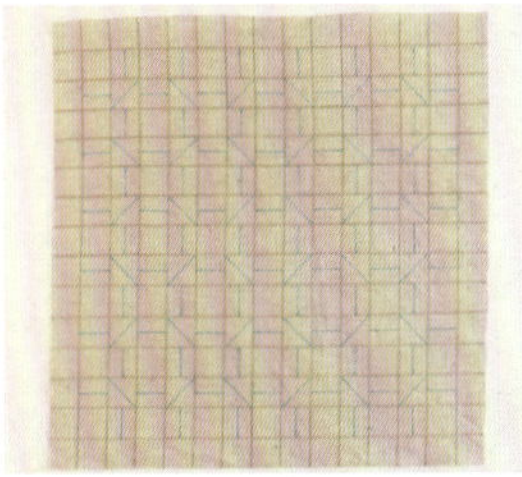

01 Draw a grid on the WS of the fabric. Draw lines connecting the areas that will be scooped together, as shown on page 89.

‣ Bring A and B together.

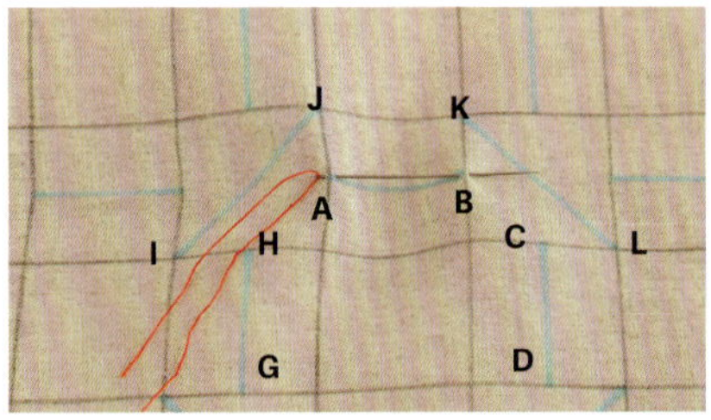

02 Thread the needle and tie a finishing knot with a single strand of thread. Pick up a stitch from outside the square to inside at A, then pick up B. Each stitch should be about 0.2cm long.

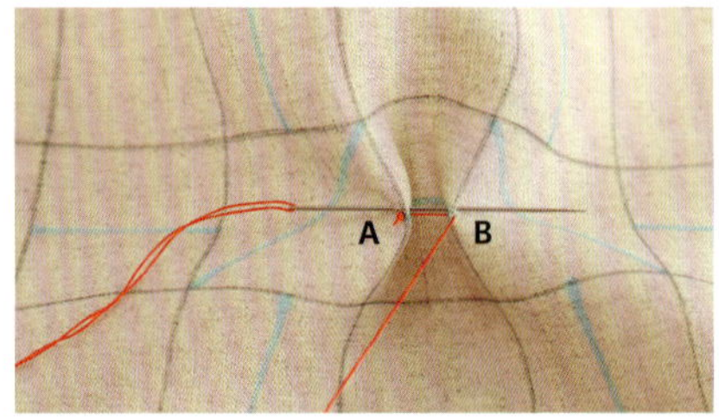

03 Pull the thread tight bring A and B together and sew AB with one stitch.

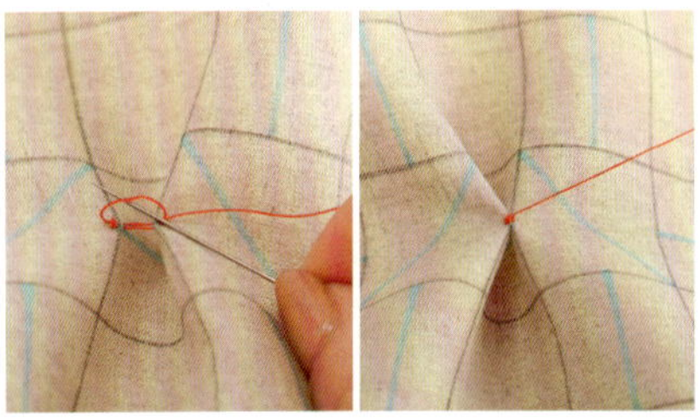

04 Pull the thread to form a small loop. Pass the needle through the loop. Pull the thread tight to lock the stitch and secure the fabric.

‣ Pass the thread from AB to C.

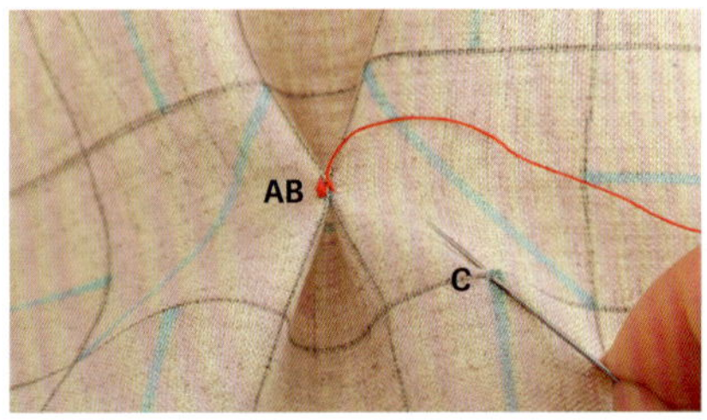

05 Pick up a stitch from inside the square to outside at C.

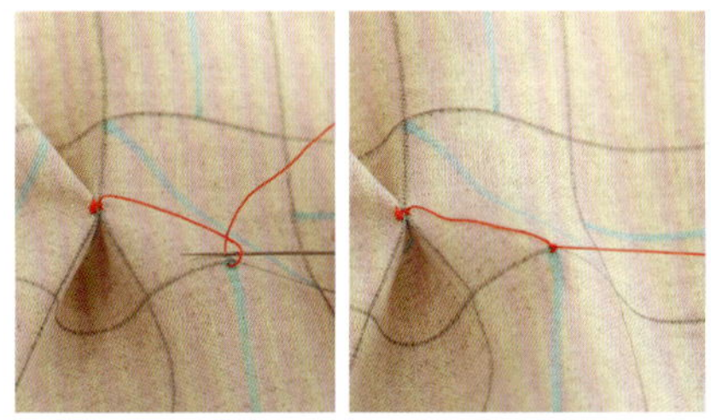

06 Without pulling the thread all the way through, pass it over the thread that you just pulled to create a loop, then bring the needle back through the loop. Pull the thread and tie a knot.

‣ Bring C and D together.

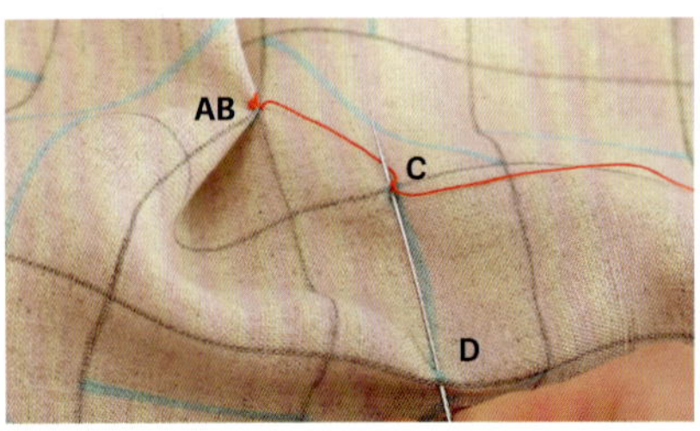

07 Pick up a stitch from outside the square to inside at D, then pick up C again.

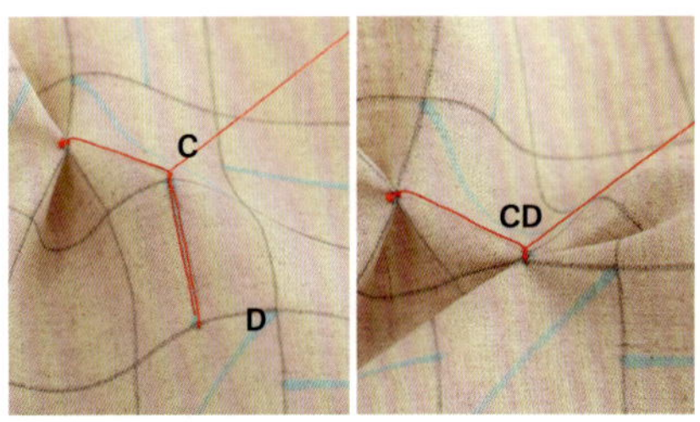

08 Pull the thread tight to bring C and D together. You will see two strands of thread running vertically.

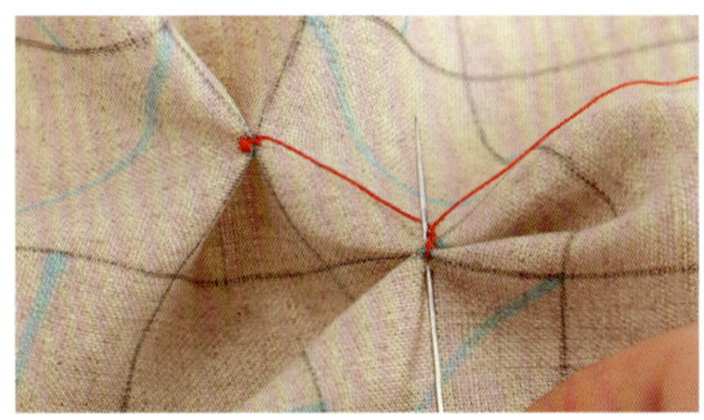

09 Sew CD together with one stitch.

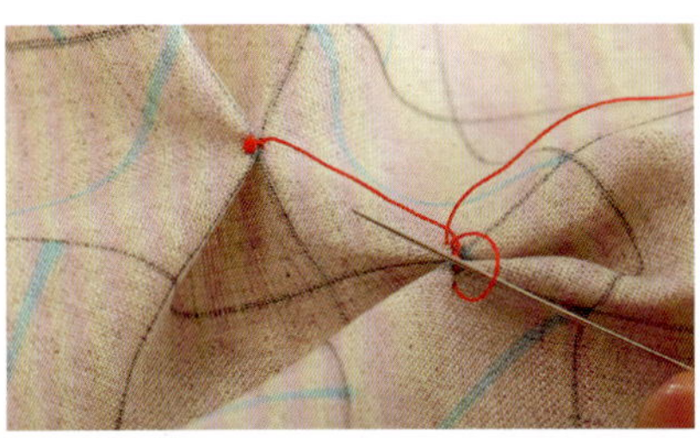

10 Pull the thread, creating a small loop just before pulling it tight. Pass the needle through the loop from bottom to top. Pull the thread tight to secure the stitch.

‣ Pass the thread from CD to E.

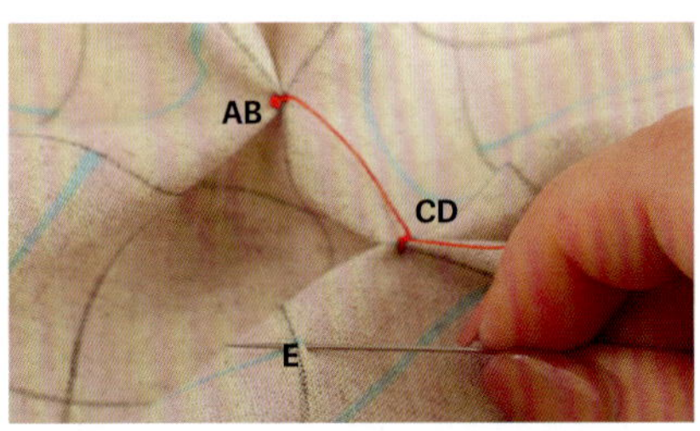

11 Pick up a stitch from outside the square to inside at E.

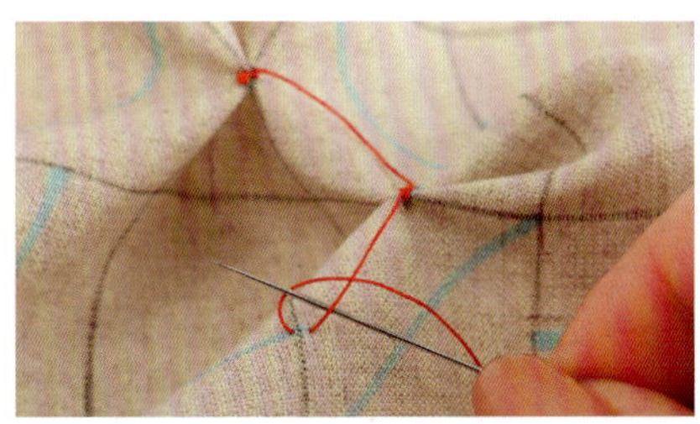

12 Without pulling the thread all the way through, pass it over the thread that you just pulled to create a loop, then bring the needle back through the loop. Pull the thread and tie a knot.

‣ Bring E and F together.

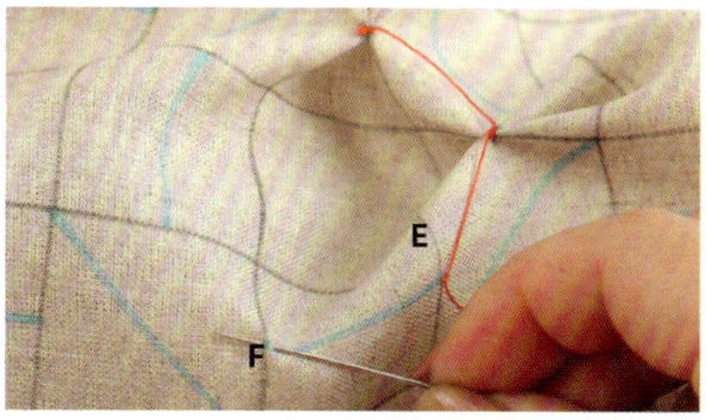

13 Pick up a stitch from inside the square to outside at F.

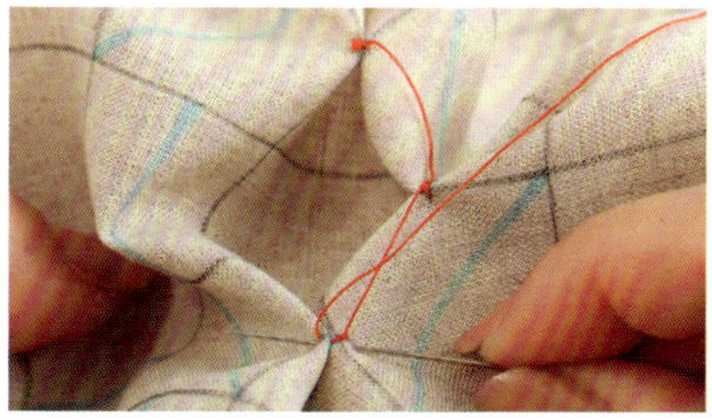

14 Pull the thread tight to bring E and F together and sew EF with one stitch.

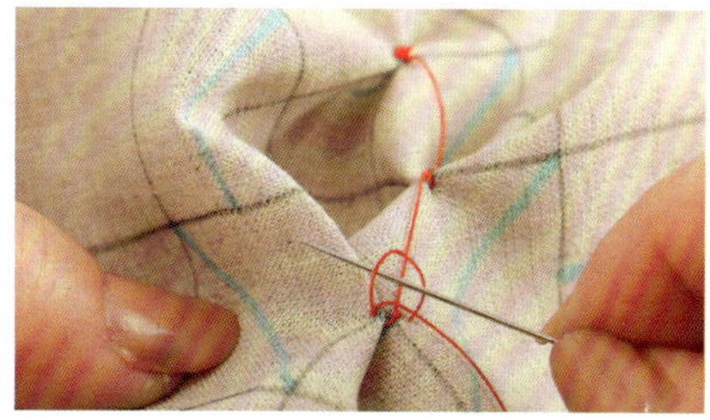

15 Pull the thread, creating a small loop just before pulling it tight. Pass the needle through the loop from bottom to top. Pull the thread tight to secure the stitch.

‣ Pass the thread from EF to G.

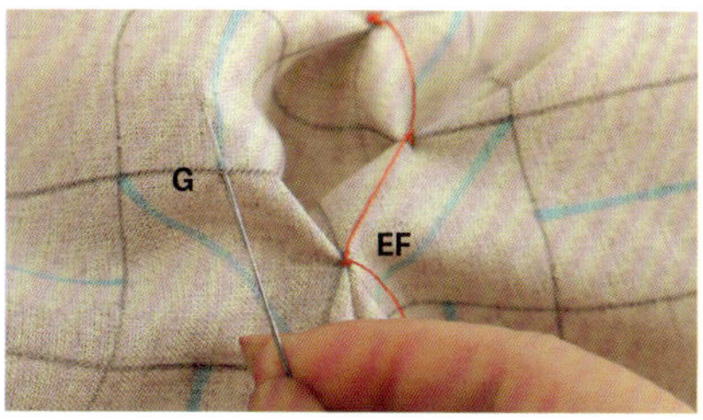

16 Pick up a stitch from outside the square to inside at G.

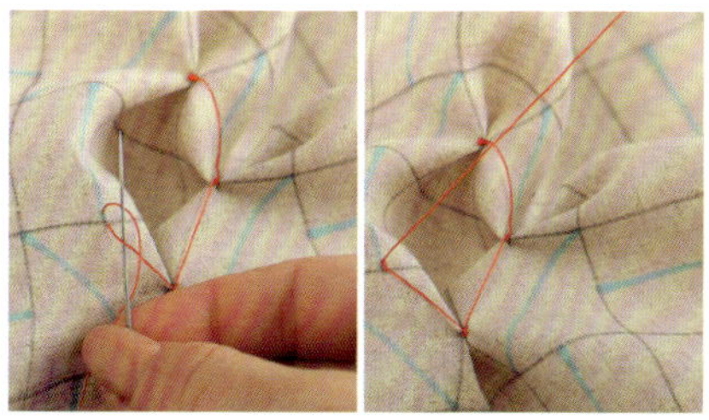

17 Without pulling the thread all the way through, pass it over the thread that you just pulled to create a loop, then bring the needle back through the loop. Pull the thread and tie a knot.

‣ Bring G and H together.

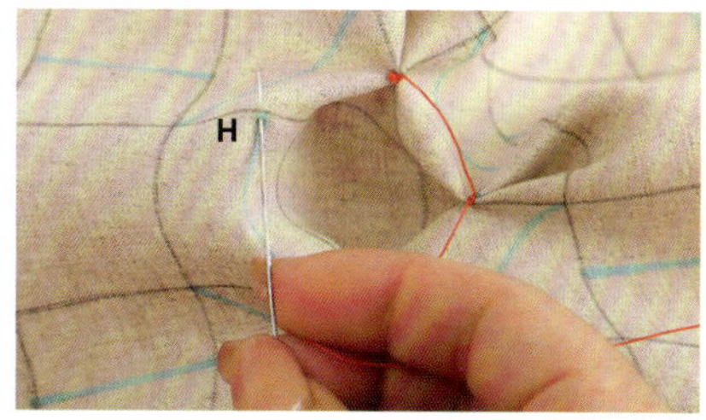

18 Pick up a stitch from inside the square to outside at H.

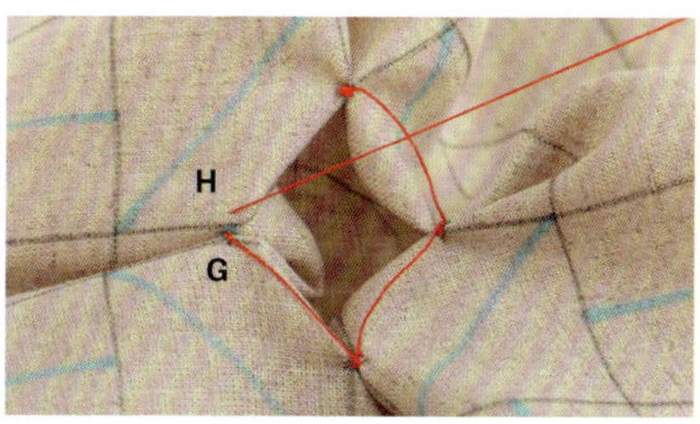

19 Pull the thread tight to bring G and H together.

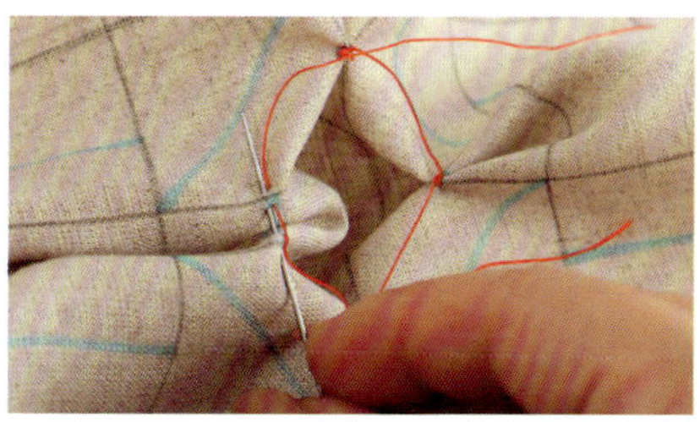

20 Sew GH together with one stitch.

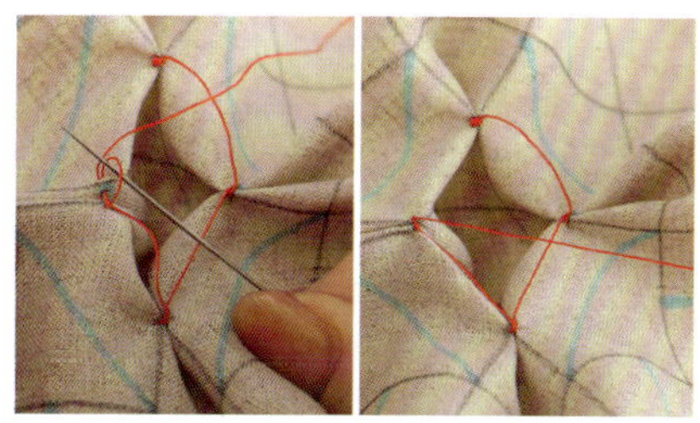

21 Pull the thread, creating a small loop just before pulling it tight. Pass the needle through the loop from bottom to top. Pull the thread tight to secure the stitch.

‣ Pass the thread from GH to I.

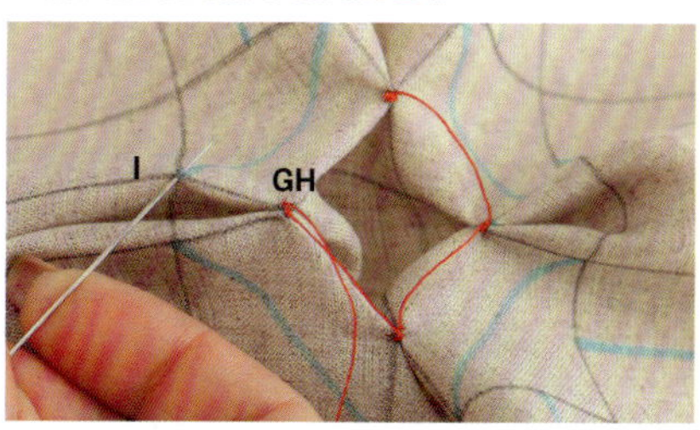

22 Pick up a stitch from outside the square to inside at corner I.

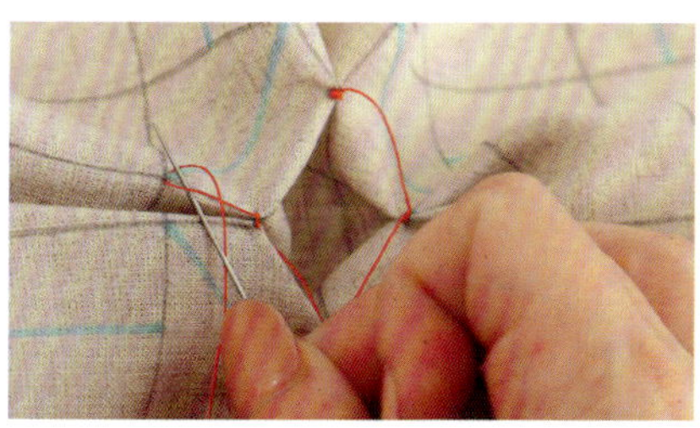

23 Without pulling the thread all the way through, pass it over the thread that you just pulled along the gridline to create a loop, then bring the needle back through the loop. Pull the thread and tie a knot.

‣ Bring I and J together.

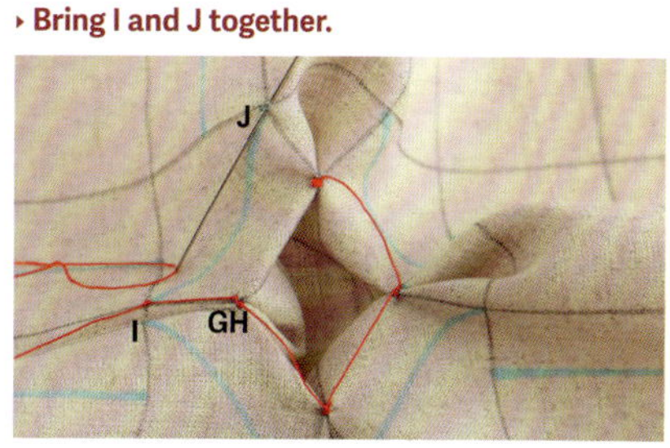

24 Pick up a stitch from inside the square to outside at corner J.

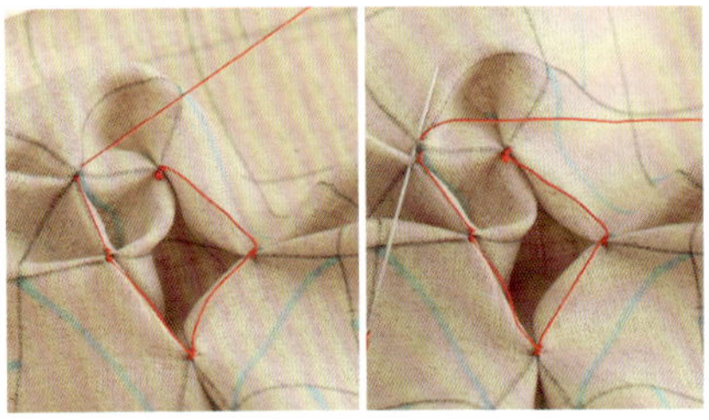

25 Pull the thread tight to bring corners I and J together and sew the joined corners IJ with one stitch.

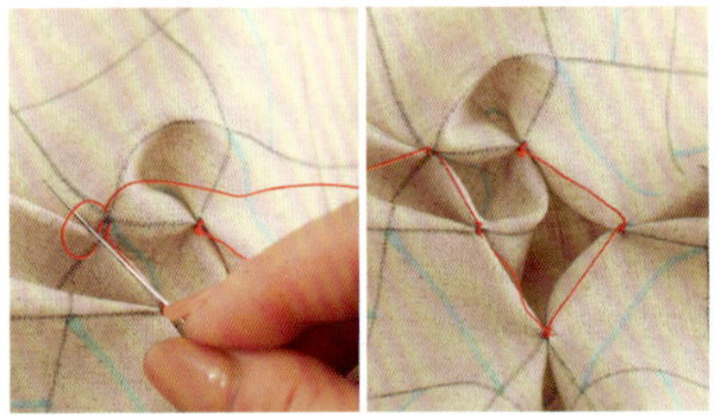

26 Pull the thread, creating a small loop just before pulling it tight. Pass the needle through the loop from bottom to top. Pull the thread tight to secure the stitch.

‣ Pass the thread from IJ to K.

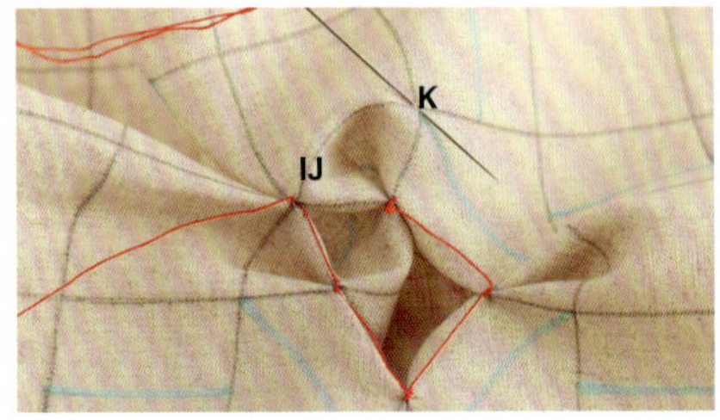

27 Pick up a stitch from outside the square to inside at corner K.

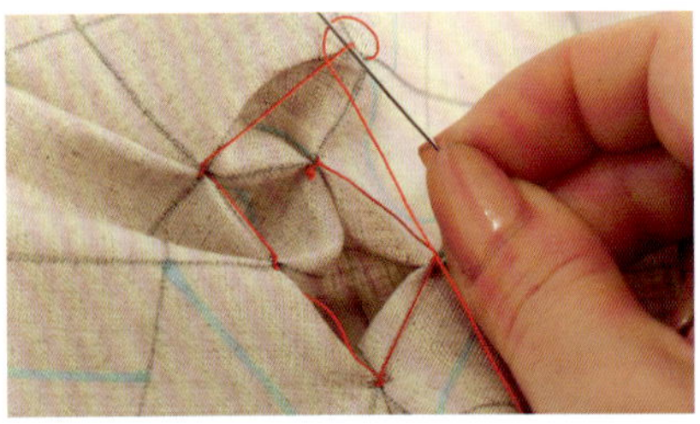

28 Without pulling the thread all the way through, pass it over the thread that you just pulled to create a loop, then bring the needle back through the loop. Pull the thread and tie a knot.

‣ Bring K and L together.

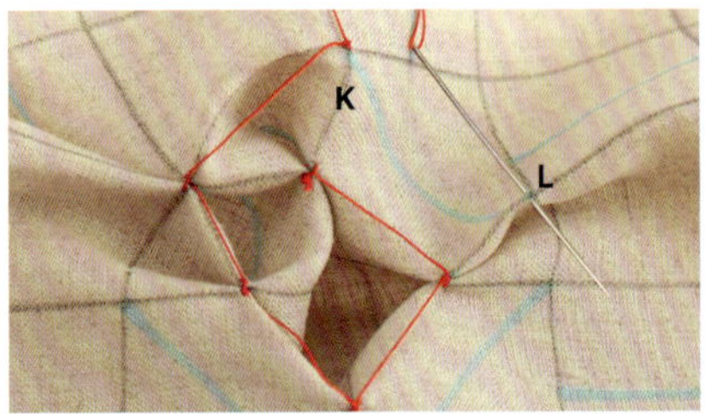

29 Pick up a stitch from inside the square to outside at corner L.

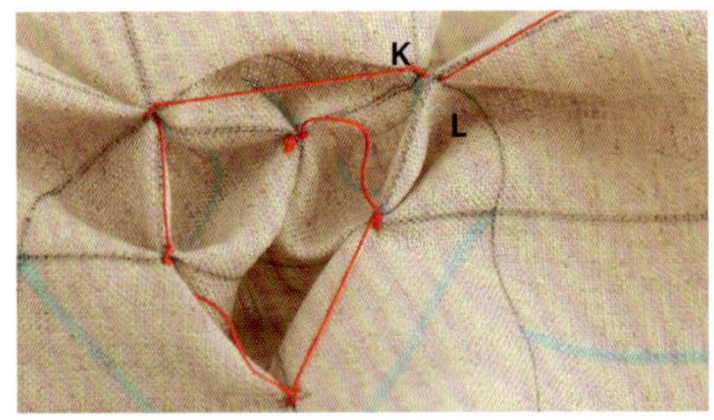

30 Pull the thread tight to bring corners K and L together.

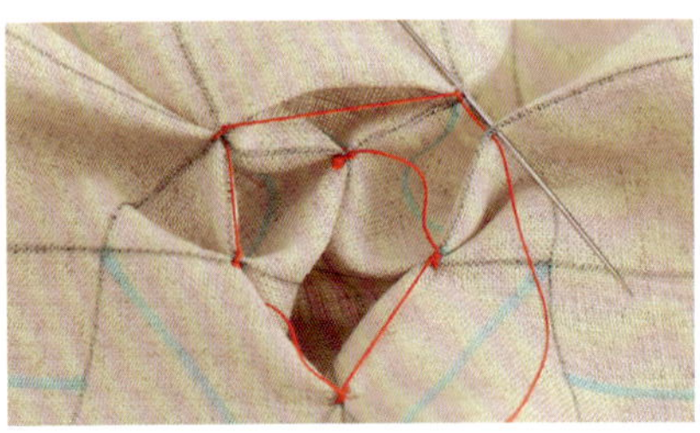

31 Sew the joined corners KL together with one stitch.

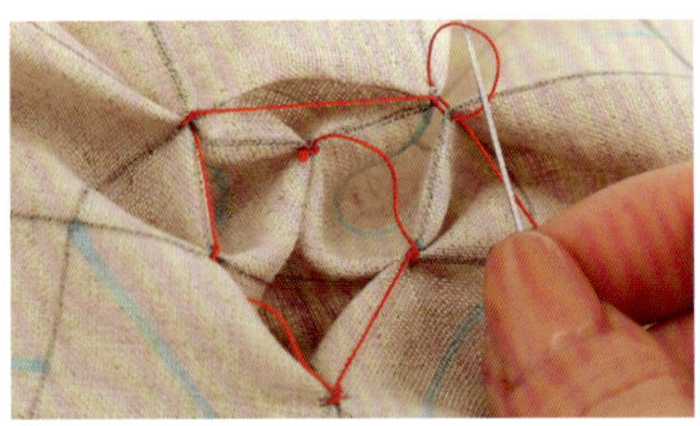

32 Pull the thread, creating a small loop just before pulling it tight. Pass the needle through the loop from bottom to top. Pull the thread tight to secure the stitch.

‣ One section is complete.

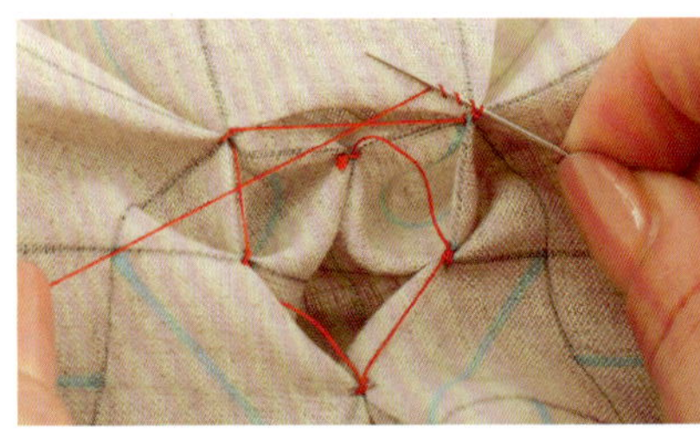

33 Tie a finishing knot and cut the thread. You have now created one section.

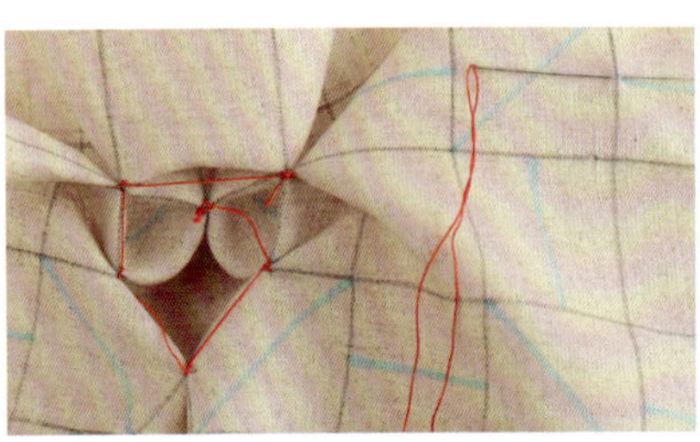

34 Stitch the next section. It is the same pattern, so repeat this process from A.

‣ Seven sections are complete.

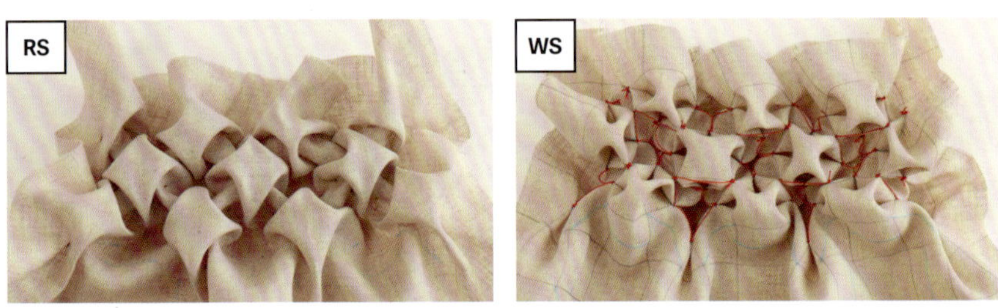

35 This is what it looks like after you have finished stitching seven sections. Stitch one section at a time.

Four Corners

This stitch scoops up fabric
by picking up all four corners
of squares in a grid in a certain order.

FLOWER

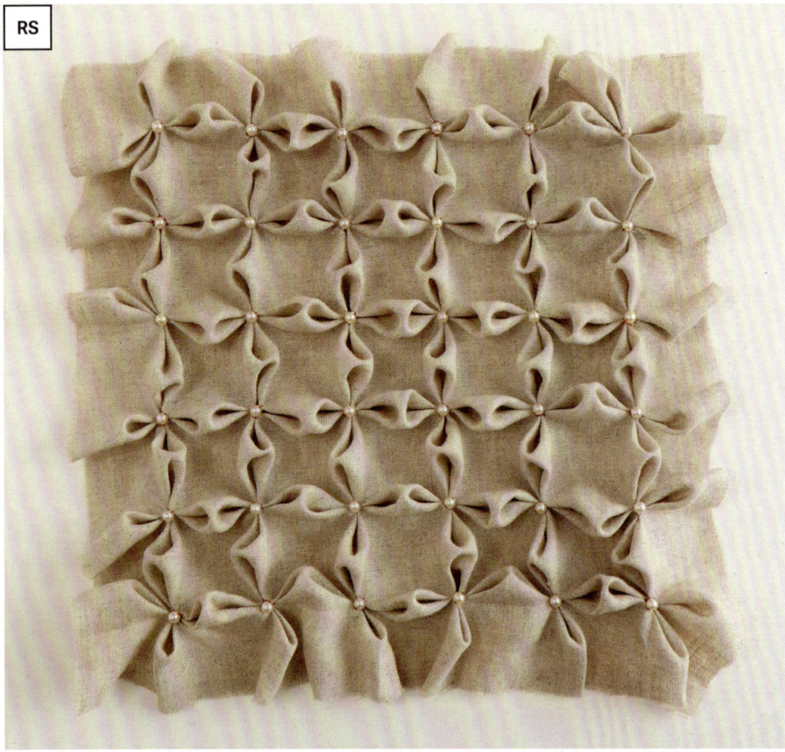

■ Original Fabric Size

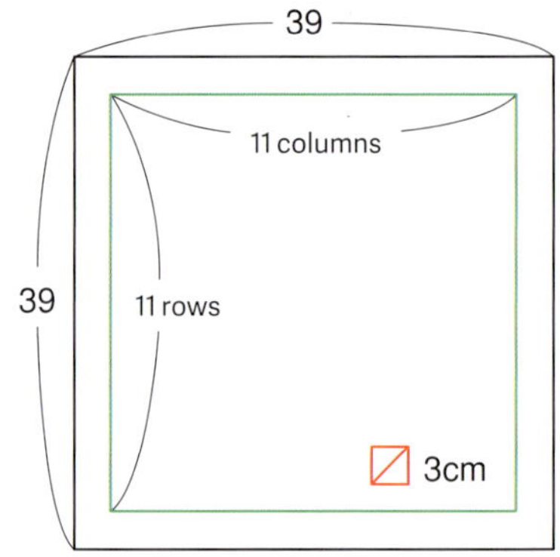

■ Fabric's Stretch Level

★★☆☆☆

■ Pressing

- Not required to finish

■ Notes

- Finish one column at a time
- The WS is also interesting
- Use beads in the design

The **red** lines show where you should pick up and tighten the thread on the WS (solid lines) and RS (dashed lines). The **light blue** dashed lines show where you should pass the thread. **Green** letters and arrows indicate stitching order. **Gray** arrows indicate direction.

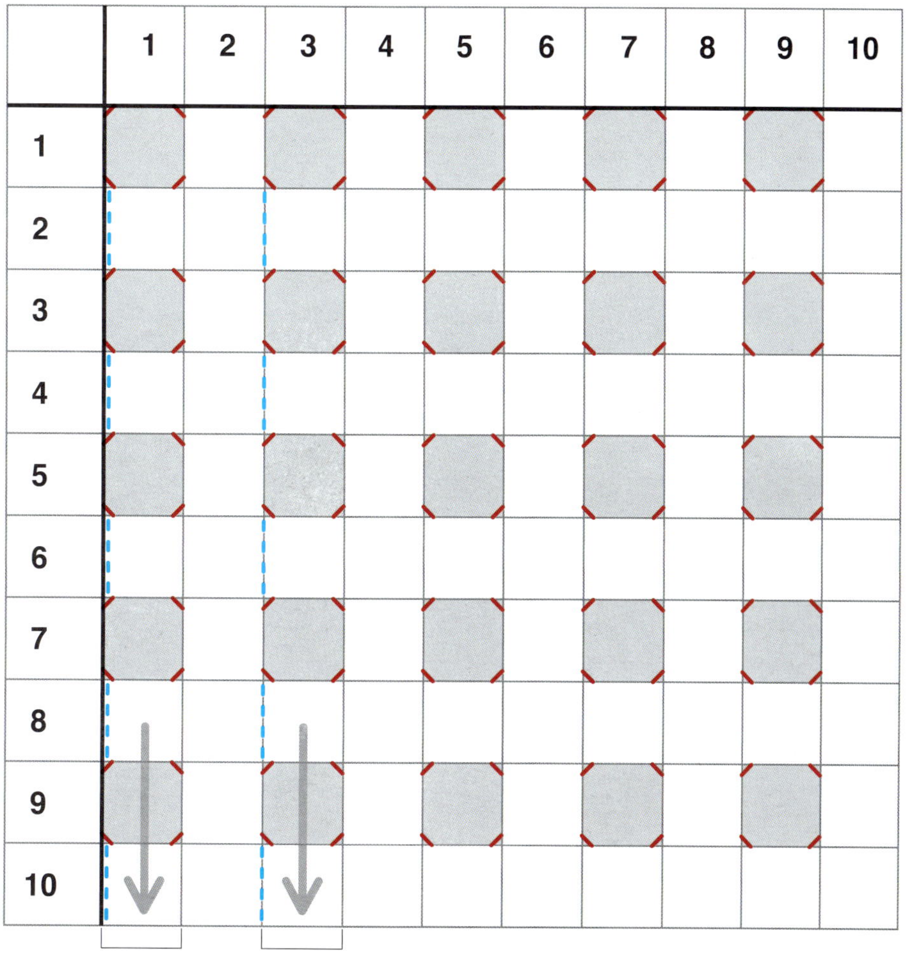

Finish one column at a time.

■ Stitching Instructions

1. Insert the needle into A, pass the thread to the RS, and bring it out at B.
2. Pass the thread to the corner on the WS, insert the needle into C, pass the thread to the RS, and bring it out at D.
3. In the same way, pass the thread to the corner on the WS, insert the needle into E, pass the thread to the RS, and bring it out at F. Repeat until you bring the needle out at H.
4. Insert the needle into corner I, thread it through a bead on the RS, bring it out at J, and pull the thread tight.
5. Next to where you brought the needle out at J, insert it into the bead on the RS, and bring it out at I. Tie a finishing knot.
6. Pick up a stitch at corner K, pass the stitch, pick up a stitch at corner L, and secure the stitch.
7. Insert the needle into M, pass the thread to the RS, and bring it out at N. M is now the same as A, so just repeat the process for the rest of the column.
8. When you reach the end of the column, tie a finishing knot and cut the thread. Skip a column and begin stitching the next column from the top using the same process.

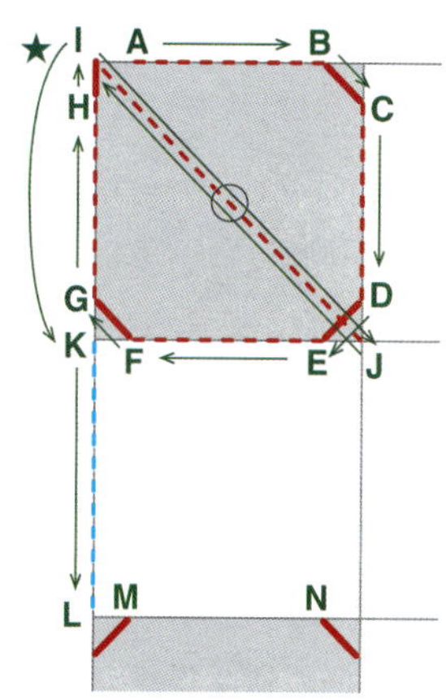

★: Finishing knot

01 Draw a grid on the WS of the fabric. Draw lines at the corners, as shown on page 95.

▸ Pass the thread from A to H.

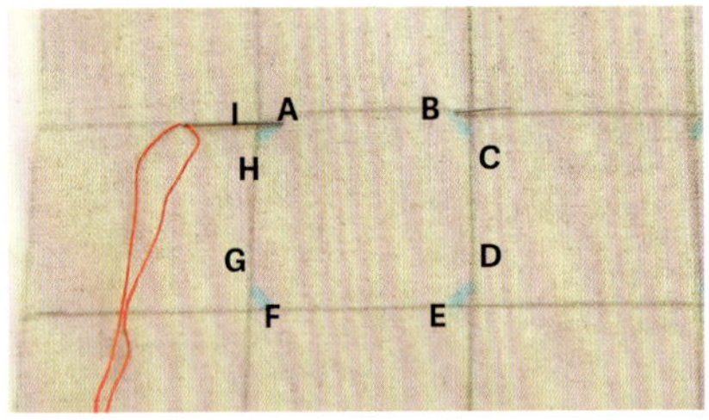

02 Thread the needle and tie a finishing knot with a single strand of thread. Insert the needle into A, pass the thread to the RS, and bring it out at B.

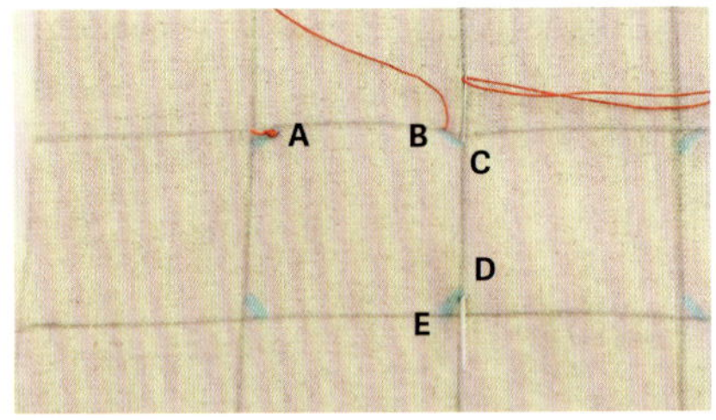

03 Pass the thread around the corner on the WS, insert the needle into C, pass the thread to the RS, and bring it out at D.

▸ Thread a bead on the RS.

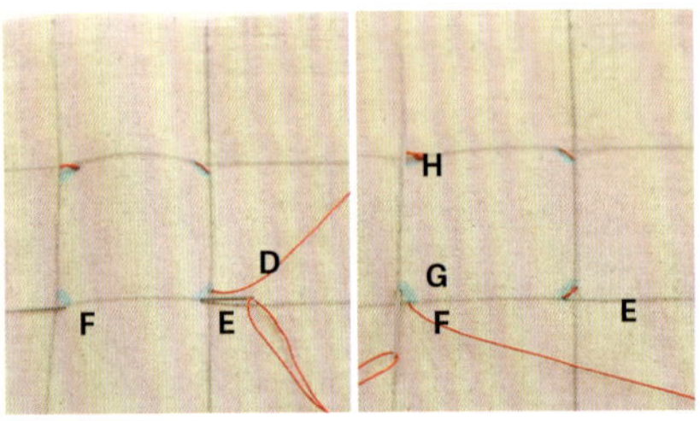

04 Pass the corner on the WS, insert into E, pass to the RS, and bring it out at F. Repeat to bring the needle out at H.

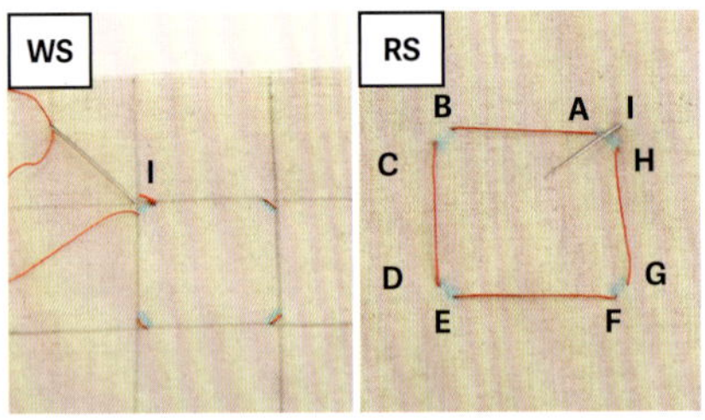

05 Insert the needle in corner I and bring it out on the RS.

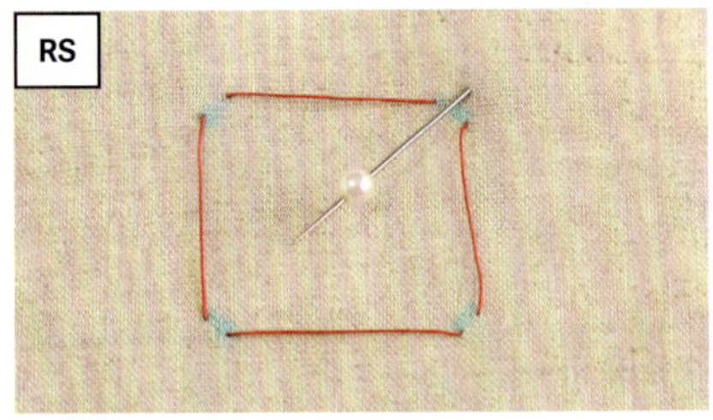

06 On the RS, thread a bead onto the needle.

▸ Bring A through J together.

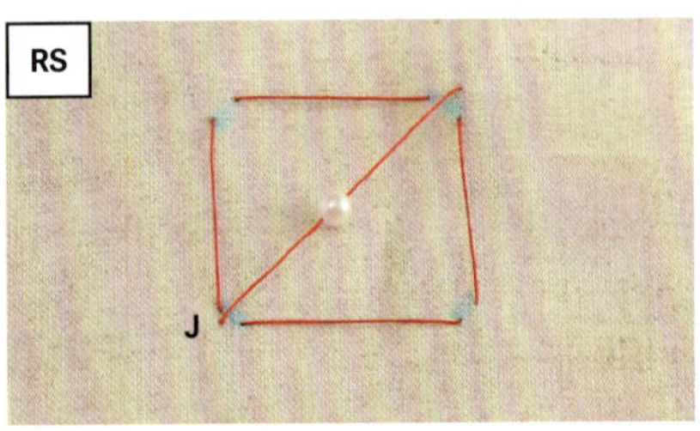

07 Insert the needle in corner J and bring it out on the WS.

08 Pull the thread tight, bring A through H together, and trap the bead between the layers of fabric.

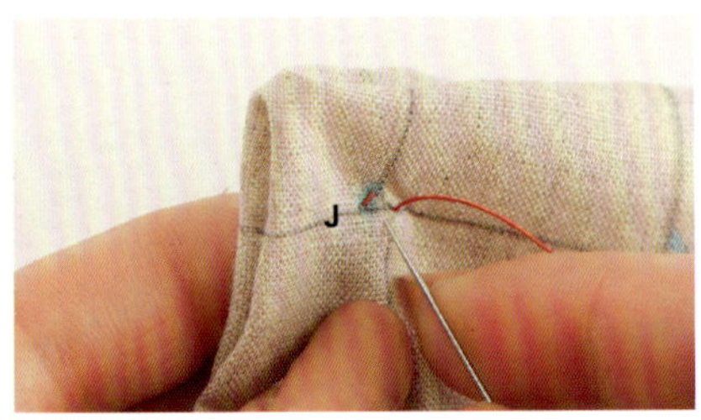

09 Insert the needle next to where it was brought out at J.

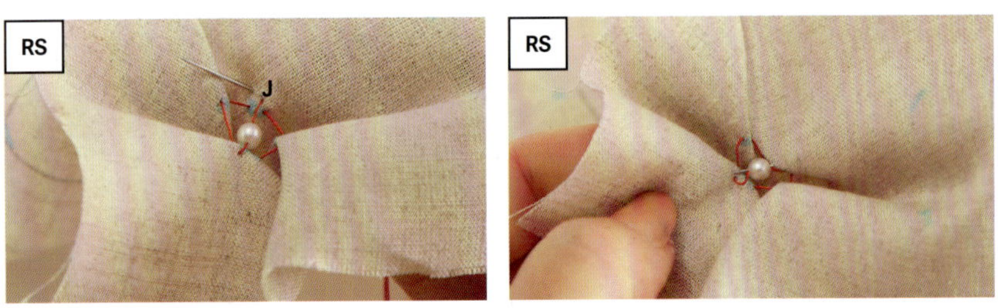

10 Bring the needle out on the RS, pass it through the bead, then insert the needle at I.

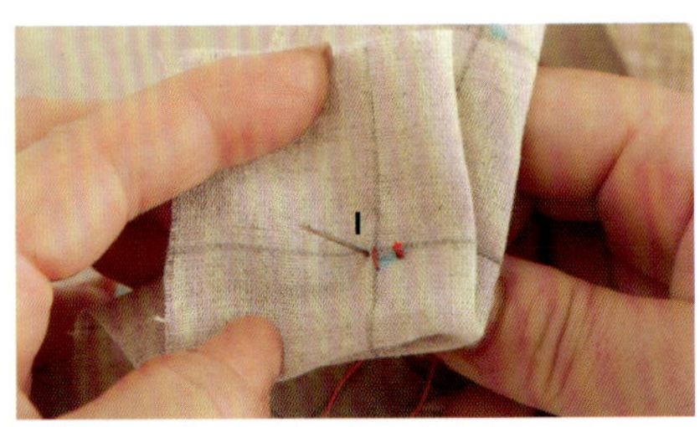

11 Bring the needle out at corner I on the WS.

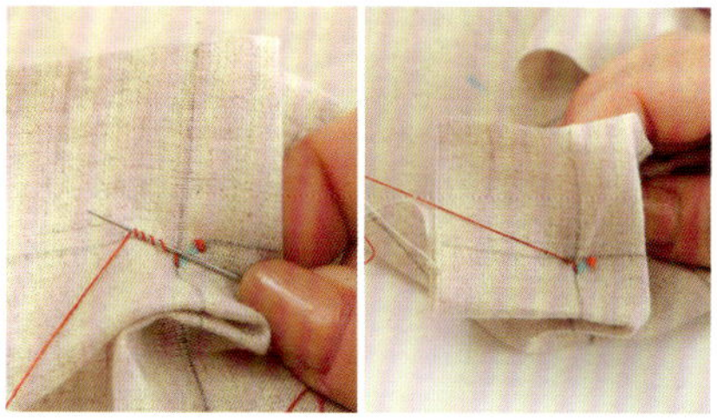

12 Tie a finishing knot to secure the fabric. Do not cut it.

Pass the thread from I to K.

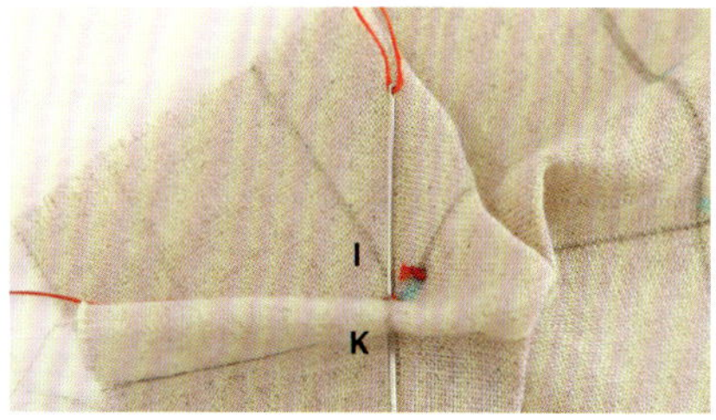

13 Insert the needle at corner I and bring it out at K directly beneath it.

Pass the thread from K to L.

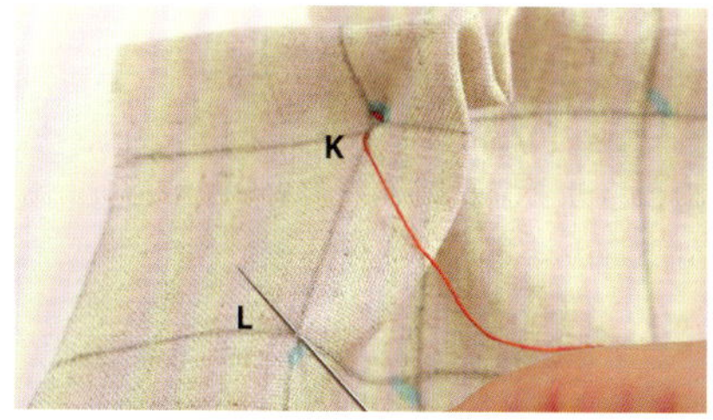

14 Pick up a stitch from inside the square to outside at corner L.

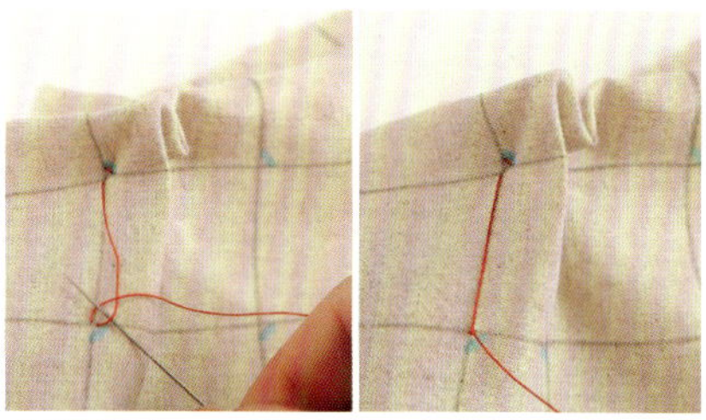

15 Without pulling the thread all the way through, pass it over the thread that you just pulled to create a loop, then bring the needle back through the loop. Pull the thread and tie a knot.

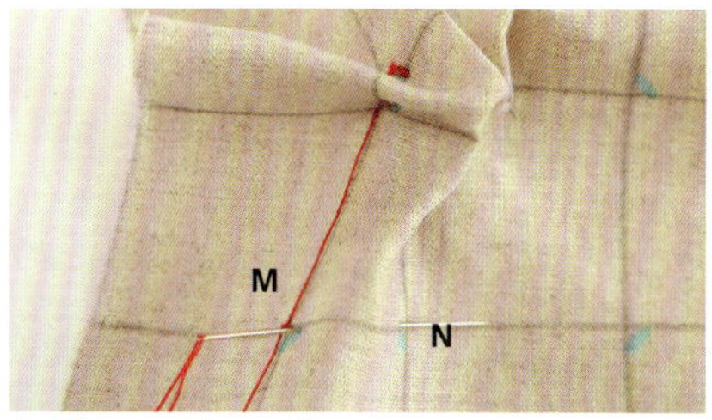

16 Insert the needle at M, pass the thread to the RS, and bring it out at N. M is now the same as A, so repeat this process to the end of the column.

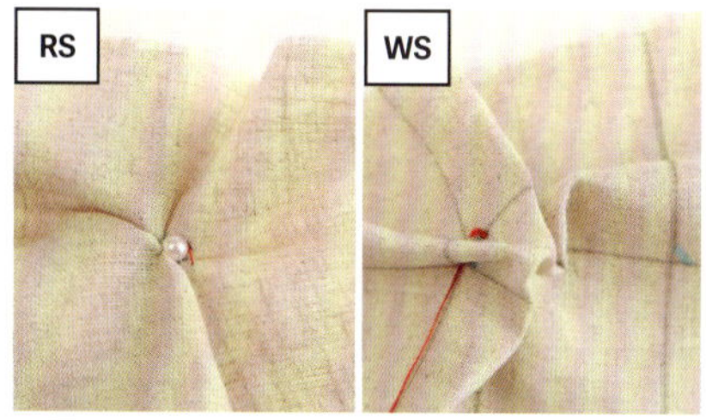

17 When looked at from the RS, the fabric is now drawn tightly around the bead.

One column is complete.

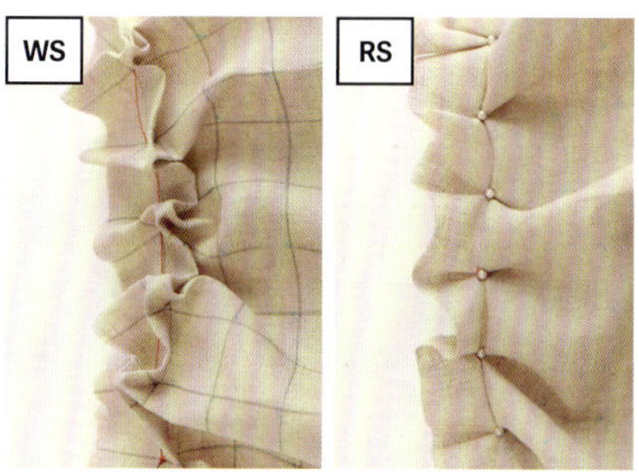

18 At the end, tie a finishing knot and cut the thread. It will look like this.

Two columns are complete.

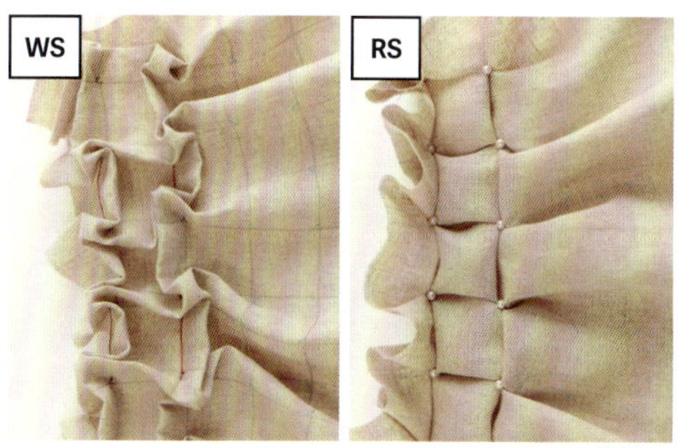

19 When you have stitched two columns, the shape becomes more defined.

Push the fabric.

20 Once you have stitched everything, use your fingers to push the pleats on the WS to the RS.

21 A triangular petal shape will appear, so use an awl to neatly pull it out and shape it.

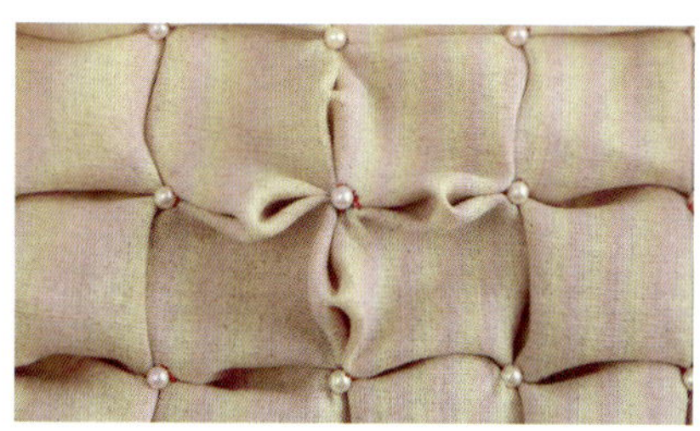

22 Arrange the smocking around the bead so that the four petals stand out.

HOURGLASS

RS

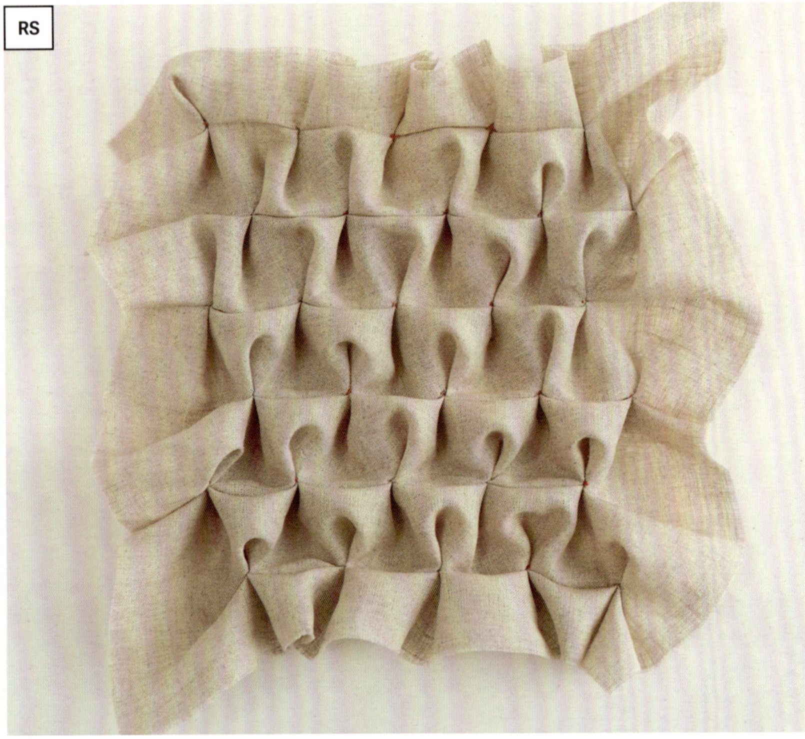

WS

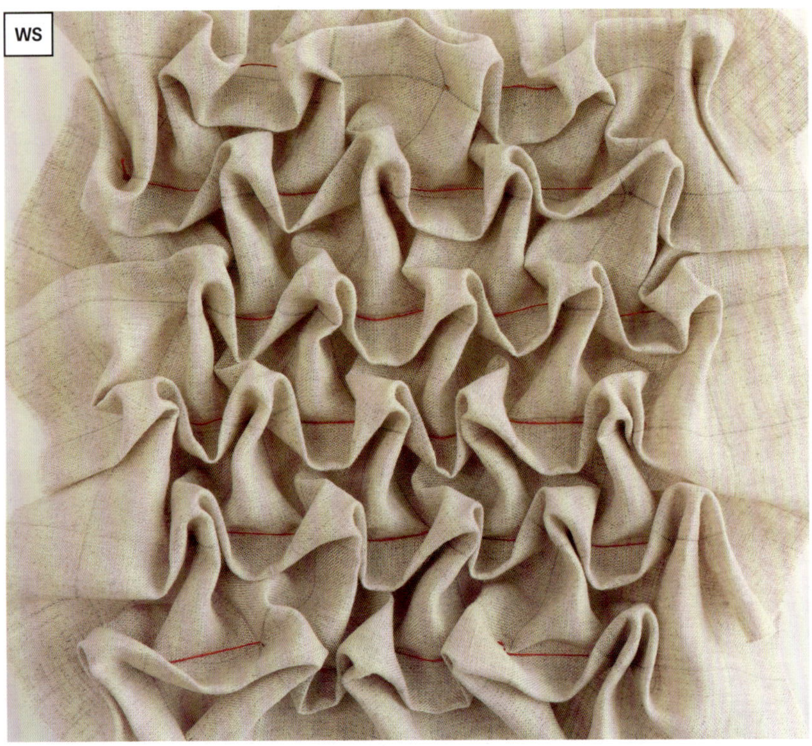

Original Fabric Size

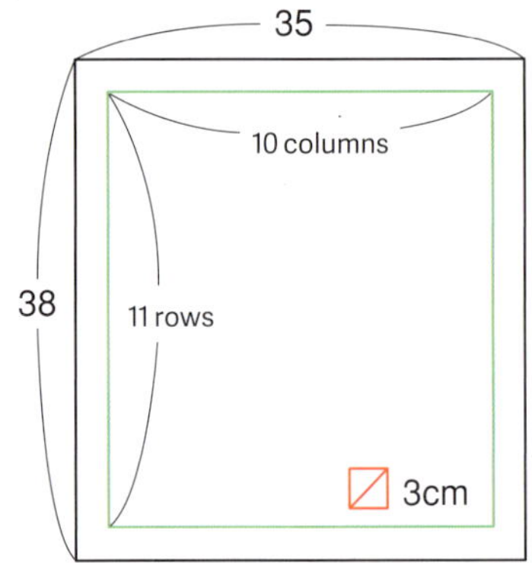

Fabric's Stretch Level

★★★☆☆

Pressing

- Not required to finish

Notes

- Finish one row at a time
- Proceed horizontally
- Goes well with check and stripe fabric
- Technique almost the same stitching as Flower (page 94)

The **red** lines show where you should pick up and tighten the thread on the WS (solid lines) and RS (dashed lines). The **light blue** dashed lines show where you should pass the thread. **Green** letters and arrows indicate stitching order. **Gray** arrows indicate direction.

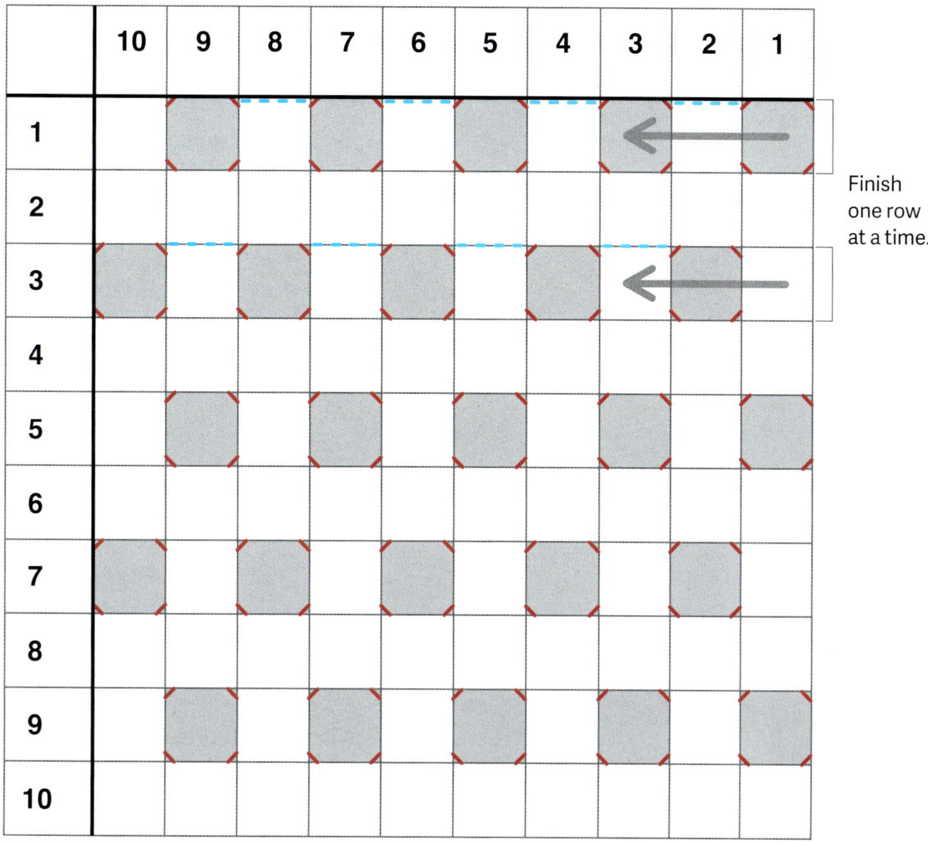

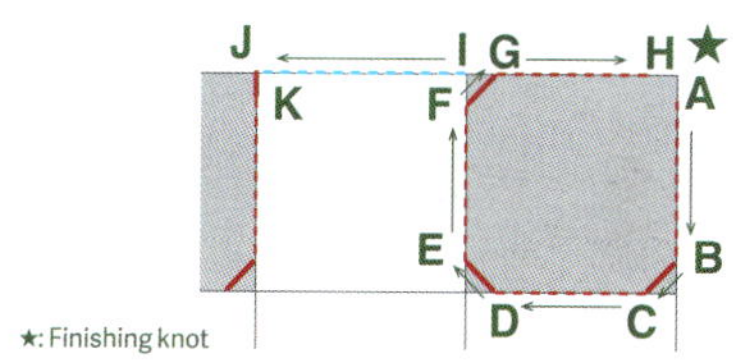

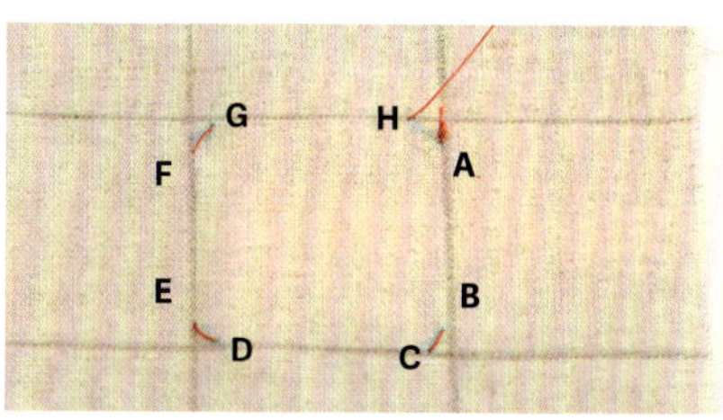

01 Follow **Steps 01–04** of Flower (page 96). Note that the square is rotated.

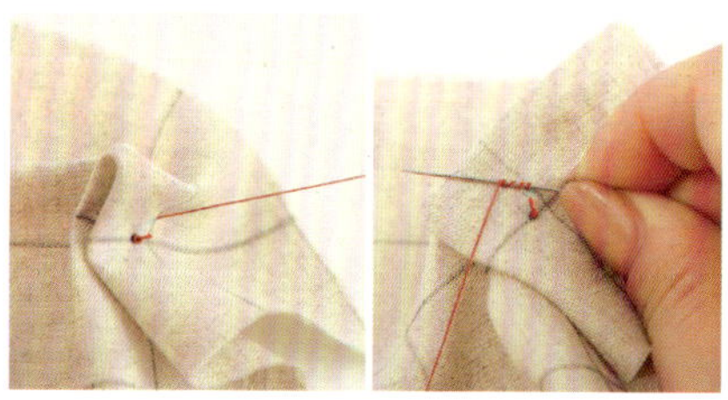

02 Pull the thread tight and tie a finishing knot at H.

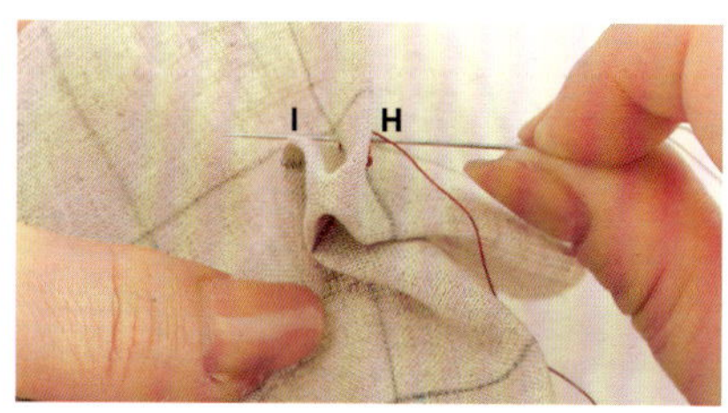

03 Insert the needle at H and bring it out at corner I.

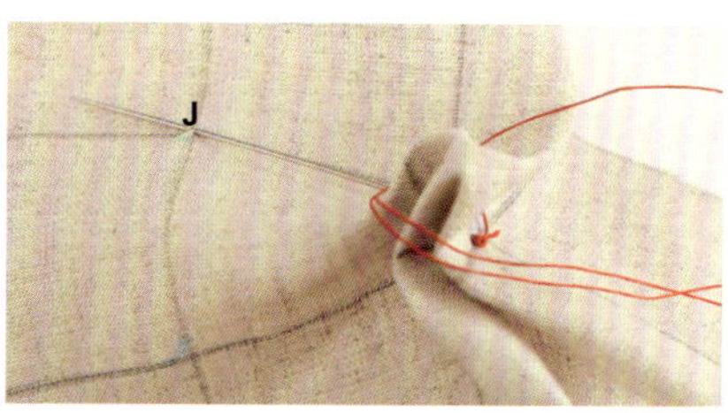

04 Pass the thread along the gridline and pick up a stitch at corner J.

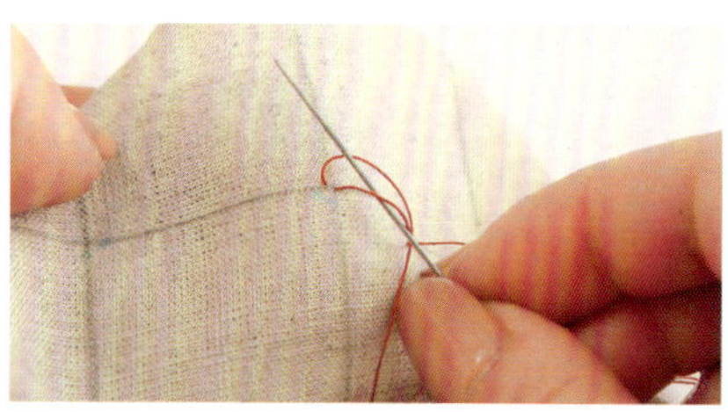

05 Pass it over the thread that you just pulled to create a loop, then bring the needle back under the thread and tie a knot.

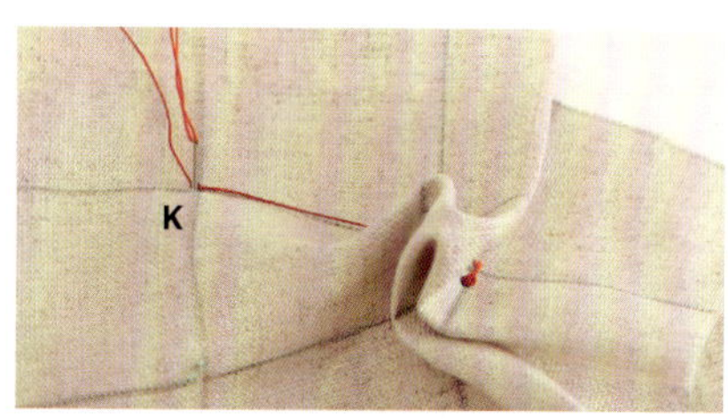

06 K is now the same as A, so repeat this process for the rest of the pattern.

DIAMOND

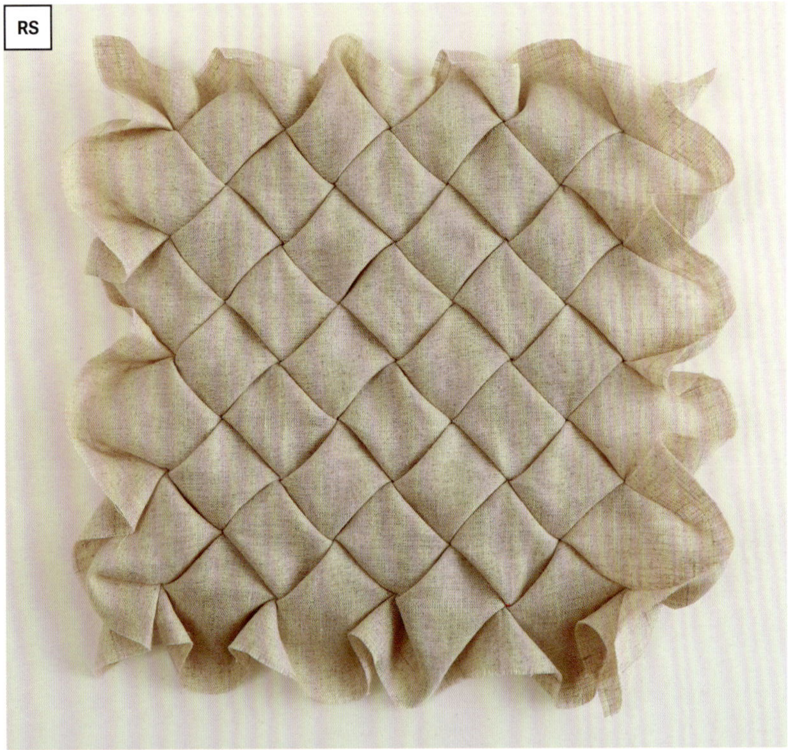

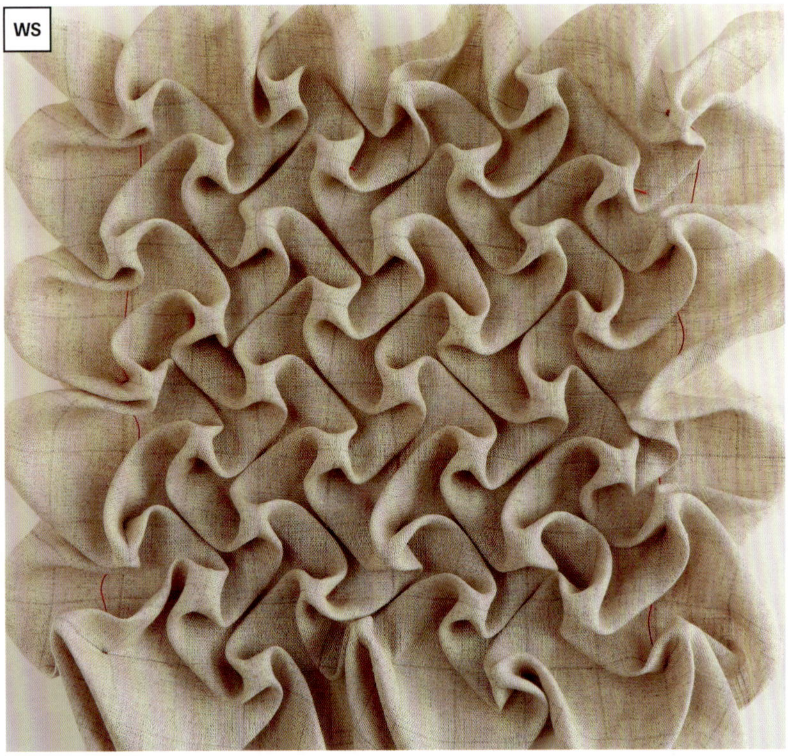

■ Original Fabric Size

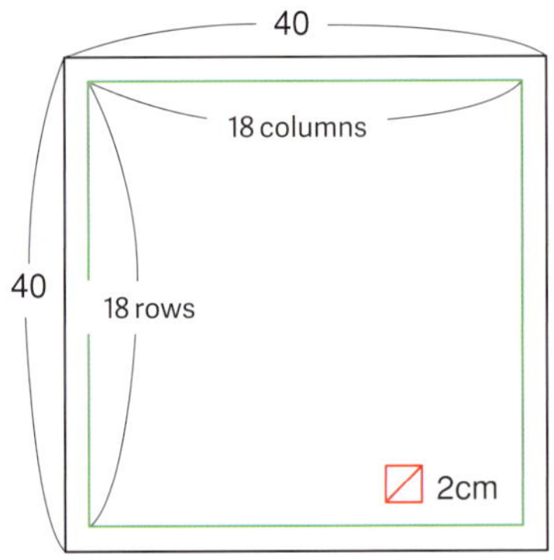

■ Fabric's Stretch Level

★★☆☆☆

■ Pressing

- Not required to finish

■ Notes

- Finish two columns at a time
- The WS is also interesting
- Stitch the corners of the grid into diamond shapes
- Goes well with polka-dot and check fabric
- You can add beads, like in Flower (page 94)

The **red** lines show where you should pick up and tighten the thread on the WS (solid lines) and RS (dashed lines). The **light blue** dashed lines show where you should pass the thread. **Green** letters and arrows indicate stitching order. **Gray** arrows indicate direction.

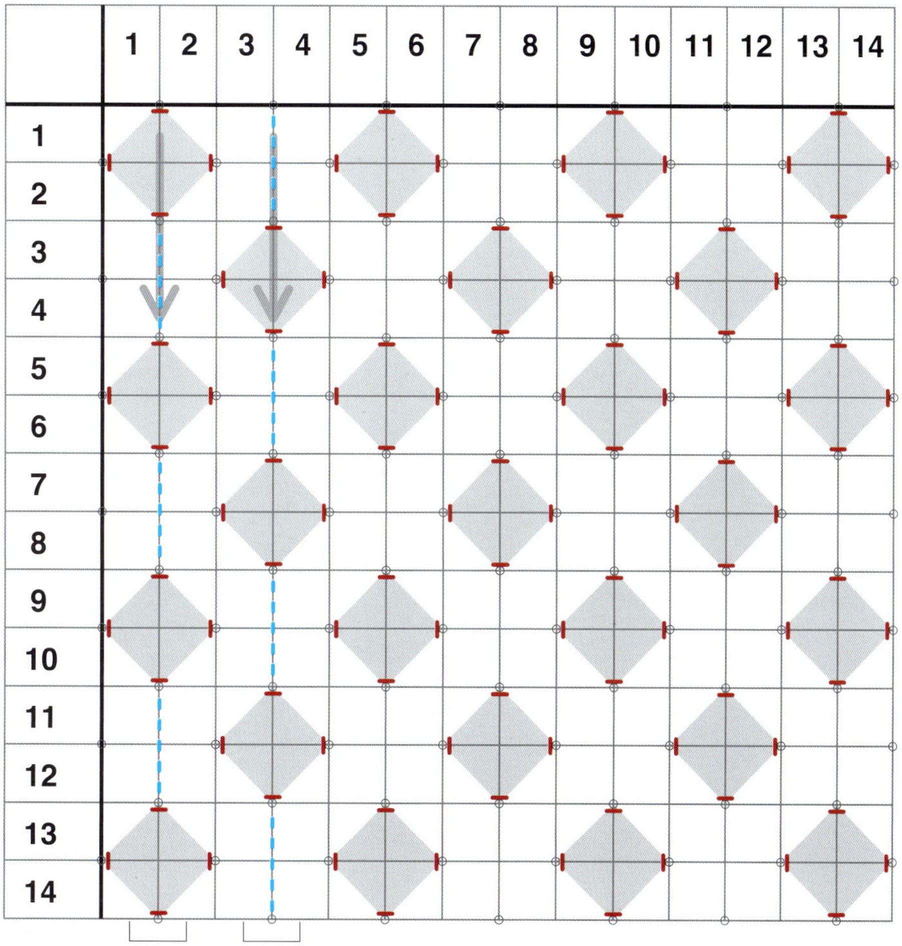

Finish two columns at a time.

■ Stitching Instructions

1. Insert the needle into A, pass the thread to the RS, and bring it out at B.
2. Pass the thread to the corner on the WS, insert the needle into C, pass the thread to the RS, and bring it out at D.
3. In the same way, pass the thread to the corner on the WS, insert the needle into E, pass the thread to the RS, and bring it out at F. Repeat until you bring the needle out at H.
4. Pull the thread tight and tie a finishing knot.
5. Insert the needle into corner I, bring it out at J, pass the stitch, pick up the stitch at corner K, and secure the stitch.
6. Insert the needle at L, pass the thread to the RS, and bring it out at M. L is now the same as A, so just repeat the process for the rest of the column.
7. When you reach the end of the column, tie a finishing knot and cut the thread. Begin stitching the next column from the top using the same process.

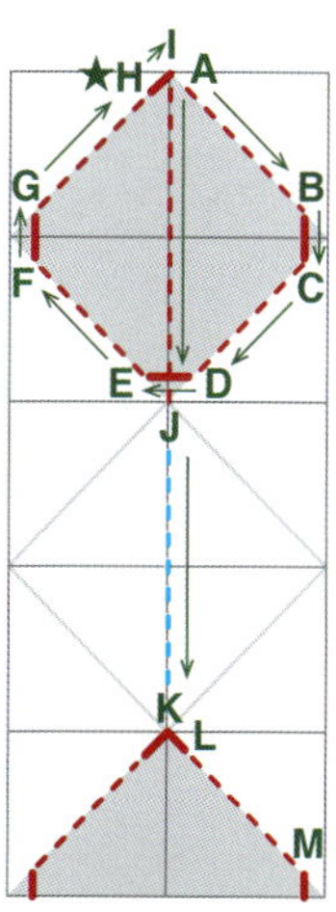

BOX

RS

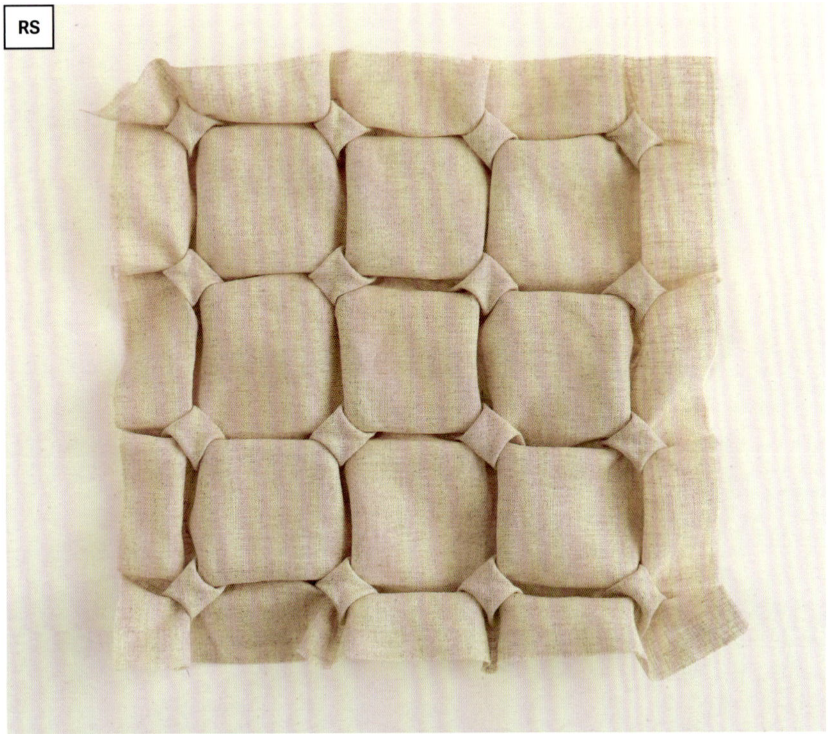

WS

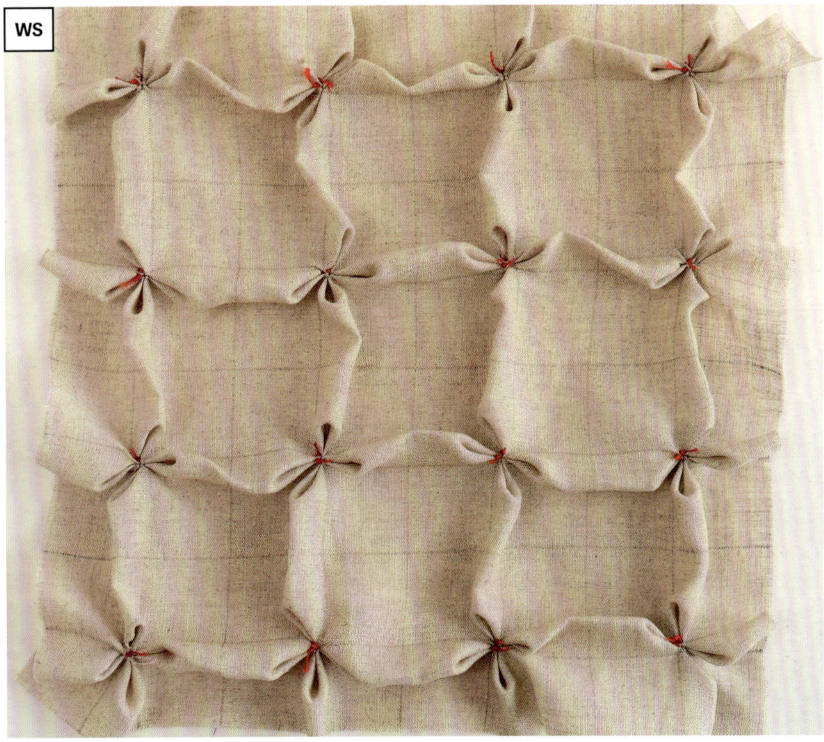

■ Original Fabric Size

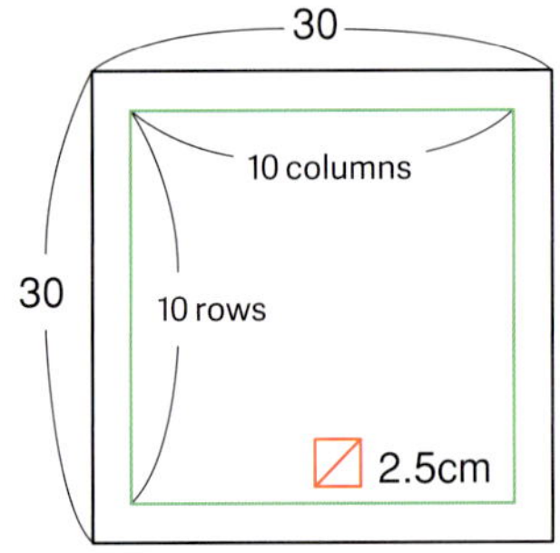

■ Fabric's Stretch Level

★☆☆☆☆

■ Pressing

- Could be pressed depending on the desired finish

■ Notes

- Finish one section at a time
- Since there will be gaps, instead of continuing to pass the thread, tie a finishing knot each time and cut the thread
- Technique is the same stitching as Flower (page 94), but the pattern focuses on the reverse side
- The pattern changes depending on whether the seams are bumpy or concave

The **red** lines show where you should pick up and tighten the thread on the WS (solid lines) and RS (dashed lines). **Green** letters and arrows indicate stitching order.

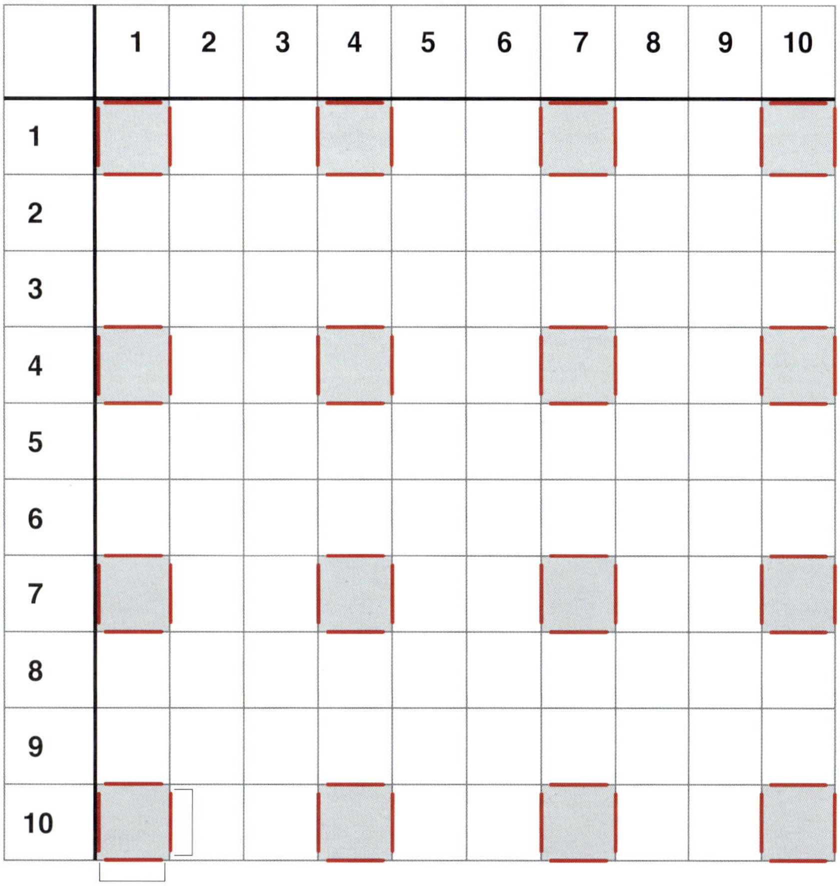

Finish one marked section at a time.

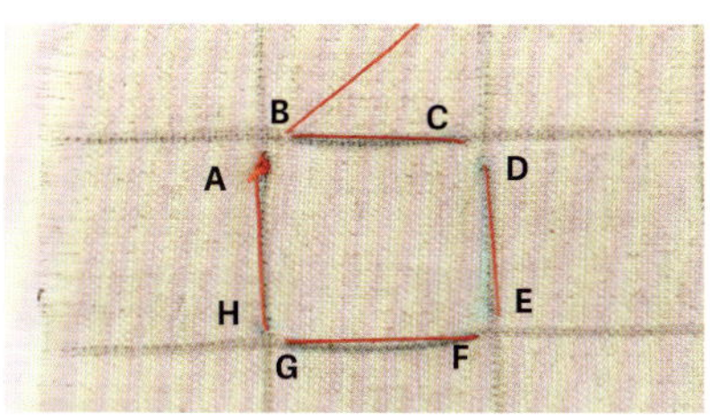

01 Insert the needle at A and bring it out at B. Pass the thread on the WS and insert the needle at C. Repeat until you bring the needle out at J(B). AB has two strands of thread.

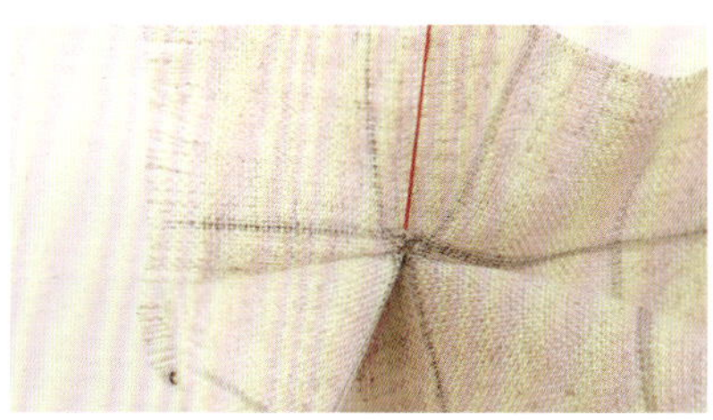

02 Pull the thread tight.

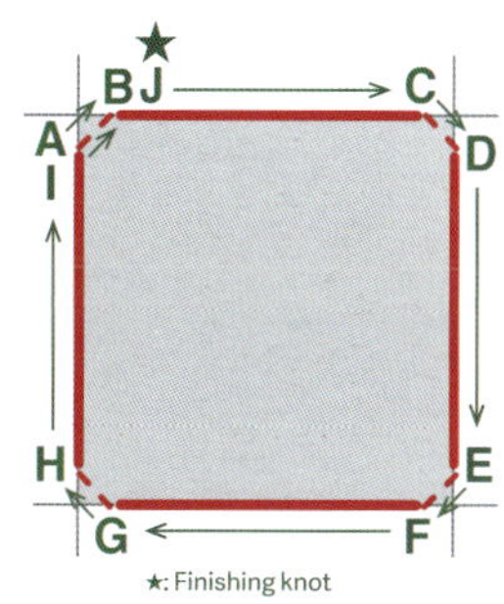

03 Tie a finishing knot and cut the thread.

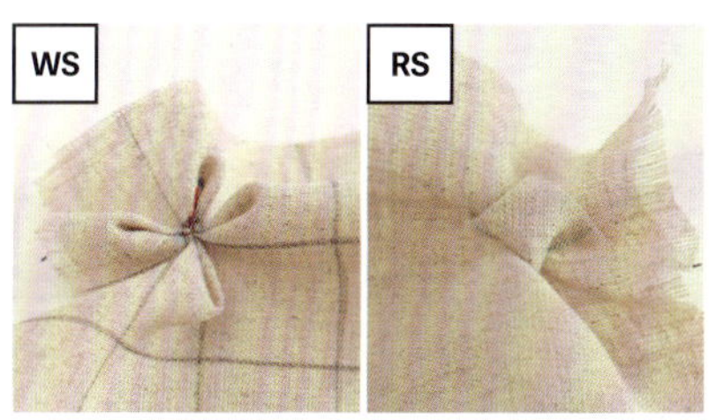

04 On the WS, a flower-like pattern forms, while on the RS, a diamond pattern appears. Repeating this creates squares between the sections.

MAKING A SHOULDER BAG

Finished Size: 24 × 18 × 2 cm

■ Materials

- Main fabric (DARUMA FABRIC: Clay cotton nylon gabardine): 104 × 80 cm
- Lining fabric (sheeting): 50 × 30 cm
- Fusible interfacing: 100 × 10 cm
- D-rings: 2 pieces, 2.1 cm inner dimension
- Magnetic button: 1.2 cm diameter

Note: The instructions use a different fabric than on page 21. Also, red thread is used for clarity, but when sewing, use a matching color.

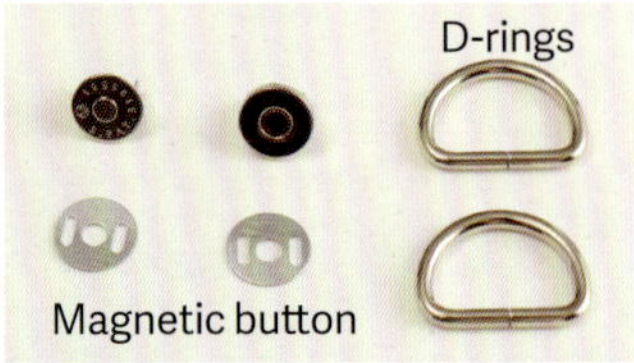

Measurement unit: cm
All seam allowances not specified are 1cm
Pattern pieces are shown with seam allowances included
The lattice smocking diagram shown from the WS

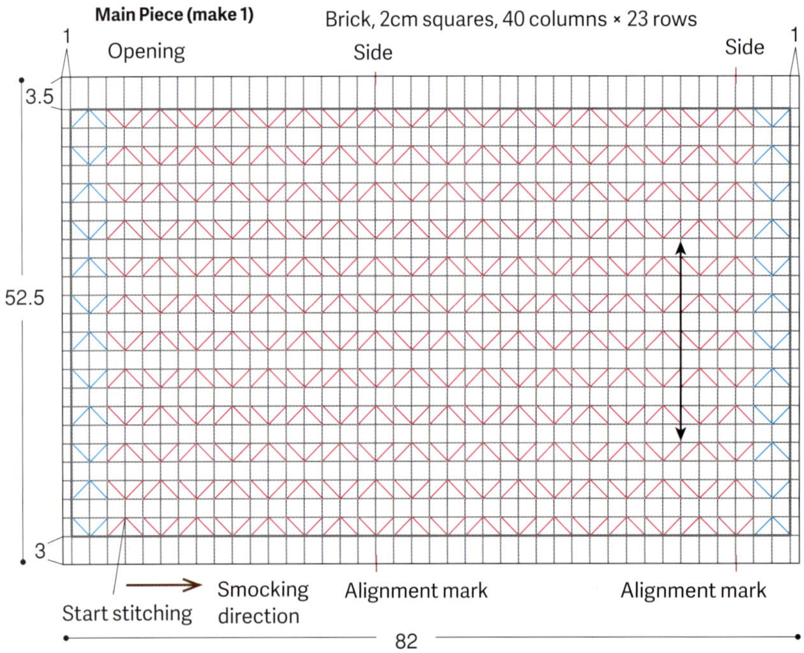

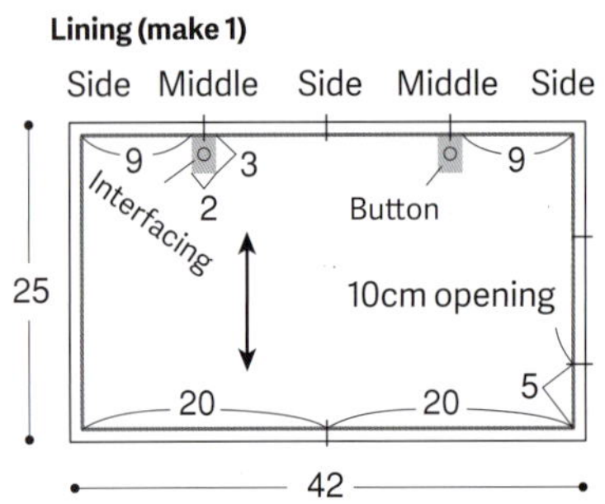

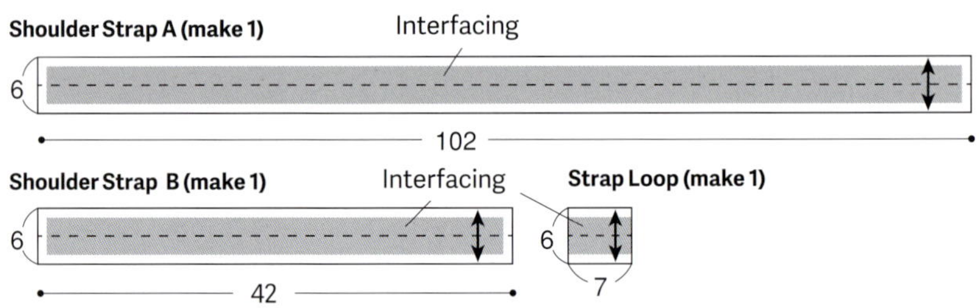

01 Press the main fabric and cut it. Draw lines on the WS. The two columns of on both ends (light blue lines in diagram) are where you'll smock after joining the ends. Draw alignment marks on the sides.

02 Cut the lining and draw lines and alignment marks. Prepare (10) 3 × 2cm pieces of fusible interfacing. Attach them one by one where indicated on the diagram, making two stacks of five pieces.

03 Cut Shoulder Straps A and B and the Strap Loop. Fuse the interfacing to the WS and cut to the finished size. Leave only two ends of the Strap Loop as raw edges.

04 Stitch the Brick pattern (pages 68–71). Leave the two columns on either side; start from the bottom left of the third column. Rotate 90 degrees and stitch. You'll need about 1.2m of thread per row.

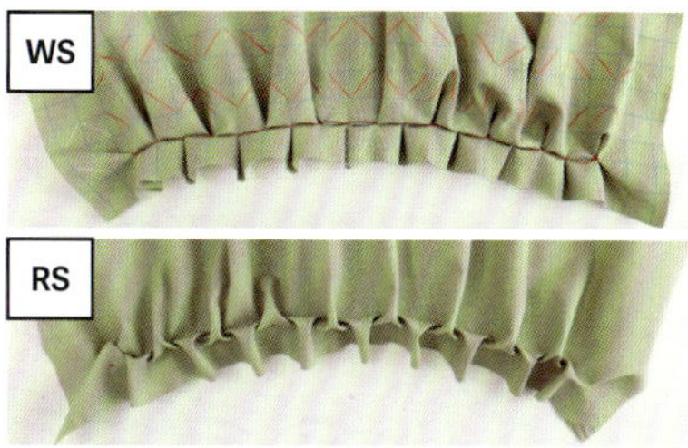

05 The first row is complete. Leave the two columns (rows) on the side open and tie a finishing knot.

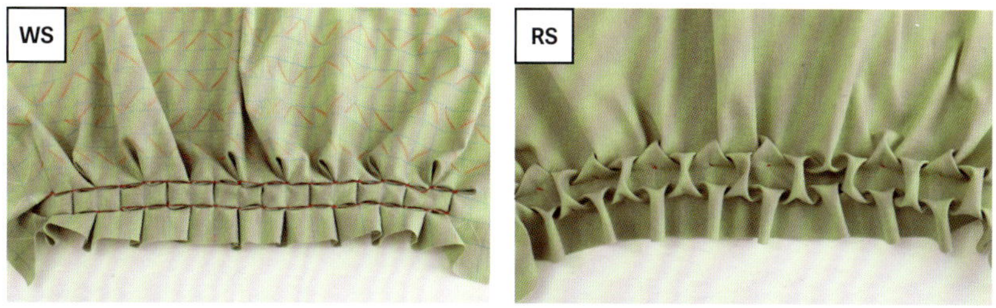

06 Three rows are stitched. The Brick pattern is beginning to emerge. In this way, stitch up to the 23rd row, leaving the two columns on the other side open.

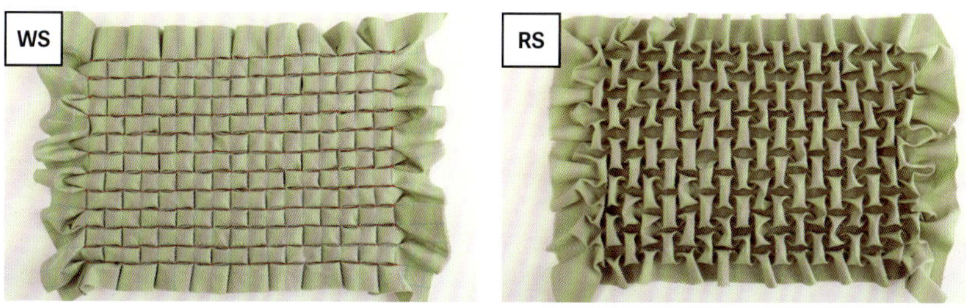

07 The main body is completely stitched. Only two rows on each side and a seam allowance (2 squares wide) remain.

08 Shape it so that the pattern appears, then press it from the RS. Slowly apply steam until it is slightly puffy.

09 Fold pleats along the guide lines at the top and bottom and iron them, leaving both ends untouched.

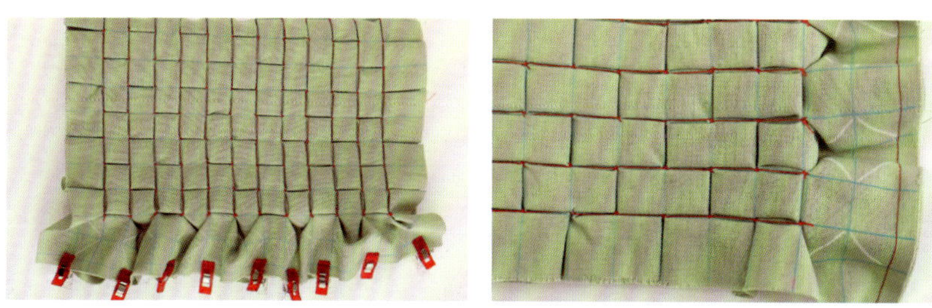

10 With RS together, sew the ends with a 1cm seam allowance. I used clips to secure the fabric in place, but you can also use pins.

Making a Shoulder Bag

11 Press the seam open with an iron. Place an ironing glove inside and press firmly. You can also use a rolled-up towel.

12 Stitch the four remaining rows at the ends. Turn the main piece sideways and begin from the edge. Scoop at the lower-right corner to the upper-left corner. Pull the thread tight to bring them together.

13 Pick up one stitch at the lower-left of the next grid square. In the seam allowance area, stitch from above the seam allowance.

14 Pull the thread tight to bring the corners together.

15 Pick up a stitch at the next lower-left corner, pass the thread without pulling it tight, and secure the stitch. Pick up a stitch in the top-right corner of the same square and pull the thread tight.

16 Pick up the bottom-right corner of the last square and pull tight. This completes one row. Stitch the next row as shown on page 68, completing all 23 rows.

17 This is what it looks like after you have finished stitching. Now the smocking on the edges are connected.

18 Turn the fabric RS out, straighten the pattern in the four columns, and press.

19 Turn it out again. With RS together, sew the bottom at the side seam marks. Adjust the pleats and sew with a 1cm seam allowance.

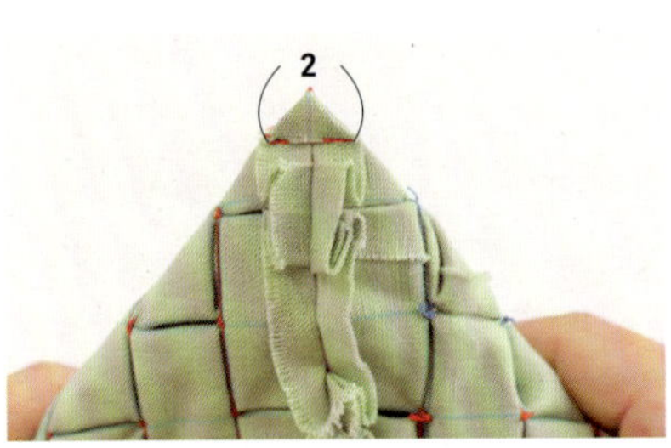

20 Press the bottom seam open, align it with the side seam, fold it into a triangle, and sew the gusset 2cm in from the edge.

21 Press the bottom seam open with an iron.

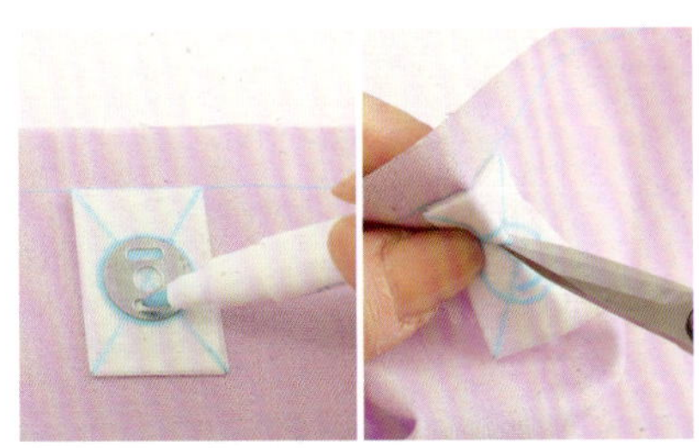

22 Align one side of the button with the center of the interfacing, mark the position, and use scissors to make a cut at the mark.

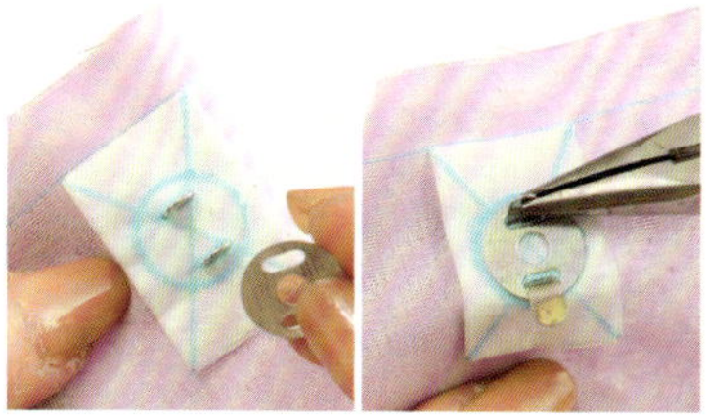

23 Insert the button through the slit. Attach the plate and bend the prongs with pliers. Attach the other side of the button to the other side of the lining.

24 Fold the lining piece in half RS together. Stitch the sides and bottom, leaving an opening for turning at one side. The seam allowance is 1cm.

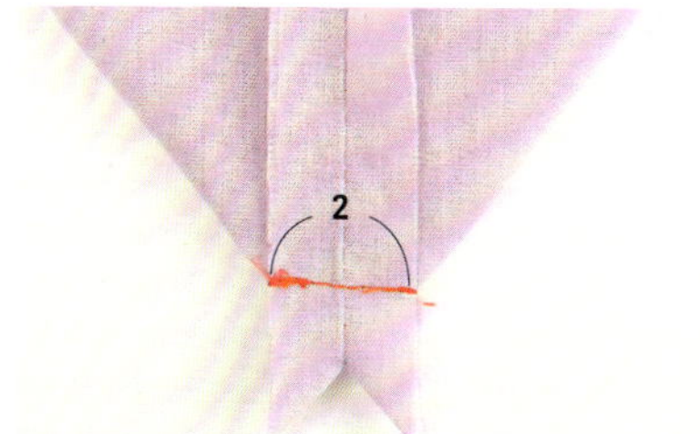

25 Press the seam allowances open and sew a 2cm boxed corner to form the gusset.

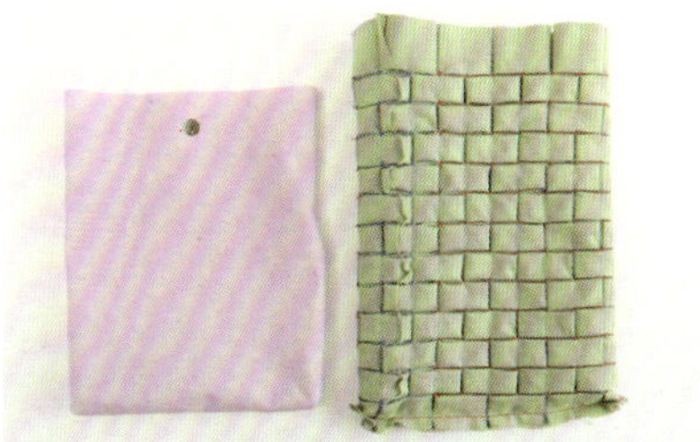

26 Turn the lining RS out. The main body and lining are now complete.

27 Insert the lining into the main body, which makes them RS together. Match the side seams of the main body and the lining.

28 Stitch around the opening with a 1cm seam allowance.

29 Turn the lining RS out through the opening.

30 Insert the lining back into the main body, so they are now WS together, and align the bottoms. The smocking will sit partially on the inside.

31 Place an ironing glove inside and press the opening.

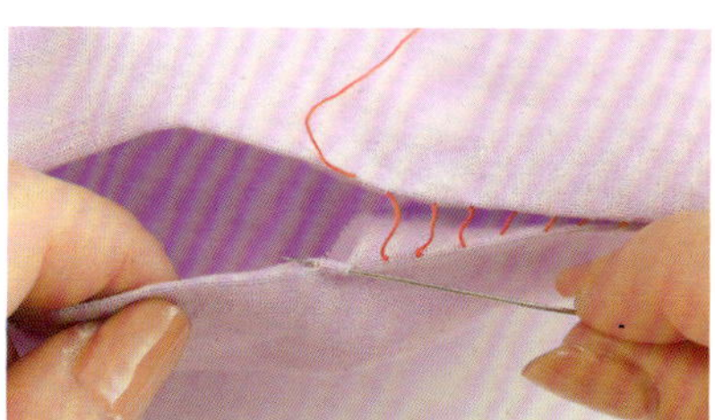

32 Close the lining opening with a ladder stitch. Catch the seam allowances alternately and stitch straight across.

33 For both Shoulder Straps A and B, fold in half lengthwise, then fold the 1cm seam allowances inward and press. The finished width of the strap is 2cm.

34 Open the shoulder strap flat and clip the corners. Make diagonal clips at the center fold as well.

Making a Shoulder Bag

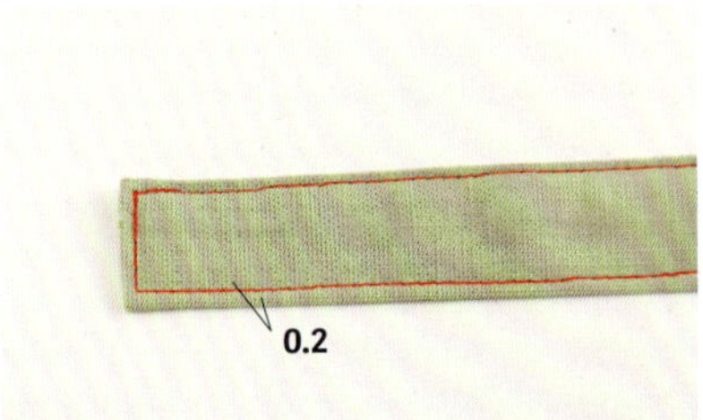

35 Fold the seam allowances inward again and fold the strap in half. Stitch 0.2cm from the edge all the way around. First stitch the folded side, then stitch down the center. This prevents shifting.

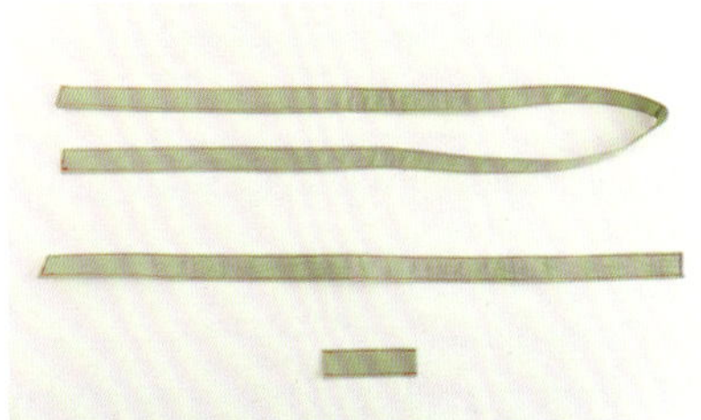

36 Make two shoulder straps. Sew the Strap Loop in the same way, but do not stitch the short ends; leave them as raw edges.

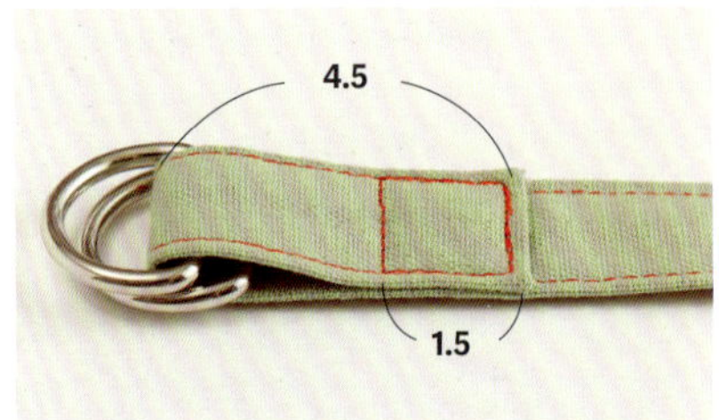

37 Thread two D-rings onto Strap A, fold it back, and stitch in a square to secure.

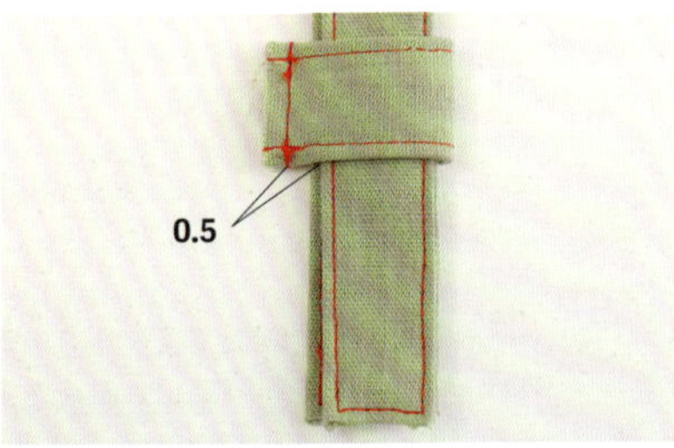

38 Fold Strap B in half and layer it. Repeat with the strap loop. Stitch a 0.5cm seam allowance on the strap loop.

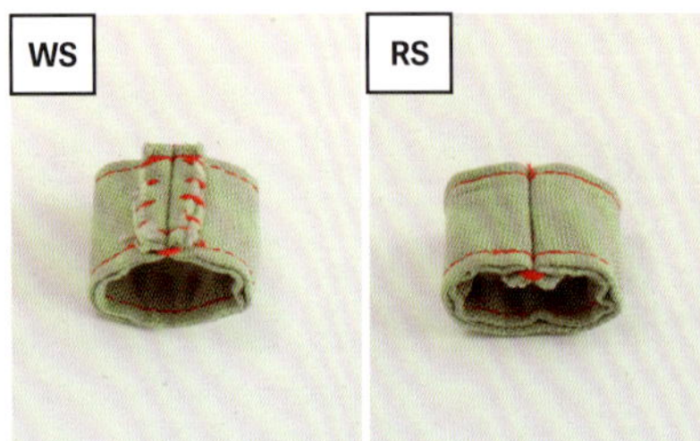

39 Press the seam allowances of the strap loop open and topstitch so it does not fold back. Turn it RS out.

40 Sew the shoulder straps onto the main body. Position and attach the straps according to the marks.

41 Layer the end of the shoulder strap 4cm down from the top edge. Mark a point on the strap 0.5cm down from the opening.

42 Stitch a square over the existing stitching of the strap, using the mark from step 41 as a guide.

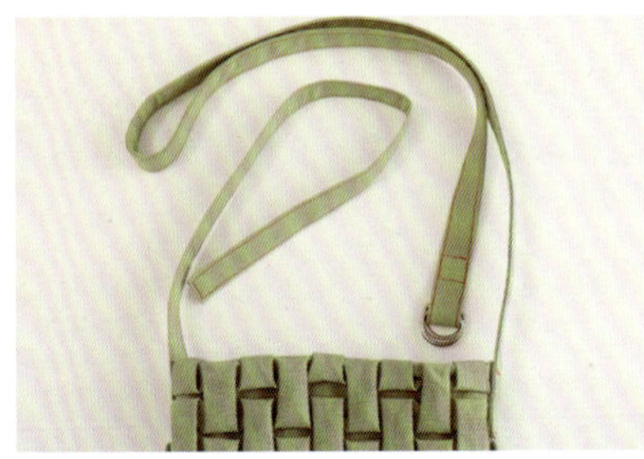

43 Shoulder Straps A and B are now attached to the main body.

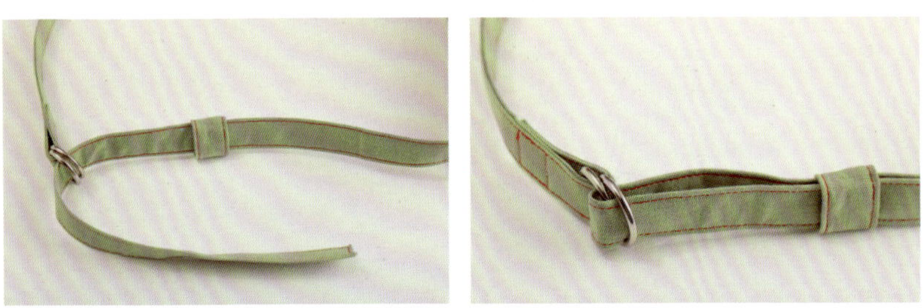

44 Thread Strap B through the strap loop, then pass it through both D-rings on Strap A. Fold Strap B back and pass it through one D-ring again, then thread it back through the loop.

45 The bag is complete.

How to Make the Projects

- The numbers used throughout this book are in metric to maintain the dimensions provided by the author. All the numbers in centimeters (cm).
- The measurements given in the cutting layouts and diagrams include seam allowances. Please cut the fabric accordingly. The standard seam allowance is 1 cm unless otherwise specified.
- Seam lines and stitching lines are depicted using both solid lines and dashed lines.
- Fabric measurements are given as width × length. A small margin of excess has been included in the cutting measurements. Finished project dimensions are given as height × width × depth.
- Refer to the technique page for the stitching instructions of each lattice smocking pattern.
- The lattice smocking diagrams are shown from the wrong side (WS).
- Use fabrics that are easy to work with. The fabrics used in this book are listed by name and supplier; please refer to them as needed.
- Finished dimensions may vary slightly from the measurements shown in the diagrams.

P. 13 Bone One-Handle Bag

Finished Size: 27 × 24 × 12cm

■ Materials

- Main fabric (Artemondo: Orpheus leather-look satin): 70 × 70cm
- Lining fabric (linen): 70 × 70cm

■ Notes

- For the smocking, do not carry the thread; fasten off each time and cut the thread. Refer to page 58 for the Bone stitching instructions.
- When cutting the fabric, fold it on the bias and cut in a circular shape.
- When finishing by stitching the inside of the pleats, stitch all the way through to the lining and fasten off on the inside of the pleat.

■ Instructions

1. Stitch the Bone smocking pattern.
2. Sew the gusset and join the front and back pieces RS together.
3. Sew the lining in the same way.
4. Place the main body and lining RS together and sew around the opening.
5. Attach the ends of the handles to the main body and lining.
6. Stitch down the inside of the handle pleats to secure.

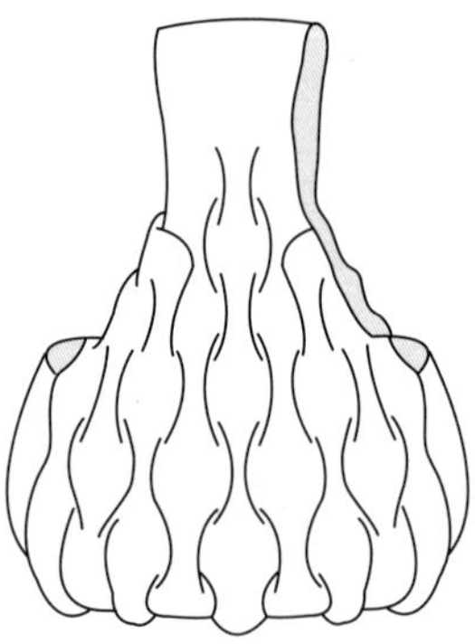

Main Piece (make 1)

BONE, 3cm squares, 21 rows × 21 columns

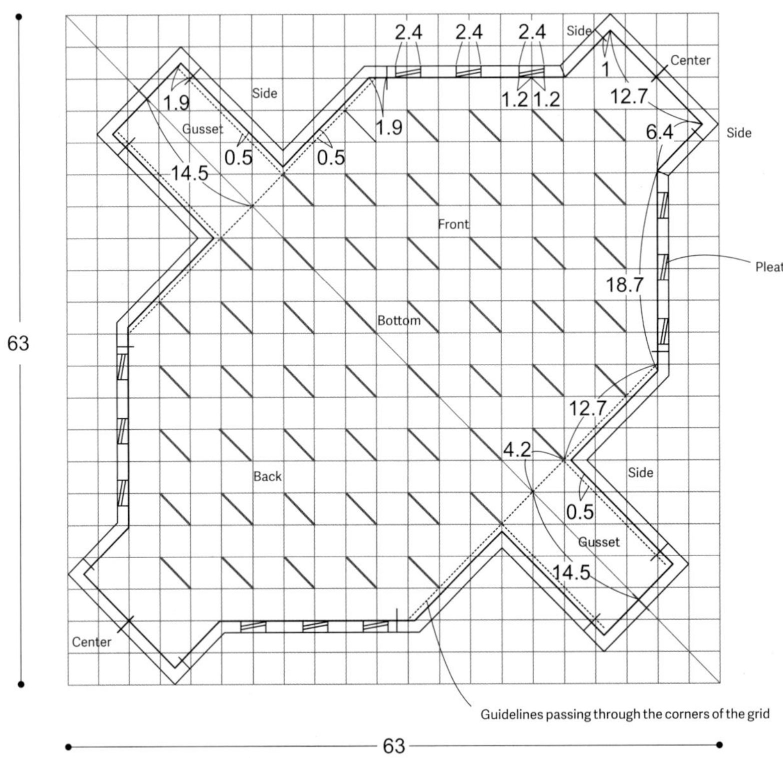

Lining (make 1)

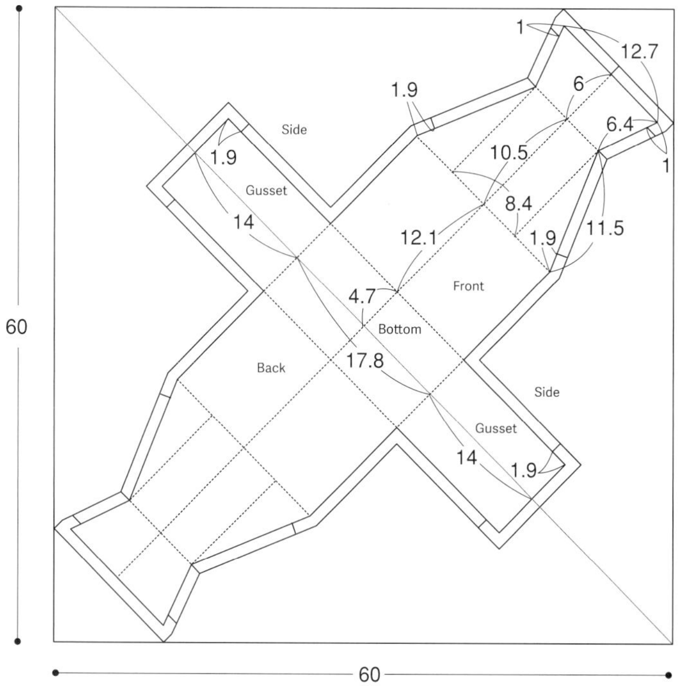

How to Make the Lining

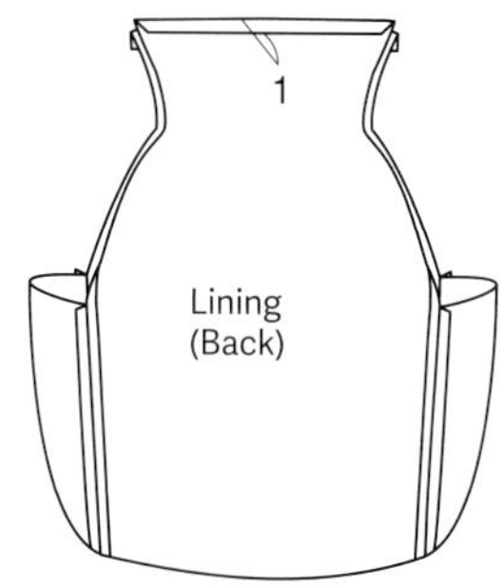

Sew in the same way as for the main piece.
Fold the end of the handle.

Instructions

①

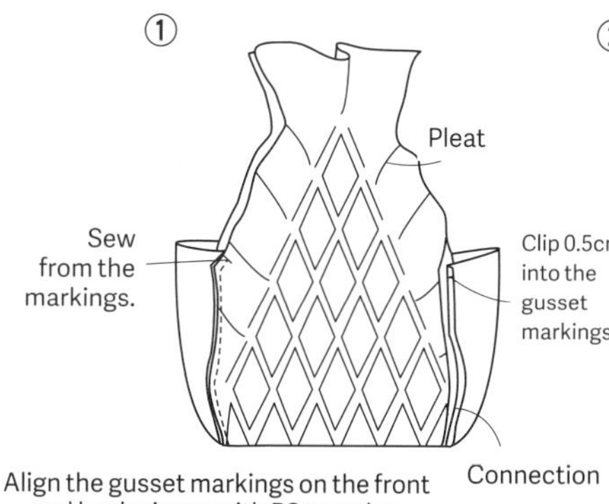

Align the gusset markings on the front and back pieces with RS together and sew the sides. Press the seam allowances open.

②

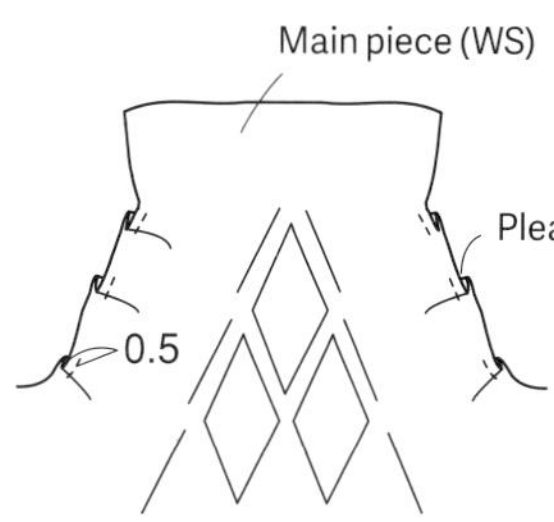

Arrange the pleats at the sides of the handles and sew by machine.

③

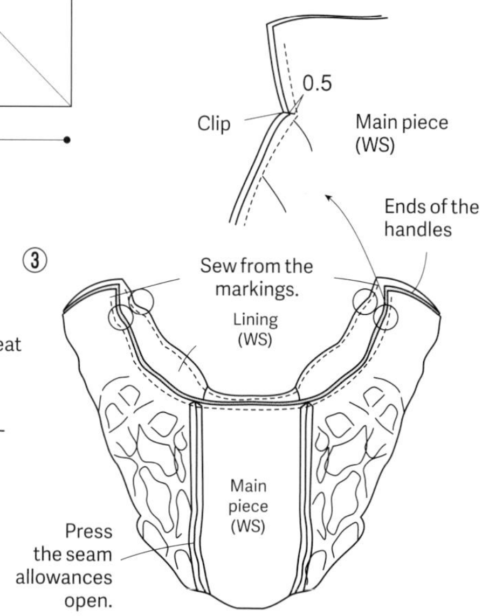

With the main body and lining RS together, sew around the opening and make cuts.

④

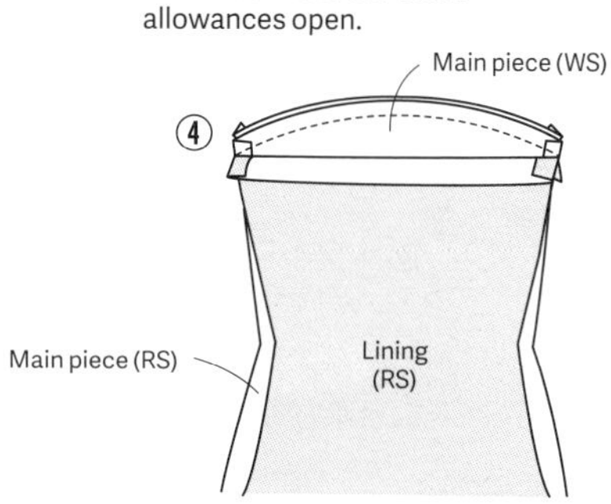

Turn the main body RS out through the handle opening.

Align the handle ends of the main body and lining with RS together and sew.

⑤

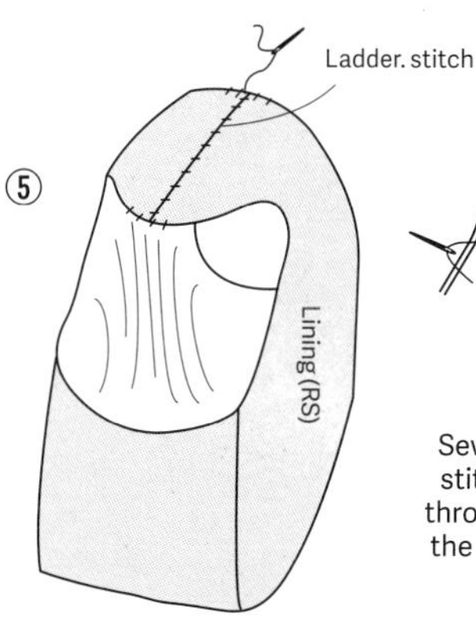

Close the opening in the lining. handle with a ladder stitch.

⑥

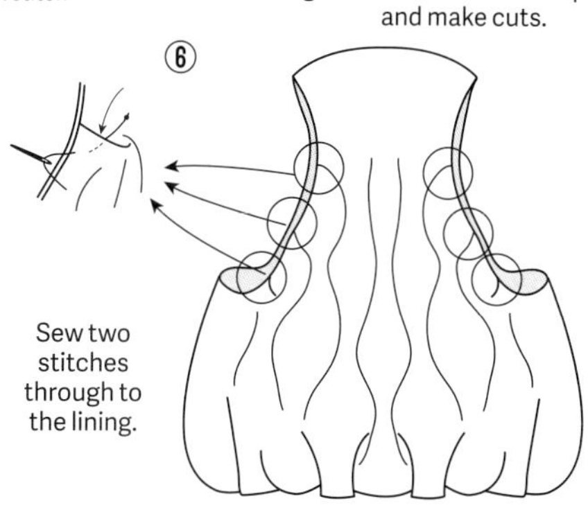

Sew down the inside of the pleats to secure them.

Photocopy at 40% (reduced size) or 250% (full size)

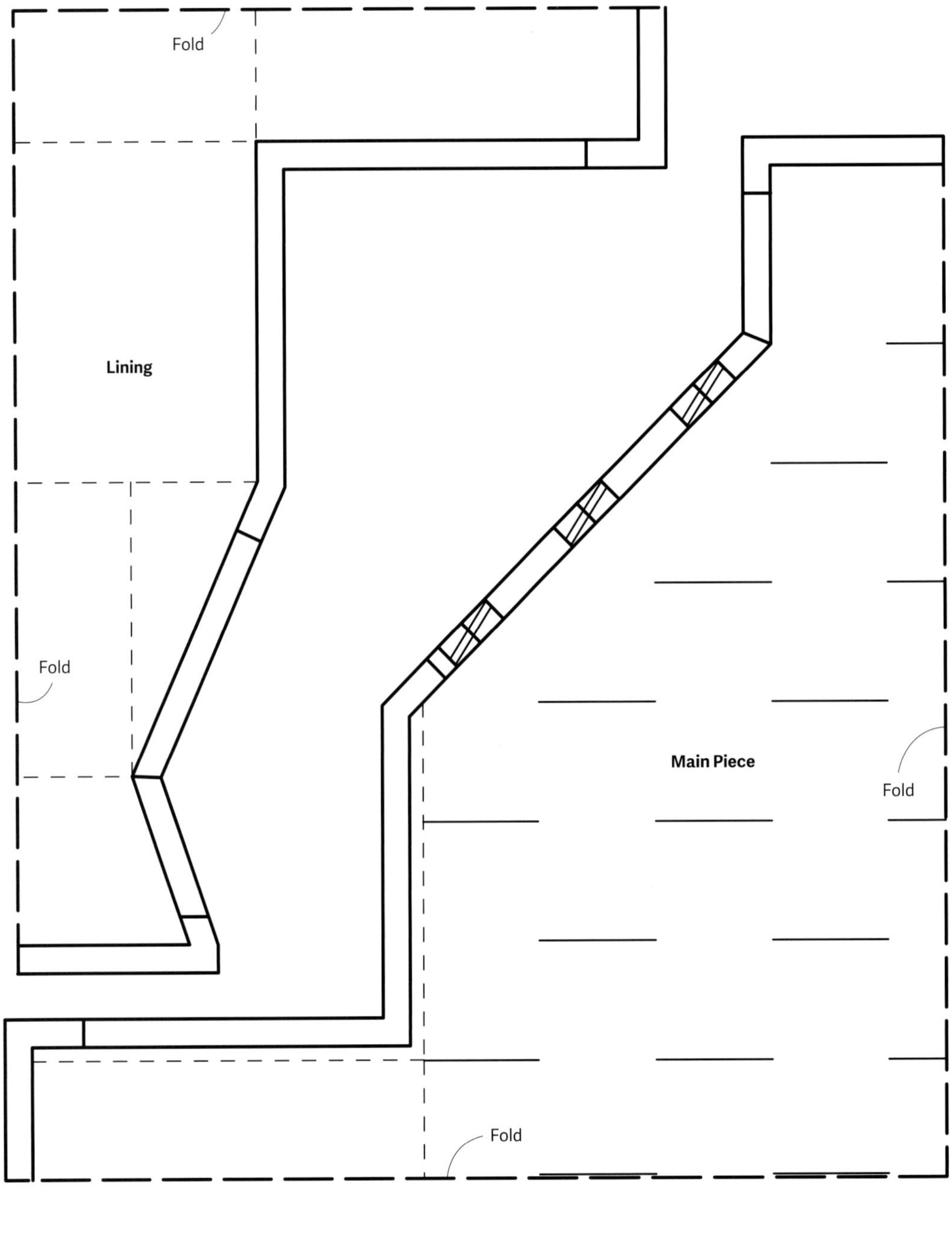

P. 14 Wave Pocket Tote

Finished Size: 35 × 28 × 2cm

■ Materials

- Main fabric (KIJINOMORI: Vintage No. 11 canvas): 108 × 80 cm
- Pocket outer fabric (DARUMA FABRIC: Frost ramie lawn): 60 × 50 cm
- Lining fabric: 80 × 50 cm
- Fusible interfacing: 100 × 20 cm
- Rivets: 8 pieces, 0.9 cm diameter

■ Notes

- For the pocket outer fabric, adjust the pleats around the edges and baste them in place first.
- When sewing the two main body pieces RS together, be careful not to catch the smocking stitching; press the folds in place by hand as you sew.
- Refer to page 60 for the Wave stitching instructions14

■ Instructions

1. Stitch the Wave smocking pattern and make the pocket outer fabric.
2. Place the pocket outer fabric and pocket lining RS together, sew, and press the seam allowances to the lining side.
3. Place the pocket lining onto the main body and sew pocket divider seam.
4. Turn the pocket to the RS and baste around the edges.
5. Place the main body pieces RS together, sew around the edges, and sew the gusset.
6. Sew the lining to the main body.
7. Insert the lining into the main body, fold the opening into thirds, and sew.
8. Make the handles, attach them, then attach the snaps.

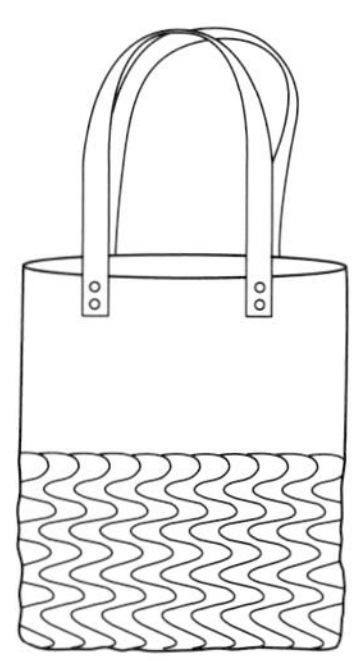

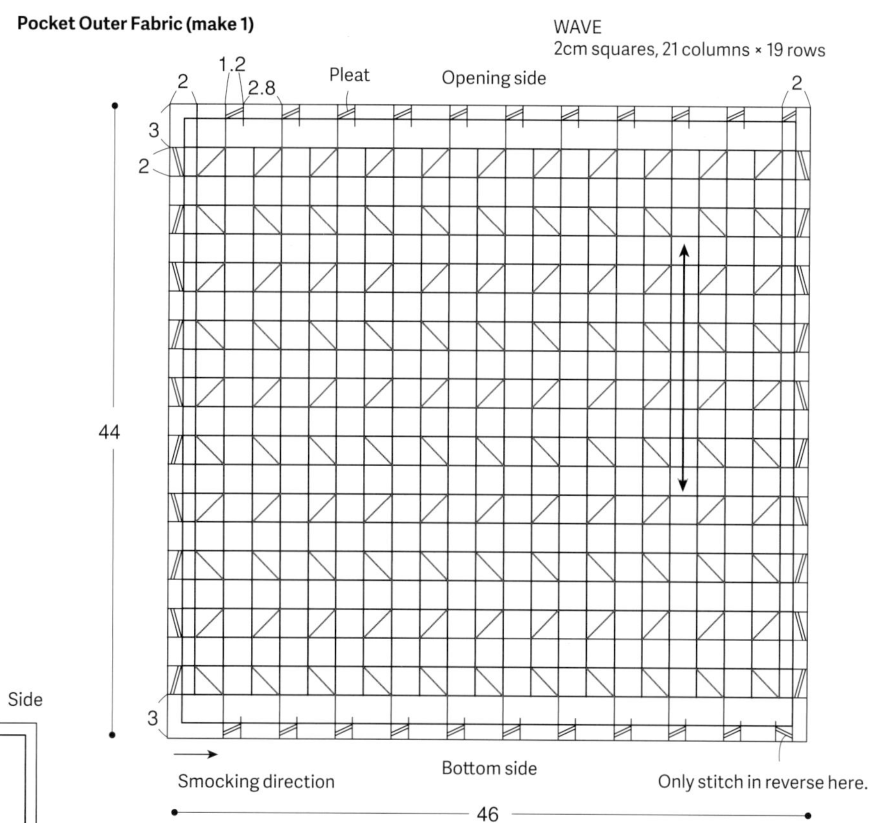

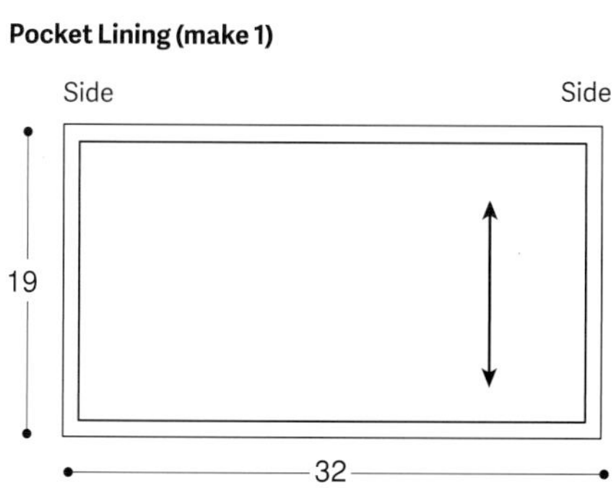

Main Pieces (make 2)

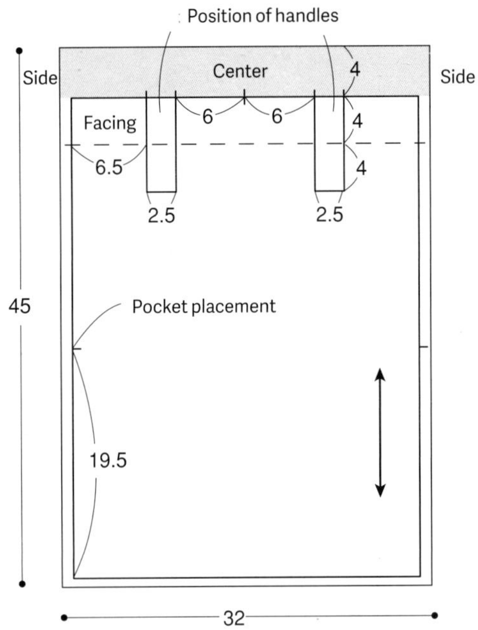

*Fuse a 32 × 4cm strip of interfacing to the seam allowance at the opening.

Main Lining (make 2)

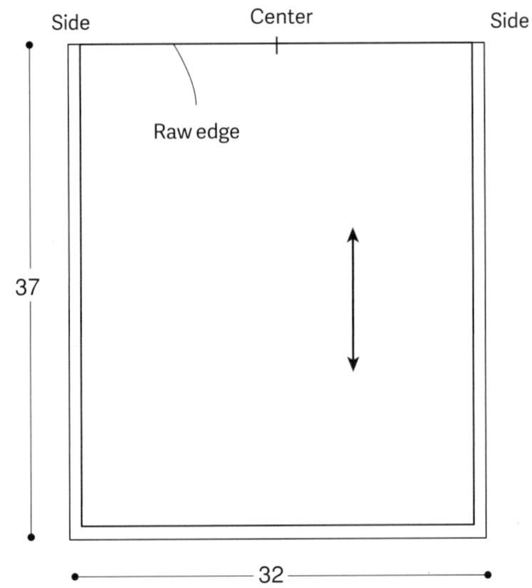

Handles (make 2)

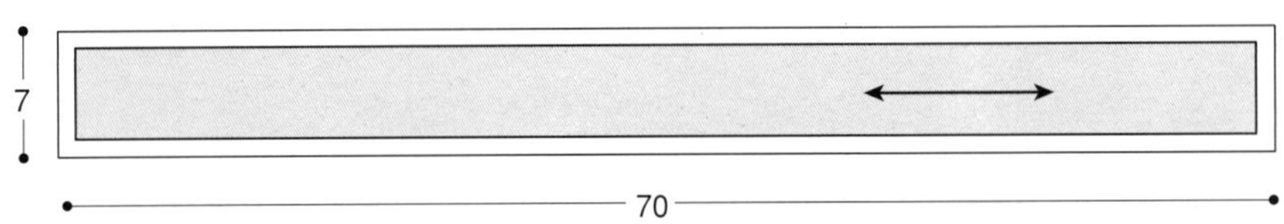

* Fuse the interfacing (leave the edges raw).

How to Make the Handles

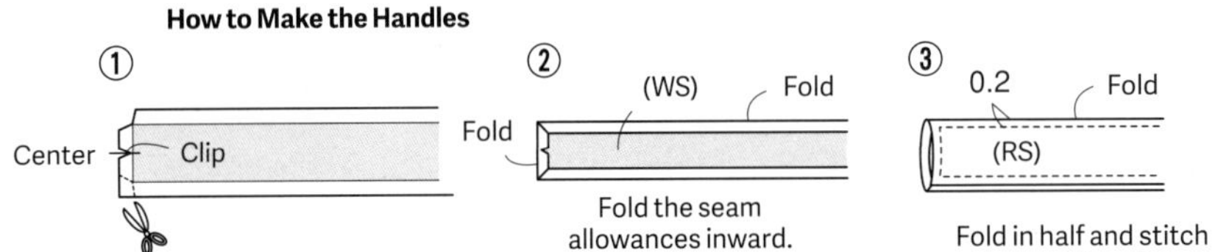

① Make a small cut at the center of the end, then trim the end.

② Fold the seam allowances inward.

③ Fold in half and stitch around the edge.

Instructions

①

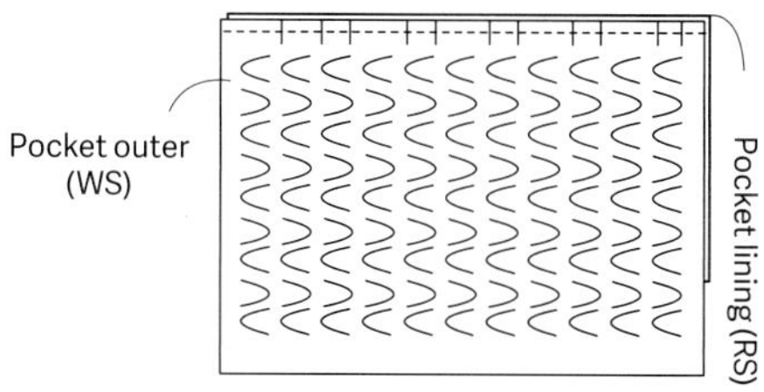

Arrange the pleats on the pocket outer fabric. Place the pocket outer and pocket lining RS together and sew along the top edge.

②

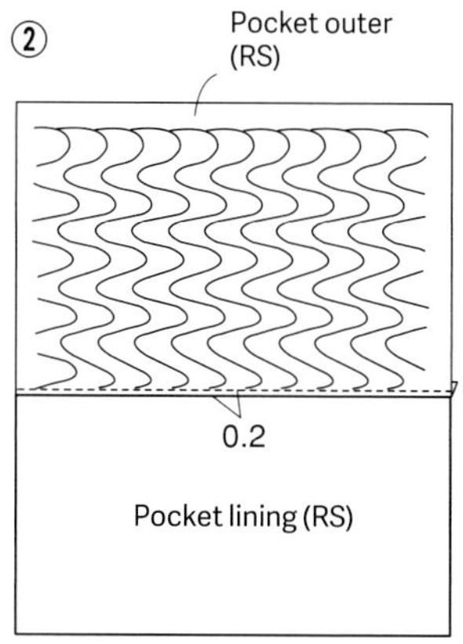

Press the seam allowance toward the pocket fabric and topstitch.

③

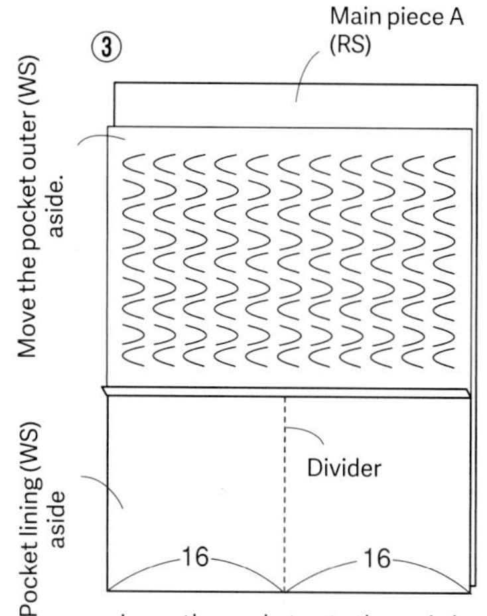

Layer the pocket onto the main body piece with RS together and sew the divider seam.

④

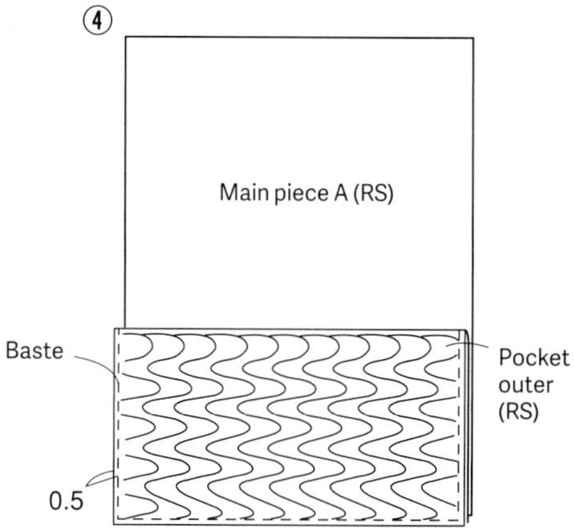

Fold the pocket outer fabric to the bottom edge of the main body. Baste around the pocket. Leave the top edge open.

⑤

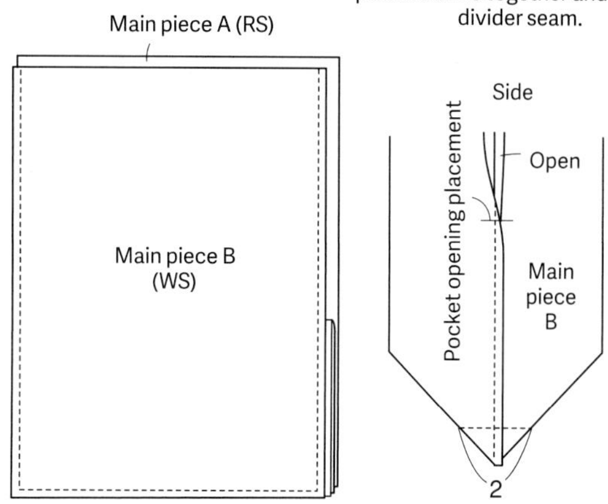

Place the second main body piece RS together with the first and sew around the edges. Sew the gusset. Trim the seam allowances and press toward the second main piece. Clip from the pocket up to the seam allowance. Sew the lining in the same way

⑥

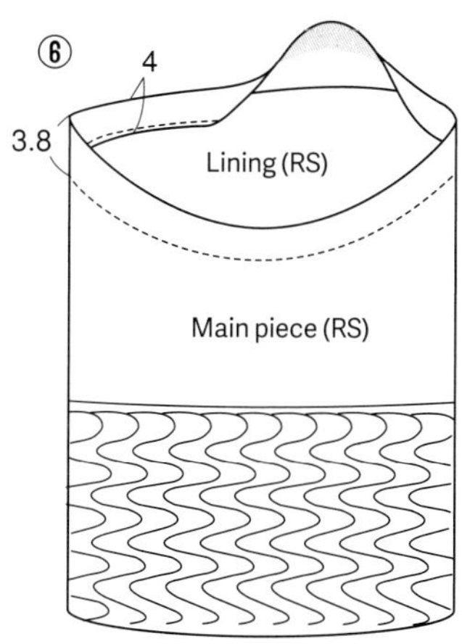

Insert the lining into the main piece, WS together. Fold the opening edge three times and stitch.

⑦

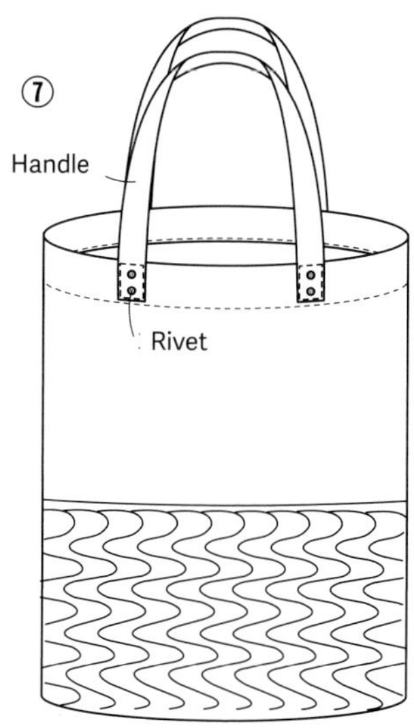

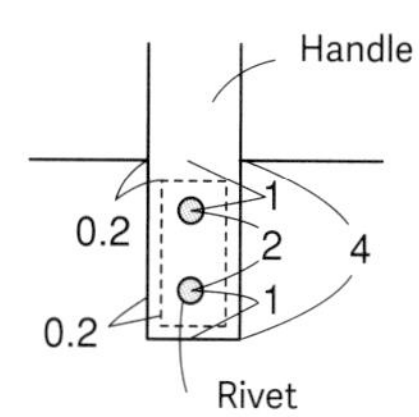

Make the handles and attach them to the main body. Attach the rivets.

P. 16 Crisscross Bone Ruffle Handle Bag

Finished Size: 24 × 44 × 4cm

■ Materials

- Main fabric (COSCLOTH: Minesoft synthetic leather): 90 × 80 cm (includes handles and tabs)
- Lining fabric (Artemondo: Irish Cross Oxford cotton): 100 × 60 cm
- Zipper: 30 cm
- Bias tape: 3.8 × 60 cm

■ Notes

- Before turning the handles RS out, insert a ruler or similar tool to create a firm base and press the seam allowances open.
- When attaching the zipper, position the pull stop on the side where the handles are attached.
- For the lining bag pleats, lengthen the machine stitch and sew, then pull the thread to create pleats before pressing.
- Refer to page 62 for the Crisscross Bone stitching instructions.

■ Instructions

1. Stitch the Crisscross Bone smocking pattern on the main body, gather the pleats, and baste in place.
2. Fold the two main body pieces in half and sew the sides and gusset.
3. Stitch the Crisscross Bone smocking pattern on the handles, sew RS together, and insert the bias tape.
4. Sew the upper and lower lining pieces together in the same way as the main body.
5. Attach the lining to the main body.
6. Attach the zipper to the opening of the main body.
7. Sew the opposite side of the handles to the main body.
8. Insert the lining into the main body and attach it around the opening.
9. Make the tabs, wrap them around the base of the handles, and stitch them in place.

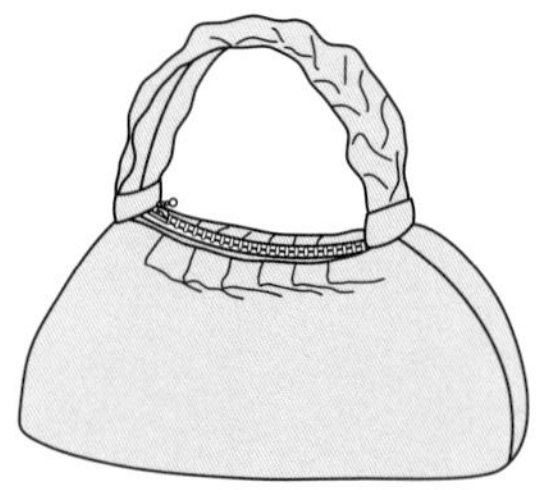

Main Piece (make 1)

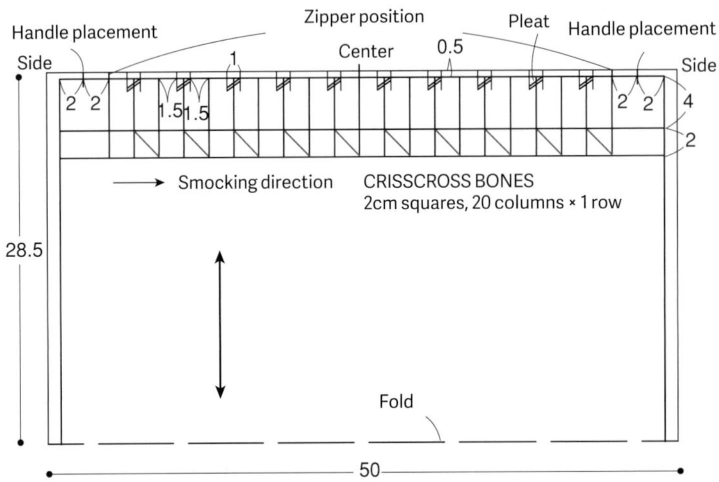

*For the smocking and pleats, draw the lines in the same direction on the WS as well (do not flip them).

Handle (make 1)

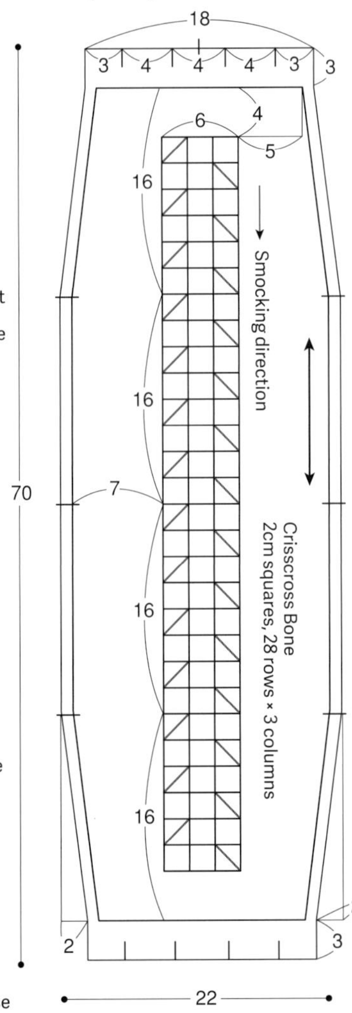

Tabs (make 2)

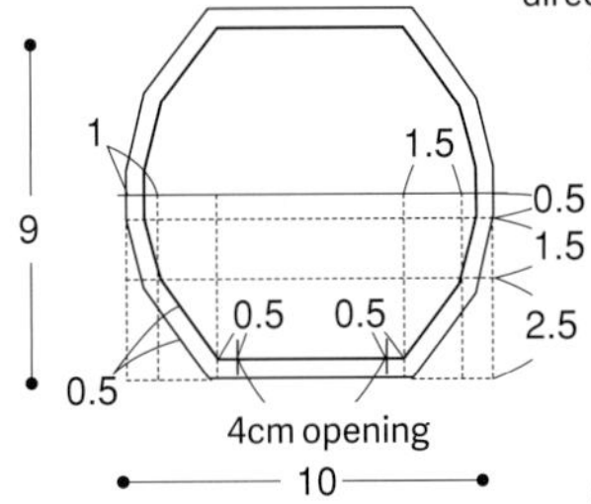

How to Make the Tabs

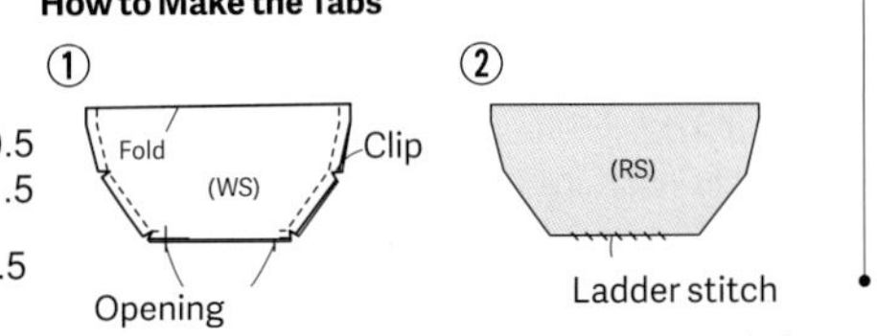

① Fold in half RS together and sew around the edge, leaving an opening for turning. Clip at a few spots.

② Turn RS out and close the opening with a ladder stitch.

Lining Pieces (make 2)

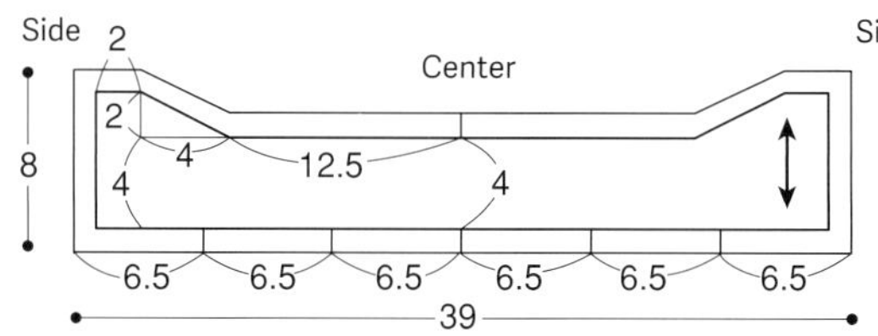

Lining Piece (make 1)

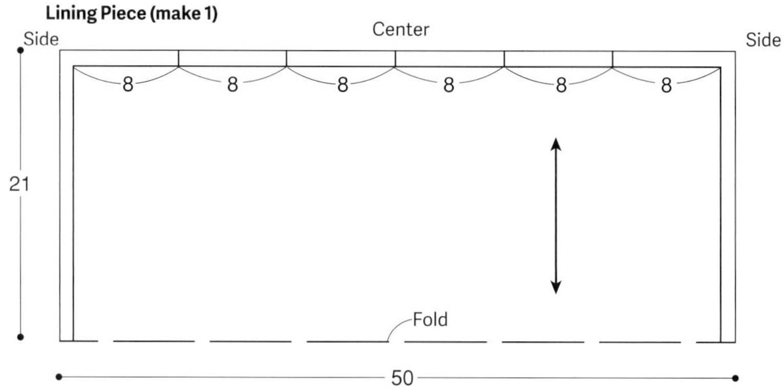

How to Finish the Lining

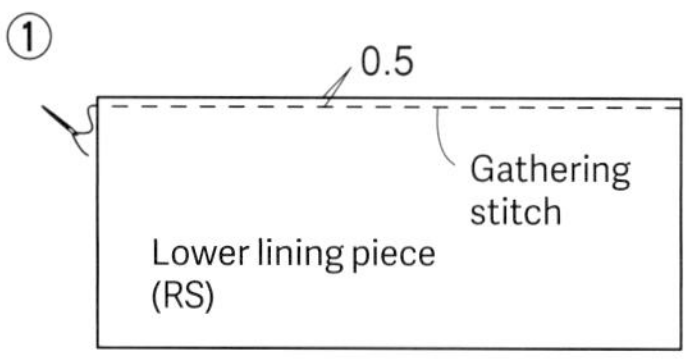

Sew gathering stitches along the top edge of the lower lining piece, pull the thread to gather it, and reduce it to 39cm to match the upper lining piece

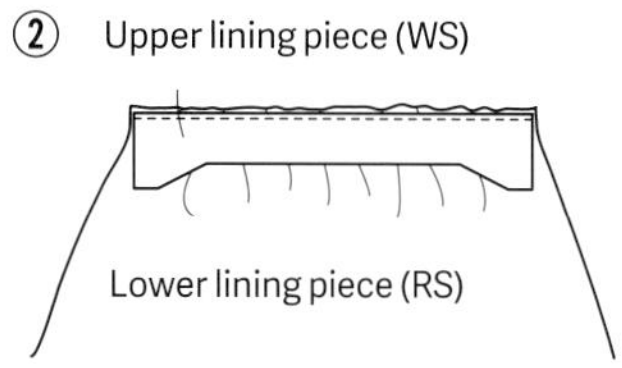

Place the upper lining and lower lining RS together and sew.

Remove the gathering stitches and press the seam allowances open.

How to Make the Handles

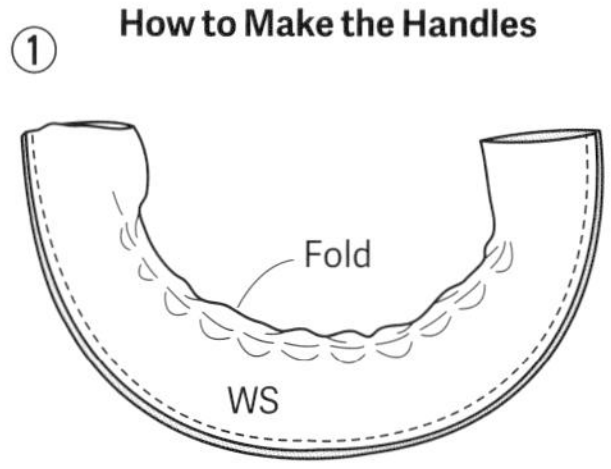

Fold the smocked handle RS together and sew it into a tube.

Press the seam allowances open and turn it RS out.

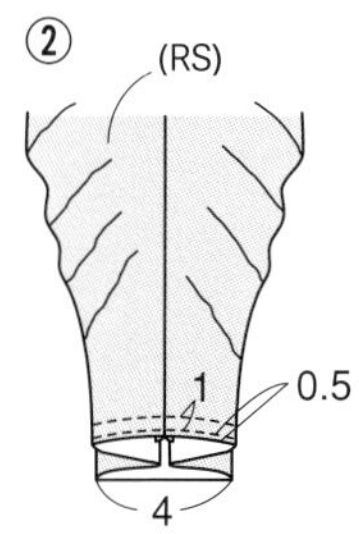

Fold as shown in the diagram and thread the bias tape through on the seam side.

Position the end so that the total length is 54cm, stitch the end in place, and trim any excess tape.

Preparation of the Zipper

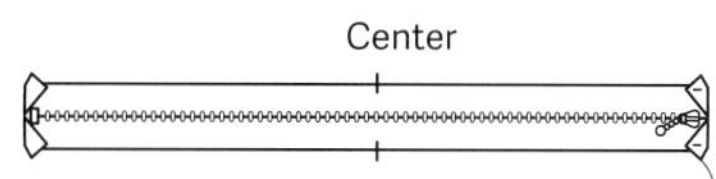

Fold the edge and secure it by stitching a triangular seam.

How to Fold the End of the Zipper

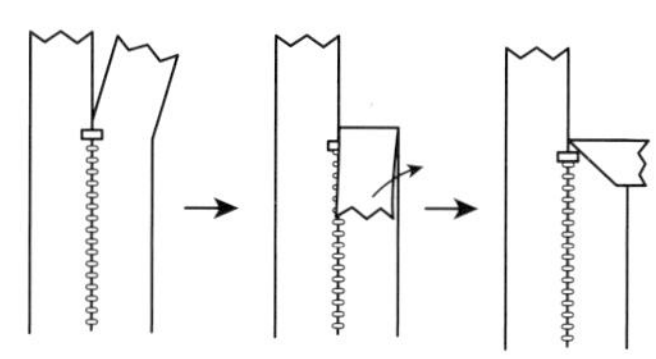

Instructions

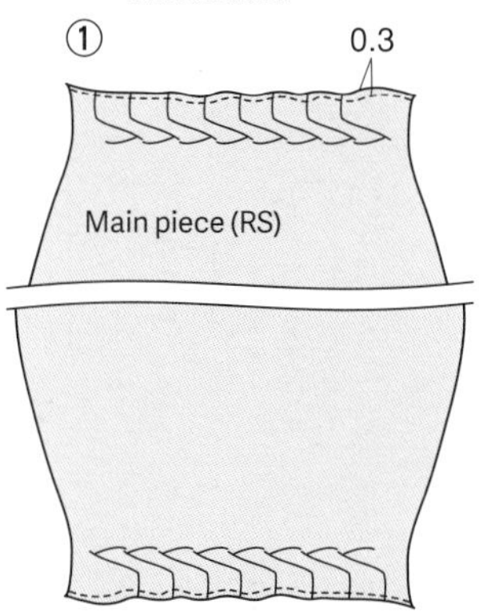

Gather the pleats along the edge of the smocked main body and baste them in place.

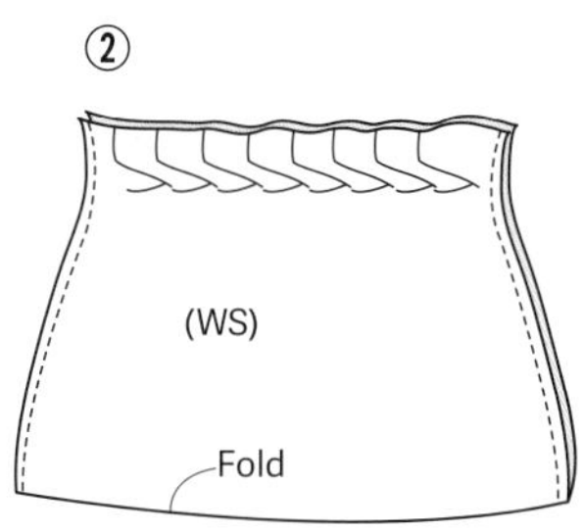

Fold in half with RS together and sew the sides. Sew the gusset. Sew the lining in the same way. Press the seam allowance at the opening of the lining to the inside.

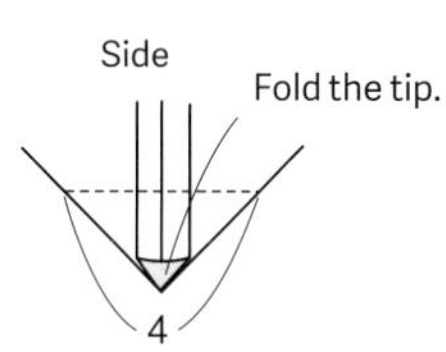

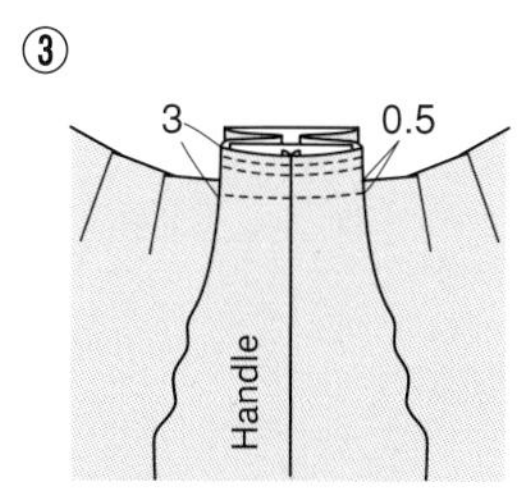

Sew the handle to one side seam of the main body only.

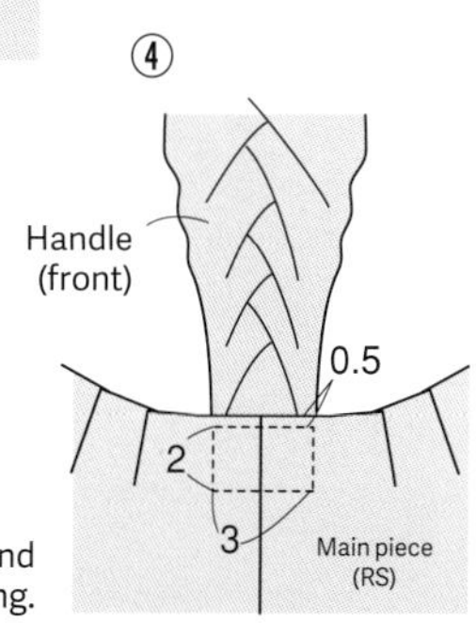

Raise the handle and secure it with topstitching.

Photocopy at 100%

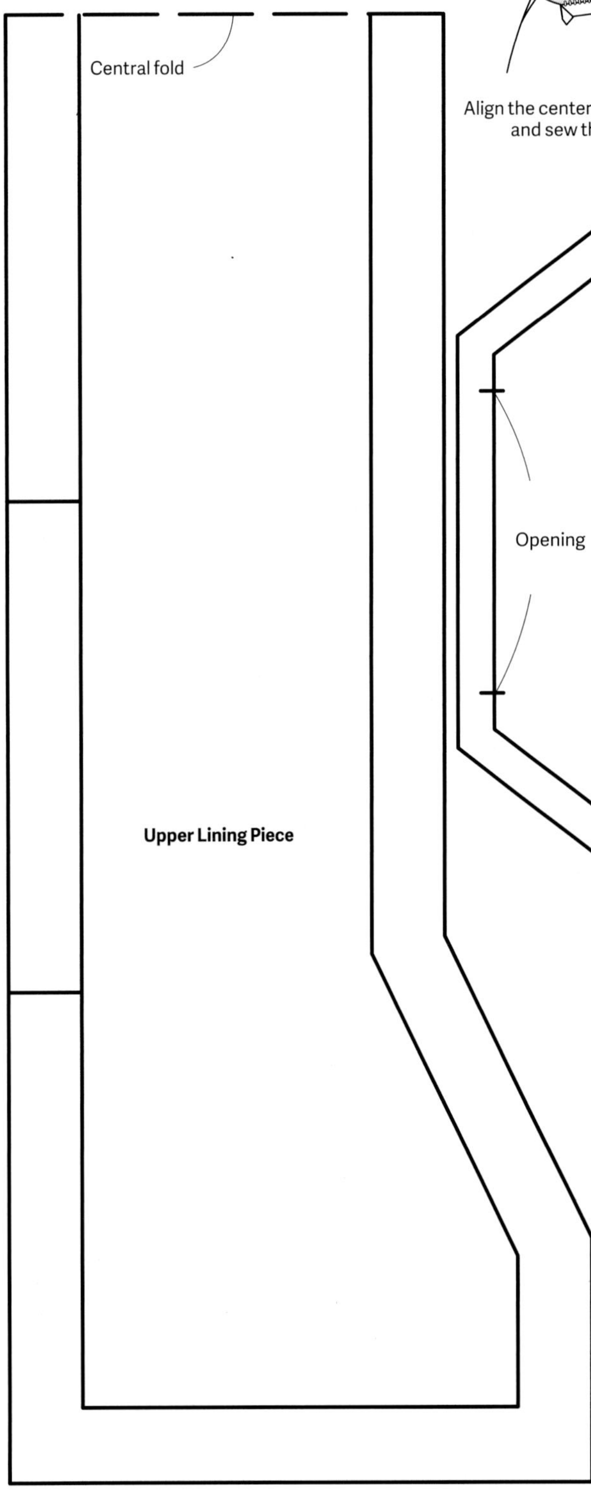

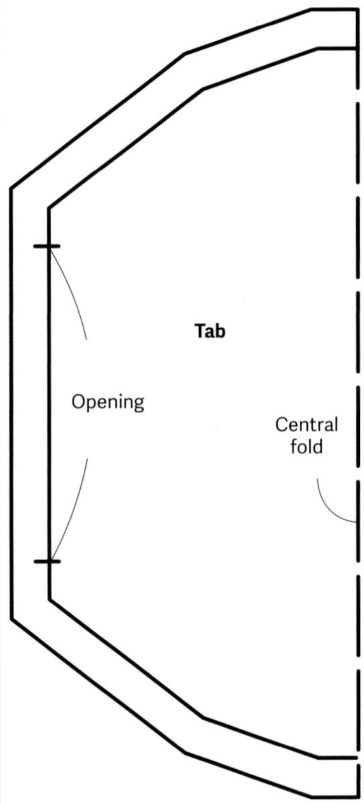

⑤

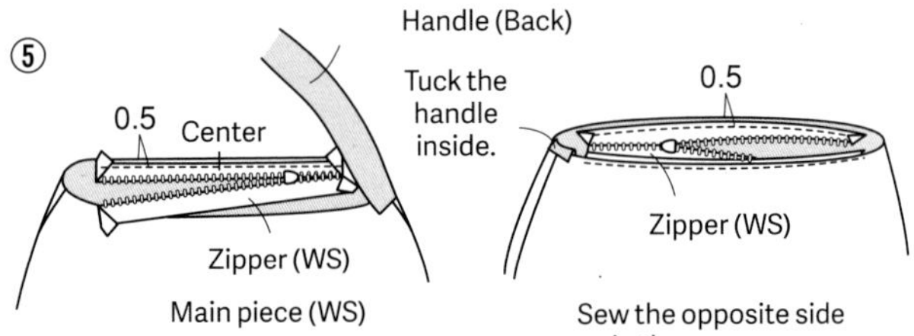

Align the centers of the main piece and the zipper, and sew them together with RS facing

Sew the opposite side in the same way.

⑥

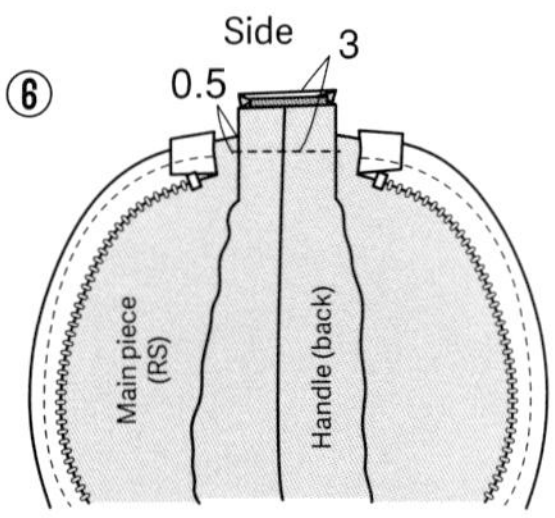

Sew the end of the handle on the opposite side seam of the main body, and stitch in the same way as step ④.

⑦

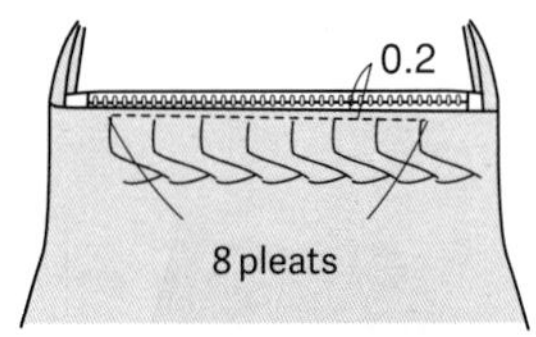

Turn the main body RS out and topstitch close to the zipper, using the width of eight pleats as a guide.

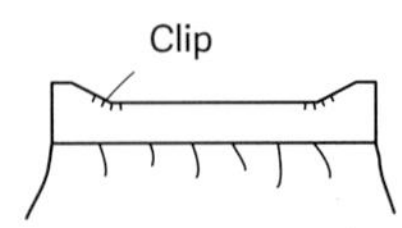

Make clips in the seam allowance along the curve of the lining opening.

⑧

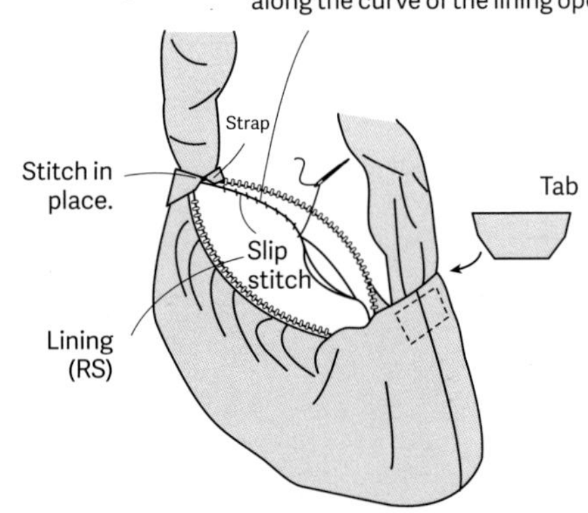

Insert the lining, slip stitch it to the zipper, wrap the base of the handle with the tab, and stitch it in place.

P. 17 Arrow Triangle Bag

Finished Size: 37 × 60cm

■ Materials

- Main fabric (linen blend): 150 × 80 cm (includes handles)
- Lining fabric (sheeting): 110 × 80 cm
- Lightweight fusible interfacing: 110 × 30 cm

■ Notes

- Fold the pleats at the opening of the main body and topstitch, then fold the pleats at both sides.
- Refer to page 64 for the Arrow stitching instructions.

■ Instructions

1. Stitch the Arrow smocking pattern on the main body, gather the pleats, and baste in place.
2. Sew the darts to make the lining.
3. Place the main body and lining RS together and sew the opening.
4. Place the two main body pieces RS together, leaving an opening, and sew around the edges. Sew the gusset.
5. Turn RS out and close the opening.
6. Make the handles and attach them to the sides of the main body.
7. Stitch the main piece to the lining at five points along the front and back.

Main Pieces (make 2)

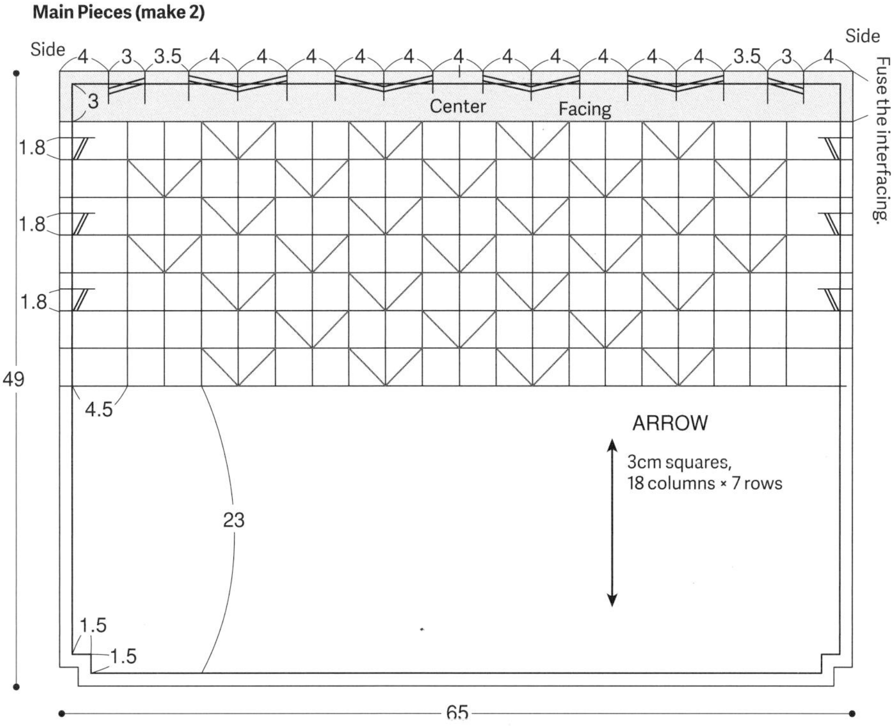

*Fuse interfacing to the facing.

Handles (make 2)

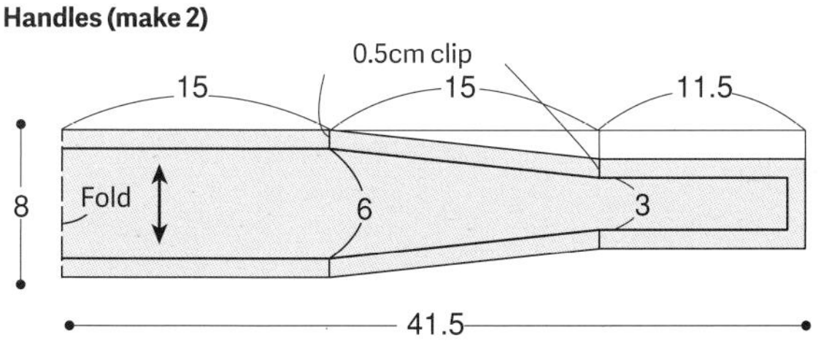

*Fuse the interfacing.

Upper Lining (make 2)

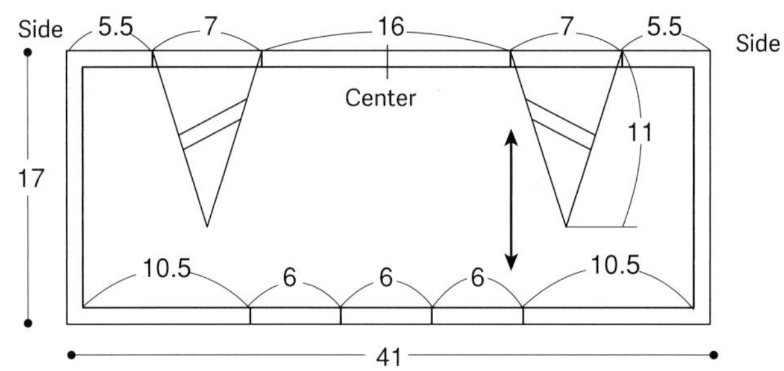

Lower Lining (make 2)

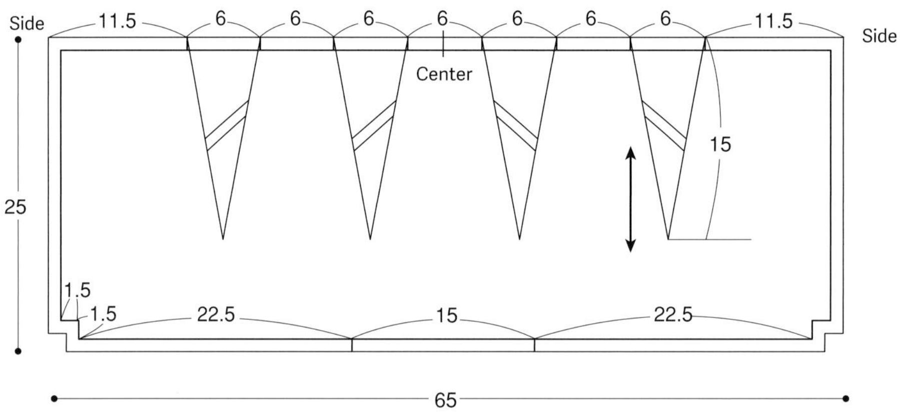

How to Finish the Lining

①

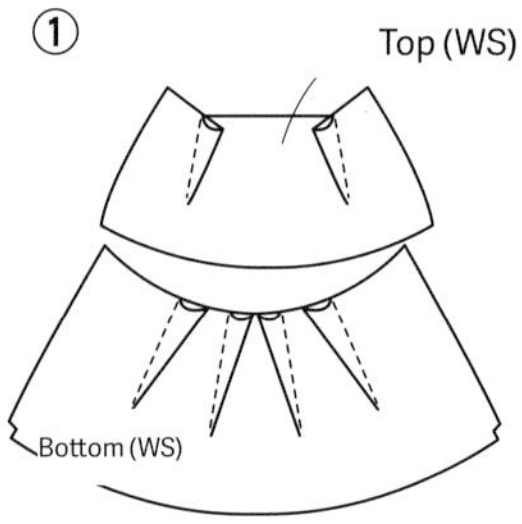

Sew the darts in the upper lining and lower lining.

②

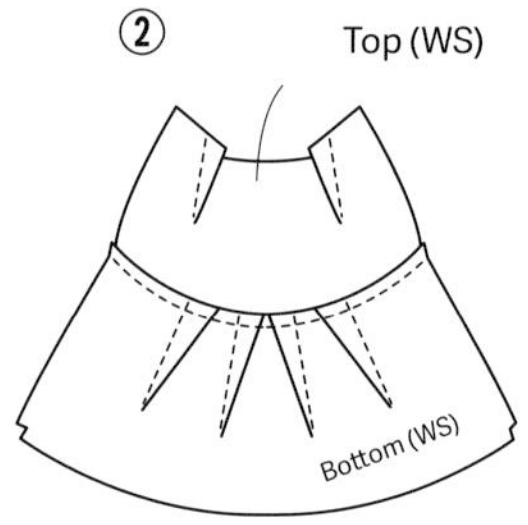

Place the upper and lower lining pieces RS together and sew, then press the seam allowance toward the upper lining.

How to Make the Handle

①

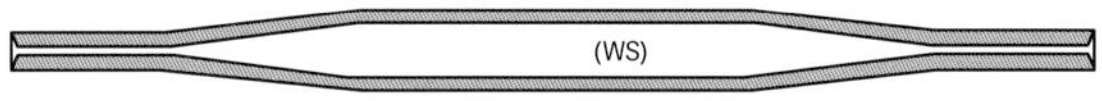

Fold the seam allowances at the top and bottom.

②

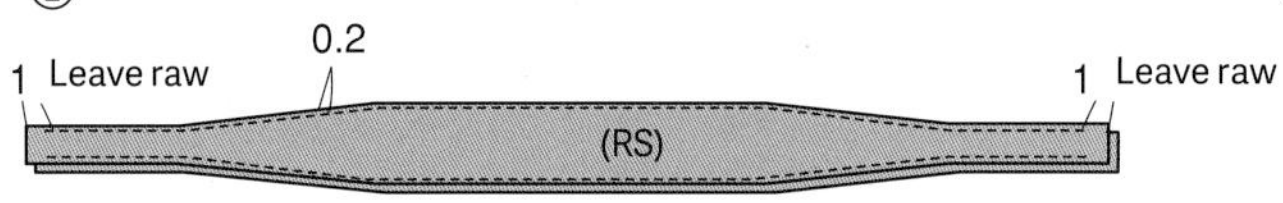

Layer with WS together facing out and sew.

③

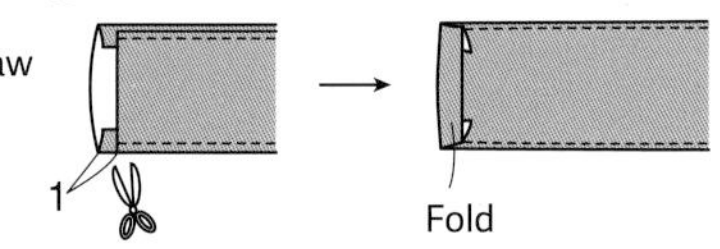

Trim the seam allowance on the side that will be inside, and fold the edge over to enclose it.

Instructions

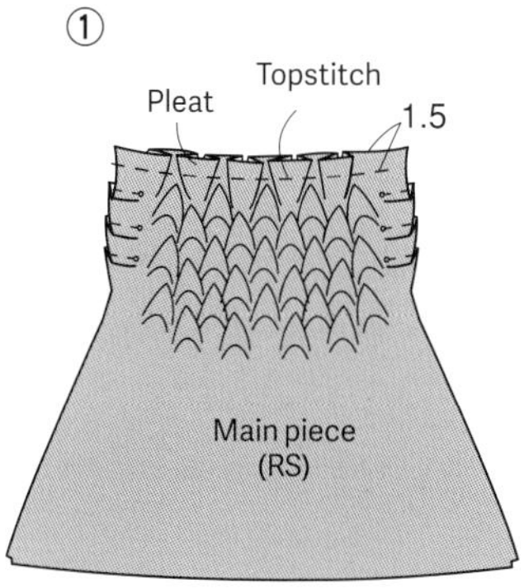

Stitch the smocking on the main piece.
Fold the pleats at the opening and topstitch.
Fold the pleats at the sides as well.

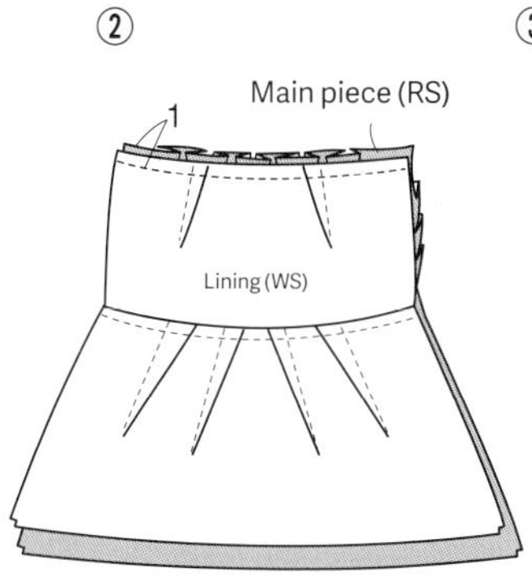

Place the main body and lining RS together and sew the opening. Press the seam allowance toward the lining.

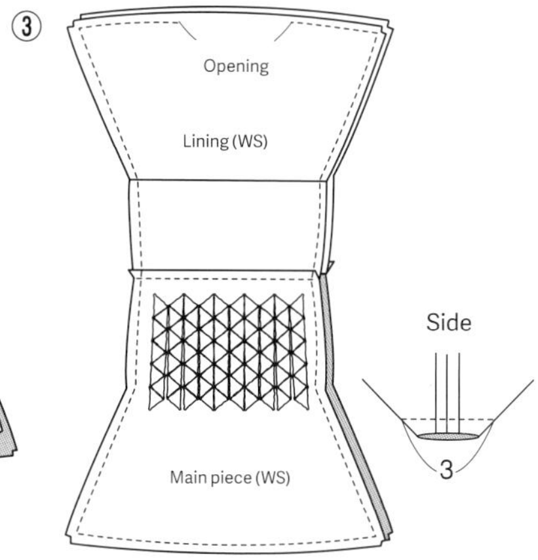

Place the two main body pieces and the two lining pieces RS together, leaving an opening, and sew around the edges. Sew the gusset. Press the seam allowances toward the main body for the outer piece and toward the lining for the lining piece.

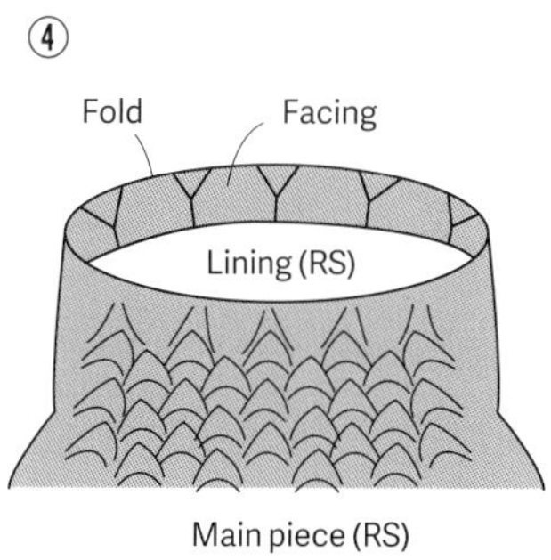

Turn RS out through the opening and close the opening with a ladder stitch. Fold the facing to the inside.

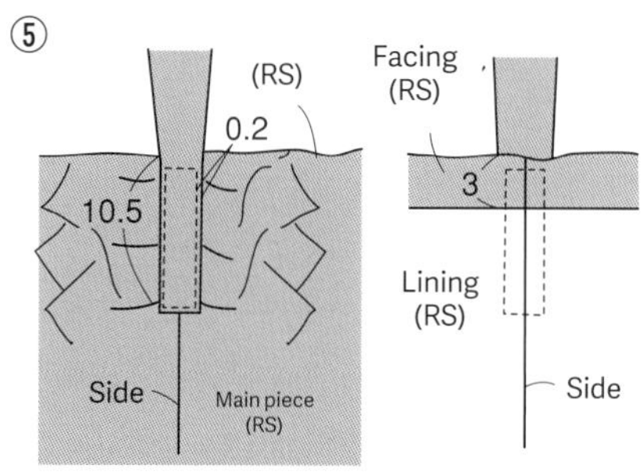

Attach the handles to both sides of the main body.

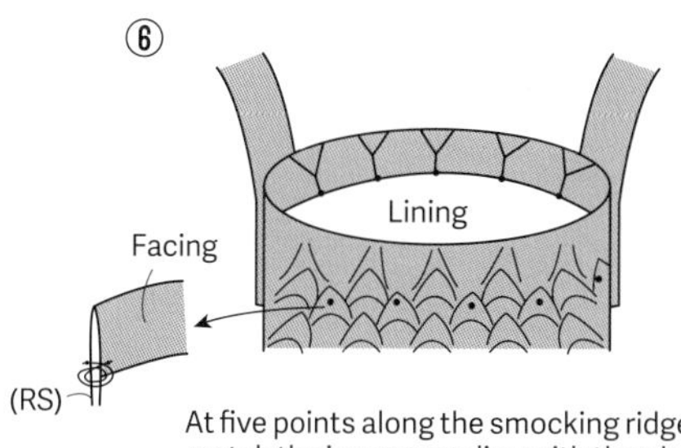

At five points along the smocking ridges, match the inner seam line with the pleat folds and stitch in place (make two stitches at each point).

P. 20 Brick and Bow Clutch

Finished Size: 11 × 18 × 4cm

■ Materials

- Main fabric (DARUMA FABRIC: Clay cotton, nylon gabardine): 60 × 50 cm
- Lining fabric (sheeting): 40 × 30 cm
- Flat knit zipper: 20 cm
- Seed beads (small round): 740 pieces

■ Notes

- After stitching the smocking, attach the zipper along the grid line.
- When sewing the side seams, fold the smocking back so it does not get caught in the stitching.
- Refer to page 66 for the Brick stitching instructions.

■ Instructions

1. Stitch the Brick smocking pattern on the main body, arrange the seam allowances, and sew the 10 pleats at the sides.
2. Attach the zipper to the opening of the main body.
3. Fold the main body in half RS together and sew the sides and gusset.
4. Sew the lining in the same way as the main body.
5. Insert the lining into the main body and slip stitch it to the zipper.
6. Secure the center of the Brick smocking to make Bows while threading the beads through as you sew.

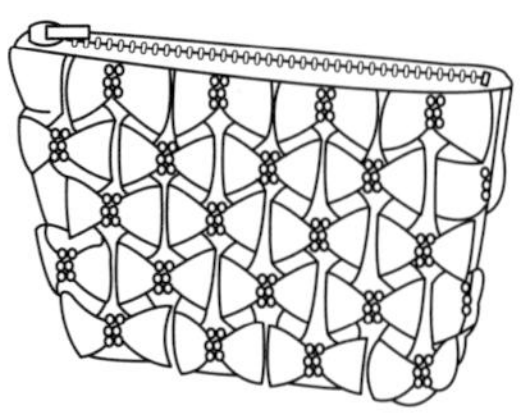

Main Piece (make 1)

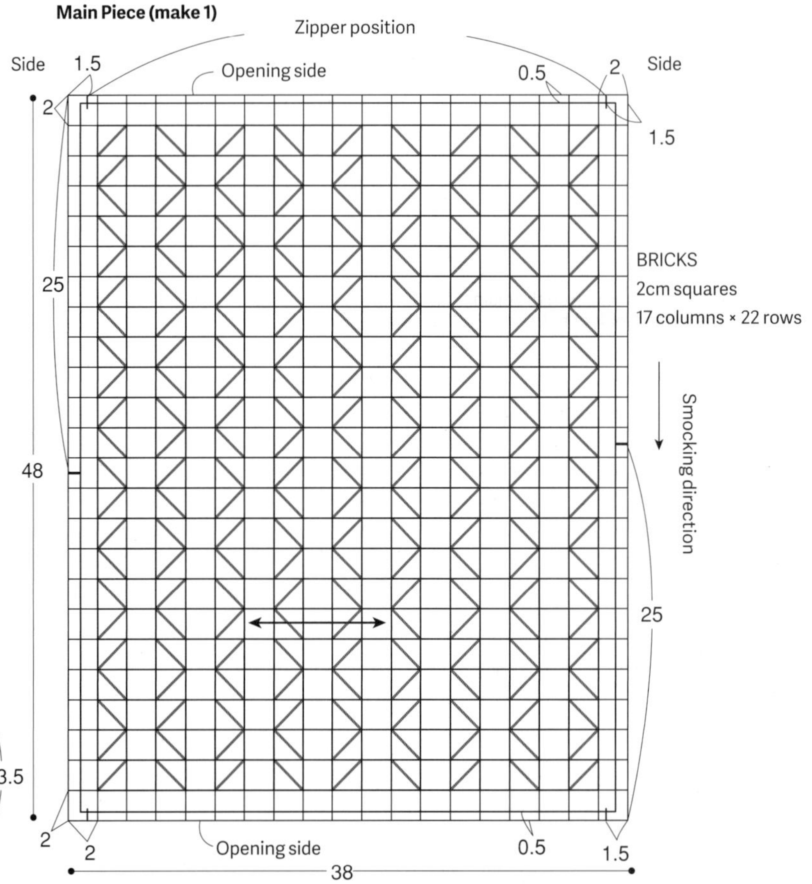

Lining (make 1)

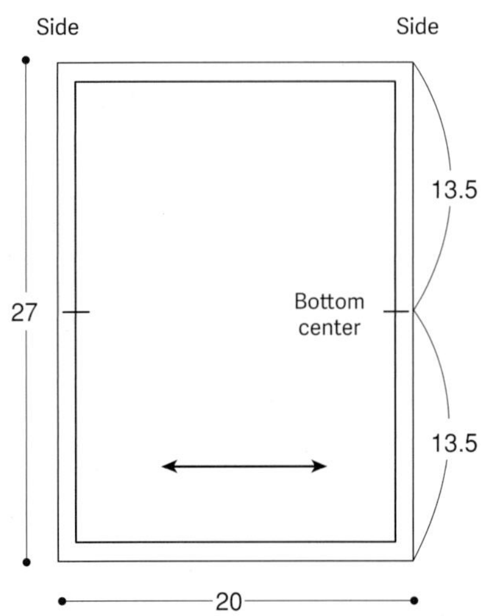

How to Make the Lining

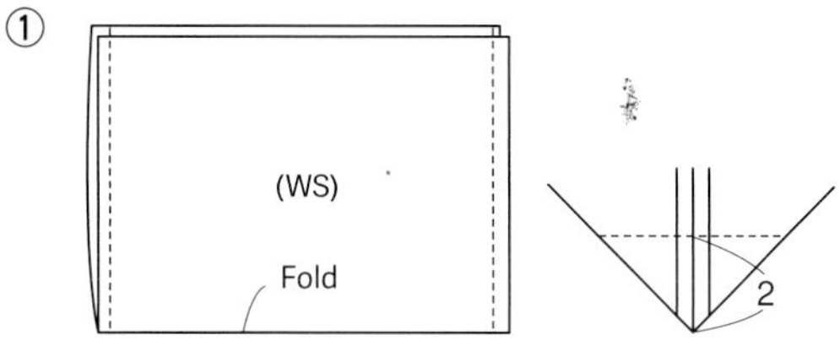

Fold the lining RS together, sew the sides, and sew the gusset.

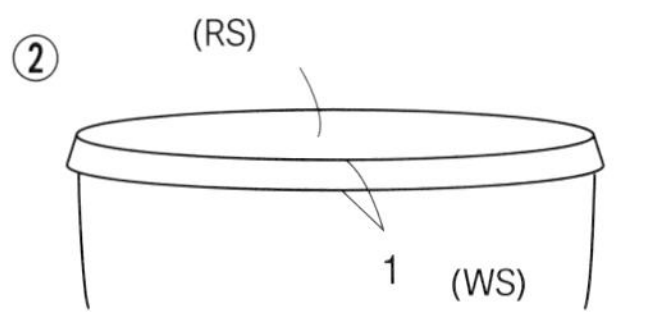

Fold the seam allowance at the opening.

Instructions

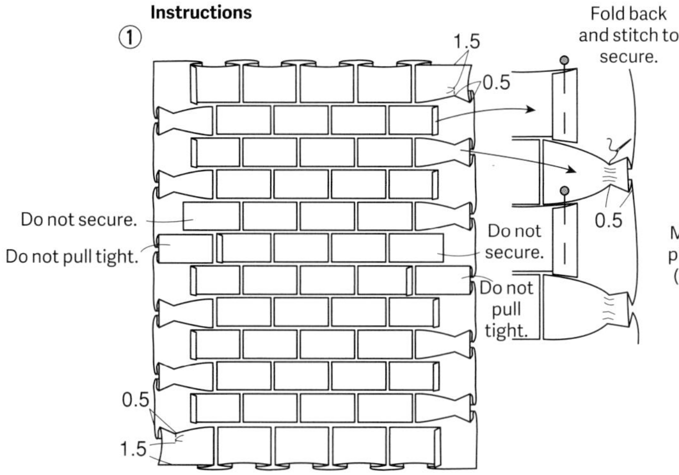

Stitch the smocking on the main piece and press with an iron. Gather the formed folds at both sides by stitching, and secure at 10 points.

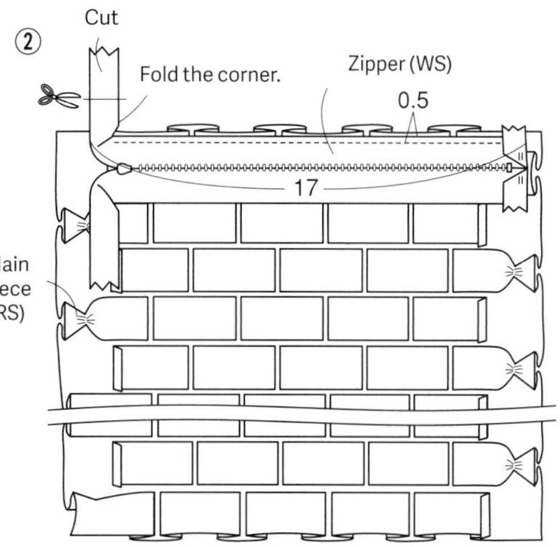

Place the zipper RS together with the opening of the main piece and sew. Sew the zipper to the opposite side of the opening in the same way.

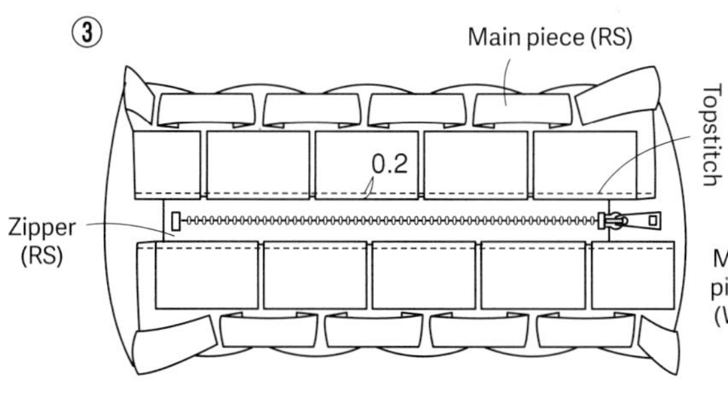

Press the seam allowances toward the main piece and topstitch from the RS to secure.

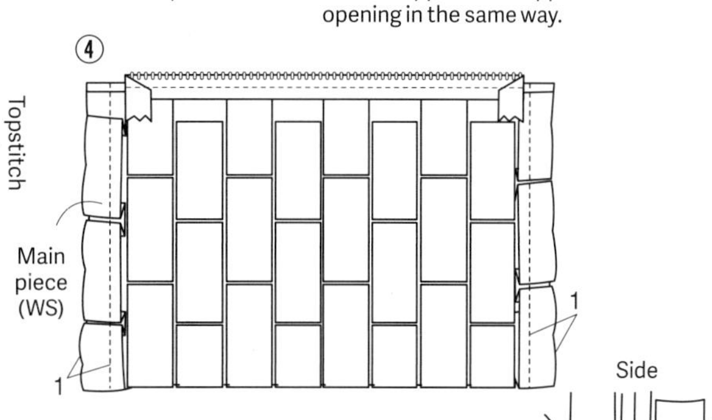

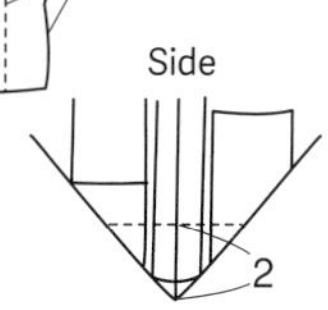

Fold the main piece RS together and sew both sides and the gusset.

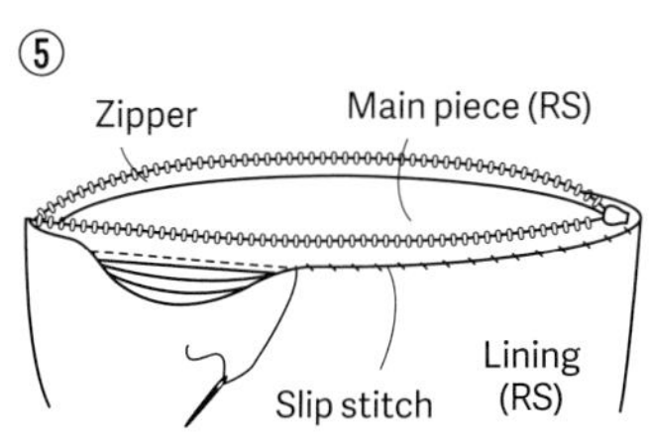

Slip stitch the lining to the zipper on the inside of the main piece.

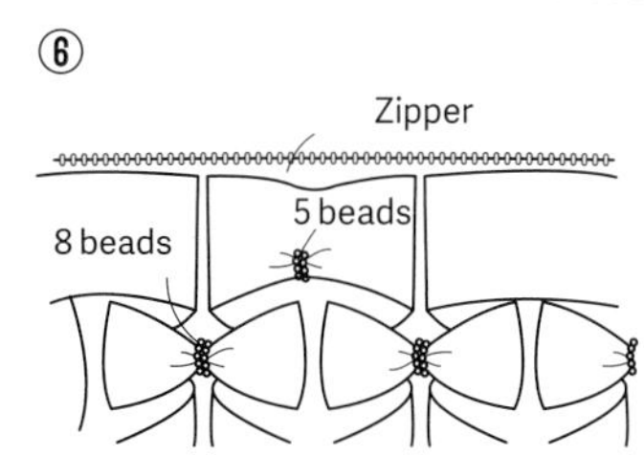

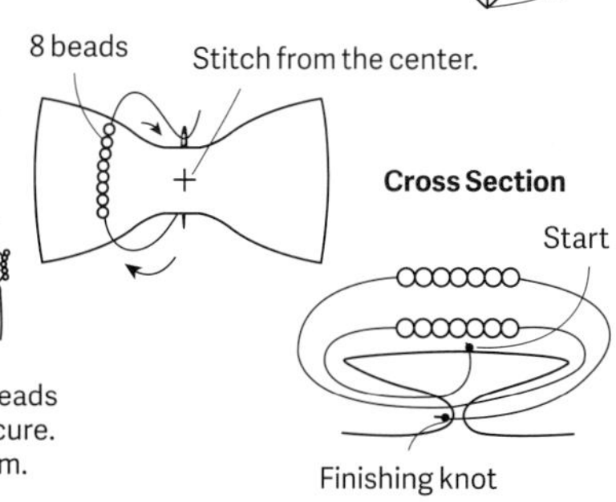

Pinch the center of each brick, thread beads through, pull to gather, and stitch to secure. Do not sew the two rows at the bottom.

P. 23 Lozenge Cushion

Finished Size: 40 × 40cm

■ Materials

- Main fabric (Artemondo: Tsumugi Cross) 150 × 60 cm
- Cushion insert: 40 × 40 cm

■ Notes

- The smocking uses a large grid, so do not carry the thread across; knot and cut the thread each time.
- Overlock (zigzag) stitch the entire perimeter of the front piece and three sides of the back piece (excluding the opening side).
- Refer to page 76 for the Lozenge stitching instructions.

■ Instructions

1. Overlock the edges of the front and back main pieces.
2. Stitch the Lozenge smocking pattern on the front piece and arrange the pleats. Leave one column unstitched on both sides and stitch it last.
3. Make two back pieces.
4. Place the front and back pieces RS together and sew around the edges.
5. Stitch the smocking on the remaining two ends, turn RS out, and shape neatly.

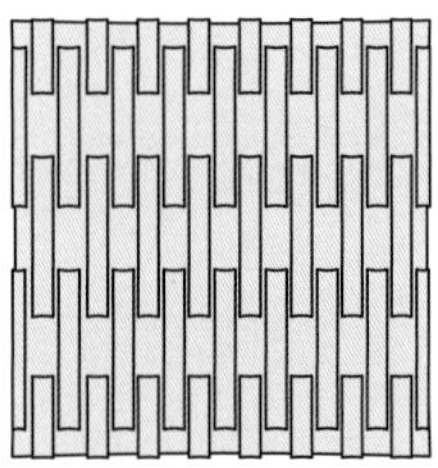

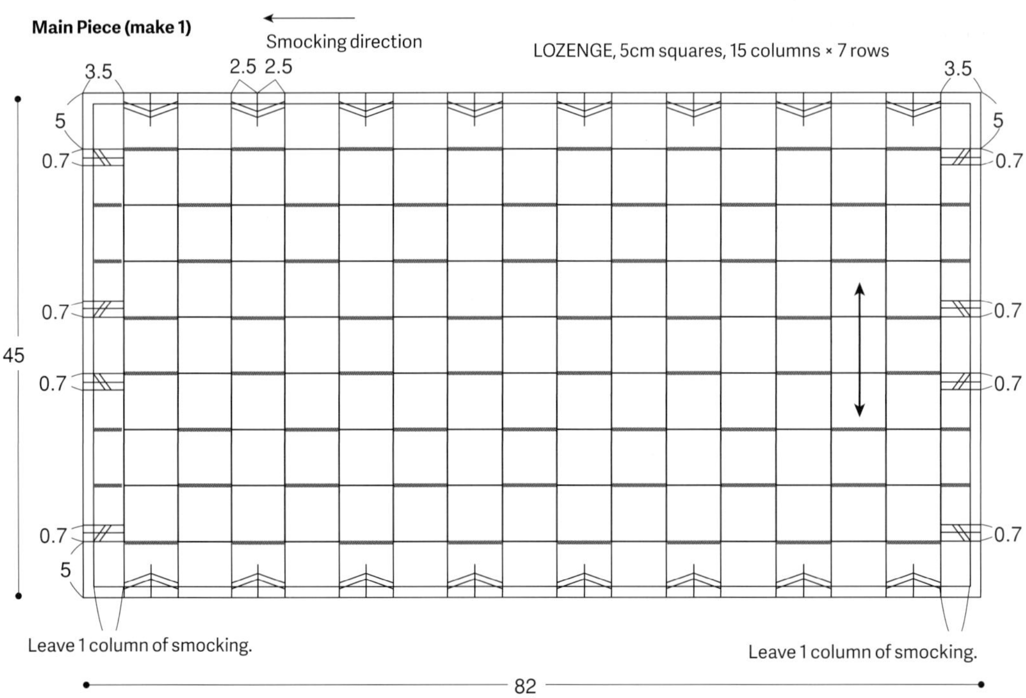

Back Main Pieces (make 2)

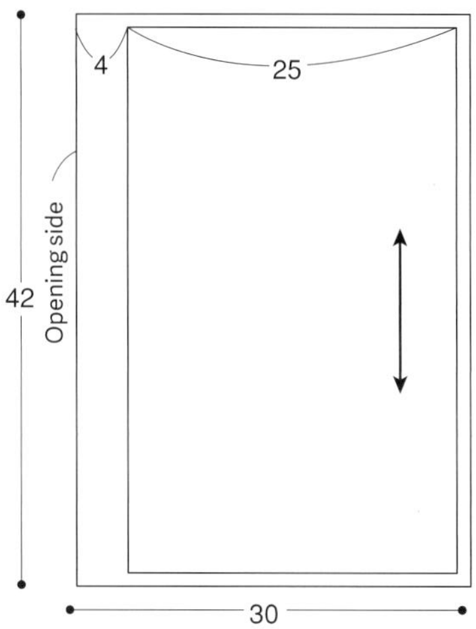

How to Make the Back of the Main Piece

①

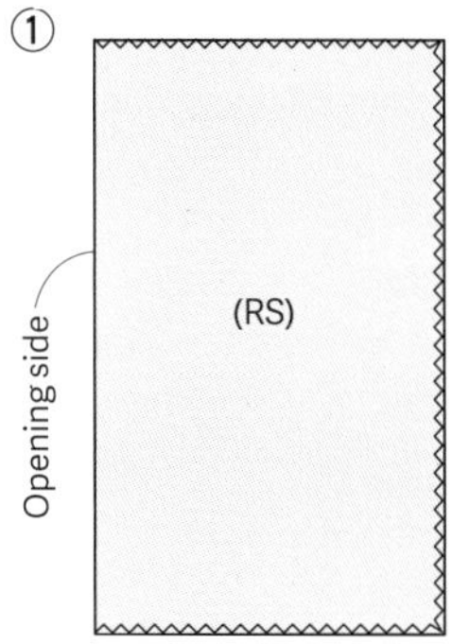

Finish three sides with a serger (zigzag stitch).

②

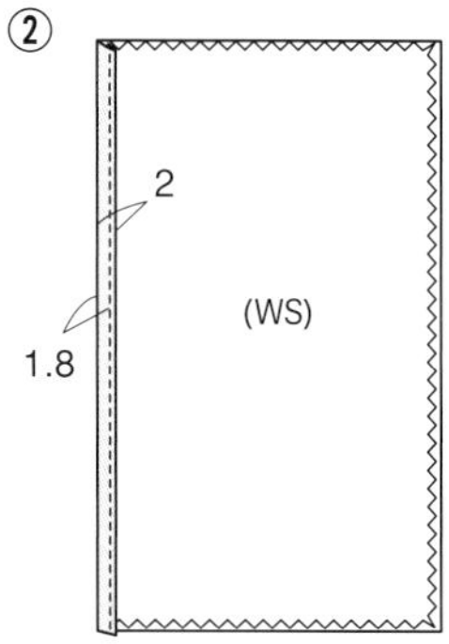

Fold the opening side into thirds (double-fold hem) and stitch.

Instructions

①

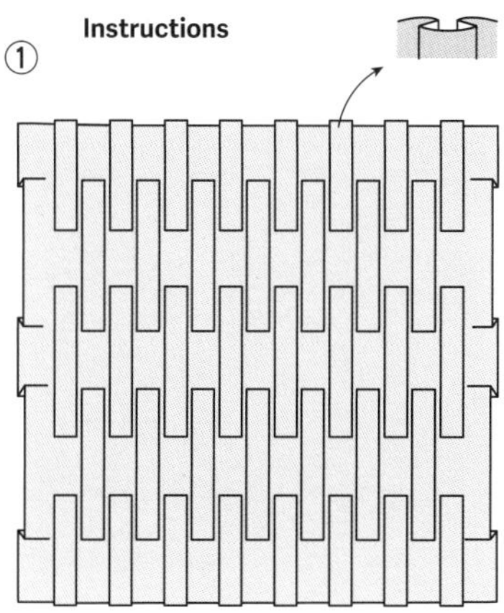

Stitch the smocking on the front main piece and form the pleats at the top, bottom, left, and right.

②

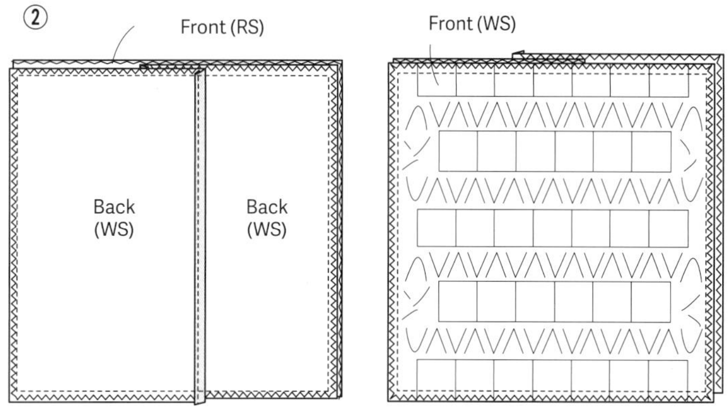

Place the front and back main pieces RS together and sew around the edges, starting from the front.

③

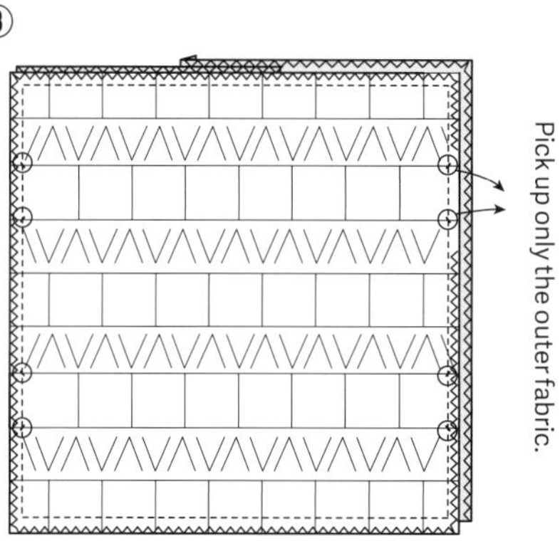

Stitch the smocking at the eight remaining points on both ends.

④

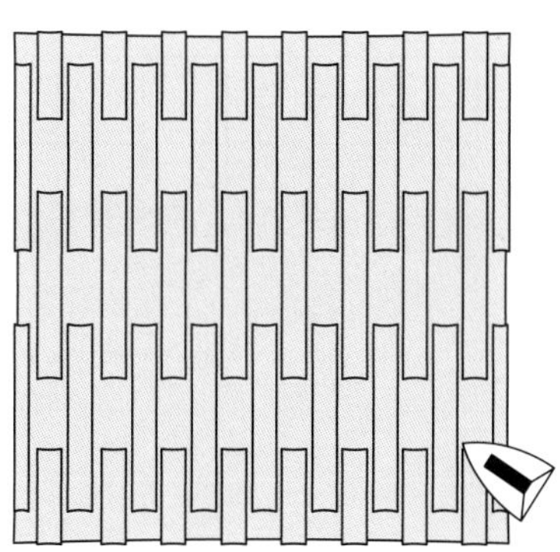

Turn to the RS and press both ends. Insert the pillow.

P. 25 Shell Circle Cushion

Finished Size: 40cm diameter × 15cm deep

■ Materials

- Main fabric (wool gauze): 90 × 180 cm (including covered buttons)
- Buttons: 2 pieces, 5 cm diameter
- Hand-sewing thread
- Heavy-weight thread
- Stuffing

■ Notes

- When gathering the top and bottom with running stitches, use four strands of thread, each 2 m long.
- Refer to page 54 for the Shell stitching instructions.

■ Instructions

1. Stitch the Shell smocking pattern. Leave four squares unstitched on each side.
2. Place RS together, leave an opening, and sew in a circle.
3. Press the seam allowances open, then stitch the remaining smocking sections.
4. Sew around the opening with running stitches and gather it up tightly.
5. Sew to secure the pleats, folding them consistently in one direction as you work.
6. Turn RS out and tighten the threads.
7. Make the covered buttons, sew them to the center of the main body, and close the opening with a slip stitch.

Covered Buttons (make 4)

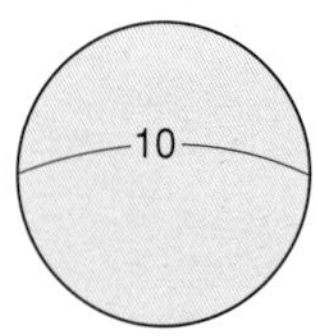

Cut on the straight grain.

How to Make the Covered Buttons

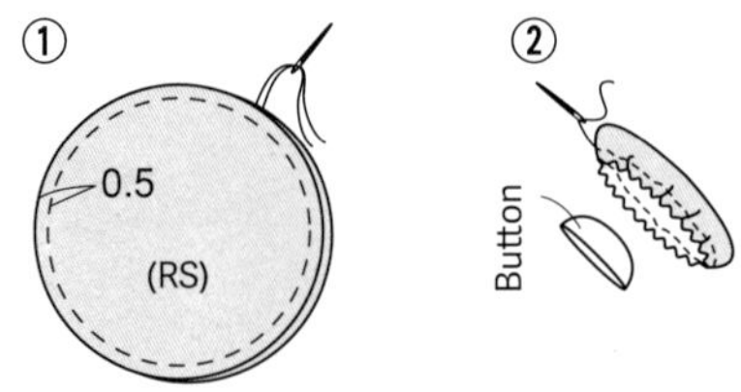

① Layer two pieces together and sew a running stitch around the edge.

② Wrap the fabric around the button form, pull the running stitch tight, and secure it.

Main Piece (make 1)

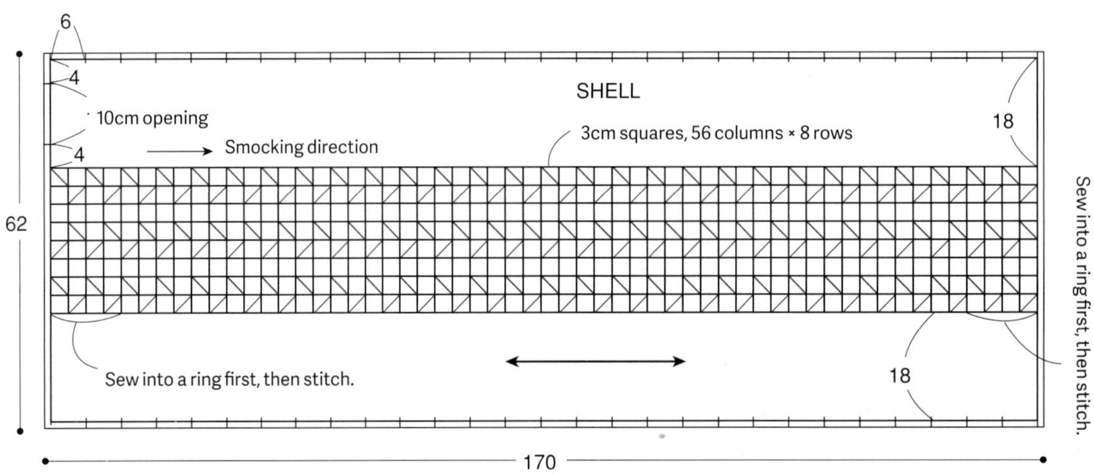

Instructions

①

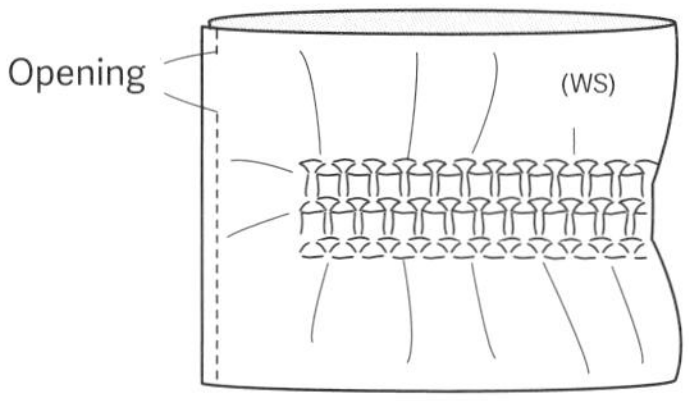

Fold in half with RS together and sew into a ring.

②

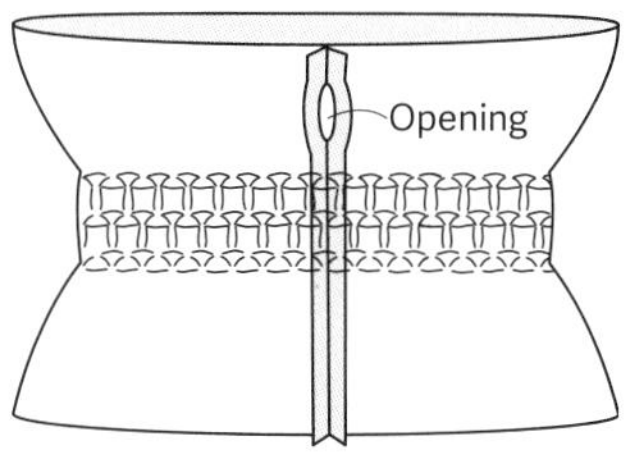

Press the seam allowances open, then stitch the remaining smocking sections.

③

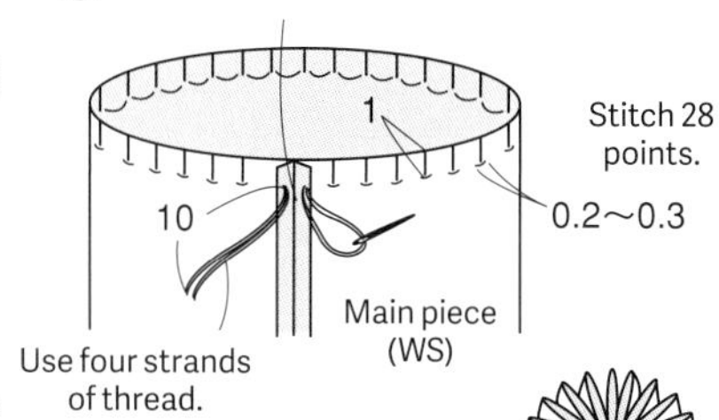

Start at the seam allowances. Using the markings as a guide, sew gathering stitches, pull tight, and adjust the formed folds before tying off the thread.

Tie off the remaining thread.

④

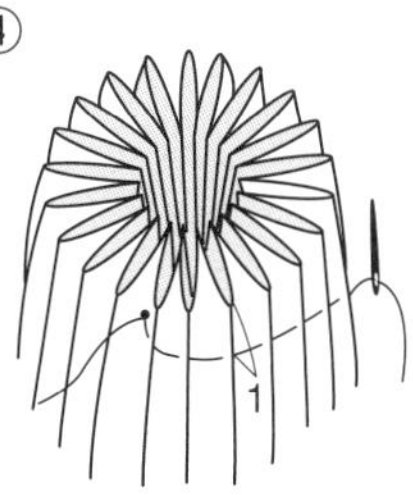

Pick up the outer edge of each of the 28 formed folds as you go around once. While keeping the folds all leaning in the same direction, pull tight and tie off the remaining thread.

⑤

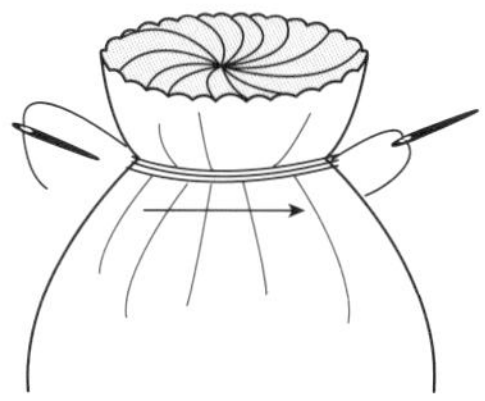

As in step ④, wrap the thread around and secure it with several stitches. Pull tight at both the top and bottom.

⑥

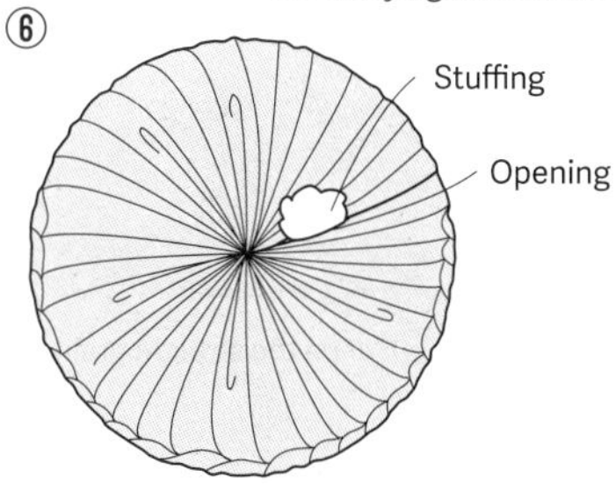

Turn RS out through the opening and stuff firmly.

⑦

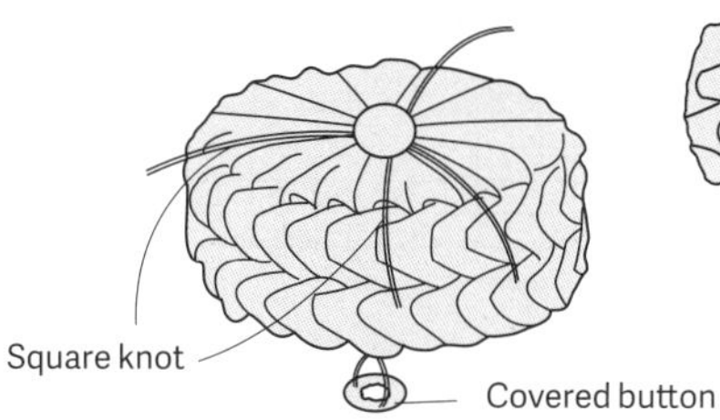

Pull thread through the center of the top and bottom of the main body and sew the covered button on, working the thread back and forth to secure. Tie off the remaining thread and close the opening with a slip stitch.

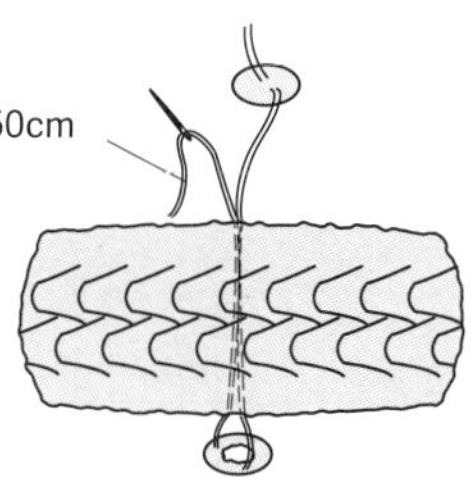

Prepare two sets of thread. Thread each through separately and tie a firm knot to secure.

P. 26 Flower Drawstring Bag

Finished Size: 23 × 22 × 20cm

■ Materials

- Main fabric (COSCLOTH: Frost Satin): 140 × 60 cm (includes handles and facing)
- Lining fabric (sheeting): 110 × 40 cm
- Medium-weight fusible interfacing: 100 × 10 cm
- Cord: 220 cm long, 0.3 cm diameter
- Beads: 107 pieces, 0.3 cm diameter

■ Notes

- In areas along the top edge of the smocking that are not continuous, do not carry the thread across; fasten off each time.
- Refer to page 94 for the Flower smocking instructions.

■ Instructions

1. Fold the main body in half RS together, and sew the sides and gussets.
2. Stitch the Flower smocking pattern on the main piece, threading beads as you sew.
3. Make the handles and facing.
4. With the main piece RS up, fold back the facing and sew it RS together.
5. Turn RS out and topstitch the opening.
6. Sew the main piece and lining RS together.
7. Turn RS out and close the opening with a ladder stitch.
8. Topstitch the opening and sew the cord casing.

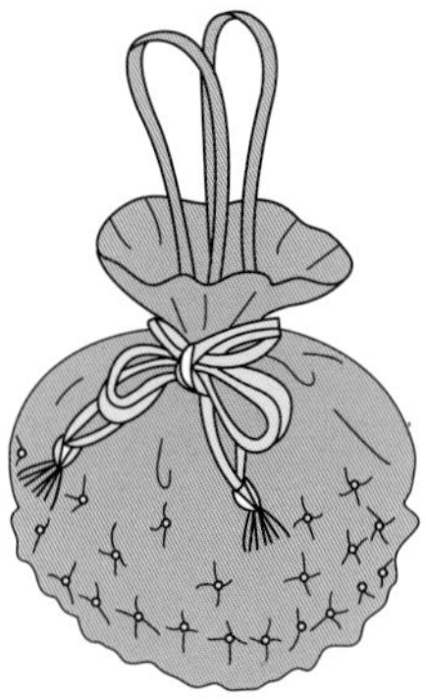

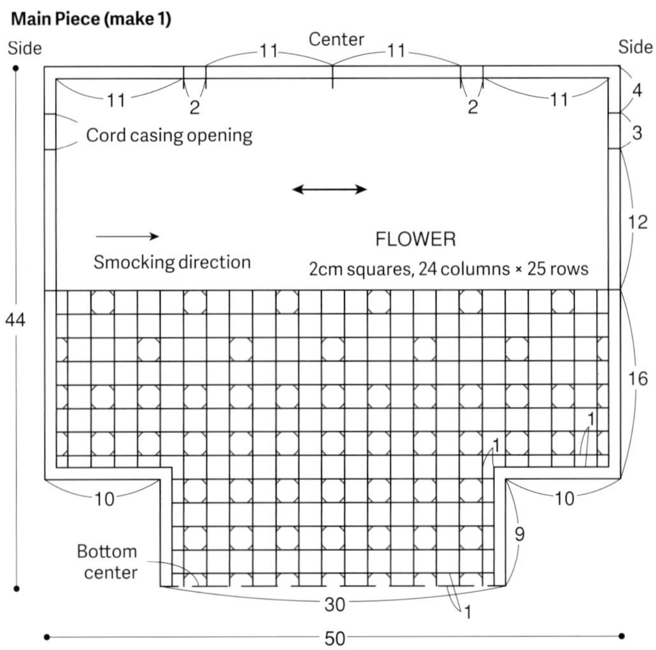

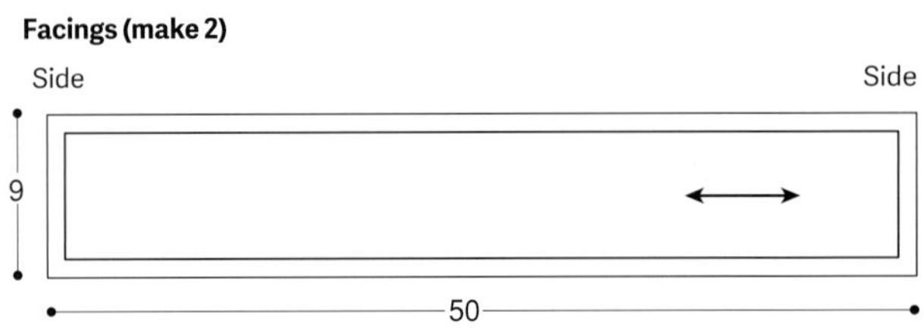

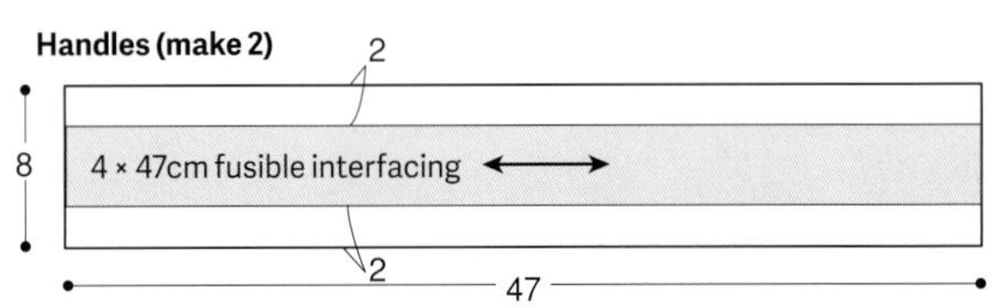

*Fuse the interfacing.

Lining (make 2)

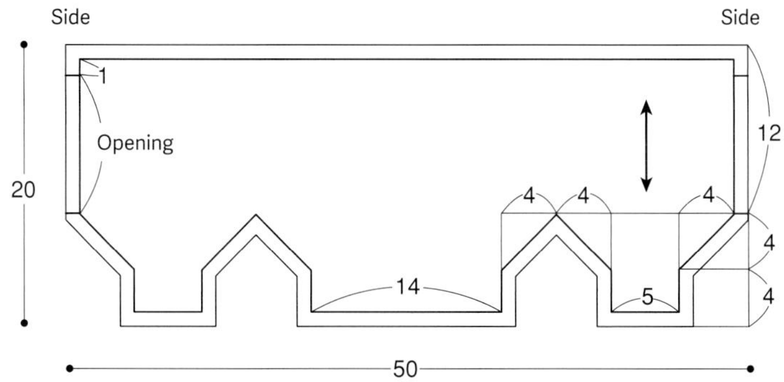

Bottom Lining (make 1)

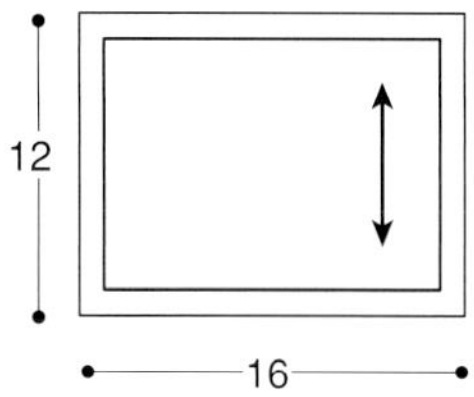

How to Make the Handle

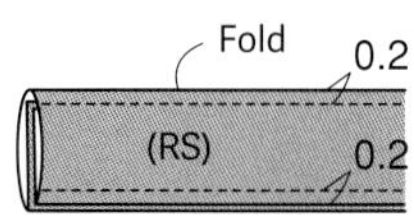

Fold four times and stitch.

How to Make the Facing

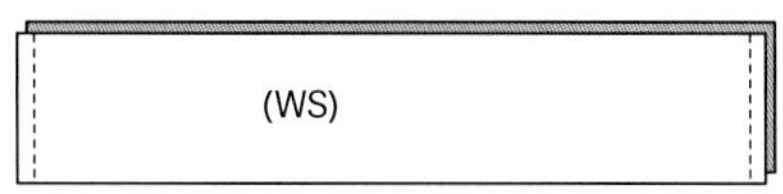

Place RS together and sew both long edges.

How to Make the Lining

①

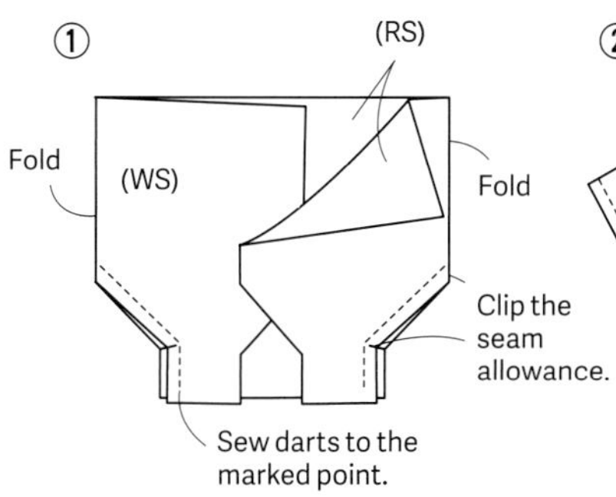

Fold both sides RS together and sew the darts.

Sew to the marked point without sewing into the seam allowance.

②

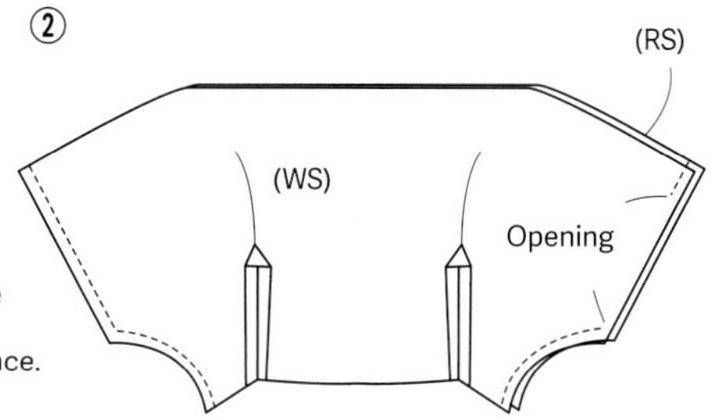

Place the two pieces RS together and sew both sides.

③

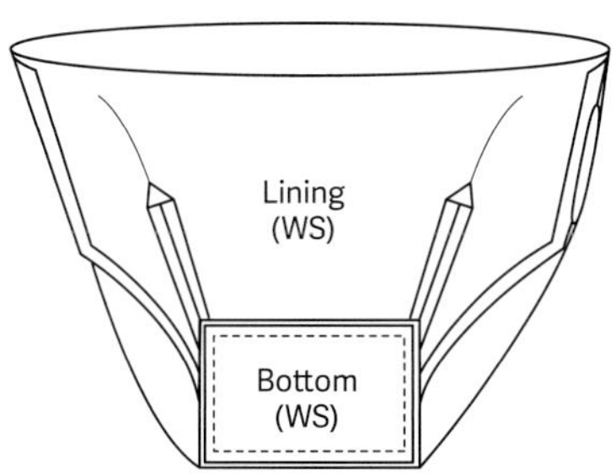

Place the lining and bottom lining RS together and sew. Press the seam allowances toward the bottom.

Instructions

①

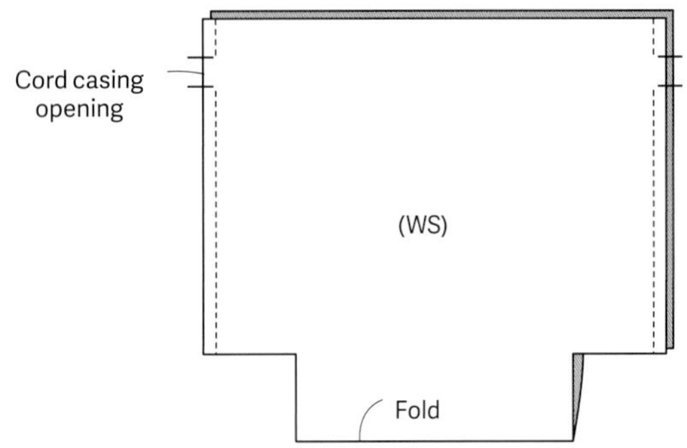

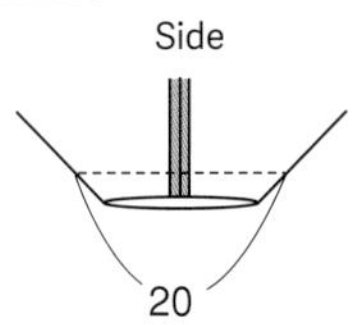

Fold the main body RS together, leaving the cord casing opening, and sew the sides and gussets. Press the seam allowances open.

②

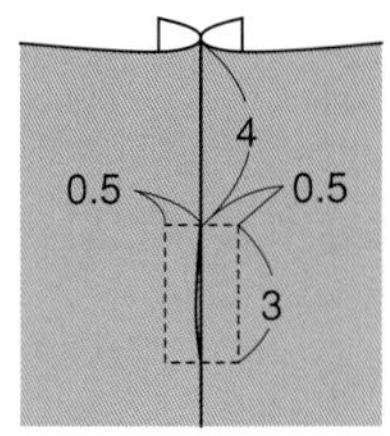

Topstitch the cord casing opening at the top and bottom.

③

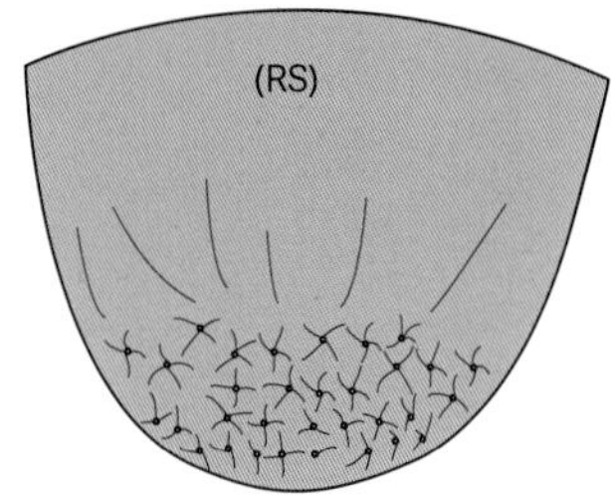

Stitch the smocking. On the RS, bring out and shape the flower petals.

④

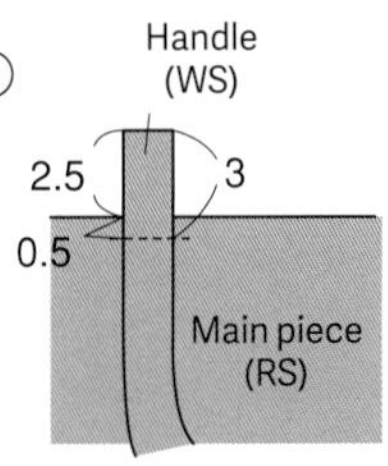

Baste the handles in place at the top edge of the main body.

⑤

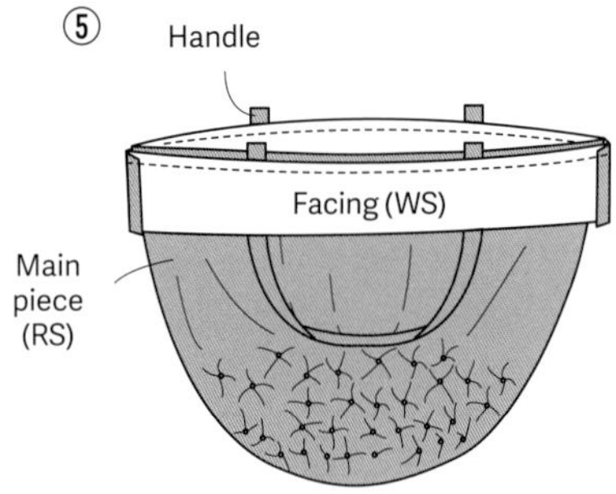

Place the facing RS down on the top edge and sew around the opening.

⑥

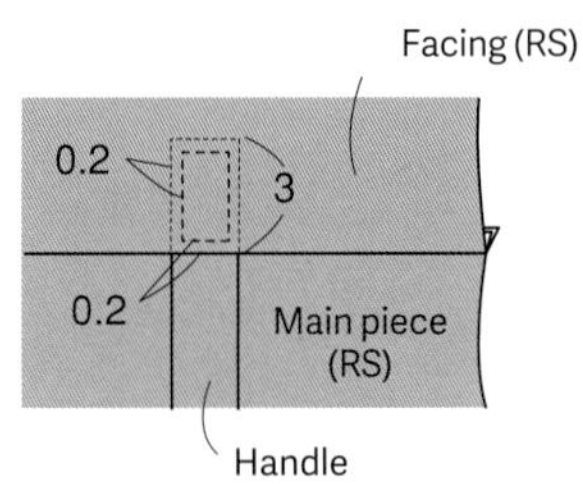

Turn the facing to the RS and sew it down, securing the handles in place.

⑦

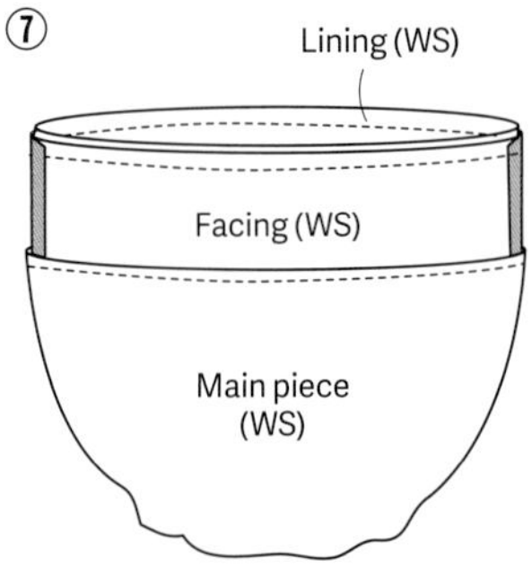

Place the main body and lining RS together and sew around the opening. Turn RS out and close the opening with a slip stitch.

⑧

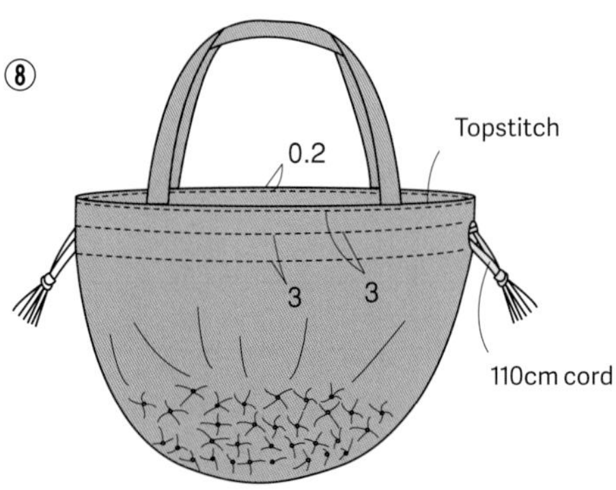

Topstitch around the opening and sew the cord casing closed. Thread the cord through from both sides.

P. 31 Heart Chain Clutch

Finished Size: 17 × 23 × 6cm

■ Materials

- Main fabric (Artemondo: Orpheus leather-look satin): 140 × 70 cm (including tabs and cord casing)
- Lining fabric (sheeting): 110 × 30 cm
- Woven fusible interfacing: 100 × 30 cm
- Bag base shaper: 22 × 6 cm
- Cord: 180 cm, 0.3 cm diameter
- Zipper: 40 cm
- D-rings: 2 pieces, 1.5 cm
- Lobster swivel clasps: 2 pieces, 3.1 cm
- Chain handles: 60 cm, 0.9 cm thick

■ Notes

- When attaching the bag base shaper, apply a thin layer of fabric glue before securing it.
- When sewing the bottom to the body, sew to the marking and clip into the seam allowance of the bottom, working gradually from the base and easing it into place.
- Refer to page 74 for the Heart stitching instructions.

■ Instructions

1. Stitch the Heart smocking pattern on the main piece.
2. Make the tabs and the cord casing.
3. Attach the zipper to the gusset, then sew the tabbed bottom to it.
4. Sew the cord casing onto the gusset.
5. With RS together, sew the body and the gusset together.
6. Make the inner pocket and attach the lining.
7. Secure the lining to the inside of the body.
8. Attach the chain.

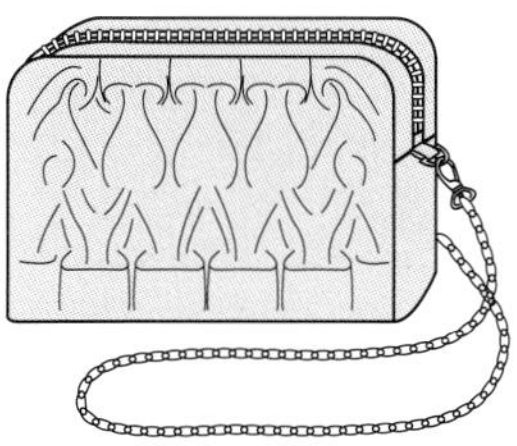

Back Main Piece (make 1), Lining (make 2)

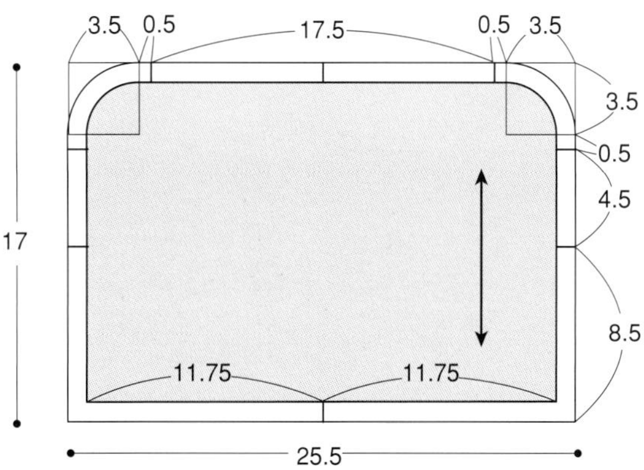

*Apply the fusible interfacing to the back of the main piece only.

Tabs (make 2)

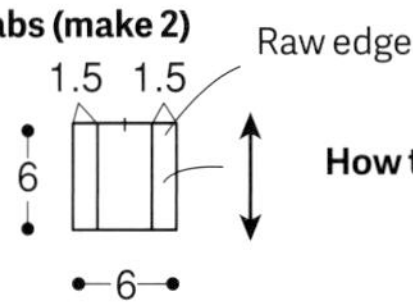

How to Make the Tab

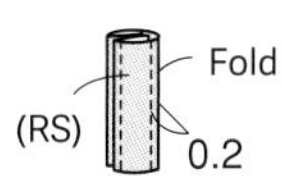

Fold the seam allowance, fold in half, and sew both ends.

Front of Main Piece (make 1)

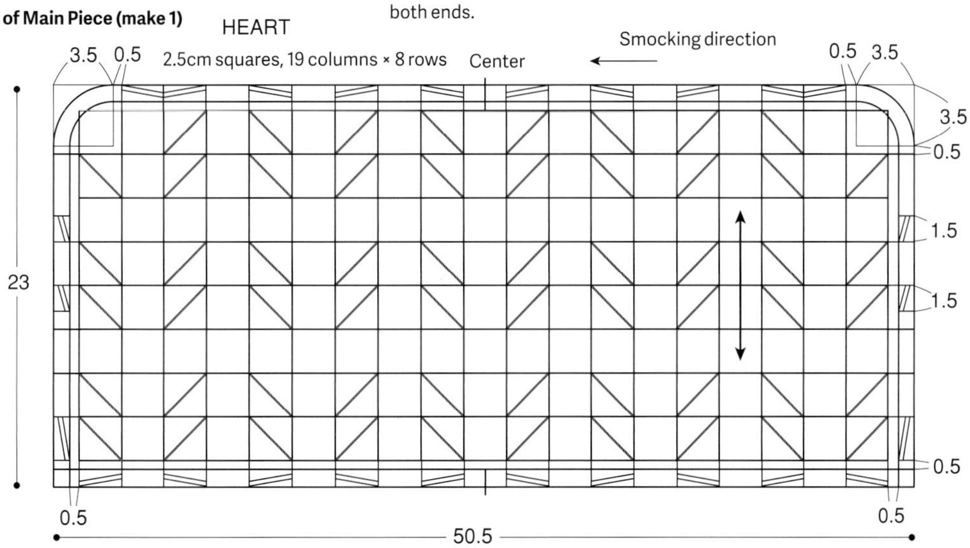

Cord Casing (make 2)

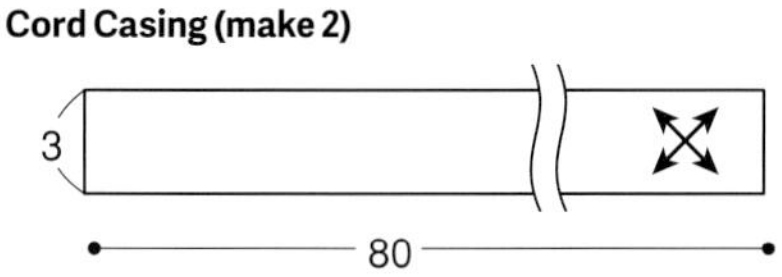

How to Make the Cord Casing

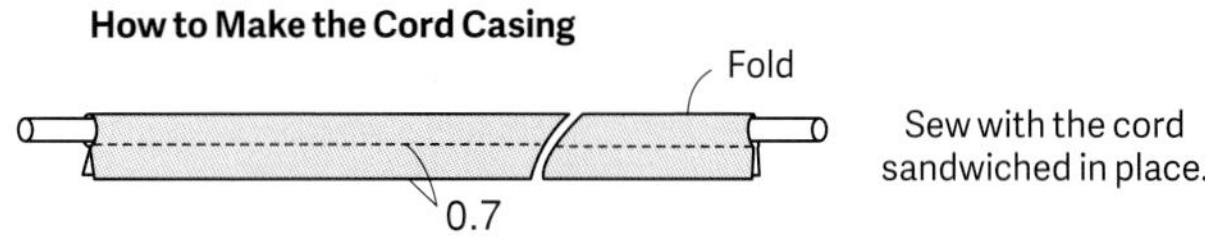

Main Zipper Gusset (make 2), Lining Zipper Gusset (make 2)

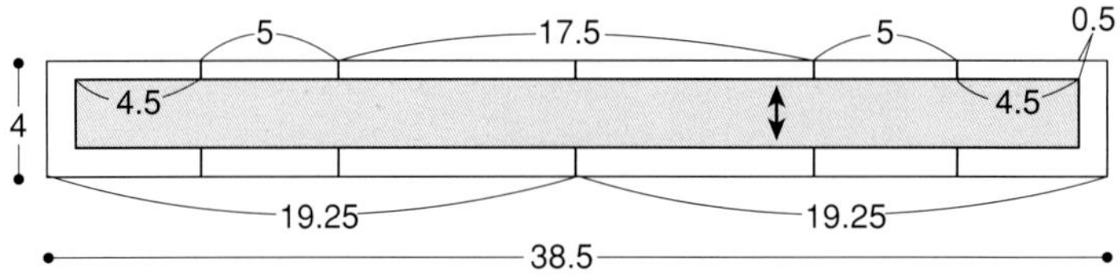

*Fuse the interfacing (raw edge) to to only the main zipper gusset.

Inner Pocket (make 1)

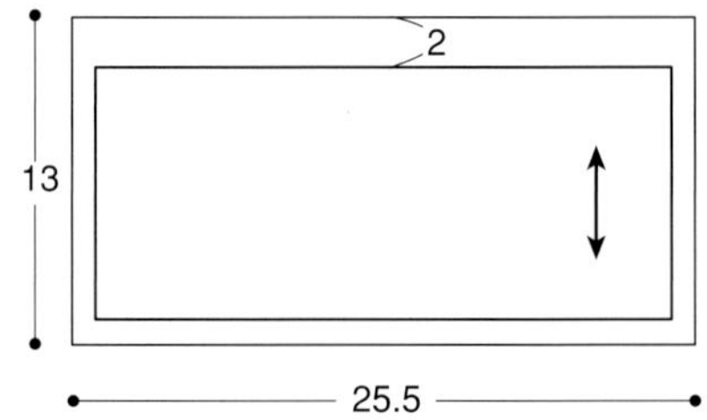

Main Piece Bottom (make 1), Lining Bottom (make 1)

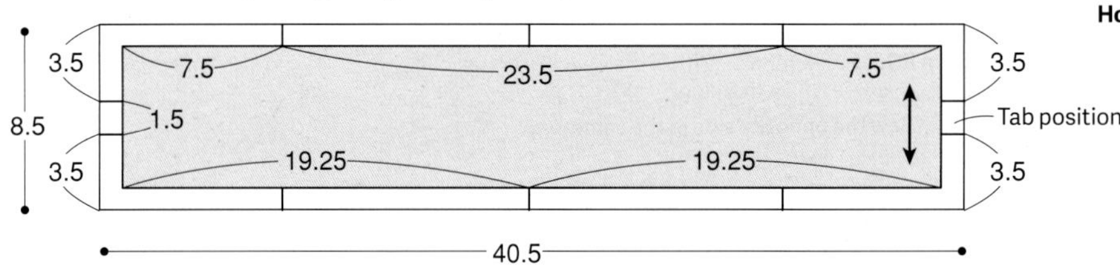

*Fuse the interfacing to only the main piece bottom.

How to Make the Inner Pocket

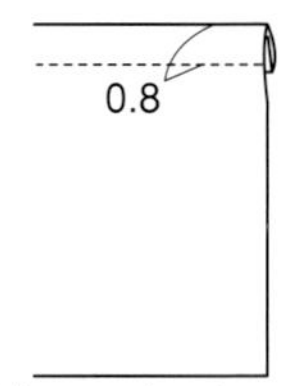

Fold the opening three times and stitch.

How to Make the Zipper Gusset

①

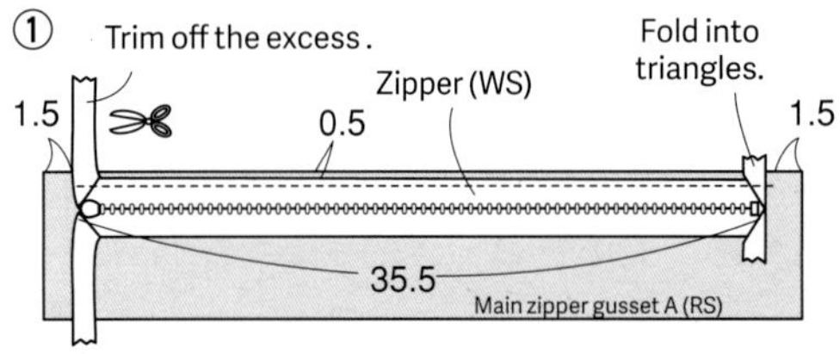

With the RS together, sew the zipper to the first main zipper gusset. Cut off the excess zipper fabric. Sew the other side to the second main zipper gusset.

②

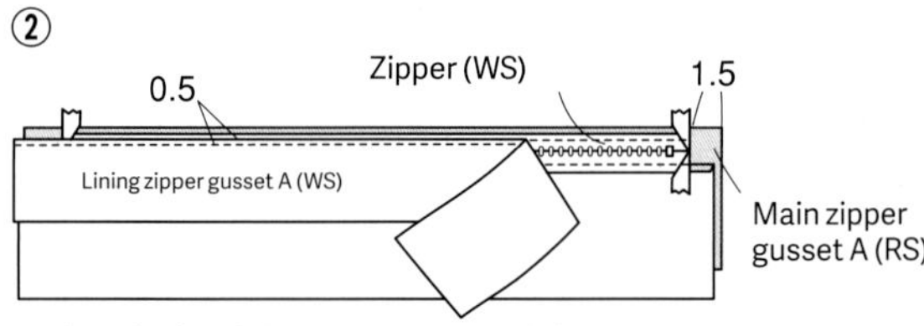

Place the first lining zipper gusset RS down on the second main zipper gusset and sandwich the zipper between them. Sew the opposite side.

③

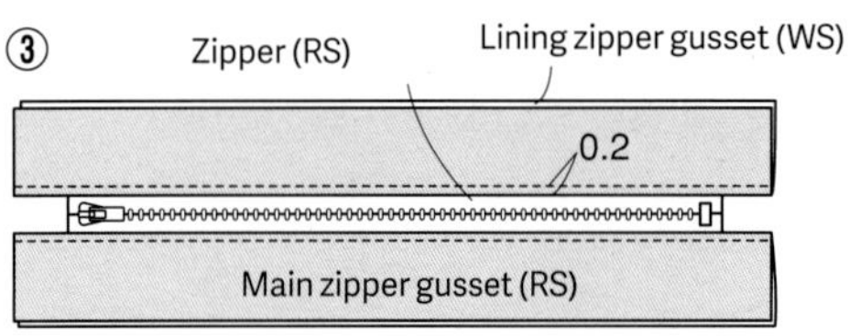

Turn RS out, press the seam allowance toward the lining zipper gusset, and secure with topstitching.

How to Fold the End of the Zipper

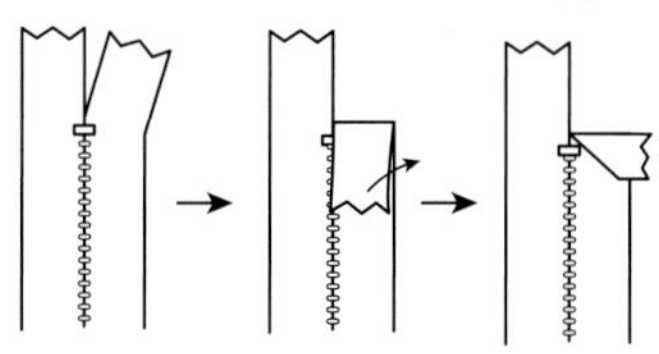

① **How to Make the Gusset**

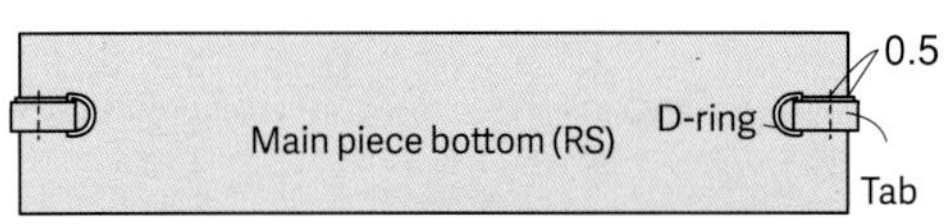

Baste the tabs with D-rings attached to both ends.

②

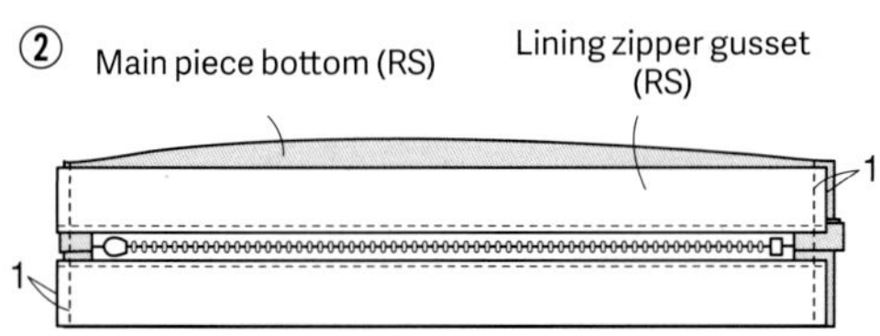

Place the zipper gusset and the main piece bottom RS together and sew the sides for a continuous round.

③

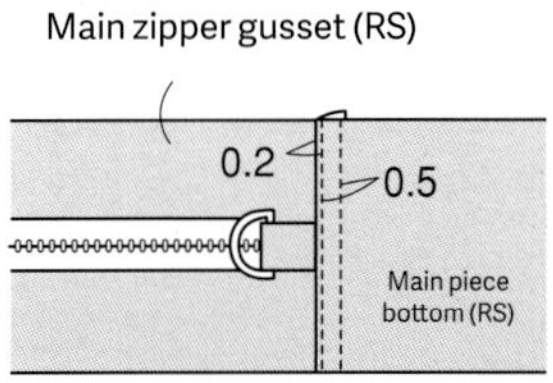

Turn RS out, press the seam allowance toward the main piece bottom, and secure with topstitching.

How to Make the Lining

①

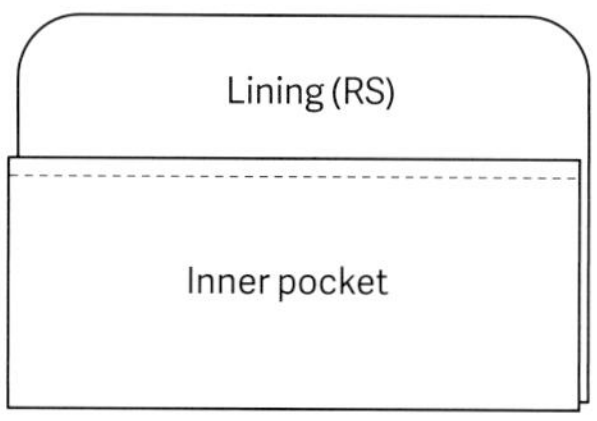

Layer the inner pocket onto the lining.

②

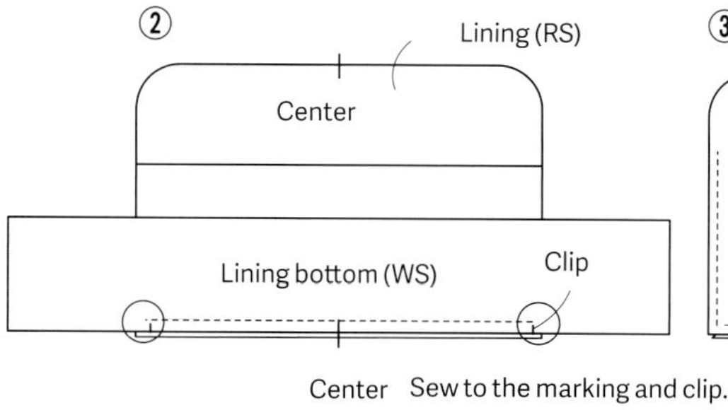

Align the centers of the lining and lining bottom, place them RS together, and sew from the opening to the marking.

Sew the opposite side in the same way.

③

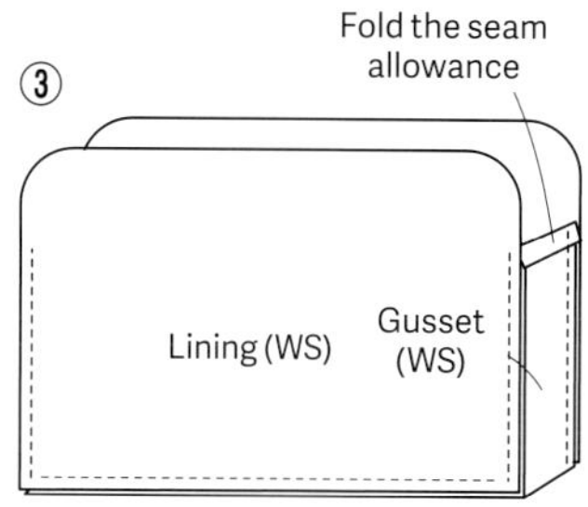

Join both ends of the gusset to the lining.

Instructions

①

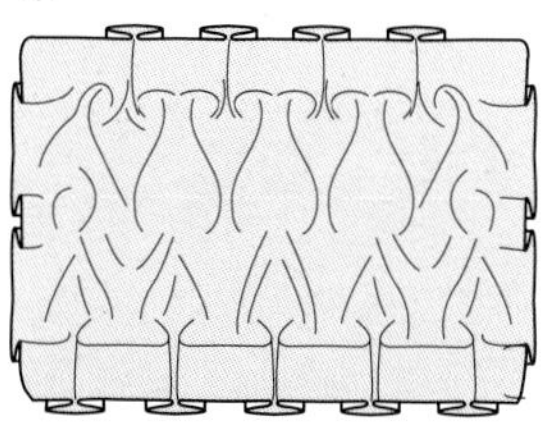

Smock the main piece front and arrange the surrounding pleats.

②

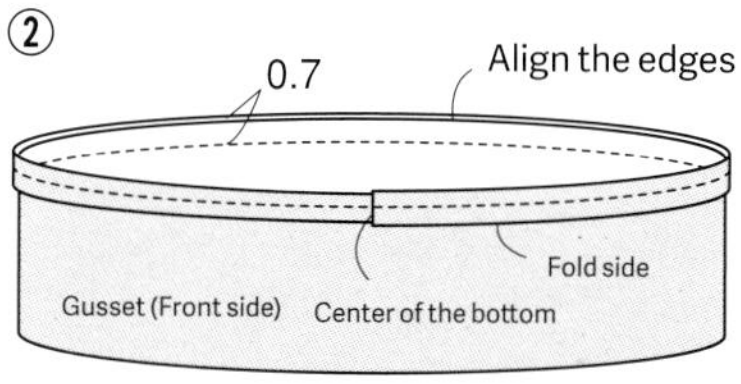

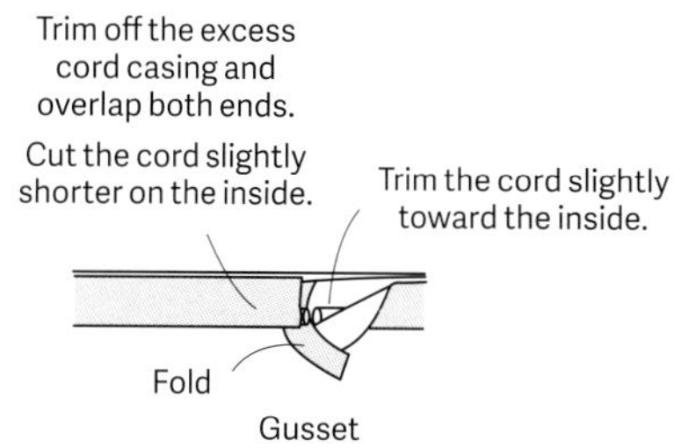

Attach cord casing to the gusset and sew in place.

Sew the opposite side in the same way

③

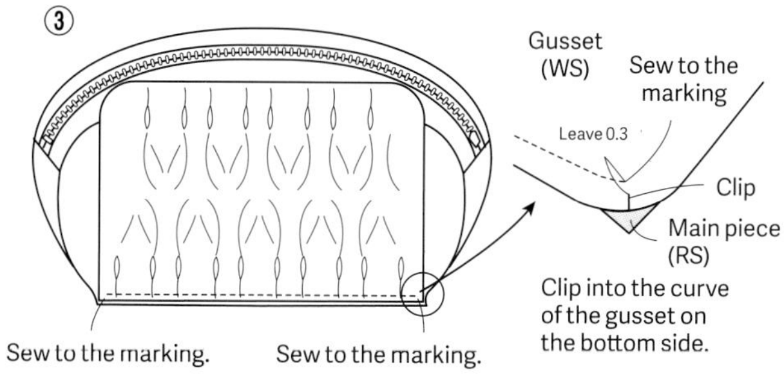

Clip into the curve of the gusset on the bottom side.

Align the main piece front and back with the gusset RS together and sew the bottom up to the markings.

④

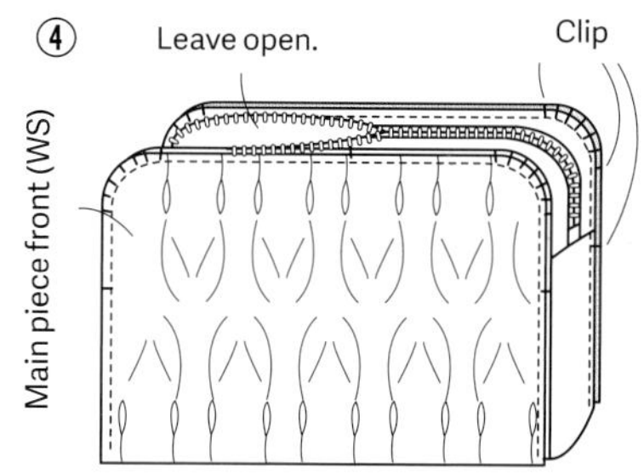

Sew the side seams, and in the same way, sew the zipper gusset section.

Clip into the seam allowance at the markings and at the curved corners.

⑤

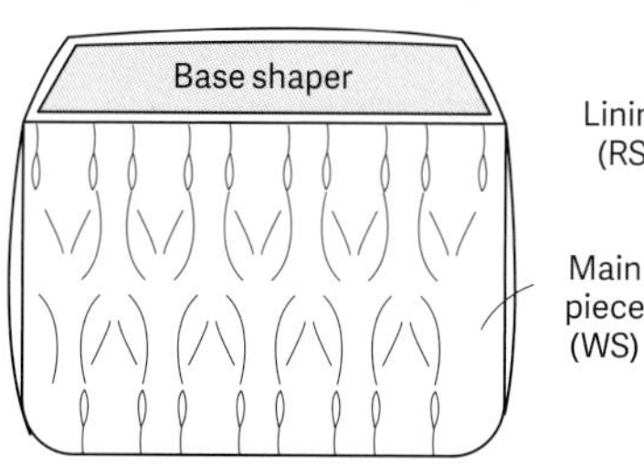

Apply a thin layer of glue to the bottom and attach the base shaper.

⑥

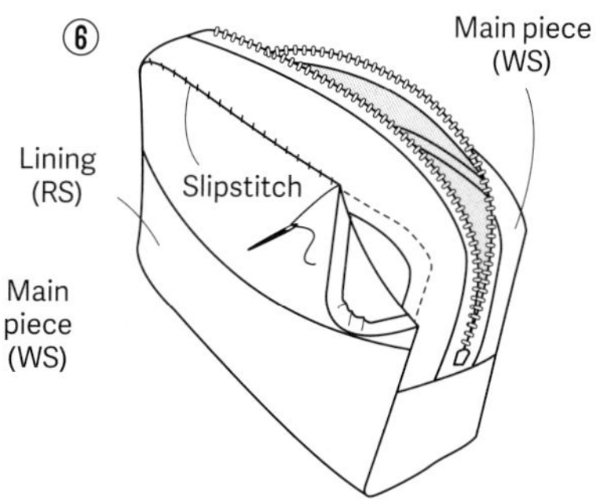

Place the lining inside the main piece with the seam allowances folded inward, and slip stitch it in place.

Photocopy at 100%

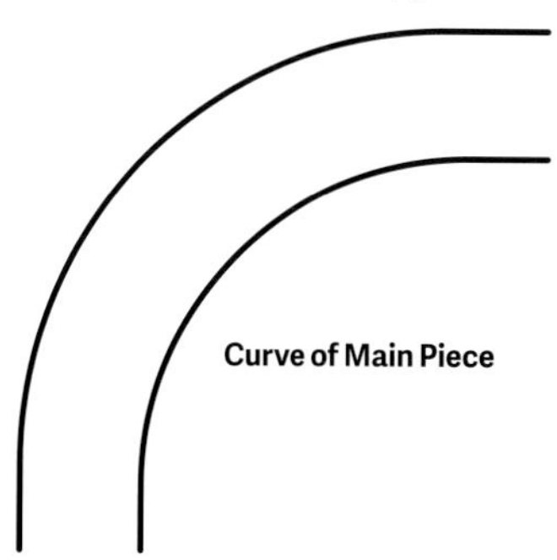

P. 29 Box Drawstring Pouch

Finished Size: 14 × 10 × 10cm

■ Materials

- Main fabric (Artemondo: Irish Cross Oxford cotton): 70 × 40 cm
- Lining fabric (sheeting): 50 × 30 cm
- Knit fusible interfacing: 50 × 20 cm
- Fusible interfacing: 10 × 10 cm
- Cord: 110 cm, 0.25 cm diameter
- Green round beads: 2 pieces, 0.8 cm
- Silver square beads: 2 pieces, 0.5 cm

■ Notes

- Use knit interfacing for the side sections of the main piece; use regular-weight interfacing for the bottom.
- Leave one column of smocking unstitched on both sides, then stitch the pieces together before completing the smocking.
- Refer to page 102 for the Box stitching instructions.

■ Instructions

1. Sew the four lining pieces together.
2. Place the main piece and the lining RS together and sew the opening.
3. Leave one column unstitched on both sides of the main piece and stitch the Box smocking pattern. Pull the threads and shape the piece, stopping at the marked points.
4. Fold the main piece RS together and sew, leaving both the opening and the cord casing openings unstitched.
5. Complete the remaining smocking and shape the pleats at the bottom of the main piece.
6. Place the main piece and lining RS together and sew.
7. Turn RS out and close the opening with a slip stitch or ladder stitch.
8. Sew the cord casing, thread the cord through, and attach the beads.

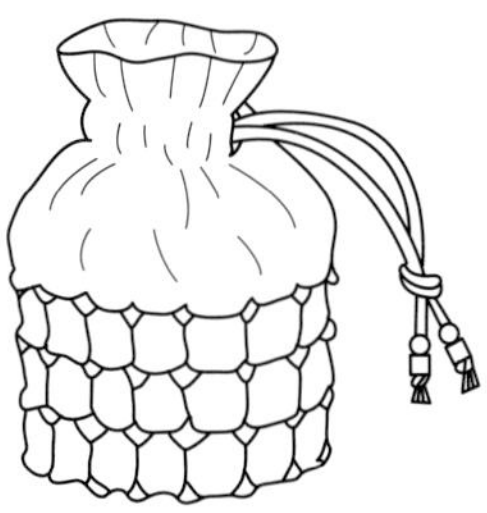

Photocopy at 100%

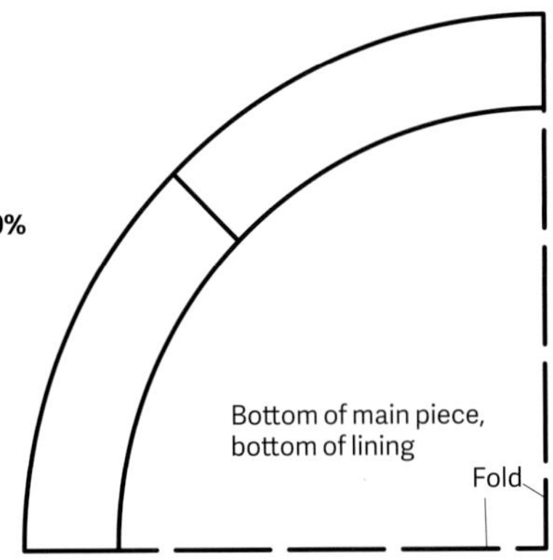

Main Piece (make 1)

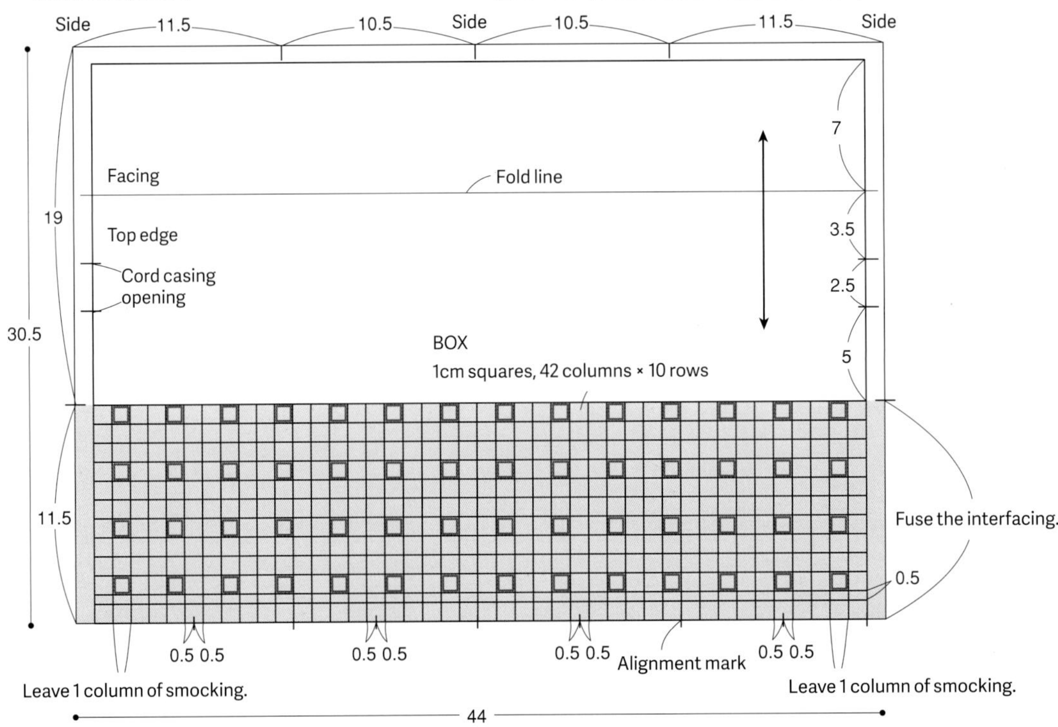

Lining (make 4)

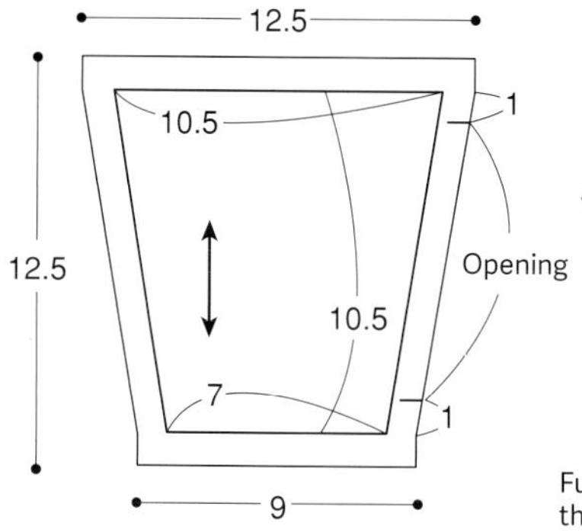

Main Piece Bottom (make 1), Lining Bottom (make 1)

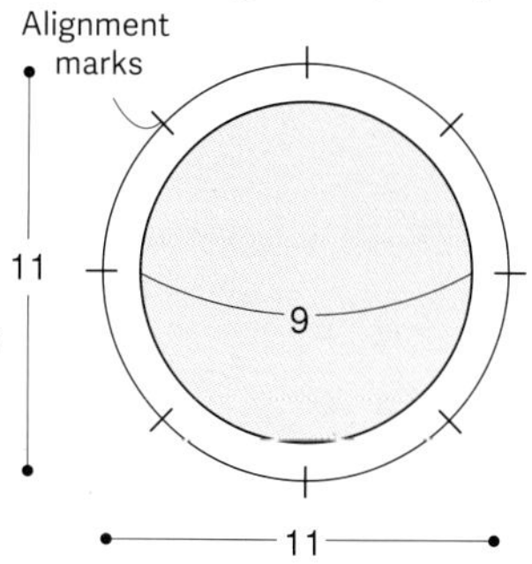

Fuse the interfacing to only the bottom of the main piece.

How to Make the Lining

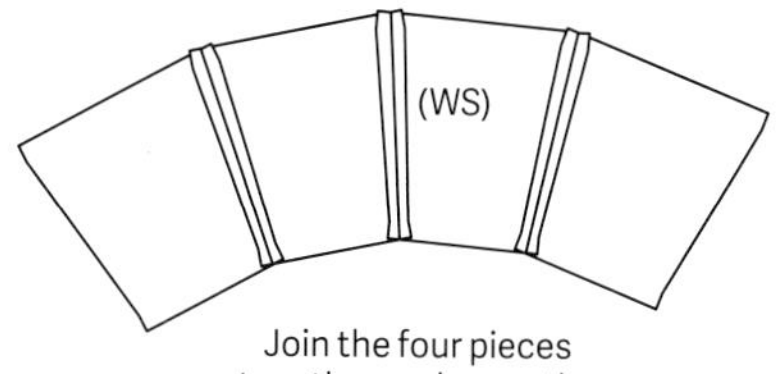

Join the four pieces together and press the seam allowances open.

How to Make the Bottom of the Bag

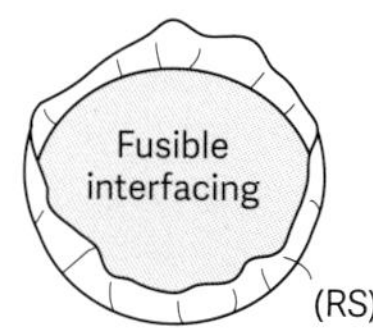

Fold the seam allowance.

Instructions

①

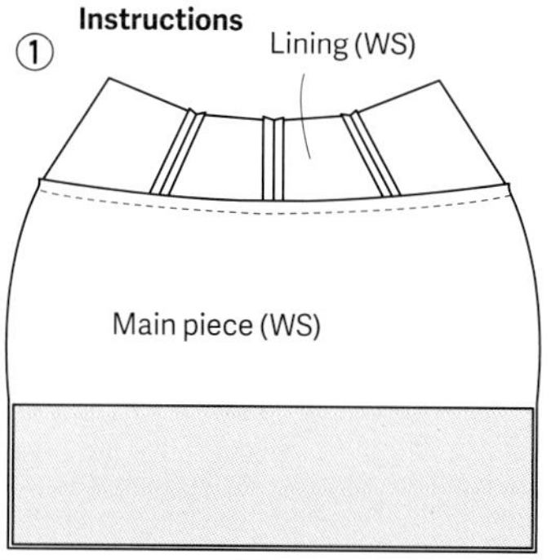

Sew the opening of the main piece and the lining together with RS facing.

Press the seam allowance toward the lining.

②

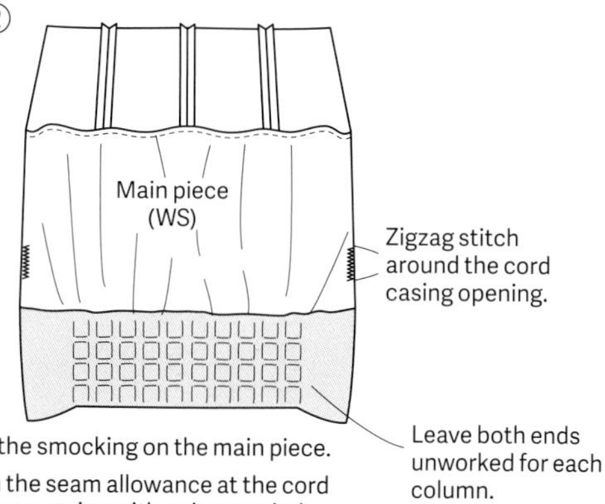

Work the smocking on the main piece.

Finish the seam allowance at the cord casing opening with a zigzag stitch.

Leave one column at each end unworked.

③

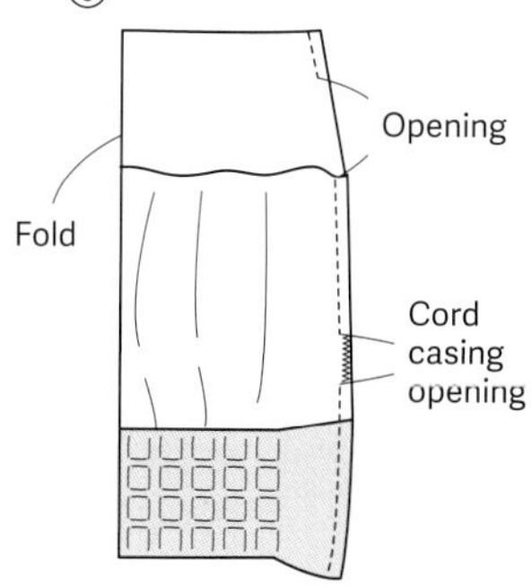

Fold in half with RS together, leaving the opening and the cord casing opening unstitched, and sew the side seams.

④

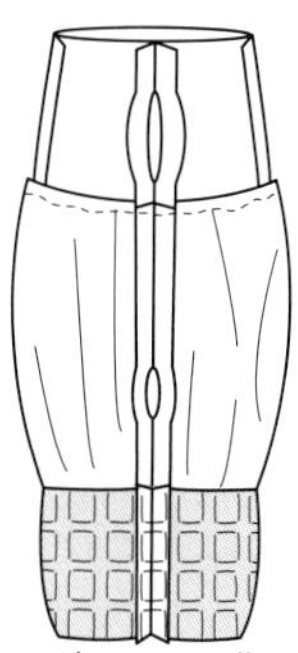

Press the seam allowances open and stitch the remaining two columns of smocking.

⑤

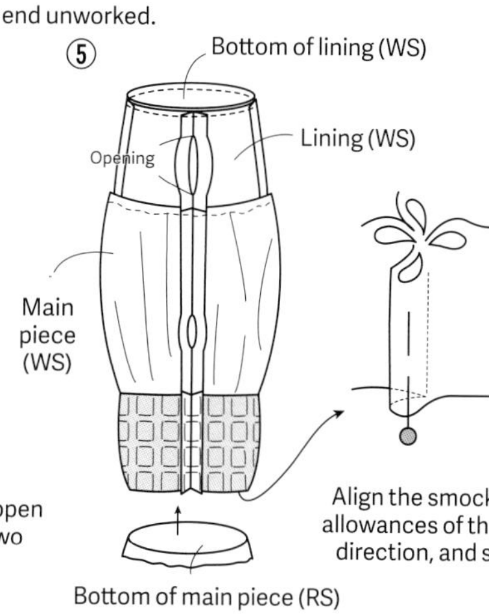

Align the smocking, press the seam allowances of the bottom toward one direction, and secure with basting.

Sew the main body to the main bottom, and the lining to the lining bottom, each with RS together.

Turn RS out through the opening.

⑥

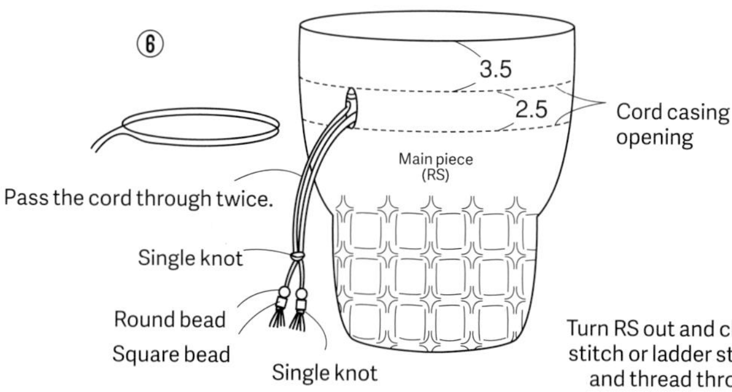

Turn RS out and close the opening with a slip stitch or ladder stitch. Make the cord casing and thread through the casing opening.

P. 32 Diamond Ruffle Pouch

Finished Size: 15.5 × 21cm

■ Materials

- Main fabric (Kiyohara: Sheeting Dot Print 5 mm / Gingham Check 6 mm): 110 × 40 cm each
- Lining fabric (sheeting): 110 × 20 cm
- Zipper: 20 cm
- Seed beads (size 6/0): 218 pieces

■ Notes

- Determine the dimensions of the main piece according to the size of the fabric print.
- After attaching the zipper to the opening of the main piece, trim off any excess.
- For the smocking, leave one outer round and stitch while adding beads; afterward, stitch the remaining round without beads. Finally, attach beads to that outer round.
- Refer to page 100 for the Diamond stitching instructions.
- For how to stitch the beads, refer to Flower instructions on page 96.

■ Instructions

1. Stitch the Diamond smocking pattern on the main piece.
2. Arrange the pleats and baste along the outside of the stitching lines.
3. Sew along the stitching lines.
4. Attach the zipper to the opening of the main piece.
5. Place the main piece RS together and sew around the frill.
6. Turn RS out and stitch around the frill and along the stitching lines.
7. Turn inside out and sew the sides and the bottom.
8. Turn RS out and attach.
9. Create the lining. Whipstitch it to the zipper on the inside of the main piece.

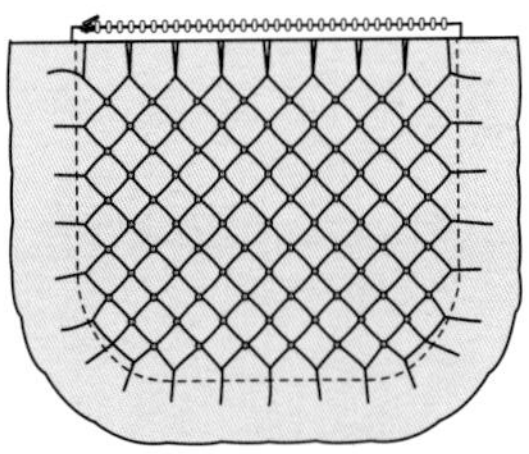

Main Piece with Polka Dots (make 2)

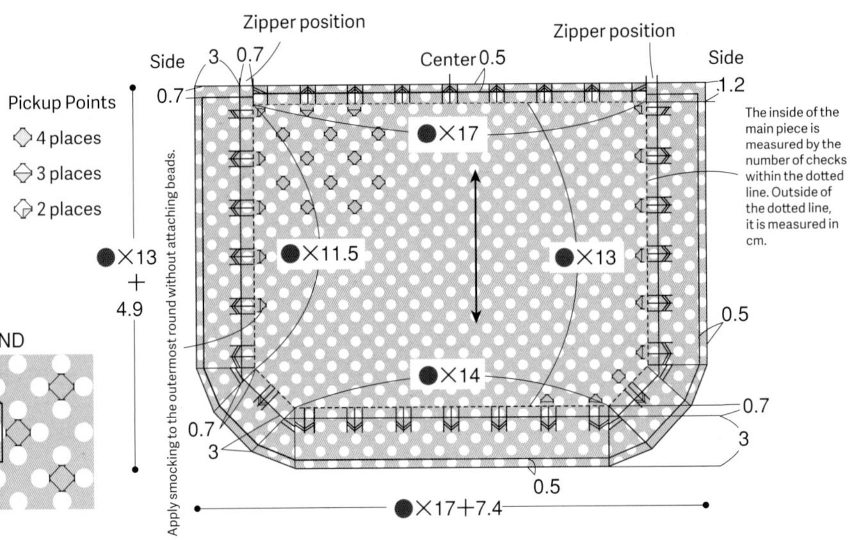

About the Drawing

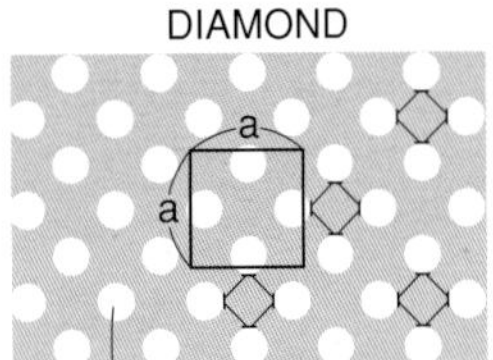

Count this ● as 1 polka dot.

Main Piece with Checks (make 2)

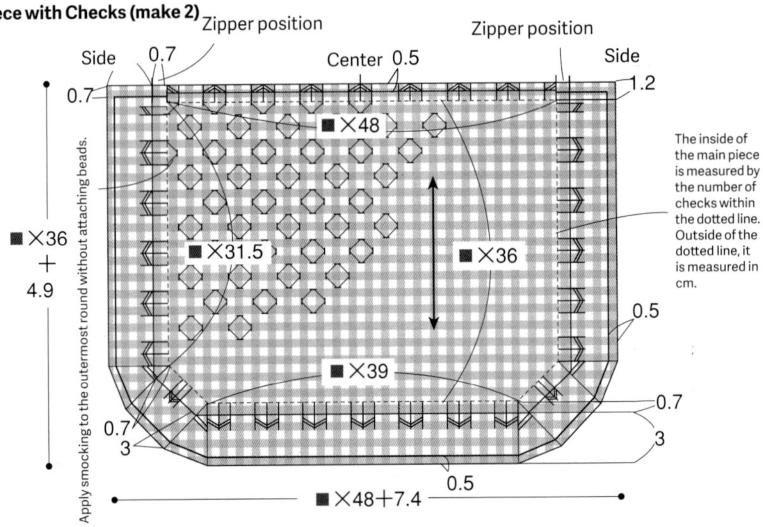

* Around 2cm is fine for a. In the project it is 1.9cm.

About the Drawing

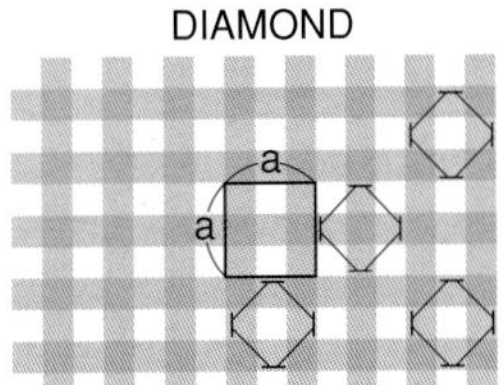

Count this ■ as 1 check.

Lining (make 2)

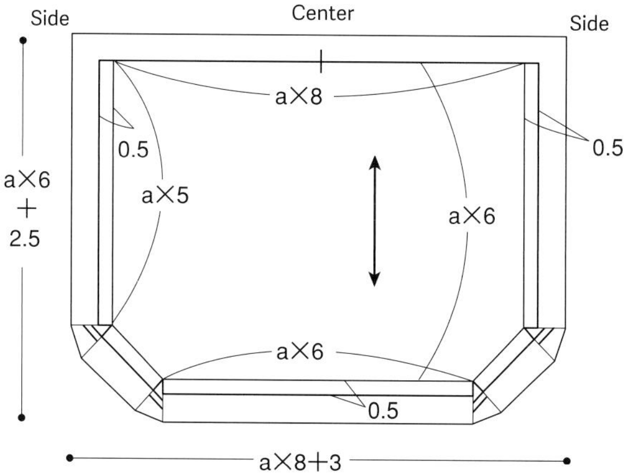

*For the lining, calculate a from the size of the fabric.

How to Make the Lining

① 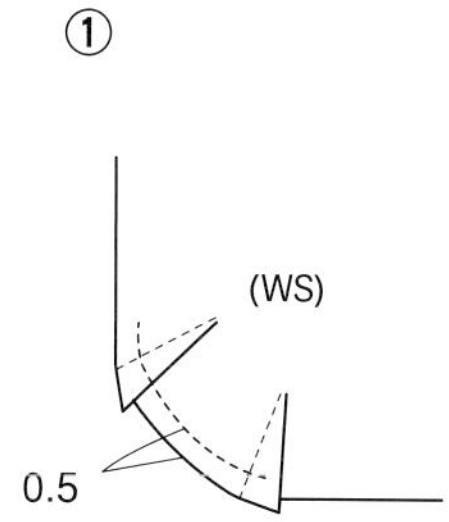

Sew darts.

② 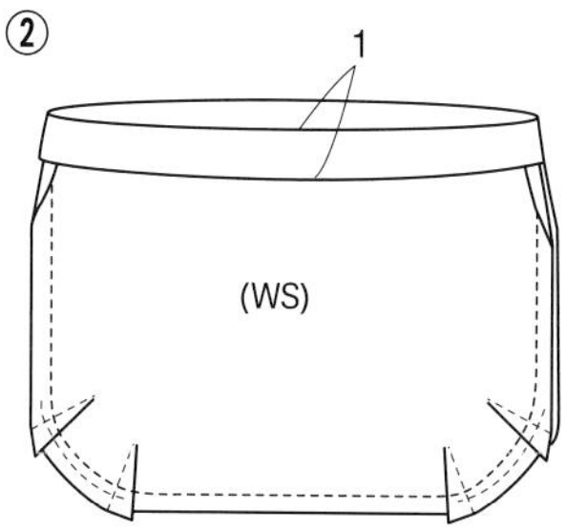

Sew all the way around and fold the seam at the opening.

Instructions

① 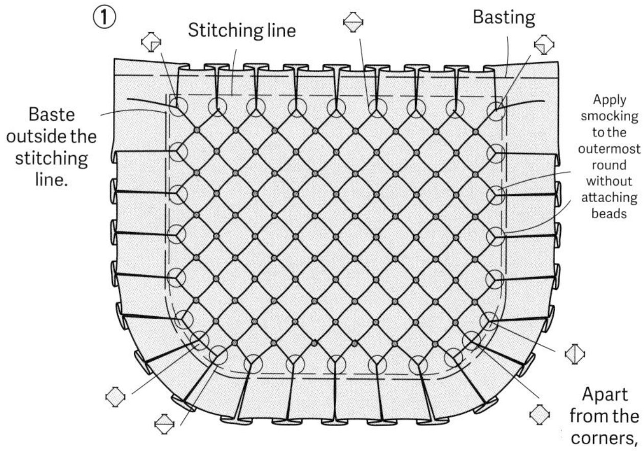

Stitch the smocking on the main piece while attaching beads.
On the outer edge, stitch without beads, changing the pickup positions and the number of pickups according to the diagram.
Fold the surrounding pleats and baste them in place.

② 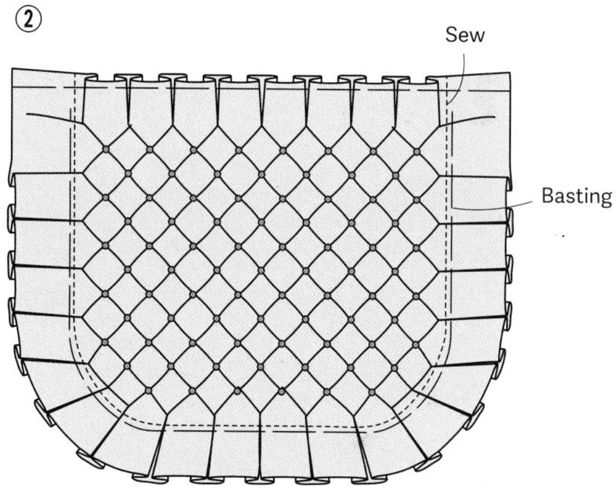

Stitch in a U shape along the stitching line.

③ 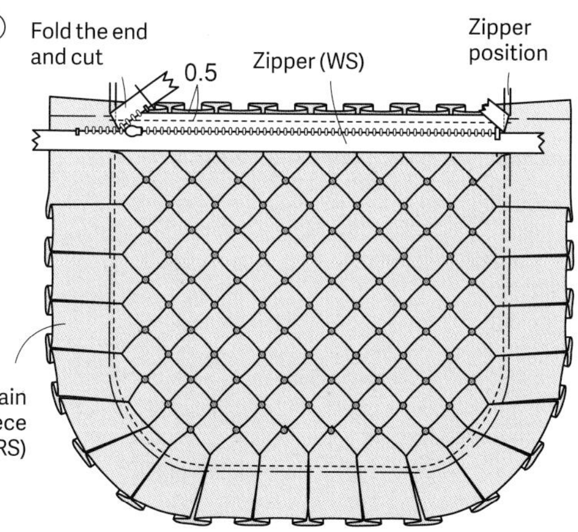

Place the zipper RS together with the opening of the main piece.
Fold both ends at the zipper position and sew.
Sew the opposite side in the same way.

④ 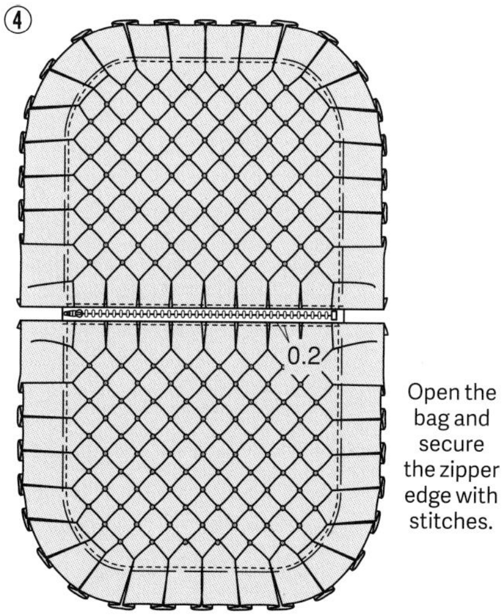

Open the bag and secure the zipper edge with stitches.

Instructions

⑤

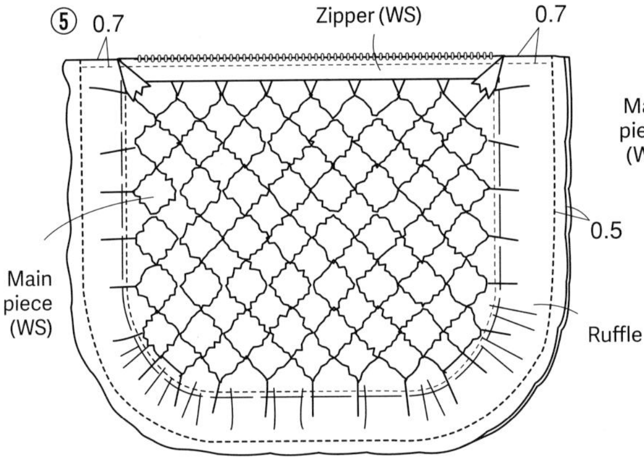

Place RS together and sew around without forming pleats, stretching slightly to create a ruffle.

⑥

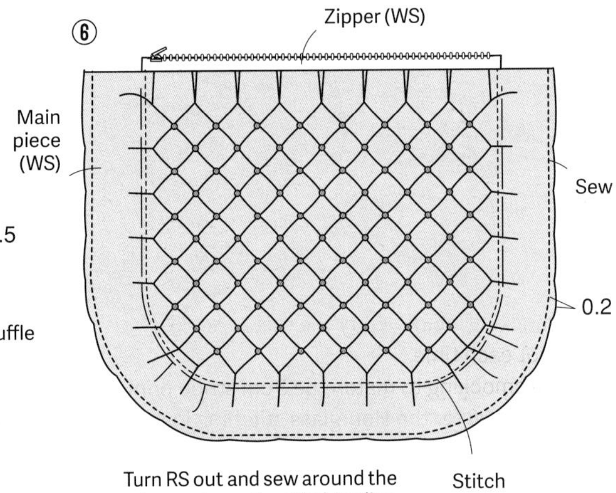

Turn RS out and sew around the edge and over the stitching line from Step ②.

⑦

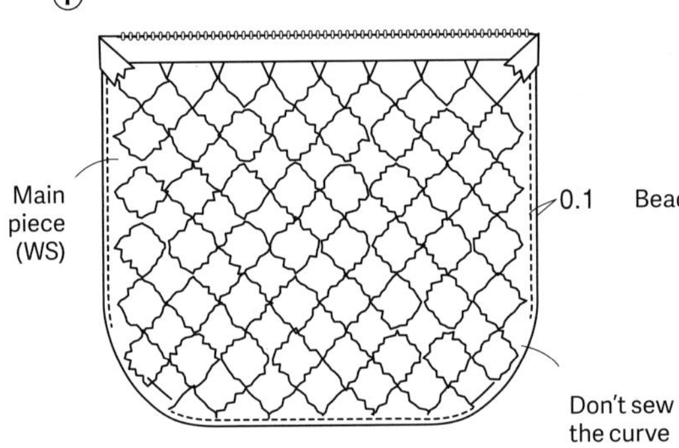

Turn WS out and sew the sides and the bottom.

⑧

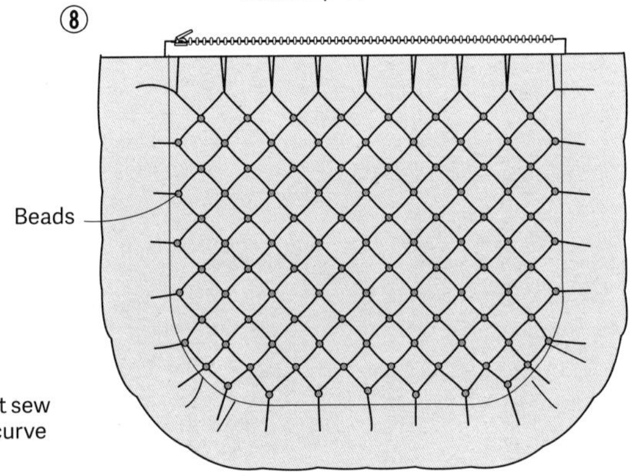

Turn RS out and sew on the beads around the outermost round that was previously left unworked.

⑨

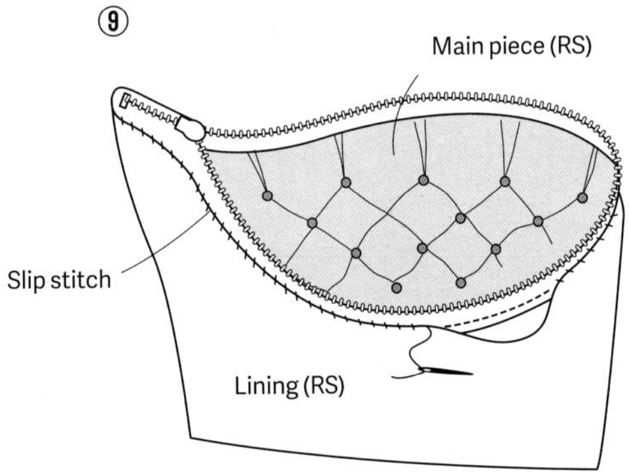

Turn WS out, place the lining over the main piece, and slip stitch to the zipper.

P. 34 Hourglass Crescent Bag

Finished Size: 25 × 37 × 6cm

■ Materials

- Main fabric (Artemondo: Café Stripe Oxford cotton): 70 × 70cm
- Lining fabric (cotton voile): 110 × 40cm
- Knit fusible interfacing: 100 × 60cm
- Pearl beads: 20 pieces, 0.8cm
- Circle handles: 2 pieces, 10cm inner diameter

■ Notes

- When smocking, do not carry the thread across; secure it with a knot each time.
- Stitch the smocking to match the 3cm stripe print.
- Refer to page 98 for the Hourglass stitching instructions.

■ Instructions

1. Stitch the Hourglass smocking pattern on the main piece.
2. Sew the sides at the handle-opening positions of the main piece.
3. Sew a running stitch around the opening and pull to gather.
4. Place one lining piece and the lining gusset RS together and sew.
5. Place the lining body and the lining gusset RS together and sew.
6. Place the main piece, lining upper gusset, and lining lower gusset RS together, leaving an opening, and sew.
7. Position the handles at the opening, place the main piece and lining RS together, and sew both sides.
8. Turn RS out through the opening, close with a ladder stitch, and press the lining down from above.
9. Pinch the seam position of the lining, sew, and attach the pearl beads.

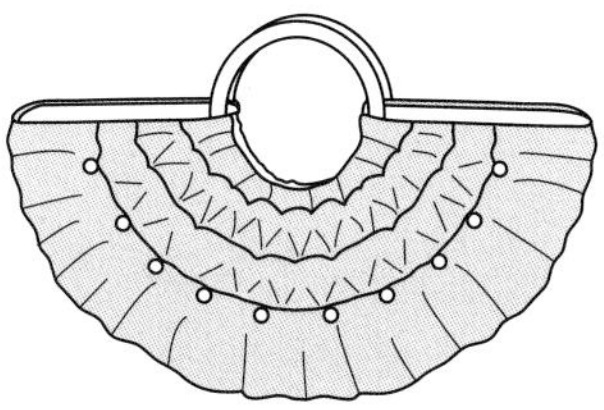

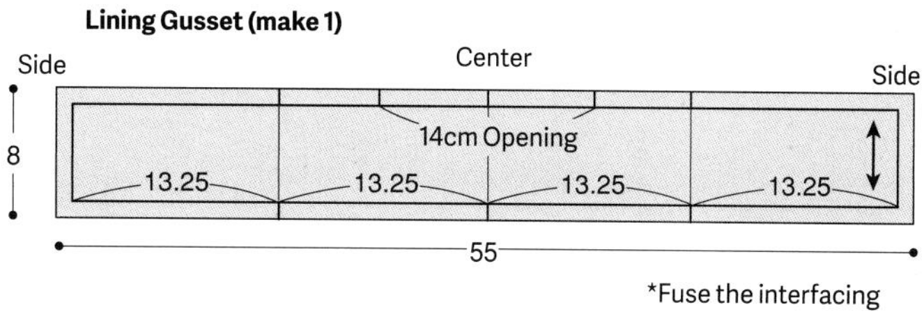

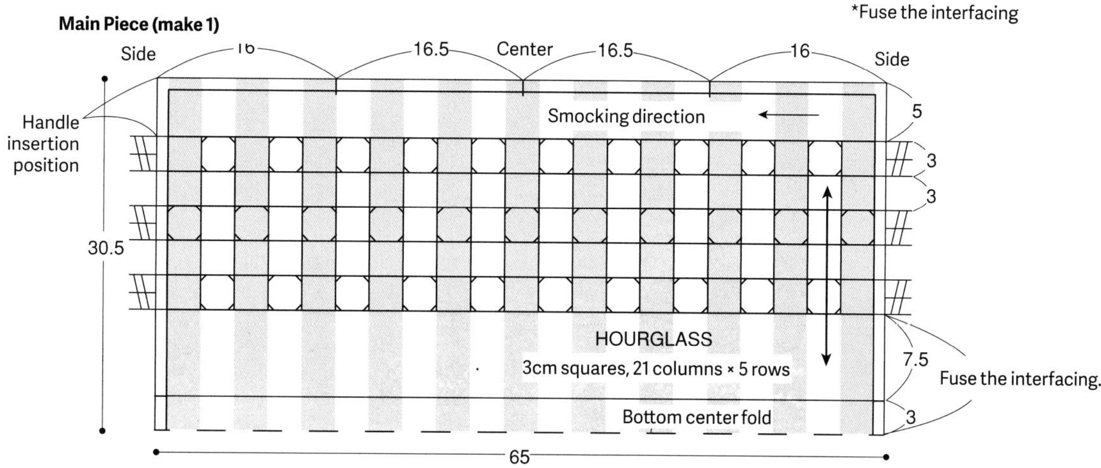

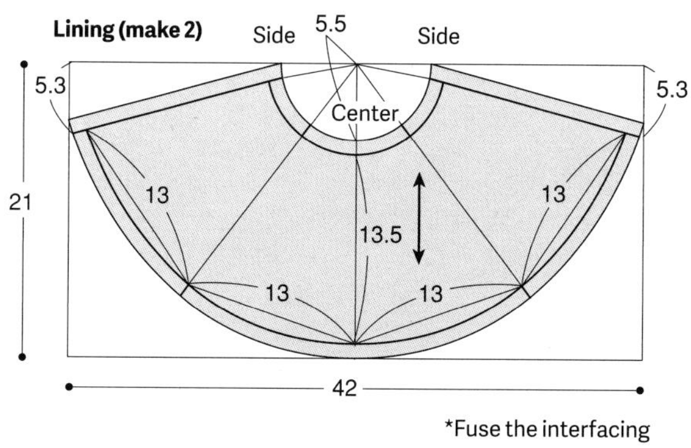

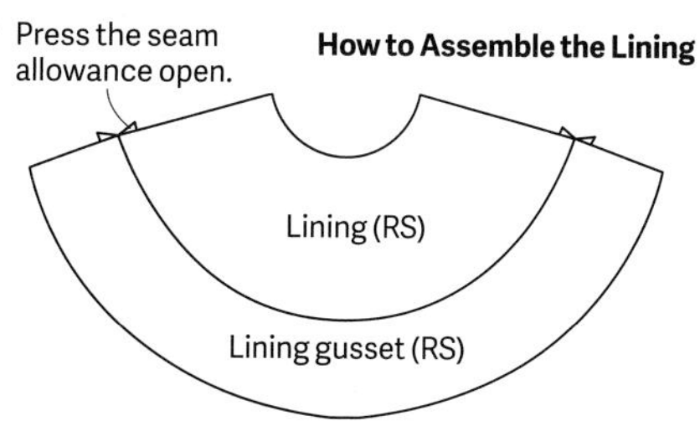

Place the lining and the lining gusset RS together and sew.
Turn RS out and press the seam allowances open.

Instructions

①

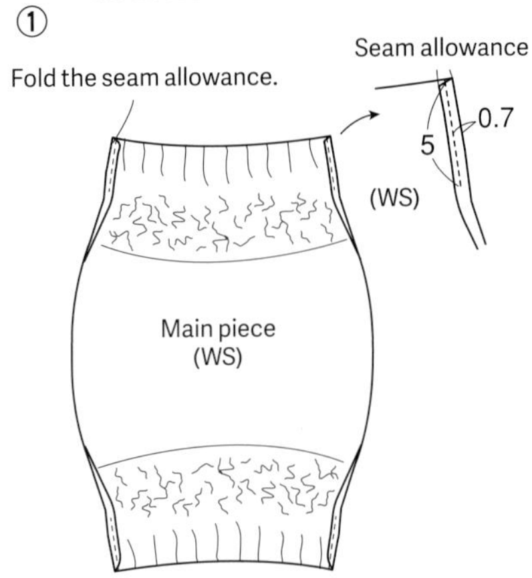

Stitch the smocking, then fold and sew the seam allowances at the handle openings on both sides.

②

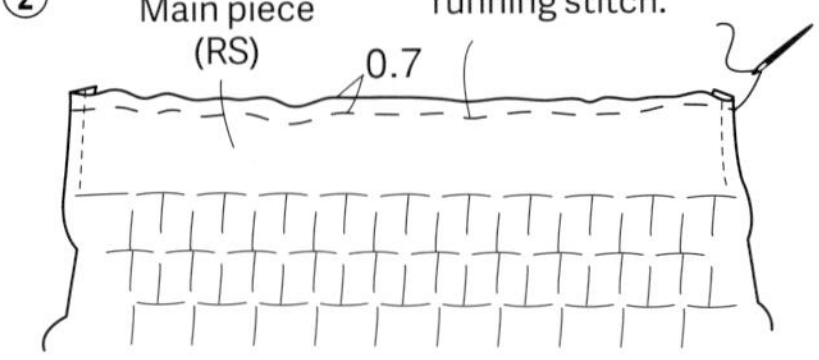

Sew a running stitch along the opening edge, draw it up, and adjust it to 17.5cm.

③

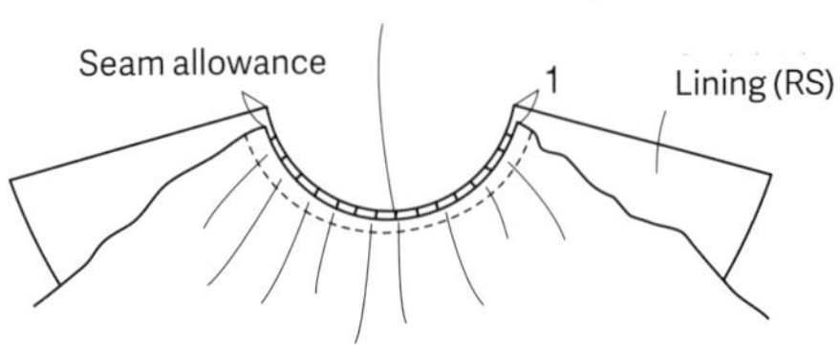

Place the main piece and the lining RS together and sew the opening.

Press the seam allowance toward the lining

④

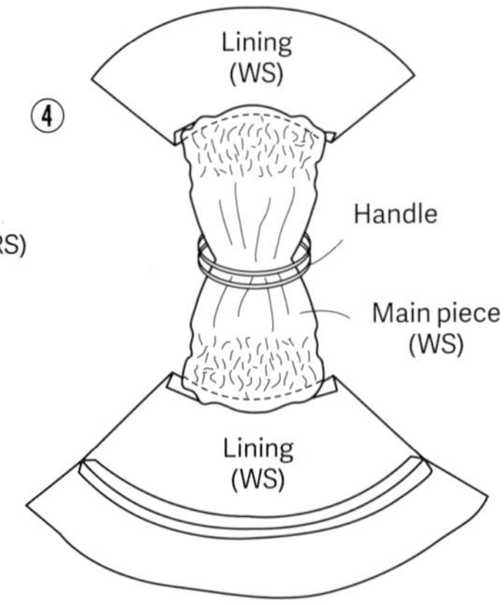

Sew the other lining piece to the opposite side as well, then thread the handle through

⑤

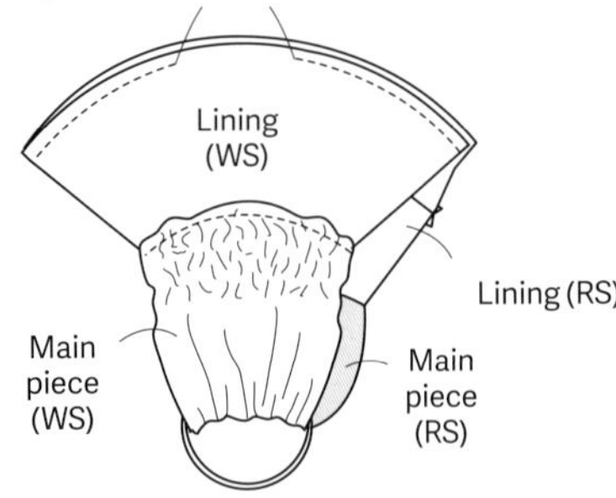

Place the lining and the lining gusset RS together and sew, leaving an opening.

Press the seam allowances open.

⑥

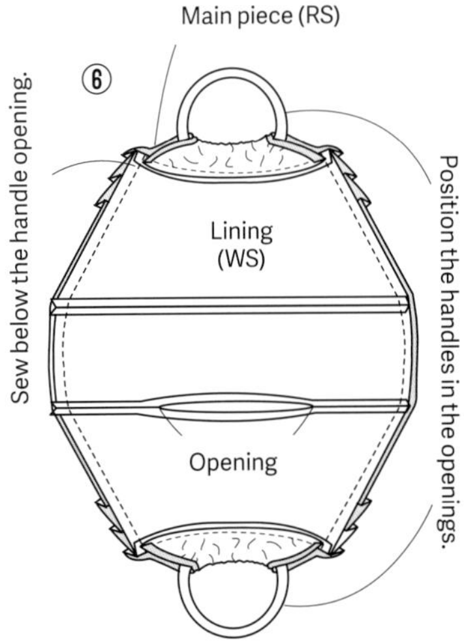

Move the handles, place the main piece and lining RS together, and sew both sides.

⑦

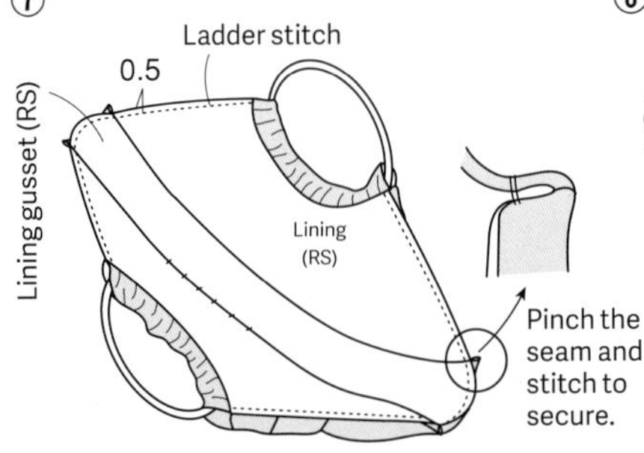

Turn RS out through the opening and close it with a ladder stitch.

Topstitch the lining to secure it in place.

Sew the seam of the lining gusset.

⑧

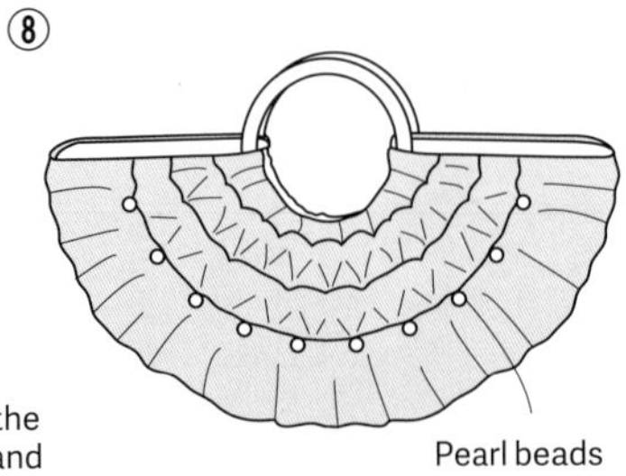

Pinch the seam and stitch to secure.

Sew pearl beads onto the tips of the smocking.

Photocopy at 75% (reduced size) or 133% (full size)

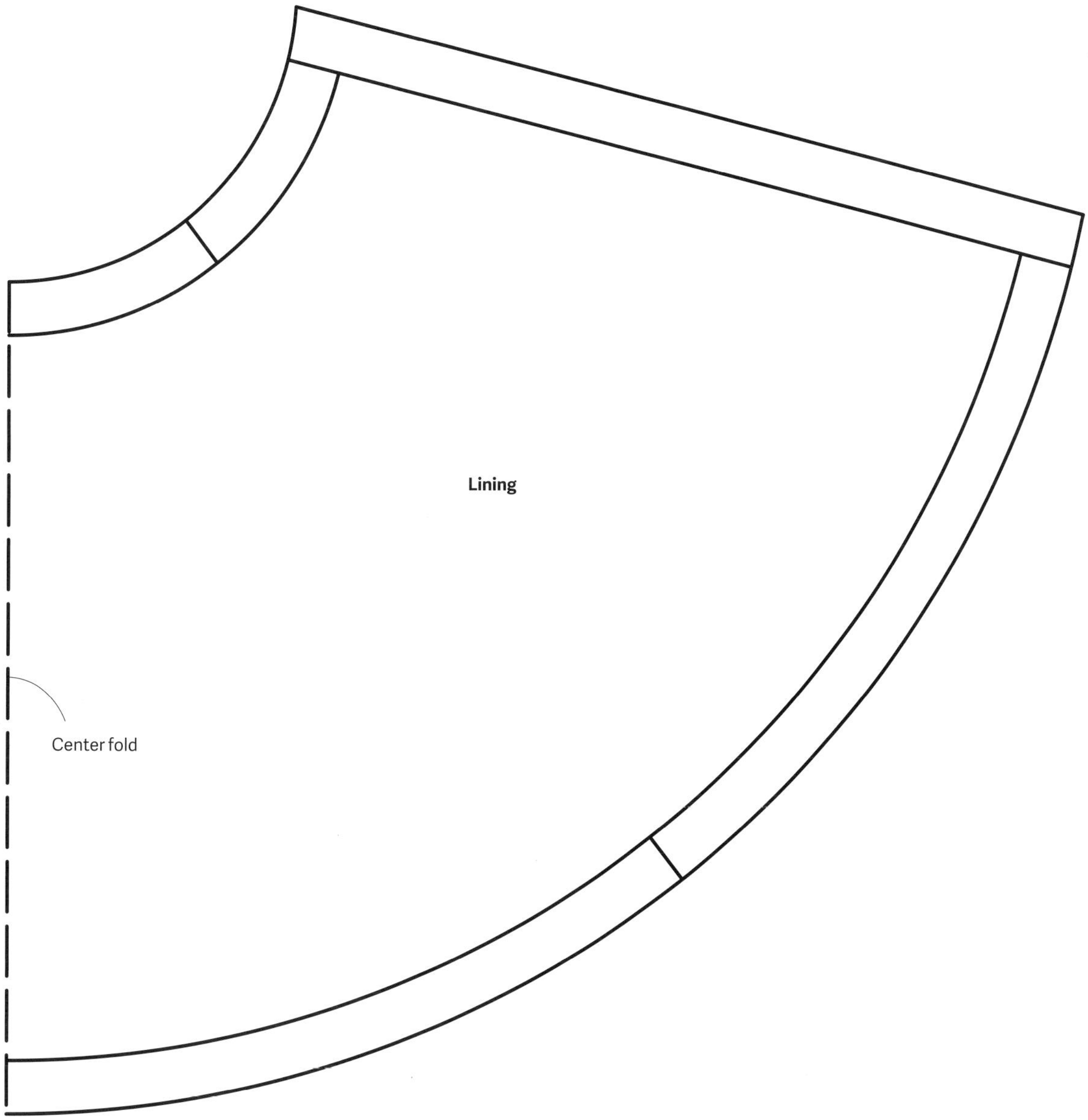

P. 35 Rattan Bamboo-Handle Bag

Finished Size: 33 × 33 × 11cm

■ Materials

- Main fabric (Solpano: yarn-dyed cotton/rayon/silk twill multiborder): 90 × 50 cm (including tabs)
- Lining fabric (cotton-linen): 110 × 30 cm (including main body bottom)
- Knit fusible interfacing: 110 × 40 cm
- Fusible interfacing: 110 × 40 cm
- Bamboo handbag handles: 2 pieces, 13 × 20 × 1.5 cm
- Handle hardware: 4 pieces, 1.5 cm inner dimension

■ Notes

- For the smocking, apply a steam iron to gradually shape and flatten the fabric.
- Apply the knit interfacing to the main piece and the standard-weight interfacing to the upper lining, main piece bottom, lower lining, and tabs.
- If the handles cannot be inserted after assembly, thread them through while temporarily basting the tabs in place.
- Refer to page 80 for the Rattan stitching instructions.

■ Instructions

1. Work the Rattan smocking pattern onto the main piece, leaving the ends unstitched.
2. Sew the main piece into a loop with RS together, then complete the remaining smocking stitches.
3. Sew the main piece and the main piece bottom with RS together.
4. Make the lining.
5. Make the tabs.
6. Gather the opening of the main body into pleats and baste the tabs in place.
7. Place the main body and the lining RS together and sew, leaving an opening at the top.
8. Turn RS out, trim the opening, and topstitch the opening.
9. Attach the handles.

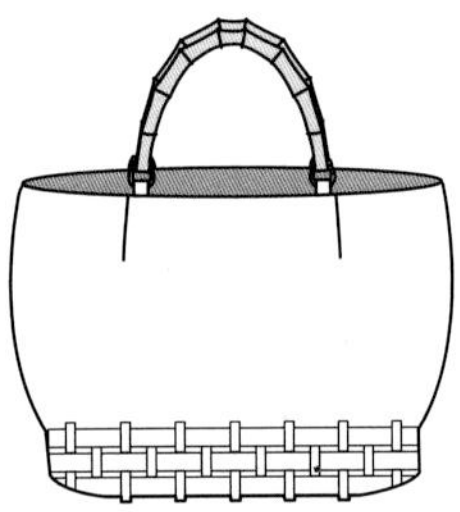

Main Piece (make 2)

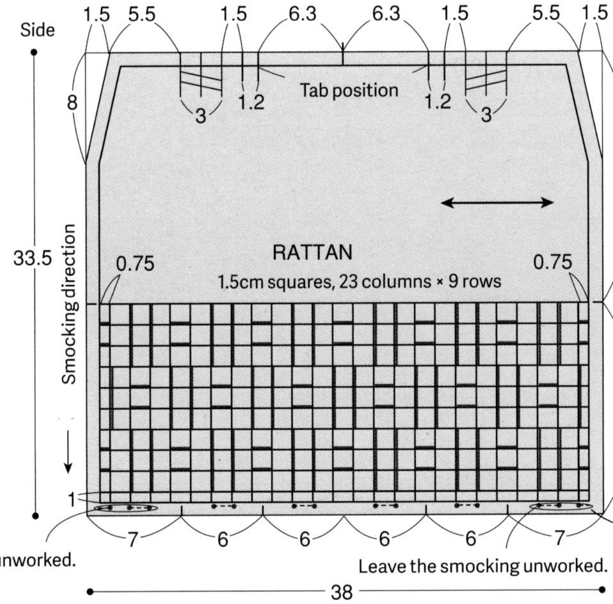

How to Finish the Ends

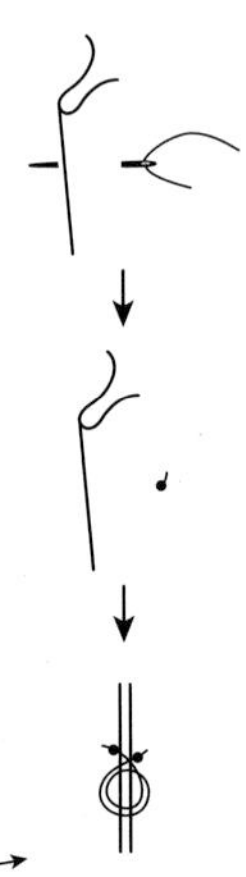

Pinch and scoop twice, then tie a finishing knot on the opposite side to where you started stitching.

Main Piece Bottom (make 1), Lining Bottom (make 1)

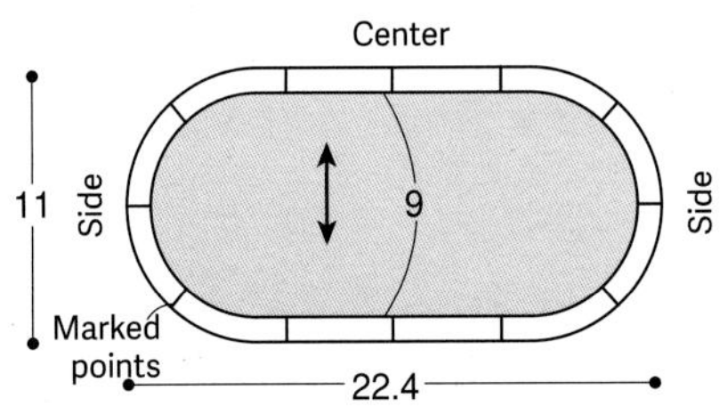

*Fuse the interfacing (raw edge).

Tab (make 1)

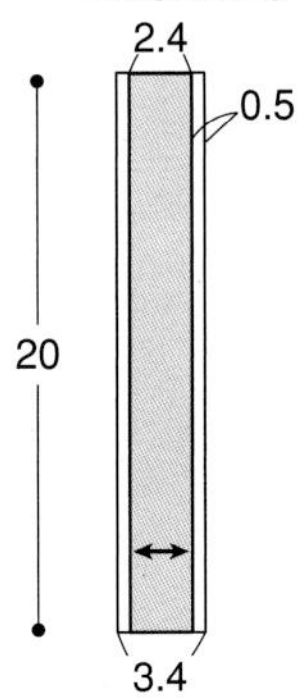

How to Make the Tab

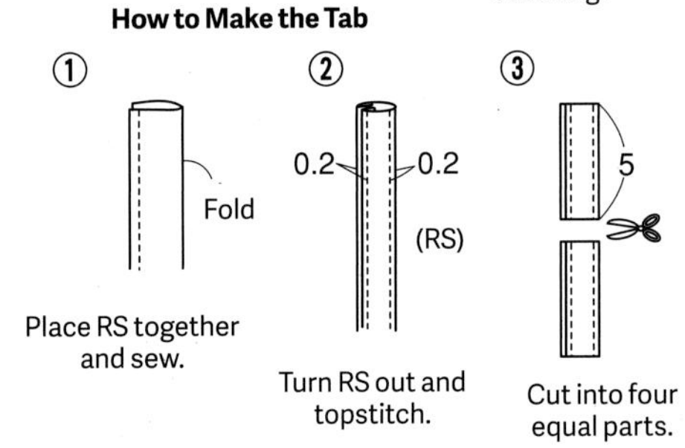

Upper Lining (make 2)

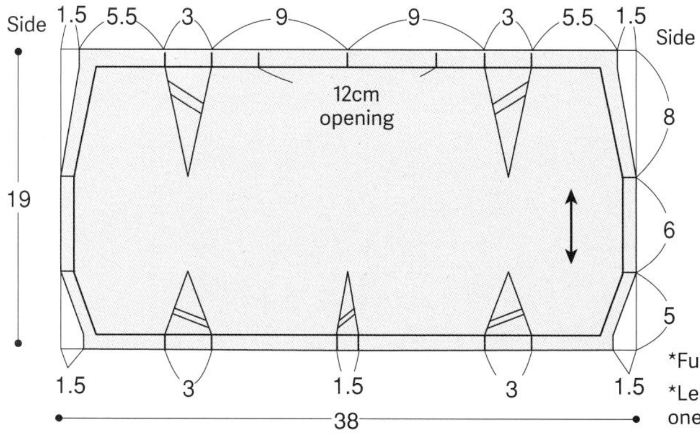

*Fuse the interfacing.

*Leave an opening on only one of the pieces.

Lower Lining (make 2)

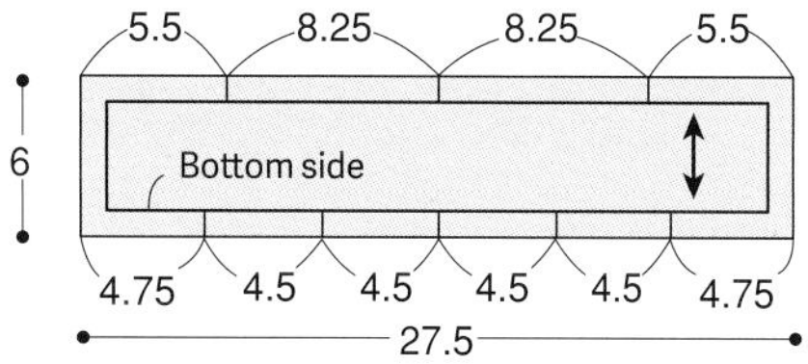

*Fuse the interfacing.

How to Make the Lining

①

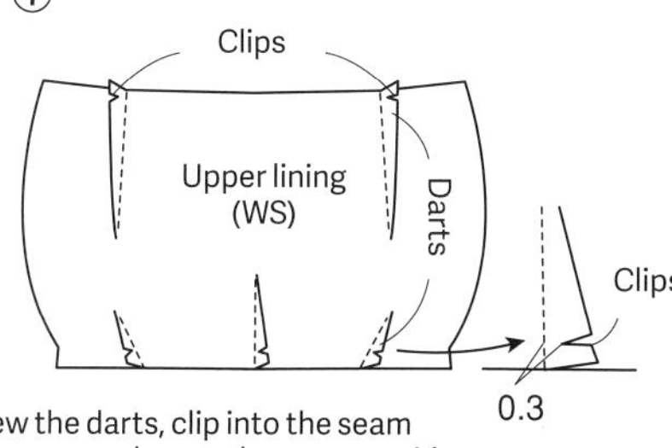

Sew the darts, clip into the seam allowances, and press them to one side.

②

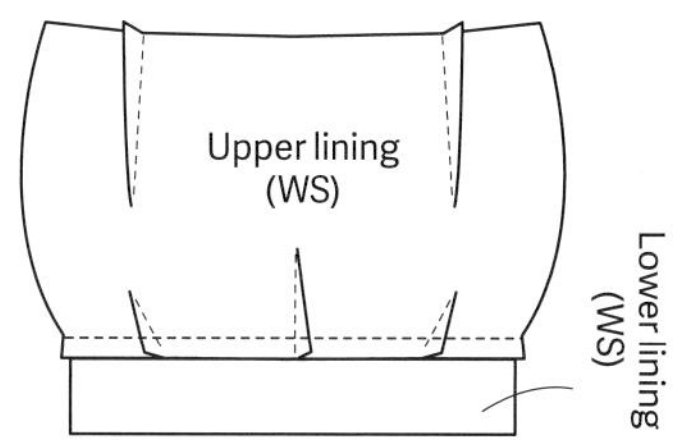

Place the upper and lower lining RS together and sew.

Press the seam allowances downward.

Make two of these.

③

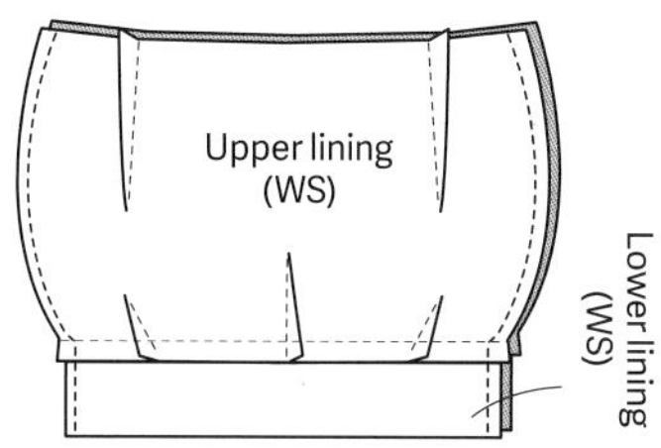

Place the two lining pieces RS together and sew both side seams.

Press the seam allowances open.

④

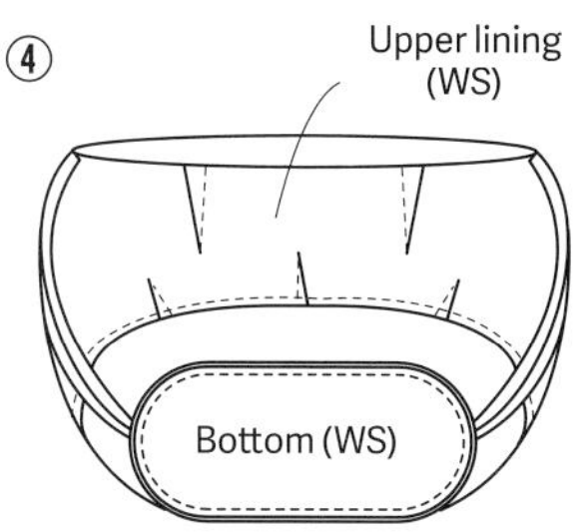

With RS together, sew the bottom to the lining.

Instructions

①

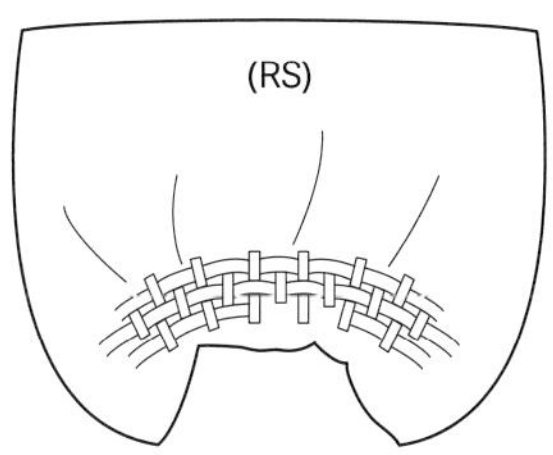

Work the smocking on the main piece, leaving both ends unstitched.

②

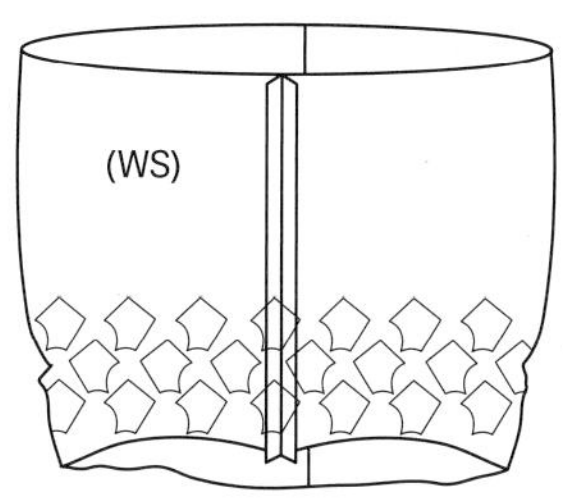

Place RS together and sew into a circle.

Press the seam allowances open, then complete the remaining smocking.

③

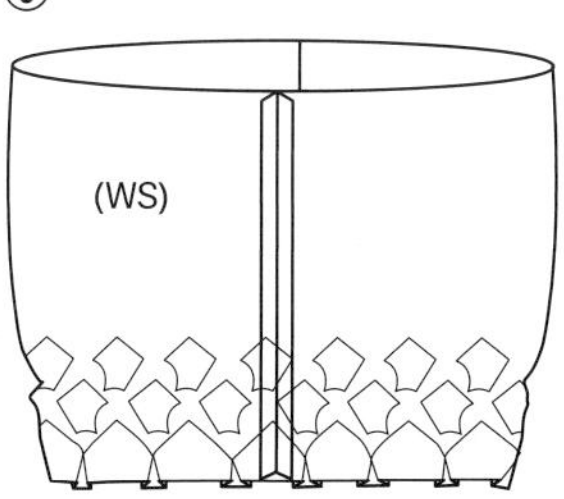

Adjust and shape the pleats on the bottom side.

④

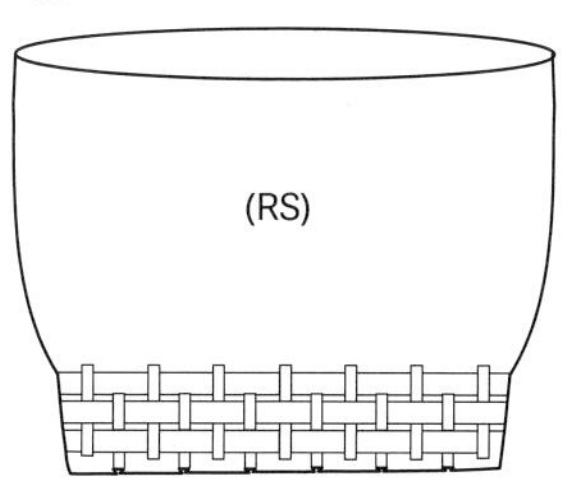

From the RS, apply steam gradually until the surface becomes flat.

⑤

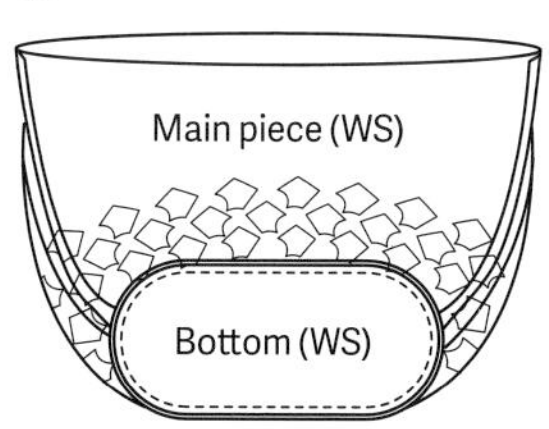

Place the main piece and main piece bottom RS together and sew.

Main Piece (make 1)

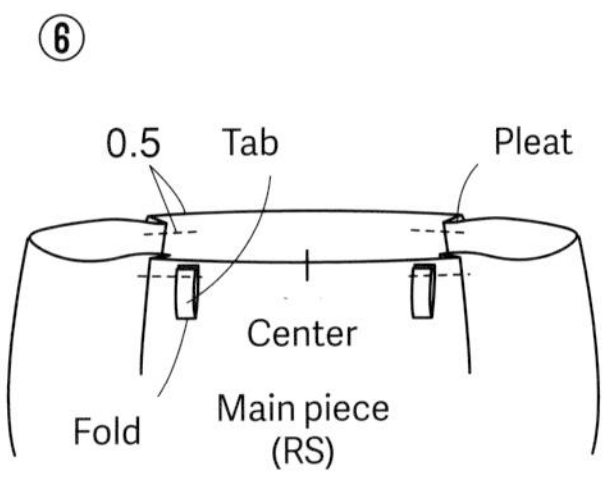

Fold the pleats at the opening of the main body, overlap the tab folded in half, and baste in place.

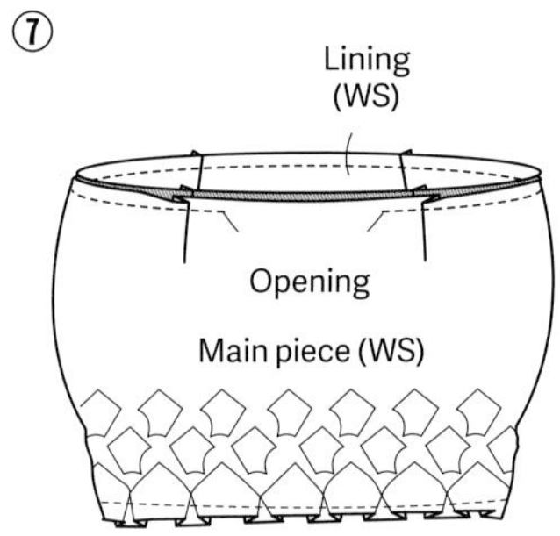

Place the main body and the lining RS together and sew around the top edge, leaving an opening.

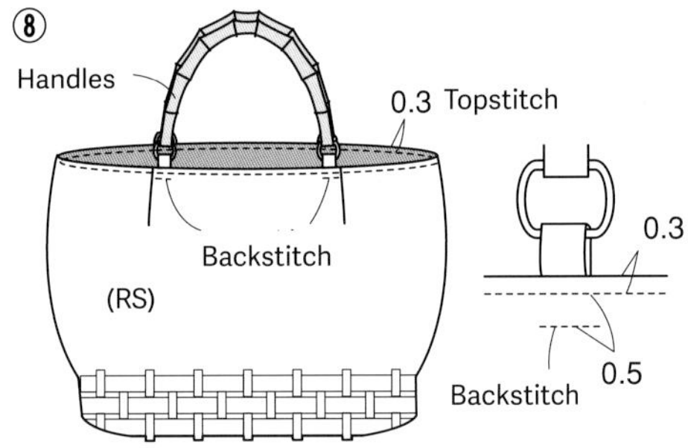

Turn RS out and shape the opening.
Topstitch around the opening.
Topstitch the tabs in four places.
Attach the handles.

Photocopy at 100%

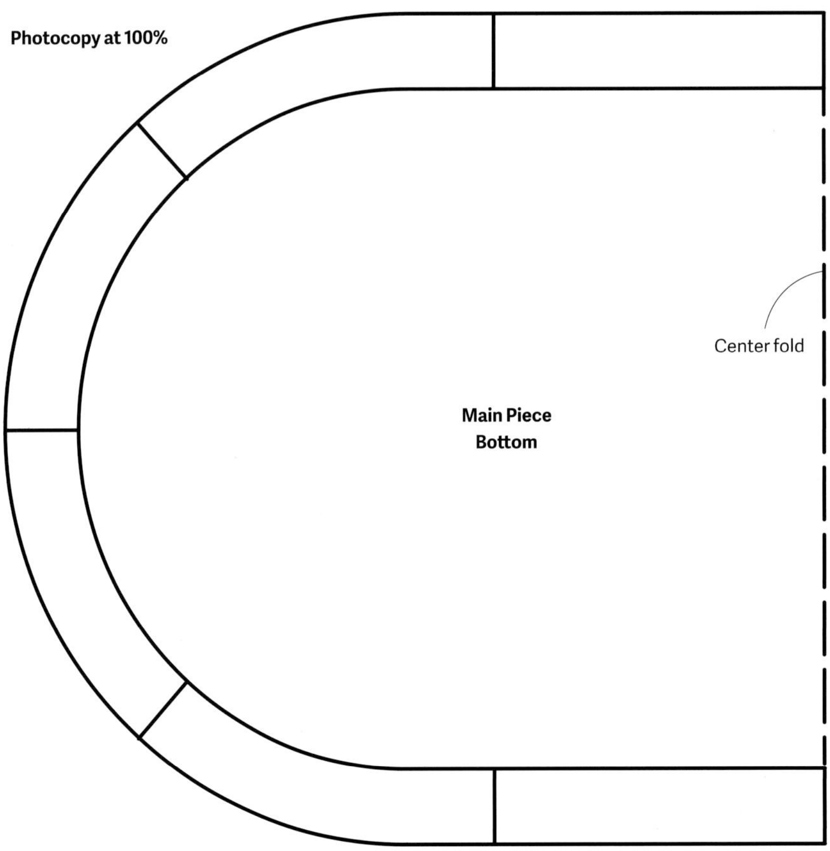

P. 36 Dragon Scale Drawstring Bag

Finished Size: 19 × 19 × 19cm

■ Materials

- Main fabric (nunocoto fabric: Diagonal strip big Oxford cotton): 110 × 80 cm (includes casing)
- Lining fabric (sheer): 110 × 30 cm
- Heavyweight fusible interfacing: 20 × 20 cm
- One-sided fusible quilt batting: 20 × 20 cm
- Cord: 170 cm, 0.5 cm diameter
- Wooden beads: 30 pieces, 0.8 cm
- Metal aglet: 4 pieces, 1 cm, 0.5 cm diameter

■ Notes

- Leave six squares of smocking at both ends of the main piece, sew into a tube, and then complete the remaining smocking.
- Use heavyweight fusible interfacing for the main piece bottom and one-sided fusible quilt batting for the lining bottom.
- Refer to page 84 for the Dragon Scale stitching instructions.

■ Instructions

1. Leave both ends and stitch the Dragon Scale smocking pattern on the main piece.
2. Fold the main piece in half RS together and sew into a circle, then stitch the remaining smocking.
3. Place the main piece and the main piece bottom RS together and sew.
4. Sew the lining into a circle and sew the cord casing.
5. Stitch the cord casing onto the lining.
6. Place the main piece and lining RS together and sew the opening.
7. Turn RS out and close the opening.
8. Attach wooden beads to the ends of the cord.
9. Thread the cord through the casing opening and attach the loop ends.

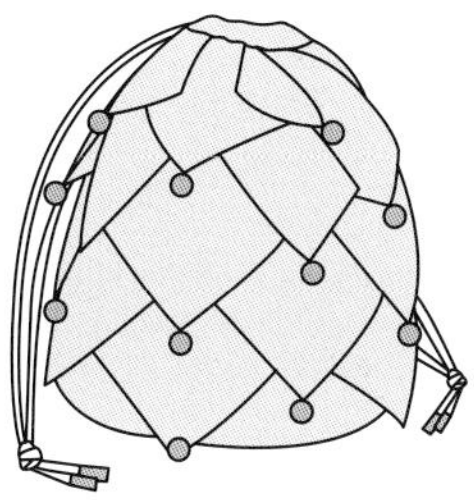

How to Finish the Ends

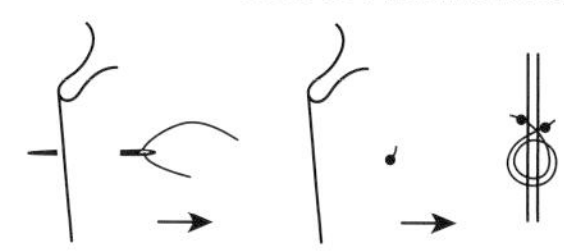

Take two stitches through the pleat, then secure it by tying off on the side opposite where you started.

Main Piece (make 1)

DRAGON SCALES
3cm squares, 30 columns × 13 rows

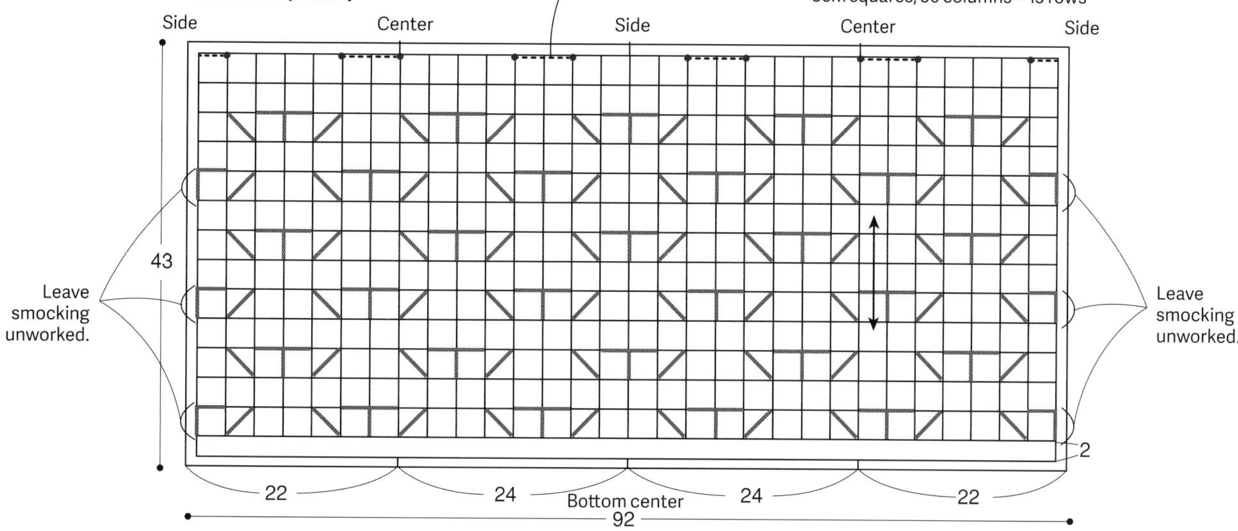

Main Piece Bottom (make 1)

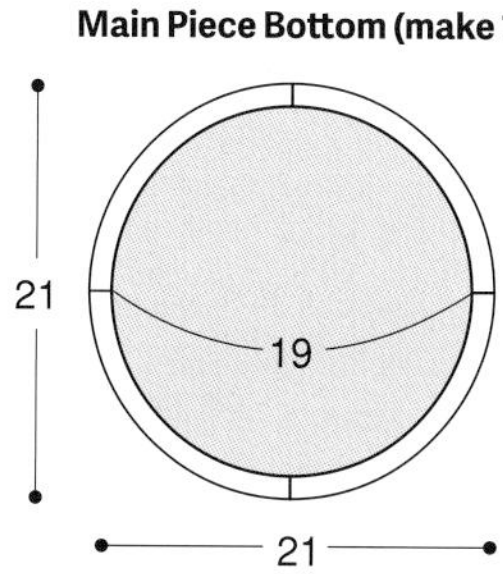

Cord Casing (make 2)

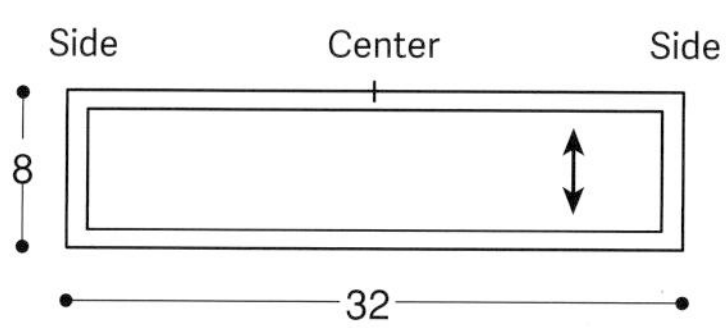

*Fuse the interfacing (raw edge).

Lining (make 1)

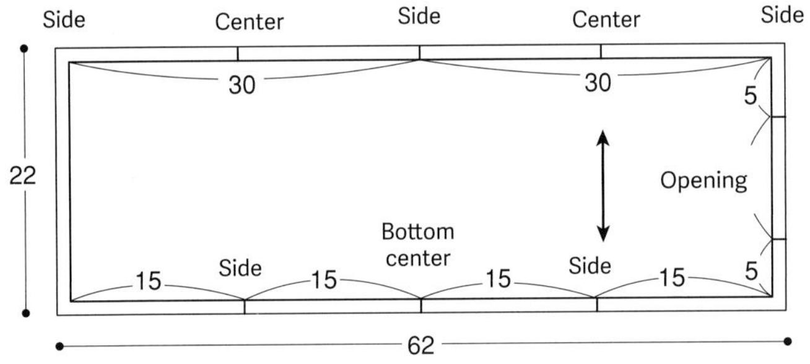

Lining Bottom (make 1)

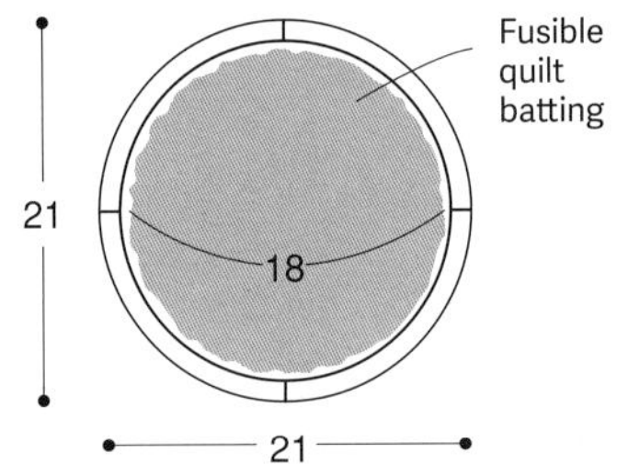

How to Make the Lining

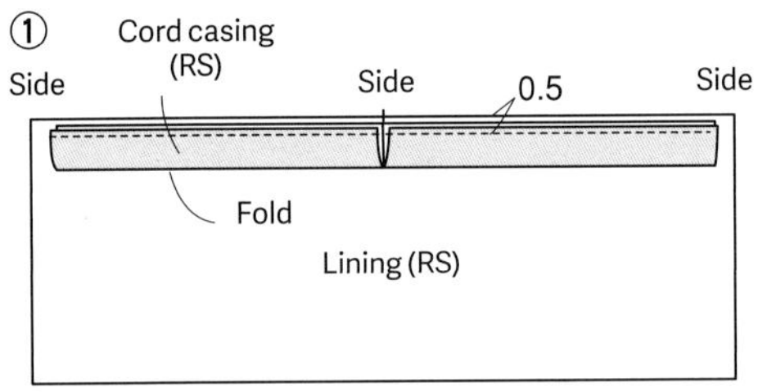

Join the side seams of the lining and folded cord casing together and sew in place.

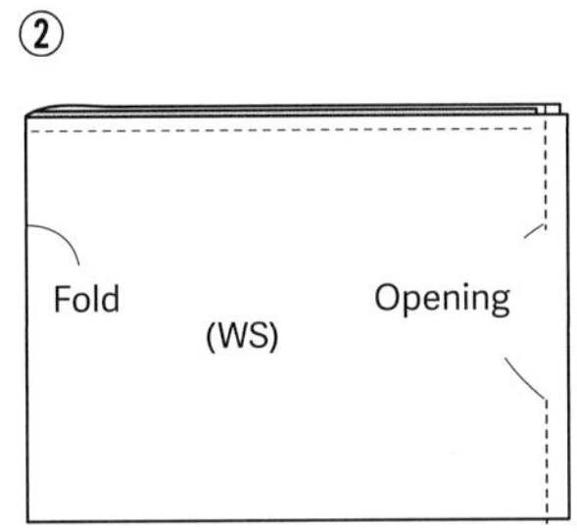

Fold RS together, sew the side seams, leave an opening, and press the seam allowances open.

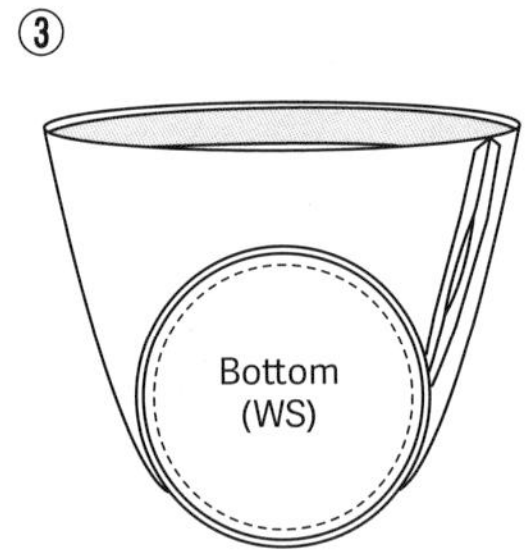

Place the lining and the main piece bottom RS together and sew.

Photocopy at 100%

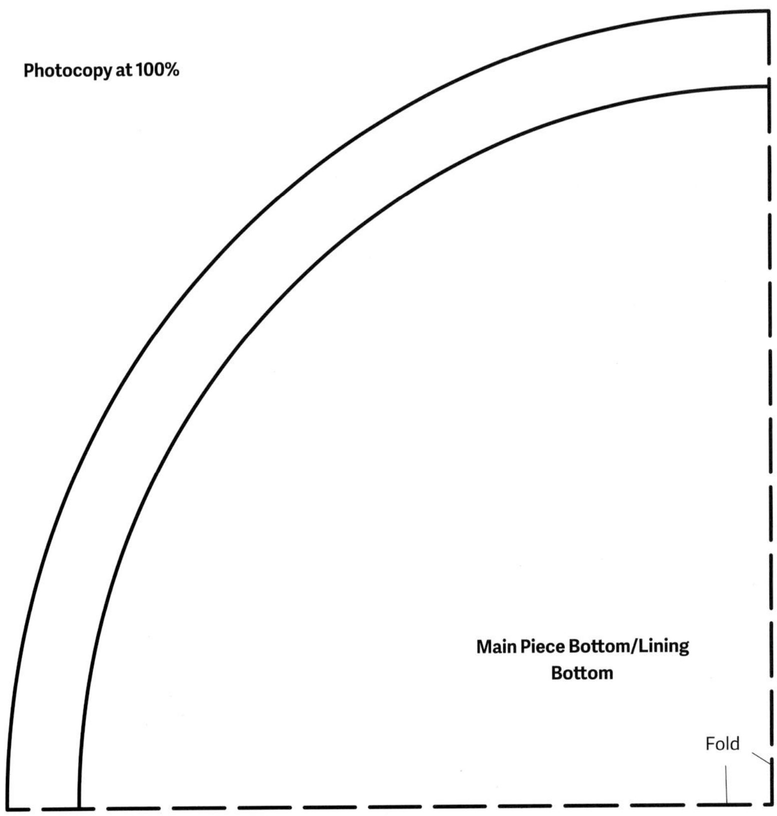

How to Make the Cord Casing

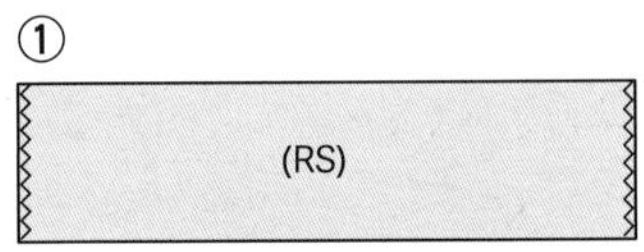

Finish both ends with an overlock stitch (zigzag stitch).

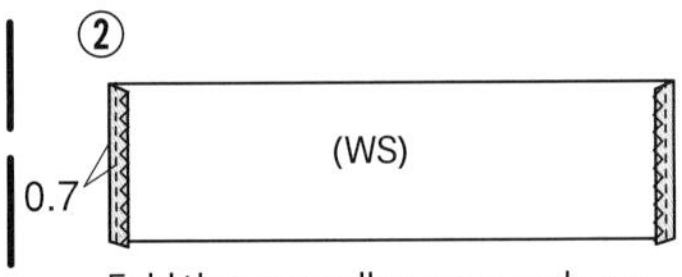

Fold the seam allowance and sew.

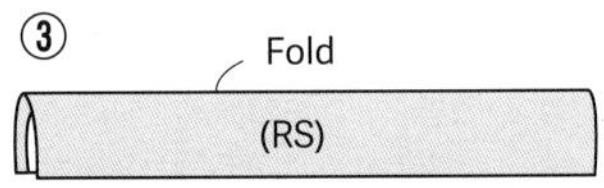

Fold into half.

Instructions

①

Leave 6 blocks at both sides unworked, stitch the remaining smocking, and press with an iron.

②

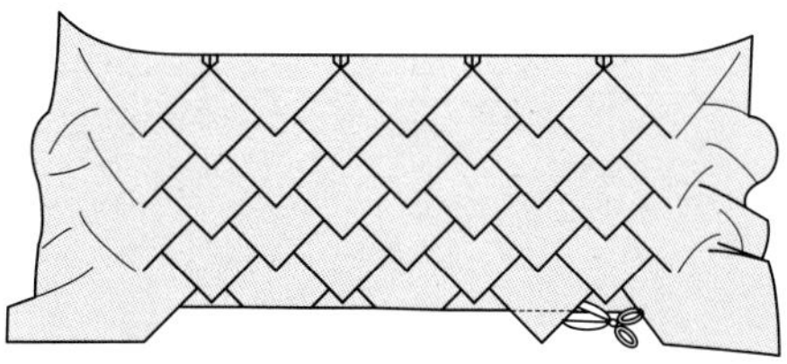

Trim the protruding folds at the top and bottom.

③

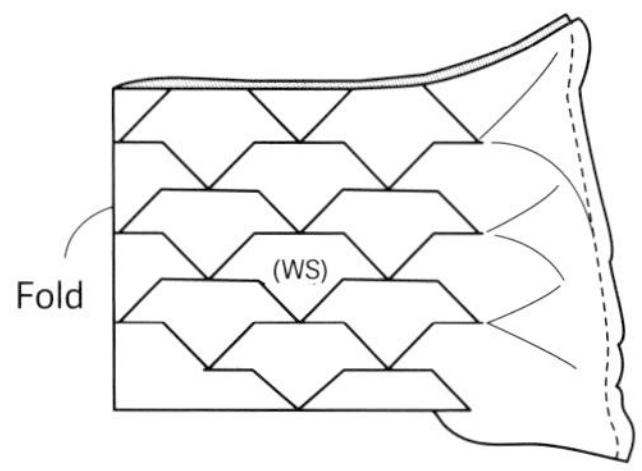

Fold RS together into a circle and sew; press the seam allowance open.

④

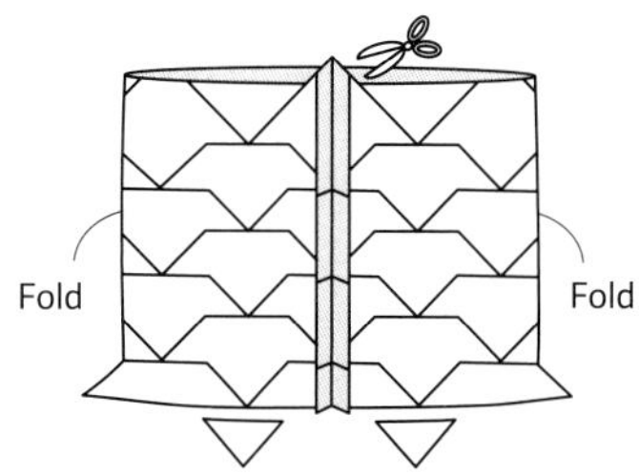

Stitch the unworked 6 blocks of smocking, and trim the protruding folds at the top and bottom.

⑤

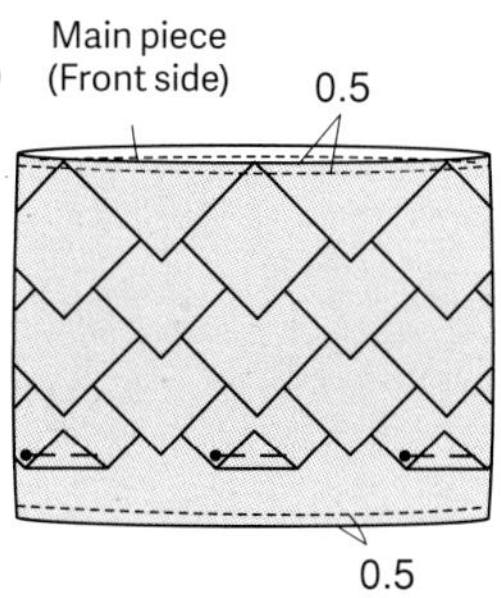

Topstitch around the top and bottom edges.

Be careful not to catch the lower folds in the stitching.

⑥

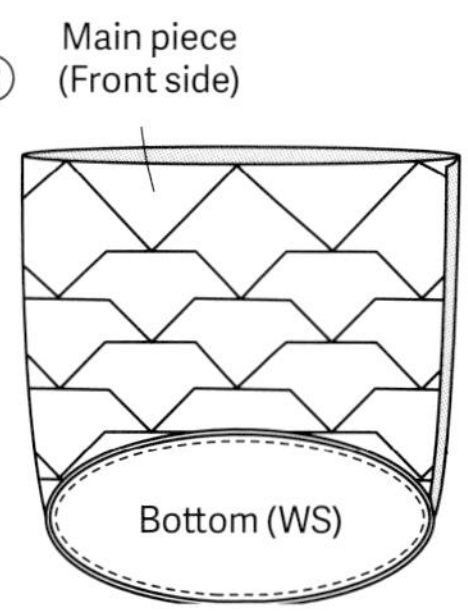

Place the main piece and main piece bottom RS together and sew.

Press the folds in the same way as in step ⑤.

⑦

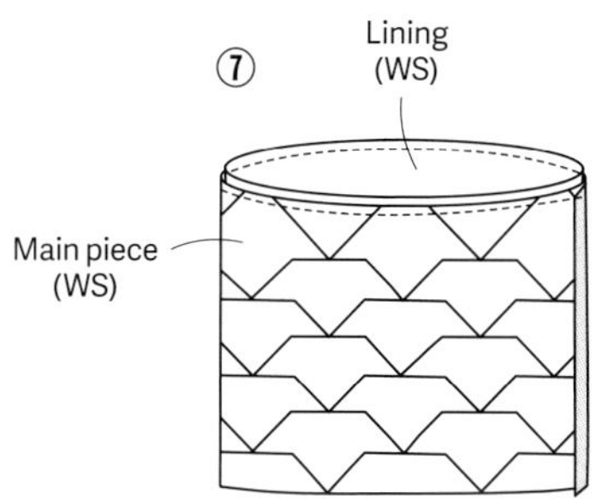

Place the main body and lining RS together and sew the opening.

Turn RS out through the opening and close it with a ladder stitch.

⑧

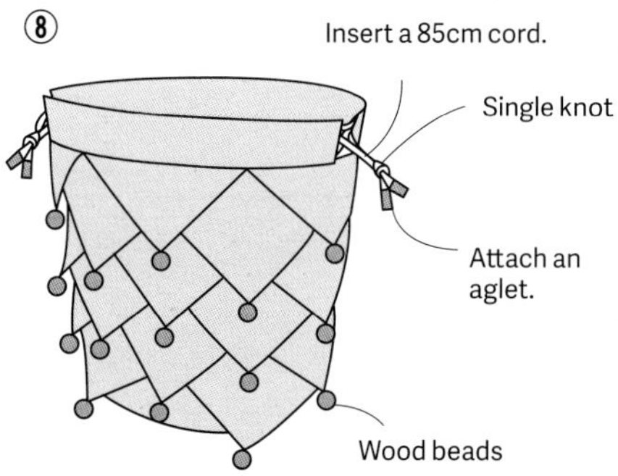

Pass the cord through, and sew on wooden beads at the tips of the formed folds.

P. 39 Puzzle Wall Art

Finished Size: 29 × 29 × 2cm

■ Materials

- Main fabric (Artemondo: Irish Cross Oxford cotton): 70 × 70cm
- Organza (COSCLOTH: Chambray Soft Organza): 70 × 70cm
- Canvas or frame: 27.3 × 27.3 × 2cm
- Double-sided tape

■ Notes

- When attaching the main fabric to the canvas, pull the fabric39 lightly to align the corners before fixing it in place.
- After securing the pleats, hammer them down firmly from above to secure them.
- On the back side, you may secure the edges with staples first and then apply masking tape over them.
- Refer to page 88 for the Puzzle stitching instructions.

■ Instructions

1. Layer the organza over the main fabric and baste them together.
2. Stitch the Puzzle smocking pattern.
3. Wrap the fabric around the canvas and secure it in place.

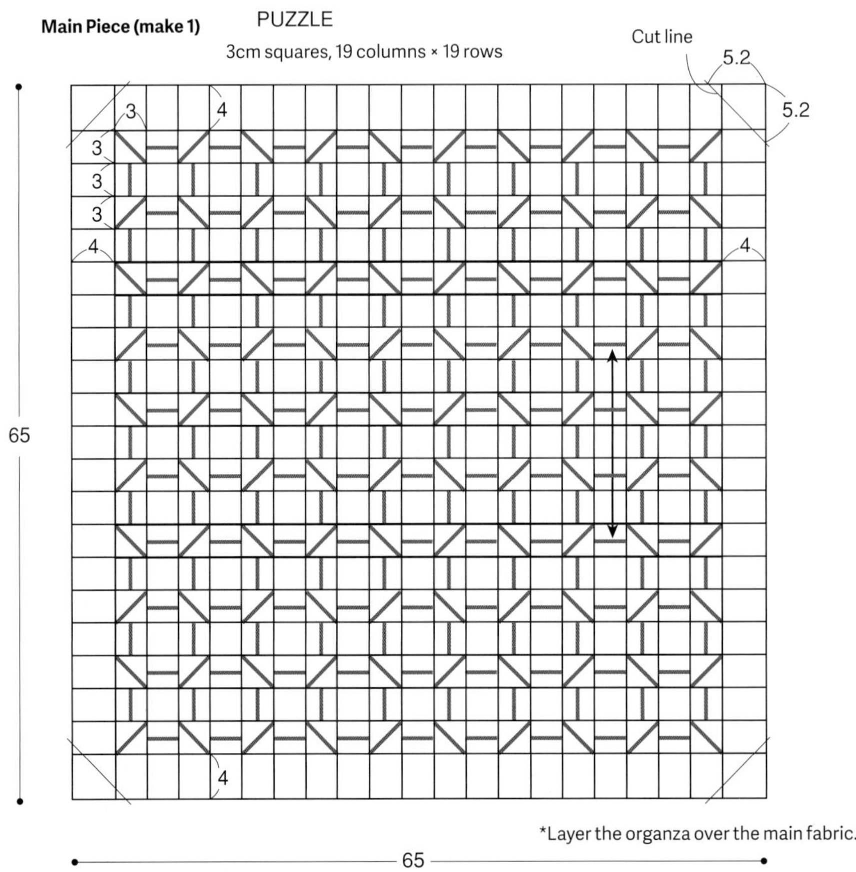

How to Prepare the Main Piece

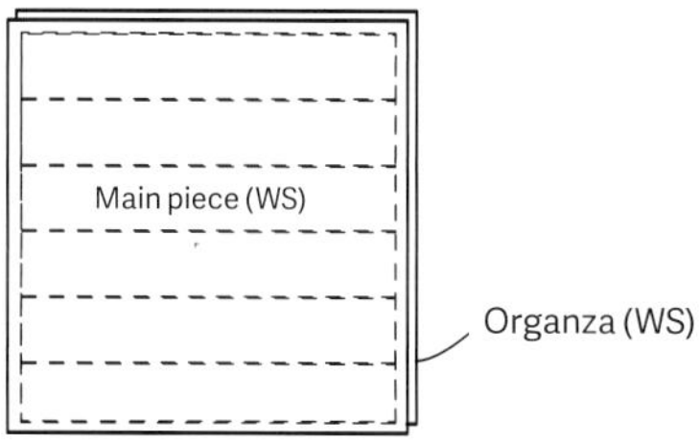

Layer the organza over the main fabric and baste around the perimeter and inside.

Instructions

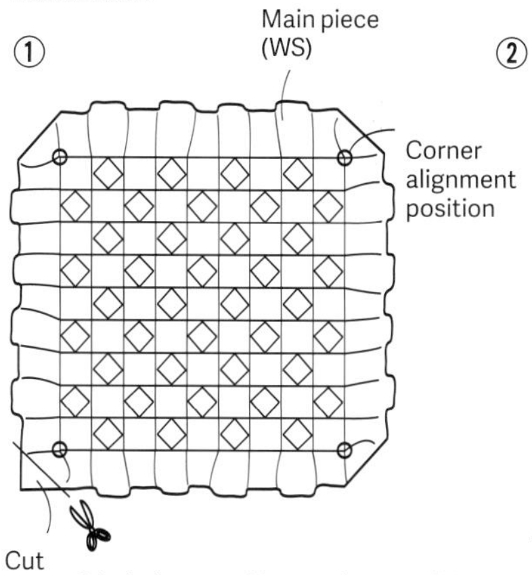

Stitch the smocking on the main fabric.

Remove the basting stitches except around the perimeter and trim the corners.

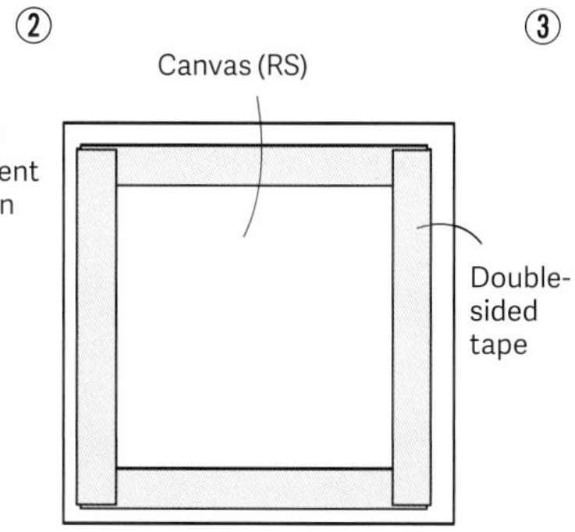

Apply double-sided tape to the canvas or frame.

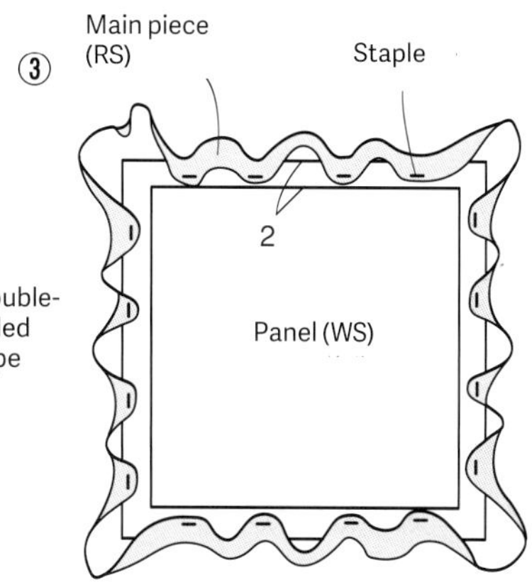

Using the smocking grid as a guide, pull the fabric taut and align the corners.

Fold the seam allowance around the perimeter and staple at the indented sections of the pleats.

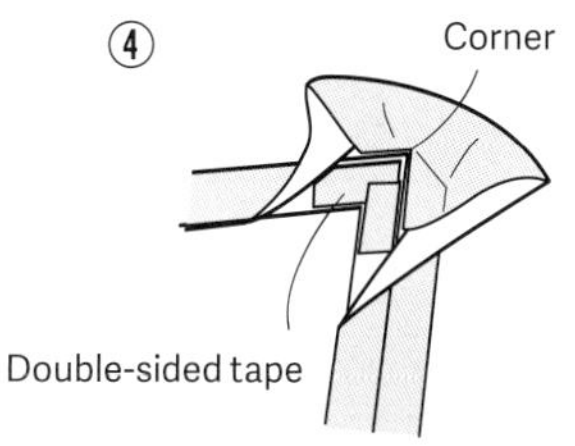

Apply tape to the corners and secure them to the inside.

Fold in the sides so they follow the angle of the corners.

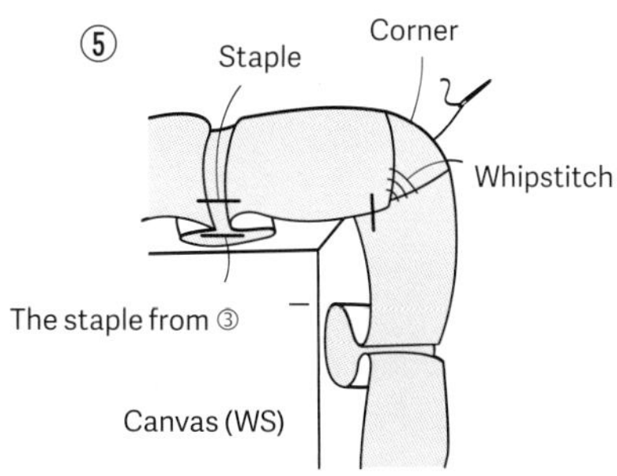

Fold the corners and staple them.

Fold the perimeter pleats and staple them.

Pleat the corner pleats under and stitch them together.

INDEX

Note: Page numbers in *italics* indicate projects.

A

arrow patterns and stitching, 64–65
Arrow Triangle Bag, *17–19, 119–21*
awl, 40

B

bags and totes
  about: customizing patterns, 44; making shoulder bags, 104–8; materials for, 41; tools for, 40
  Arrow Triangle Bag, *17–19, 119–21*
  Bone One-Handle Bag, *12, 13, 110–12*
  Box Drawstring Pouch, *28, 29, 134–35*
  Brick and Bow Clutch, *20, 22, 122–23*
  Brick Shoulder Bag, *21, 22*
  Crisscross Bone Ruffle Handle Bag, *16, 116–18*
  Diamond Ruffle Pouch, *32–33, 136–38*
  Dragon Scale Drawstring Bag, *36–37, 145–47*
  Flower Drawstring Bag, *26–27, 128–30*
  Heart Chain Clutch, *30, 31, 131–33*
  Hourglass Crescent Bag, *34, 139–41*
  Rattan Bamboo-Handle Bag, *35, 142–44*
  Wave Pocket Tote, *14–15, 113–15*
beads, 41
blue dashed lines, 10
Bone One-Handle Bag, *12, 13, 110–12*
bone patterns and stitching, 58–59
Box Drawstring Pouch, *28, 29, 134–35*
box patterns and stitching, 102–3
braid patterns and stitching, 52–53
Brick and Bow Clutch, *20, 22, 122–23*
brick patterns and stitching, 66–71
Brick Shoulder Bag, *21, 22*
bubble patterns and stitching, 72–73

C

clips, sewing, 40
clutches. *See* bags and totes
corduroy, finishing with, 43
crisscross bone patterns and stitching, 62–63
Crisscross Bone Ruffle Handle Bag, *16, 116–18*
cushions
  about: customizing patterns, 44; tools and materials for, 40–41
  Lozenge Cushion, *23–24, 124–25*
  Shell Circle Cushion, *25, 126–27*
customizing patterns, 44

D

dashed lines, blue, 10
diagonal and straight lines. *See* patterns and stitching
diagrams, stitching. *See* stitching diagrams
diamond patterns and stitching, 100–101
Diamond Ruffle Pouch, *32–33, 136–38*
double lattice patterns and stitching, 78–79
Dragon Scale Drawstring Bag, *36–37, 145–47*
dragon scale patterns and stitching, 84–87
drawstrings for bags, 41
D-rings, 41

F

fabric
  about, 42–43; to use, 41
  finishing differences by type (corduroy, satin, sheeting), 43
  fusible interfacing with, 41
  for linings, 41
  pressing, 11
  stitching diagrams, 9, 10
  stretch level, illustrated, 42
  washing (smocked), 11, 42
Flower Drawstring Bag, *26–27, 128–30*
flower patterns and stitching, 94–97
four corners, 93–103
  about: overview of, 93
  box, 102–3
  diamond, 100–101
  flower, 94–97
  hourglass, 98–99
fusible interfacing, 41

H

handles, for bags, 41
Heart Chain Clutch, *30, 31, 131–33*
heart patterns and stitching, 74–75
hera marker, 40
Hourglass Crescent Bag, *34, 139–41*
hourglass patterns and stitching, 98–99

I

interfacing, fusible, 41
iron and ironing board, 40

L

lattice patterns and stitching, 46–51. *See also* double lattice patterns and stitching
lattice smocking
  about: this book and, 8
  basics, 9–11
  explained, 6
  markings, 9
  passing thread, 11
  patterns (*See* four corners; patterns and stitching; *specific patterns*)
  pressing fabric, 11
  seam allowances, 11

stitching diagrams, 9
thread for, 9
types, and other names for, 6
washing, 11
leaf patterns and stitching, 56–57
lines, stitching, 10
Lozenge Cushion, *23–24, 124–25*
lozenge patterns and stitching, 76–77

M

magnetic snaps, 41
marking tools, 40
markings, 9
materials and tools, 40–41. *See also* fabric

N

needles, sewing, 40

P

patterns and stitching. *See also* four corners
about: diagonal and straight lines and, 45
arrow, 64–65
bone, 58–59
braid, 52–53
brick, 66–71
bubble, 72–73
crisscross bone, 62–63
double lattice, 78–79
dragon scale, 84–87
heart, 74–75
lattice, 46–51 (*See also* double lattice)
leaf, 56–57
lozenge, 76–77
puzzle, 88–92
rattan, 80–83
shell, 54–55
wave, 60–61
pillows. *See* cushions
pink and red lines, 10
pins and pincushion, 40
pressing fabric, 11
projects
about: customizing patterns, 44; guidelines for making, 109; lattice smocking basics and, 9–11; making shoulder bags, 104–8; tools and materials for, 40–41 (*See also* fabric)
Arrow Triangle Bag, *17–19, 119–21*
Bone One-Handle Bag, *12, 13, 110–12*
Box Drawstring Pouch, *28, 29, 134–35*
Brick and Bow Clutch, *20, 22, 122–23*
Brick Shoulder Bag, *21, 22*
Crisscross Bone Ruffle Handle Bag, *16, 116–18*
Diamond Ruffle Pouch, *32–33, 136–38*
Dragon Scale Drawstring Bag, *36–37, 145–47*
Flower Drawstring Bag, *26–27, 128–30*
Heart Chain Clutch, *30, 31, 131–33*
Hourglass Crescent Bag, *34, 139–41*
Lozenge Cushion, *23–24, 124–25*
Puzzle Wall Art, *38–39, 148–49*
Rattan Bamboo-Handle Bag, *35, 142–44*
Shell Circle Cushion, *25, 126–27*
Wave Pocket Tote, *14–15, 113–15*
puzzle patterns and stitching, 88–92
Puzzle Wall Art, *38–39, 148–49*

R

Rattan Bamboo-Handle Bag, *35, 142–44*
rattan patterns and stitching, 80–83
red and pink lines, 10
ruler, 40

S

satin, finishing with, 43
scissors, 40
seam allowances, 11
sewing tools, 40
sheeting, finishing with, 43
Shell Circle Cushion, *25, 126–27*
shell patterns and stitching, 54–55
shoulder bags, making, 104–8. *See also* bags and totes
stitching diagrams
about, 9
blue dashed lines, 10
lines explained, 10
red and pink lines, 10
specific patterns (*See* patterns and stitching)
straight and diagonal lines. *See* patterns and stitching

T

thread
about, 9, 40, 41
how to pass, 11
thread wax, 40
tools and materials, 40–41. *See also* fabric
tracing wheel, 40

W

wall art, puzzle, *38–39, 148–49*
washing smocked fabric, 11
wave patterns and stitching, 60–61
Wave Pocket Tote, *14–15, 113–15*
wax, thread, 40

ABOUT THE AUTHOR

After graduating from fashion design school, Miyuki Uemura worked at La Droguerie. She began her career as an independent crafter in 2011. Unconstrained by specific genres, she conveys the joy of handmade creations by blending a diverse range of techniques. She hosts private lessons and workshops at her studio in Osaka, and her work is regularly featured in magazines and other publications.
Website: https://www.hazelutt.net/
Instagram: @cherry_hazelutt